JOHN DEWEY

THE MIDDLE WORKS, 1899–1924

Volume 8: 1915

Edited by Jo Ann Boydston
With an Introduction by Sidney Hook

Carbondale and Edwardsville
SOUTHERN ILLINOIS UNIVERSITY PRESS
London and Amsterdam
FEFFER & SIMONS, INC.

LB
875
.D34
v.8

CENTER FOR EDITIONS OF
AMERICAN AUTHORS
AN APPROVED TEXT
MODERN LANGUAGE
ASSOCIATION OF AMERICA
®

Editorial expenses for this edition have been met in part by grants from the National Endowment for the Humanities. Publishing expenses have been met in part by grants from the John Dewey Foundation and from Mr. Corliss Lamont.

Library of Congress Cataloging in Publication Data   (Revised)

Dewey, John, 1859–1952.
  The middle works, 1899–1924.

  Vol. 8 has introd. by Sidney Hook.
  Includes bibliographies and indexes.
  CONTENTS: v. 1. 1899–1901.—v. 2. 1902–1903.—v. 3.
1903–1906.—v. 4. 1907–1909.—v. 5 1908.—v. 6. 1910–
1911.—v. 7. 1912–1914.—v. 8. 1915.
  1. Dewey, John, 1859–1952. 2. Education—Philosophy. I.
Title.
LB875.D34 1976   370.1'092'4   76–7231
ISBN 0–8093–0882–7 (v. 8)

The Middle Works, 1899–1924

Advisory Board

CONTENTS

INTRODUCTION

By Sidney Hook

The period covered by the publications in this volume reveals John Dewey at the height of his philosophical powers. His greatest works were still to come—*Democracy and Education, Experience and Nature, The Quest for Certainty* and *Logic: The Theory of Inquiry*—but the themes elaborated therein were already sounded and developed with incisive brevity in the articles and books of this banner year.

For purposes of exposition we shall consider Dewey's views under five rubrics—metaphysics, logic, theory of knowledge, the history of ideas with particular reference to the influence of philosophy on politics and vice versa, and theory and practice in education. These are themes suggested by the important articles "The Subject-Matter of Metaphysical Inquiry," "The Logic of Judgments of Practice," "The Existence of the World as a Logical Problem," and the two books *German Philosophy and Politics* and *Schools of To-Morrow* which constitute the bulk of this volume.

I

The question of what metaphysics is and whether pragmatists are entitled to have one, like all large questions in philosophy, depends upon the meaning assigned to the term. I recall that at the official defense of my doctoral dissertation on *The Metaphysics of Pragmatism* (subsequently published with an introduction by Dewey) Professor Wendell T. Bush, one of Dewey's admiring colleagues at Columbia, protested that the phrase was a contradiction in terms. His point was that the pragmatic method was a way of eliminating metaphysical questions and not another way of reintroducing them into the strife of systems that constituted so much of the history of philosophy. This position was shared by some other philosophers who were part of the

pragmatic movement and was attributed to leading pragmatists by sympathetic as well as hostile critics.

It is a position which, like the implications of Peirce's
pragmatic maxim, Dewey at times seemed to hold. If we ask
the question of why and how any *specific* thing or event
came to be what and where it is, the answer is to be found,
if at all, in some scientific discipline. If we ask the question
about the world or universe as a whole or about "the entire
present state of things," then for Dewey it is a meaningless
question. The quest for a first cause is not a scientific quest.
All scientific inquiries concern themselves with proximate
causes. So much was common ground for all scientifically
oriented philosophies towards metaphysical and religious
systems of thought that sought to establish universal necessary truths about everything that is or may be conceived. It
ruled out those traditional views of metaphysics that sought
to deduce from allegedly first principles or self-evident
axioms what the structure of things must be, or indeed that
any particular thing—God, man or beast—must exist.

But it is clear that Dewey, to some extent influenced by
F. J. E. Woodbridge, held another view of metaphysics, a
more empirical view, that was compatible with a whole-
hearted acceptance of the claims of the several sciences in
the broadest sense alone to determine what was true or false
about any particular occurrence or configuration of events.
Whatever the sciences tell us about the world,—and there
are no legitimate rivals or substitutes for the sciences—*that*
the world possesses the characters, features, or traits so discovered is an ultimate and irreducible fact. "Ultimate" here
has no temporal reference, and "irreducible" when attributed
to any trait assumes that the trait in question or some
synonym for it will show up in every analysis. At the time
when Dewey wrote the essay on "The Subject-Matter of
Metaphysical Inquiry," as well as when he published *Experience and Nature*, the description and analysis of the
ultimate, irreducible, generic traits of existence is what he
understood by the word "metaphysics." In his mind despite
the multiple usages of the term "metaphysics," his conception of its subject-matter had no commerce with any other
conception of metaphysics that purported to describe what

the world or experience *must* be. "A statement that the world is thus and so cannot be tortured into a statement of how and why it must be as it is."

At the time Dewey wrote his essay on "The Subject-Matter of Metaphysical Inquiry," according to which that subject-matter consisted of the generic traits of existence—traits "found in any and every subject of scientific inquiry," he was not so much concerned with demarcating metaphysics as a discipline for further development as he was with criticizing certain conceptions of biological evolution. These conceptions argued that although the properties of life may ultimately be analyzed satisfactorily by the methods of physico-chemical science, it would still be legitimate to say that the cosmic process as a whole was potentially or latently vital in character. By the same reasoning we could say that the cosmos was potentially or latently conscious. On such a view it could be claimed that life and mind and the laws of their emergence were part or aspects of the original constitution of the world and that the course of evolution was necessarily and inescapably what it turned out to be. The upshot of this position would be quite congenial to some modern forms of religion and theology.

Dewey argues that this conclusion, which admittedly could never be established by any scientific inquiry, depends upon an unacceptable conception of metaphysics that regards the world as a whole or in its totality as a legitimate subject of inquiry. In characterizing his own contrasting conception of metaphysics as a study of such generic traits as specificity, interaction, and change in existences, Dewey assimilates his view to the Aristotelian conception of the study of existence as existence, repudiating at the same time the eulogistic adjective "divine" for such general traits of existence and the identification of "first philosophy" with theology.

Thirty-five years later Dewey rejects any assimilation of his conception of metaphysics to that of Aristotle. "Nothing can be farther from the case" than "that I use the word *metaphysical* in the sense it bears in the classic tradition based on Aristotle." He vowed "never to use the word again in connection with any aspect of any part of my own position" (*Philosophy and Phenomenological Research* 9 [1949]: 712).

The reason for Dewey's abandonment of the term *metaphysical* and cognate expressions was the penchant of critics to read into his use of the term ontological notions about the nature of the world over and above what scientific knowledge discloses. Whether Dewey would have been able to persist in his resolution to eschew all use of the term, had he continued to write, is questionable. If the reading of alien meanings by critics into the basic terms he employed were a sufficient ground for abandoning those terms, he would have never persisted in using the word "experience."

The real or important question is what Dewey meant by the term "metaphysics" when he did use it. If, as Dewey often says, only the sciences give us knowledge of the world, metaphysics is not a science like other sciences. There is no such thing as a science of existence as existence. In what sense, then, are we to take Dewey's view that the subject-matter of metaphysical inquiry is the generic traits of existence? Certainly not literally, for, aside from logical terms, there are no traits that can intelligibly be attributed to all existences. There are no characters that turn up in every universe of discourse whether it is "space," "time," "contingency," "causality," "mind," "life," or "energy." And those that have some semblance of universality like "individuality" and "continuity," "identity" and "difference" turn out to be systematically ambiguous expressions whose meaning alters as we go from one field to another. The very variety of metaphysical views about the nature of the world, the failure to reach any cumulative agreement about what exists, and the absence even of a common method of resolving differences suggests the implausibility of the assimilation of metaphysics to a science distinctive from all others. This is perfectly compatible with the recognition that historically what have been regarded as metaphysical notions have had an important heuristic role in the development of the natural and social sciences.

The central meaning that Dewey gives to metaphysics, it seems to me, is clearly manifest in *Experience and Nature*. Metaphysics is the study of those traits of experience and nature which have special relevance to the career of human life on earth. It is philosophical anthropology in its broadest sense. Although there are certain verbal inconsistencies in Dewey's discussion of the theme when we consider his writings as a whole, I suggest that this key will prove most fruitful in clarifying obscurities, revealing his intent, and disclosing his vision of the place of man in the world.

During the later years of Dewey's career, metaphysics, especially of the variety that made claims to deduce by reason what the nature of nature must be, fell into desuetude. This was a consequence not of the influence of Dewey's philosophy but of the impact of logical empiricism and the ordinary language reorientation that followed hard on Wittgenstein's publications. In recent years there has been a revival of interest in metaphysics which on analysis turns out to be little more than an exercise in conceptual revision of the basic categories of understanding, comparable to a redrawing of the map of thought or knowledge. There is no incongruity between this conception of metaphysics and Dewey's own since Dewey recognizes that with the emergence of new needs, interests, and hopes what is of central importance to man may change and in that light the world may appear and be described differently.

Such redrawing of the map of thought in contradistinction to the revision of categories within the special fields of the sciences does not lead to the discovery of new knowledge. The metaphysician does not use his map to go anywhere, to solve problems, or to disclose unsuspected nooks and crannies in the world that all future map makers will have to include on their maps whatever the notation or scale they employ. The map expresses his vision of how all things in the world hang together, and it necessarily bears the mark of the map maker.

II

As in the case of his views about the nature of metaphysics, Dewey's views about the nature of logic underwent development. They received their most systematic development in his *Logic: The Theory of Inquiry* but the central conceptions were already expressed in earlier writings. Most notable are his articles on "The Logic of Judgments of Practice," which were published in the *Journal of Philosophy, Psychology and Scientific Methods* in 1915 and then revised, considerably amplified, and reprinted the following year in his *Essays in Experimental Logic.* I have developed this view at length in chapter nine, "The Quest for 'Being'" in my book *The Quest for Being* (New York: St. Martin's Press, 1961).

Dewey's conception of logic is probably the most difficult aspect of his thought for those who approach it with traditional views of the nature of logic. Such views in the main regard logical traits as either forms of the mind, considered as an immaterial or psychical existence, or as inherent in the ontological structure of the world, antecedent to anything that exists or can be conceived. Dewey's approach takes its point of departure from the fact that thinking and therefore logical thinking makes a difference to the world, a fact which none of the traditional notions can plausibly explain. Logical traits are objective features of existence that arise in the course of human inquiry. They may be regarded as forms of human discourse only if discourse is considered in its broadest sense in relation to the multiple forms of behavior with which it is related. It is a naturalistic approach to logic which recognizes the continuity between man and nature, and involves a behavioristic view of ideas, mind, and consciousness. Most conflicting conceptions of logic find Dewey's approach unintelligible because they seek to interpret what is said in their own terms, which express a standpoint that ignores the fact that thinking or rational behavior or its failure makes some concrete difference to what occurs in the world. Or like Russell they dismiss Dewey's logical theories as so much dubious psychology irrelevant to genuine problems of logic—which, aside from the fact that this extends the scope of psychology beyond any they previously considered under its rubric, begs the questions at issue.

Nonetheless even in its own terms there are many difficulties and problems as well as paradoxical consequences in

Dewey's logical theories and as yet there have been no developments of his position in this area even by those sympathetic to his views. His work so far stands as a lonely monument rather than as a beacon to other inquiries in the field.

Dewey begins the exposition of his logical views by considering "judgments of practice" which are differentiated
from other judgments in virtue of their specific subject-
matter, e.g., "He had better consult a physician." He then
goes on to enumerate six implications of the subject-matter
of judgments of practice—the first of which is that an objective "incomplete situation" is present, the second that the
proposition "is itself a factor in the completion of the situation" and the third that "it makes a difference how the given
is terminated." In the course of his explications Dewey dis-
tinguishes judgments of practice from "descriptive judgments" which do not affect the development of subject-
matter. This distinction is unnecessarily confusing because,
after exploring the ways in which the subject-matter judgments of practice are distinguished from other judgments,
Dewey suggests that all scientific and descriptive statements
of matter of fact are or may be interpreted as judgments of
practice, that all "have reference to a determination of
courses of action to be tried and to the discovery of means
for their realization." In subsequent writings Dewey makes
clear that he believes that all ideas about states of affairs are
plans of action and directly or indirectly involve reference to
something to be done in order to establish their validity. The
elaboration therefore at this point of the alleged differences
in the subject-matter of various types of propositions in inquiry seems needless. A further source of difficulty is Dewey's
contention as he develops his argument that judgments of
value are preeminently judgments of practice. Some critics
have read this to imply that all judgments of practice are
judgments of value, too, which Dewey would grant if it were
recognized that, although for any particular case in hand
one purported solution of the problem we face is better than
others, "the better" is not necessarily the morally better except where the subject-matter of inquiry is a moral problem.

A further difficulty in Dewey's account of judgments of
practice seems to have been his use of the term "situation"

when he says that these judgments imply an "incomplete situation." What does the term "situation" embrace? Is it the present only or the history leading up to the present? Is it everything on the horizon or only things, events, and persons in immediate juxtaposition with the organism? I believe that Dewey would answer that it all depends upon what the *problem* is. The *problem*atic situation is an incomplete situation and what is relevant to the situation is whatever must be done or taken note of to render it unproblematic or resolved. Dewey asserts that some guided activity is always necessary for a successful resolution of the problem. In the course of the inquiry we discover more adequately what the situation includes.

There is one objection to Dewey's view of the judgment of practice that is made from the standpoint of a position wholly at odds with Dewey's conception of what it means for any thing or situation to be known. This disputes the contention that there is anything distinctive about judgments of practice as a logical form and asserts that they are all reducible to hypothetical judgments in which the protasis clause has been suppressed or taken for granted. "You had better see a doctor" is an incomplete expression for the hypothetical judgment, "If you want to get well, you had better see a doctor." The practical directive or advice, "This is a good time to build a house," is an incomplete expression for the hypothetical judgment, "If you want to save money, this is a good time to build a house," etc. From Dewey's point of view these hypothetical propositions do not express the concreteness, the urgency, and the specificity of the particular situation. They are *generally* useful in the type of situations of which the particular situation is an instance but in the particular case, they may not even apply. Were we to get a response from the person to whom we said, "If you want to get well, you had better see a doctor," to the effect, "I don't want to get well," we might take this as all the more reason why he *should* see a doctor—perhaps a psychiatrist. Or he might say, "Yes, I want to get well but I can't afford to see a doctor" or "What doctor should I see? None I have consulted has done me any good." What Dewey has in mind is the indefinite number of particular situations in which we are aware that something is the matter, that our past habits of response are inadequate, in which we must do something to avoid the consequences of not doing anything, in which we are not altogether certain of what must be done but are willing to try what seems most reasonable in that particular situation. The hypothetical propositions we use are, according to Dewey, cognitive resources that express what we have learned in the past. We cannot act or experience intelligently without them in any judgment of practice but by themselves they are insufficient to justify what we should *do* in this case—otherwise we would have no problematic situation since we could deduce the answers or the judgment by logical inference. The existence and indispensability of such propositions is not denied but, with respect to the relevance and weight or applicability of any one of them to the situation in hand, only the outcome or issue of the experiment can be decisive.

There is one other important misunderstanding about Dewey's judgment of practice which should be clarified if Dewey's approach is to be fairly assessed. One of the characteristics of the subject-matter of judgments of practice is that "the judgment is itself a factor in the completion of the situation carrying it forward to its solution"; another is that "its truth or falsity is constituted by the issue," so that, since "only the issue gives the complete subject-matter, in this case at least verification and truth completely coincide."

This conclusion would seem to follow from the distinctions Dewey makes between the incomplete subject-matter that challenges inquiry and the completed subject-matter that constitutes for him the object of knowledge or objective of knowledge that results from the reordering of things in experimental action.

Dewey, however, has been interpreted by some critics as believing not only that it is the singular reconstituted situation which is known in virtue of the directed operations but that all the hypothetical propositions that have entered as means and instrumentalities in reaching the result are known in the same sense, and literally made true in the act of using them. For example, H. T. Costello argues that according to Dewey not only does the judgment of practice produce or make the truth in this particular situation, but the hypothetical relations on which we rely in our experiment are also made in the course of the experiment—which is absurd. That is to say, when we judge it is better to build a house instead of renting an apartment and proceed to do so, our judgment and the actions to which it leads are responsible not only for the completed house but for the tools—hammers, saws, nails and what not, without which the house could not be constructed. Or to use Costello's illustrations: not only is the judgment of the cook to make a cake by combining the ingredients in certain novel proportions causal towards making the cake, Dewey would have us believe that the cook not only makes the cake but also the hypothetical connections between the ingredients, and presumably the relation between $NaCl_2$ and its salty taste. Similarly, if I experiment to see what happens when I pour sulphuric acid on copper and make copper sulphate, Costello interprets Dewey as concluding: "You have made sulphuric acid and copper make copper sulphate" (*Journal of Philosophy, Psychology and Scientific Methods* 17 [1920]: 554–55).

If this were what Dewey meant, his philosophy would be a form of magical idealism. For Dewey the whole history of previous inquiry and commonsense reflective activity results in conclusions that we must use in particular situations. Their truth in *this* particular context is not at issue, only their relevance and usefulness in settling or solving the problem. They are compared to the instruments or means which we must use to bring any desired end into being. At most any particular inquiry tests the relevance and validity. It is only because we do *not* make the if-then relationships between the antecedent and estimated consequences in our deliberation on the use of these instrumental propositions that we can justify our reliance upon them. It is true that Dewey's theory leads to a semantic paradox from the point of view of those who regard these instrumental propositions as "truths." However, since there are many difficulties involved in calling them "true," this should not foreclose consideration of Dewey's proposal that, all things considered, there is less difficulty in employing the term "truth," defined as "warranted assertability," for what is known—for the object of knowledge, i.e., the particular reconstituted situation that results from using the outcomes of previous inquiries, than in calling propositions that are used in inquiry "true."

Nonetheless there are serious difficulties in Dewey's analysis which stem from his belief that what we have knowledge of in a preeminent sense is the specific, concrete case in which all abstractions—theoretical knowledge—are applied. A captain of a ship lost at sea may make port by navigating with concepts drawn from the Ptolemaic system. If we follow Dewey here we shall not regard the propositions that express the Ptolemaic theory as "true." Nor even the propositions that express the Copernican theory. But even if we do not use the term "true," we seem to be under the obligation to recognize the greater validity of the Copernican theory, granted that considered as means or tools the Copernican propositions are more reliable and fruitful than the Ptolemaic propositions. One asks why this is so? And it is hard to escape an answer that suggests that what explains it is that the Copernican theory is truer.

III

Dewey's essay "The Existence of the World as a Logical Problem" is important not only for the intrinsic significance of the theme—which challenges the epistemological tradition of modern philosophy—but because it initiates an intellectual exchange between Dewey and Bertrand Russell that was to continue with a kind of progressive asperity until Dewey's final years. Here is not the place to explore in detail the intellectual and personal relationships between these two towering figures of twentieth-century philosophical thought. Although both professed allegiance to scientific methods as the only reliable way of achieving truths about nature, man, and society, their interpretations of science on some key issues were profoundly different. Even where they seemed to agree, as when both professed belief in the correspondence theory of truth, the term "correspondence" meant different things to them, for Russell the identification of the object of knowledge with antecedent existence, for Dewey the coherence or fit of the planned activity which defines an idea with its anticipated outcome.

It is noteworthy that at their first meeting, when Russell was visiting Harvard in 1914, Russell was very much impressed with Dewey both as thinker and man. In letters to Lady Ottoline that have recently come to light, he writes: "To my surprise I liked him very much. He has a slow moving mind, very empirical and candid, with something of the impassivity and impartiality of a natural force." (Royce he dubs "a garrulous old bore.") Subsequently, referring to Dewey's criticisms of a paper he read before the New York Philosophical Club at Columbia on "The Relation of Sense Data to Physics," he characterizes them as very profound, and all other criticisms as worthless. This turned out to be the high point of Russell's appreciation of Dewey.

Dewey's article is a criticism of the chapter "On Our Knowledge of the External World," which was published in Russell's *Our Knowledge of the External World as a Field for Scientific Method in Philosophy*. In it Dewey argues that the attempt to prove the existence of the external world on the basis of what is allegedly given in sense experience is question-begging, in that an analysis of the terms of the question already presupposes the existence of a world external to what is given. He takes Russell's formulation of the problem and answer to it as paradigmatic for all efforts to prove the existence of the world outside the center of subjective experience. "Can the existence of anything other than our own hard data," Russell asks, "be inferred from the existence of those data?"

Dewey's analysis is important because if it is valid it not only undermines the epistemological tradition which has made a problem of the existence of the external world but also because it would call into question the validity of all phenomenalist views according to which the existence of the world is ultimately reducible to a complex of sense data of various kinds.

Dewey's primary contention is that just as soon as we specify the kind of data which are allegedly immediately given in sense perception from which we make an inferential leap to a world outside of them—whether we call them visual, auditory, tactile, olfactory, kinaesthetic or muscular—our statement already involves an implicit reference to physiological conditions and organs without which our specification would be unintelligible. We distinguish between a visual and auditory datum by reference to eyes and ears. That colors are seen with our eyes and sounds heard by our ears are synthetic propositions which presuppose the existence of the very world which Russell's question apparently would leave in doubt. Even to call the immediate data "objects of sense" rather than "objects of mind or imagination" could only be justified because of our knowledge of the difference between various physiological structures and processes.

Further, there is a difference between the existence of colors and the seeing of them. We often are unaware of the existence of colors and sounds even when certain electromagnetic vibrations are being recorded on our retina or tympanum. An act of attending or noting is necessary to bring the datum into focus, to make it a "hard datum." The "hard datum," whatever it is, is not immediate but, according to Dewey, "already stands in connection with something beyond itself."

Further, as Russell states the problem, it raises the question whether what is "momentarily seen" exists at other times. Dewey objects that we cannot identify any thing or any act as occurring now or later except by reference to a time continuum. Why be troubled as to whether we can legitimately infer from *this* time to "other times," if the intelligible reference to *this* time already requires that there be other times? Similarly when we speak of changes in our sense data, as when we perceive a red color being replaced by a blue color, unless there is a reference "to the same existence perduring through different times while changing in *some* respect, no temporal delimitation of the existence of such a thing as sound or color can be made." There would have to be other *things* in the world different from the mere color datum before we could discover when it began and when it ceased.

Dewey approves of Russell's definition of a sensible object as a correlation of an ordered series of shapes and colors with an ordered series of muscular movements but he as-

serts that the "correlations" of these series presuppose a
"space continuum" as well as time continuum which is not
given as a sense datum. Something from the external world
of common sense always keeps creeping in as we examine
the sense data presumably before us. "It may not be a very
big external world but having begged a small external world,
I do not see why we should be squeamish about extending it
over the edges."

In his criticism of Russell Dewey expresses a view not
only incompatible with Russell's specific epistemology but
with any view which would interpret the act of observation
as based on immediate truths of perception. For Dewey
historical and cultural tradition has more to do with the
actual starting point of knowledge than what is presumably
given in anything called sense knowledge. Sense perception
as a distinctive *activity* occurs within a subject-matter which
is primarily determined by a social tradition. That is to say,
the whole system of customary beliefs as they are transmitted from one generation to another, not only by speech
patterns but also by patterns of overt action, enters into what
we observe. What is given is always filtered out by our mind-
set. Sense perception tends to be dominated by the beliefs,
meanings, and habits which individuals incorporate into
their own experience with the world and their own reach for
knowledge while reacting to the speech and behavior of others. This approach of Dewey's does not deny or reduce the
value, indeed the indispensability, of sense perception but
claims that sense perception is in a derivative and mediate
position. It is a deliberately used activity to check on the
validity of beliefs but is not itself warranted knowledge.
There is no immediate knowledge, no truth by acquaintance.
Knowledge always involves an element of inference. In this
as in other matters Dewey's empiricism differentiates itself
from the sensationalistic empiricism of J. S. Mill and his
predecessors with which many English and European critics
of Dewey confuse it.

Dewey professes himself dissatisfied as an empiricist
with purely dialectical exercises, and his argument concerning the self-refuting character of attempts to prove the existence of the external world is clearly dialectical. He con-

cludes his analysis by trying to locate the source of the pseudo-problem. He finds it in the false psychological belief that the data of sense perception are given as primitive elements out of which we build up a world rather than the refined outcome of inquiries into our ordinary commonsense experiences. These data are always embedded in the world and their detection enables us to uncover connections within a world whose existence we cannot meaningfully doubt.

Dewey's position here not only undercuts the traditional epistemological problem but any view that professes to start with a wholesale skepticism or one which successively challenges the validity of any sense observation which confirms a judgment on the ground that it itself may be hallucinatory or a dream. Dewey like Peirce before him would argue that we can only use the terms "hallucinatory" and "dreamlike" intelligibly in contexts in which some experiences are accepted as non-hallucinatory or not dreams. All significant doubt rests on the assumption that some things are not doubtful at the time we profess doubt. And if we take our problems one at a time, there is no need to lapse into a vicious infinite regress.

Dewey's criticism of Russell's position brought a rejoinder from Russell that was relatively friendly but which on the chief points at issue denied Dewey's contention with some asperity. This rejoinder was in the form of a critical notice (*Journal of Philosophy, Psychology and Scientific Methods* 16 [1919]: 5–26) of *Essays in Experimental Logic,* which contained as one of its chapters Dewey's criticism. So far as I know, Dewey made no reply—which was quite uncharacteristic of him. (He may have been out of the country.) Years later when I mentioned Russell's response to him he did not recall it.

Readers are in a position to judge for themselves the validity of Russell's rejoinder. Russell complained that Dewey had misunderstood what the problem of the external world was, the sense in which Russell took hard sense data, and that Dewey was simply mistaken in asserting that the characterization of sense data as "visual" or "auditory" requires reference to either physiology or any other thing.

To this reader of Russell, his rejoinder seems to be

singularly weak. To begin with he admits that the word
"external" in considering the existence of the world as a
logical problem is unfortunate. "The word 'inferred' would
have been better." The question then becomes "Can we make
any valid inferences from data to non-data in the empirical
world?" I am quite confident that Dewey would admit that
this is a genuine question for every *specific* case of inquiry.
It all depends upon the problem. "From the scientific data we
have of this man's heart beat, temperature, blood tests, etc.,
can we validly infer the disease (the non-data) from which
he is suffering, and its outcome?" Sometimes we can and
sometimes we can't, and when we can, we cannot be certain
in our inference as we are in mathematics and logic. What
Dewey is objecting to is the question whether we can validly
infer from certain data the empirical world itself! "The world
I call 'external,'" Russell writes, "is so called only in this
sense that it lies 'outside' the group of data—'outside' in the
logical sense." Dewey would never object to this use of external. In this sense there are many external worlds but
what he denies is that we can speak meaningfully in any
specific case of *the* world.

Despite Russell's emendation the very fact that he holds
that solipsism and extreme skepticism are logically irrefut-
able—even when he asserts that he does not subscribe to
them—shows that Dewey was justified in reading Russell as
he did.

Russell denies that he has "begged" the external world
in his description of the world as given in sense data. There
is nothing in the sense data to warrant any belief that there
is anything outside of the sense data—"I have not 'begged'
my small external world any more than Columbus begged
the West Indies." (External world here refers to what is observed.) To which Dewey could have properly retorted that
Columbus didn't discover the world but only a part of it, and
that any description of the part of the world he discovered
would presuppose that there were other parts of the world in
existence. For Dewey there is as much sense in making the
existence of the external world a problem as there is for a
geographer making the existence of the world a problem.

Finally, Russell dismisses as mistaken the contention
Dewey regards as crucial in his criticism, viz., that the char-

acterization of sense data as visual or auditory already presupposes reference to something not a sense datum. According to Russell, the answer to Dewey "is that quite apart from
physiology, objects which (as they say) are 'seen' have a
common quality which enables us to distinguish them from
objects 'heard.' . . . We do not need to experiment by shut-
ting the eyes and stopping the ears in order to find out
whether the sense datum of the moment is 'visual' or 'auditory'; we know this by its intrinsic quality." Dewey would
deny that we know anything by its intrinsic quality: we
sense its quality, we know it by identifying some character of
the quality. How would we communicate to others what
sense data we have without terms like "visual" or "auditory"
or "kinaesthetic"? It is not merely a matter of convention
which leads us to say that we hear a sound and see a color
rather than see a sound and hear a color.

At one point Russell seems on the verge of agreeing with
Dewey. After noting that Dewey considers "the theory of
knowledge" as a mistake, he adds: "I suppose he would say,
what I would agree to in a certain fundamental sense, that
knowledge must be accepted as a fact, and can not be
proved from outside." But subsequently he spiritedly asserts
that "in discussing the world as a logical problem, I am dealing in a scientific spirit with a genuine scientific question, in
fact a question of physics." But if it were a genuine scientific question, it could be falsified, which would be like establishing the non-existence of the external world by something
in that world. If it were a question of psychology, the answer
would tell us more about ourselves than about the world. If it
were a question of physics, it would be found in some branch
of the subject but no book on physics, text or otherwise, concerns itself with it. In view of all this, to claim for it the
status of a genuine scientific question is odd indeed. For it
seems to call the very existence of the subject-matter from
which we start into question.

IV

Of all recent philosophers Dewey has been foremost in
stressing the important role that philosophy plays in civiliza-

tion. The dominant philosophy of an epoch both reflects the culture and society in which it arises and redirects its interests, ideals, and development. Even the vulgar Marxist view—according to which philosophy is purely epiphenomenal, merely a by-product of economic class struggles—acknowledges that a widely held philosophical outlook either tends to rationalize and preserve existing institutional ways against the challenge of the new or, like the Marxist philosophy itself, reinforces movements of change.

This dual role of philosophy—reflective and reconstructive—is apparent from the fact that the only way of distinguishing philosophy as a discipline from all other disciplines which it has nurtured and with which it has been historically entangled is to recognize that its characteristic concern from Socrates to the present has been the enunciation and critical analysis of normative values, and that whatever else the contributions of a mathematician, physicist, or biologist may be, what gives him a place in the history of philosophy is the direct or indirect bearing of his intellectual effort on the nature of the good or the better in man and society. This remains true regardless of the conception one holds about the cognitive or non-cognitive character of propositions about values. Even if one holds that such propositions express positive or negative attitudes towards states of affairs deemed good or bad these attitudes influence conduct as much as if not more than explicit ideas.

To say that a regnant philosophy reflects the dominant ideals of a culture is easy. To show in detail how this is done, to trace the leading ideas of a philosophical system to the institutional practices of the cultural matrix is very difficult. For one thing the differences between the philosophical views of those within the same family of doctrine can never be accounted for in terms of a common environment. The same conditions often spawn widely different reactions among the individuals who constitute the group or class affected by those conditions. The really significant connections are not between the individual views of a philosopher but between social movements and philosophical doctrines. Hobbes and Hume and Santayana were all conservatives in social outlook but their materialism and empiricism played a liberal and sometimes revolutionary role. T. H. Green and Brand Blanshard personally were very liberal in their social and political outlook, but their absolute idealism, by its emphasis on the rationality of the actual and the wisdom of existing social institutions, including the property system, tended to support the status quo.

Although Dewey himself never wrote a systematic study of the history of philosophy, scattered throughout his works are more or less detailed analyses of the relationships between philosophical ideas and movements and their environing social and economic conditions. Particularly illuminating are his interpretations of Greek philosophy and the ways in which its dualism between the ideal and empirical, its conception of the cosmos as an ethos, and the denigration of the practical, reflected the institution of slavery. Although not a professed historical materialist and indeed quite critical of its monistic explanatory schemes, Dewey presents a more plausible historico-materialistic account of Hellenic philosophy than any Marxist writer known to me.

As difficult as it is to explain the genesis and acceptance of a philosophy in terms of given conditions, since the same conditions may provoke acceptance or rejection by those affected by it, it is even more difficult to establish that a set of philosophical beliefs have had a decisive influence upon some momentous historical event. Where historical actions are concerned, the skein of causation is far more complex—and there are always material factors present that seem adequate to serve as proximate causes.

That some abstract ideas are efficacious in human affairs—and all philosophical ideas are abstract—is incontestable. The scientific revolution, without which there would have been no industrial revolution, is proof if any is needed. But philosophical ideas are not scientific ideas. Their efficacity is much more problematic. In *German Philosophy and Politics*, written and published during the First World War but before the entry of the United States into the conflict, Dewey attempts to explain the character of German political life in terms of the influence of German classical philosophy. Anyone unfamiliar with the book or who has not been informed of its content will experience a profound in-

tellectual shock on reading it. In it Dewey maintains that
the central ideas of Kant have decisively influenced the
mind, character, and deeds of the German nation. It is not
Hegel, not Nietzsche, not Richard Wagner and his intellectual
camp followers—but Immanuel Kant, the philosopher of the
enlightenment, who is the font and origin of that combination of self-righteousness and technical efficiency which
characterized the German frightfulness of the period, especially in its foreign policy. This is Dewey's thesis.

Dewey's argument is that Kant's sharp separation of the
world of nature in which science is supreme and man un-
free and the world of moral duty in which man is completely
free is the source, on the one hand, of ruthless efficiency in
achieving any given end, and on the other, of that self-
righteous acceptance of the commands of the categorical
imperative which results in the logic of fanaticism. Kant is
held responsible for encouraging if not molding the national
mind of Germany which pursues scientific knowledge with
unparalleled zeal unchecked by any moral ideal and a moral
idealism unchecked by the empirical consequences of its
policies in the world of everyday life.

Even those who are most sympathetic with Dewey's
philosophy and opposed as much as he was to the national
policies of Germany that contributed to the outbreak of the
First World War are likely to regard the argument as a *tour
de force*. It fails to show how and why this Kantian dualism
between the world of nature and the world of morals should
have led to a campaign of imperialistic aggression coupled
with asseverations about the majesty of the moral law as
interpreted by spokesmen for the Hohenzollern dynasty.
Logically this dualism could express itself just as well in
acceptance of the sovereignty of physical laws in nature,
and renunciation of aggression and war among nations.
Leonard Nelson, who staunchly opposed German national
policy even after war was declared, was a Kantian. The
characteristics of the German mind as described by Dewey
are, to be sure, logically compatible with Kantian dualism
but they are just as compatible with Cartesian dualism.

The alleged influence of philosophical ideas on political
practice is not a matter of logic but of empirical inquiry. If

ideas get translated into political policies it is in virtue of decisions and commitments made by individuals who occupy the strategic positions of power. Who were the movers and shakers of events in Imperial Germany—in the chancelleries, in the counting houses, in the press and other organs of public education? What was their philosophical allegiance, if any? What is the evidence that any key decision they made flowed from any philosophical commitment? It is only in this or a similar way that we can establish that philosophy exercised a specific influence on the shape of things in being or to come. Was Kant's philosophy truly "a banner and a conscious creed which in solid and definite fashion intensified and deepened" Germany's sense of its national mission and destiny? Aside from a quotation from General Bernhardi, a cavalry officer attached to the High Command, which makes a passing reference to Kant's *Critique of Pure Reason* in a fashion more edifying than historical, Dewey adduces no evidence. One could cite more frequent references to Christianity of a similar edifying character by German dignitaries.

Further there are aspects of Kant's philosophy which are completely incompatible with any advocacy of a special and unique mission for Germany (or Prussia in his day). One of Kant's formulations of the categorical imperative: "Treat humanity as an end in itself, and never as a means only," would be hard to square with any aggressive action by Germany or any other power. Indeed, on any formulation of the categorical imperative which, without indicating *what* is right or wrong in any situation, declares that what is wrong for one person to do in that situation cannot be right for another in that same or similar situation, no statesmen of the powers that fought in the First World War could find comfort. Kant himself was a cosmopolitan, an advocate of a world order of federated republican states in a world of enduring peace. His views on these themes would have been anathema to those who called the turn in the conflicts of nations had they been aware of them. And these views were far less recondite than the technical doctrines of his *Critiques*. Oddly enough when Dewey concludes his study with an eloquent plea for transcending the whole philosophy of nationalism—political, racial, and cultural—and for the establishment of international tribunals and legislatures that will limit national sovereignty and prepare the world for a free communication between the peoples of the world without any barriers, he sounds very much like Kant, without of course the transcendental mythology of two separate worlds.

Some hostile critics of Dewey have charged him with succumbing to the war fever which swept American society after the entrance of the United States into the conflict. Neither the tone nor the content justifies ascription to Dewey of any propagandistic intent, aside from the fact that his book was delivered as lectures fully two years *before* American entry into the war, and at a time when the mood of the nation was neutralist. The book must be treated primarily as an essay in the history of ideas. As such, it is curious that Dewey selected Kant as the prophet of the mission and destiny of Germany. A far better case could have been made out that Georg Friedrich Hegel fulfilled this role—perhaps not Hegel's philosophy as he himself understood it but as it was understood and applied by leading German statesmen who came after him.

Dewey seems to have been unmoved by any of the criticisms directed against his book. He was sensitive to the reproaches of those who felt he had let them down by his support of the war against Germany, particularly in the light of the hindsight of the provisions of the Treaty of Versailles which he himself strongly deplored. This led to an initial reluctance to support American involvement in the Second World War. After Pearl Harbor and Germany's declaration of war against the United States, he reissued his *German Philosophy and Politics* in 1942 with a new introduction entitled: "The One-World of Hitler's National Socialism" which is included in this volume. I wish it were possible to say that Dewey reversed his belief that the classic philosophic tradition of Germany reinforced the union of extraordinary flexibility in the use of means and fanatical tenacity and inflexibility of purpose which marked the forging of the German Empire. But alas! he maintains that despite the pronounced racial ideology of the National Socialist movement there is "an underlying continuity" between it and the dominant philosophy of the past. The Third Reich had the same faith in the national vocation of Germany as the Second Reich which had materialized from the dreams and intellectual efforts of its seers and prophets. Dewey is aware that Hitler glorified not The State, as Hegel did, but Race, and that Kant's cosmopolitanism was anathema to him, so that strictly speaking he cannot be considered a disciple of either one. Nonetheless he contends that the transformation of the primacy of *Innerlichkeit* into the primacy of *Blut und Boden* does not repudiate the philosophical heritage but was Hitler's barbarous way of overcoming the dichotomy of "the inner" and "the outer," the spiritual and the material. Had the philosophies of the classical tradition not introduced the false and artificial separation between the two worlds or kingdoms of the ideal and real, Hitler would not have been given an opportunity to impose his totalitarian One World.

Although Dewey is correct in denying that Hitler was a disciple of either Kant or Hegel, he is wrong in denying that he was a disciple of Houston Chamberlain, the renegade Englishman who gave Hitler his blessings and the rationalizations for Hitler's racism. He is wrong, unaccountably wrong, in implying that Hegel's Cunning of Reason reappears in some way as the sense of instinct in the Hitlerian mythology. It is simply an injustice to Hegel, who was free from racialism, to assert that there is "no great difficulty . . . in the way of translating Hegel's state, which he often calls 'nation,' into Hitler's Folk-community."

V

More characteristic both in interest, influence, and profundity are Dewey's views on education in the last of the major writings of 1915—*Schools of To-Morrow*. It would hardly be an exaggeration to say that the informed reader will get a strong sense of its contemporaneity. With respect to the descriptions of some of the schools in operation and especially the ideals they illustrate and Dewey's proposals for the reconstruction of elementary and secondary education, the work could have been entitled *Schools of Today*. Long before the practices were given a name we have an account of the open classroom, the classroom without walls, children more advanced teaching the less advanced, and other features of modern, progressive education.

The point of departure of the book, in whose writing Dewey's daughter Evelyn collaborated, was a description of new types of schools in various parts of the country that reflected the influence of Rousseau, Froebel, Pestalozzi, Montessori, and other educational reformers. On the basis of their results and his own philosophical and psychological analysis, Dewey indicates what reforms are required if the promise of equal educational opportunity in a democracy is to be achieved. These are merely sketched in outline. The philosophical foundations of Dewey's theory of education developed in a more systematic way were published subsequently in his *Democracy and Education.*

Schools of To-Morrow is still significant in the contrast it presents between the conventional education that was the rule at the time the book appeared and the type of education subsequently called "progressive," whose ideals and practices have had an enormous influence, variously assessed, on what is called conventional education today. The book is noteworthy because among other things it shows Dewey's awareness of the magnitude and difficulty of the educational reconstruction he was advocating.

Among the highlights of Dewey's exposition several stand out as significant because of the character of subsequent misinterpretations among critics and even followers. The first is the notion that Dewey was opposed to discipline in the way of method or subject-matter and that freedom in the classroom meant that the child was to be free to learn or not to learn anything at any time. Dewey makes clear that without authority or discipline no learning is possible but that it is the authority of method, the discipline of things, which the children must recognize if they are to achieve their best growth. Nor is Dewey arguing for an unstructured curriculum. He is opposed only to a curriculum which is imposed on the child without any relationship to his psychological nature and the stages of his development. Most systems of education in the past, he believes, have been devised to impart learning in such a way as to make the process easy for adults. In consequence the virtues of the child have been defined to stress his obedience, docility, and uncritical submission to the adult's point of view. For purposes of the child's own best growth as well as the moral imperatives of a democratic society Dewey urges the organization of a curriculum and methods of implementing it that recognize the natural activity of children and seek to channel that activity, physical and mental, into constructive tasks that will make a call upon their initiative and originality.

On psychological grounds Dewey stresses the importance of arousing the interest of the child if he is to grasp properly the subject under study or to master a task. Only too often Dewey has been interpreted to mean that schooling must be entertaining, and that the child should be left alone by the teacher to rediscover the world, so to speak, for himself without the tyranny of textbooks, homework, or any drill. But Dewey protests that schooling that is only entertaining never arouses a self-sustaining interest in anything. He is not opposed to the proper use of textbooks and the active intervention of the teachers but only to the inert use of the first as a source of mechanical assignments to be memorized, and to the activity of the teacher which is not controlled by its effects in evoking the self-activity of the students. Without an active response from students to what is presented in the classroom, one cannot tell whether they have truly learned or understood anything.

Similarly when Dewey stresses the importance of learning by doing it is always in relation to the testing of ideas or the carrying out of a plan or project, or of finding a way to make something necessary to achieve a task. Only too often has he been read as if he believed that all doing, however mindless, is a form of learning.

It is a simple and calamitous misreading of Dewey to interpret him as if he were indifferent to the three R's or what is sometimes called basic education. The call for the return to such education is not a reaction against the failure of the methods he advocated but of certain social factors over which teachers have had no control. "Reading, writing, arithmetic and geography will always be needed," Dewey writes, "but their substance will be greatly altered and added to." The student should learn facts but not facts as such in isolation "from their relation and application to each other."

Two fundamental ideas animate Dewey's philosophy of education—viz., that the findings of scientific psychology should ultimately control the methods to be used in the learning process of any discipline, and that in a democratic society all children have a right to the kind of schooling that will enable them to develop to the fullest reach of their desirable capacities.

A few observations that flow from Dewey's commitment to democracy in education are pertinent here. Dewey contends that by and large the curriculum of education in the Western world, to the extent that it was designed, reflected the interests and needs of an intellectual elite with a special home environment that provided strong support for what formal educational activity, to the extent that it existed, supplied. When popular education was introduced, on the whole only the rudiments of the traditional curriculum were offered, and they were transmitted by traditional methods. The curriculum was not modified to meet the situation in which universal compulsory mass education became the rule, and in which ultimately universal access to higher education would be a reality. Often educators of the past—like many university professors today who write about an ideal education for the young—presuppose almost unconsciously that students are destined for a life of intellectual and professional pursuits, and that their home environment is congenial to the achievement of such vocational goals. Dewey studied the new experimental schools because they were "all working away from a curriculum adapted to a small and specialized class towards one which shall be truly representative of the needs and conditions of a democratic society."

Dewey was no Utopian. He realized that in the foreseeable future most human beings would be under the obligation to earn a living. The choice of a vocation is one of the profoundest, because far-reaching, choices a human being is called upon to make. "Each individual should be capable of self-respecting, self-supporting and *intelligent* work." Education should among other things equip the individual with the skills, habits, and knowledge required for intelligent choice of his life calling. At some point education for a specific vocation is in order and not merely for the vocations that in the past constituted the traditional professions. Preparation for these professions was the chief objective of what was deemed liberal education to the degree that it extended beyond the cultivation of gentlemen of leisure.

In urging concern for education for vocations Dewey was interested in enriching the curriculum by the addition of scientific and social studies that would enlarge the spectrum of possible vocational choices. He anticipated that the increasing impact of science on industry and in time on society and government would generate new opportunities. He was careful to distinguish between vocational education, as he understood it, and the training of apprentices and other forms of manual training which were designed to prepare individuals merely for specific jobs. The latter made the workers appendages to industry for the good of industry rather than as a means to their growth. "It is comparatively easy to urge the addition of narrow vocational education for those who, it is assumed, are to be the drawers of water and hewers of wood in the existing economic régime, leaving intact the existing bookish type of education for those fortunate enough not to have to engage in manual labor in the home, shop or farm."

Dewey urged the reconstruction of education to provide individuals not only with opportunities for personal growth, for the enrichment of personal life, but also for more intelligent participation as citizens in the democratic process. That is why for him a liberal or general education, insofar as it can be distinguished from any other, must undergird and accompany all vocational and professional education.

It is or should be quite clear that the kind of educational reforms for which Dewey called were much more difficult to introduce successfully than the preservation of the practices that Dewey hoped would be replaced. For they required two things in very short supply. One was a large number of devoted and highly skilled teachers who could creatively adapt the new methods in conditions and circumstances rarely auspicious for experiment. The other was patient communities, especially in large urban centers, prepared to underwrite the expense of the small classes, special equipment and extracurricular activities entailed by a sincere effort to meet the needs of all children—communities prepared to suspend judgment until a reasonable time had elapsed and not be panicked by hysterical outcries of parents who set themselves up as authorities on professional questions concerning maturation and methods of testing achievement.

There was still another requirement that Dewey and all past American educators took for granted—that social conflicts that have always surrounded the school would not enter the classroom. Whatever the causes for the phenomenon, today in too many of our public urban schools conflict and violence are so endemic that the police are almost as much in evidence as the teachers themselves to preserve the minimal peace and order without which no genuine education is possible. A grim statistic that makes commentary unnecessary is that more than 70,000 American teachers have been subjected to physical assault in their classrooms or on and near school premises during the last school year.

Dewey would have been the first to acknowledge that without some appreciable degree of social reconstruction and social peace any educational change can have only a cosmetic character. The current outcry against the failure of the schools to teach their charges, the mounting evidence of functional illiteracy, and the spread of a permissiveness that takes on riotous proportions when a controversial issue arises, is not due to the philosophy and practices of progressive education. The philosophy, principles and practices of progressive education have received widespread lip-allegiance but they have not yet been introduced in a wholesale way in any large scale public school system with the requisite degree of community support.

Essays

THE SUBJECT-MATTER OF METAPHYSICAL INQUIRY

A number of biologists holding to the adequacy of the mechanistic conception in biology have of late expressed views not unlike those clearly and succinctly set forth in the following quotation:

If we consider the organism simply as a system forming a part of external nature, we find no evidence that it possesses properties that may not eventually be satisfactorily analyzed by the methods of physico-chemical science; but we admit also that those peculiarities of ultimate constitution which have in the course of evolution led to the appearance of living beings in nature are such that we can not well deny the possibility or even legitimacy of applying a vitalistic or even biocentric conception to the cosmic process as a whole.[1]

The problems connected with the organism as a part of external nature are referred to in the context of the quotation as scientific problems; those connected with the peculiarities of ultimate constitution as metaphysical. The context also shows that ultimate constitution is conceived in a temporal sense. Metaphysical questions are said to be those having to do with "ultimate origins." Such questions lie quite beyond the application of scientific method. "Why it [nature] exhibits certain apparently innate potentialities and modes of action which have caused it to evolve in a certain way is a question which really lies beyond the sphere of natural science." These "apparently innate potentialities and modes of action" which have caused nature as a whole to evolve in the direction of living beings are identified with "ultimate peculiarities"; and

---

1. Professor Ralph S. Lillie, *Science*, Vol. XL, page 846. See also the references given in the article, which is entitled "The Philosophy of Biology: Vitalism *vs*. Mechanism."

[First published in *Journal of Philosophy, Psychology and Scientific Methods* 12 (1915): 337–45. For article to which this was a reply, see this volume, pp. 449–59.]

it is with reference to them that the biocentric idea has a possible legitimate application. The argument implies that when we insist upon the adequacy of the physico-chemical explanation of living organisms, we are led, in view of the continuity of evolution of organisms from non-living things, to recognize that the world out of which life developed "held latent or potential within itself the possibility of life." In considering such a world and the nature of the potentiality which caused it to evolve living beings, we are forced, however, beyond the limits of scientific inquiry. We pass the boundary which separates it from metaphysics.

Thus is raised the question as to the nature of metaphysical inquiry. I wish to suggest that while one may accept as a preliminary demarcation of metaphysics from science the more "ultimate traits" with which the former deals, it is not necessary to identify these ultimate traits with temporally original traits—that, in fact, there are good reasons why we should not do so. We may also mark off the metaphysical subject-matter by reference to certain irreducible traits found in any and every subject of scientific inquiry. With reference to the theme of evolution of living beings, the distinctive trait of metaphysical reflection would not then be its attempt to discover some temporally original feature which caused the development, but the irreducible traits of a world in which at least some changes take on an evolutionary form. A world where some changes proceed in the direction of the appearance of living and thinking creatures is a striking sort of a world. While science would trace the conditions of their occurrence in detail, connecting them in their variety with their antecedents, metaphysics would raise the question of the sort of world which *has* such an evolution, not the question of the sort of world which causes it. For the latter type of question appears either to bring us to an *impasse* or else to break up into just the questions which constitute scientific inquiry.

Any intelligible question as to causation seems to be a wholly scientific question. Starting from any given existence, be it a big thing like a solar system or a small thing like a rise of temperature, we may ask how it came about. We account for the change by linking up the thing in question with other specific existences acting in determinate ways—ways which collectively are termed physico-chemical. When we have traced back a present existence to the earlier existences with which it is connected, we may ask a like question about the occurrence of the earlier things, viewed as changes from something still earlier. And so on indefinitely; although, of course, we meet practical limits in our ability to push such questions beyond a certain indefinite point. Hence it may be said that a question about ultimate origin or ultimate causation is either a meaningless question, or else the words are used in a relative sense to designate the point in the past at which a particular inquiry breaks off. Thus we might inquire as to the "ultimate" origin of the French language. This would take us back to certain definite antecedent existences, such as persons speaking the Latin tongue, others speaking barbarian tongues; the contact of these peoples in war, commerce, political administration, education, etc. But the term "ultimate" has meaning only in relation to the particular existence in question: French speech. We are landed in another historic set of existences, having their own specific antecedents. The case is not otherwise if we ask for the ultimate origin of human speech in general. The inquiry takes us back to animal cries, gestures, etc., certain conditions of intercourse, etc. The question is, how one set of specific existences gradually passed into another. No one would think of referring to latent qualities of the Latin speech as the cause of the evolution of French; one tries to discover actual and overt features which, *interacting* with other equally specific existences, brought about this particular change. If we are likely to fall into a different mode of speech with reference to human language in general, it is because we are more ignorant of the specific circumstances under which the transition from animal cries to articulate speech with a meaning took place. Upon analysis, reference to some immanent law or cause which forced the evolution will be found to be a lazy cloak for our ignorance of the specific facts needed in order to deal successfully with the question.

Suppose we generalize the situation still more. We may ask for the ultimate origin of the entire present state of things. Taken *en masse*, such a question is meaningless. Taken in detail, it means that we may apply the same procedure distributively to each and any of the things which now exist. In each case we may trace its history to an earlier state of things. But in each case, *its* history is what we trace, and the history always lands us at some state of things in the past, regarding which the same question might be asked. That scientific inquiry does not itself deal with any question of ultimate origins, except in the purely relative sense already indicated, is, of course, recognized. But it also seems to follow from what has been said that scientific inquiry does not generate, or leave over, such a question for some other discipline, such as metaphysics, to deal with. The contrary conception with respect to the doctrine of evolution is to be explained, I think, by the fact that theology used to have the idea of ultimate origin in connection with creation, and that at a certain juncture it was natural to regard the theory of evolution as a substitute or rival of the theological idea of creation.

If all questions of causation and origin are specific scientific questions, is there any place left for metaphysical inquiry at all? If its theme can not be ultimate origin and causation, is metaphysics anything but a kind of pseudo-science whose illusory character is now to be recognized? This question takes us to the matter of whether there are ultimate, that is, irreducible, traits of the very existences with which scientific reflection is concerned. In all such investigations as those referred to above we find at least such traits as the following: Specifically diverse existences, interaction, change. Such traits are found in any material which is the subject-matter of inquiry in the natural science. They are found equally and indifferently whether a subject-matter in question be dated 1915 or ten million years B.C. Accordingly, they would seem to deserve the name of ultimate, or irreducible, traits. As such they may be made the object of a kind of inquiry differing from that which deals with the genesis of a particular group of existences, a kind of inquiry to which the name metaphysical may be given.[2]

2. The name at least has the sanction of the historical designation given to Aristotle's consideration of existence as existence. But it should be noted that we also find in Aristotle the seeds (which, moreover, have at places developed into flourishing growths in his own philosophy) of the conception of meta-

It may well seem as if the fact that the subject-matter of science is always a plurality of diverse interacting and changing existences were too obvious and commonplace to invite or reward investigation. Into this point I shall not go, beyond pointing out, in connection with the present theme, that certain negative advantages in the economizing of intellectual effort would at least accrue from the study. Bare recognition of the fact just stated would wean men from the futility of concern with ultimate origins and laws of causation with which the "universe" is supposed to have been endowed at the outset. For it would reveal that, whatever the date of the subject-matter which may be successfully reflected upon, we have the same situation that we have at present: diversity, specificality, change. These traits have to be begged or taken in any case. If we face this fact without squeamishness we shall be saved from the recurrent attempts to reduce heterogeneity to homogeneity, diversity to sheer uniformity, quality to quantity, and so on. That considerations of quantity and mathematical order are indispensable to the successful prosecution of researches into particular occurrences is a precious fact. It exhibits certain irreducible traits *of* the irreducible traits we have mentioned, but it does not replace them. When it tries to do so it cuts the ground out from under its own feet.

Let me emphasize this point by comment on a further quotation.

If we assume constancy of the elementary natural processes, and constancy in the modes of connection between them—as exact observation forces us to do—there seems no avoiding the con-

---

physics rejected above. For he expressly gives the more general traits of existence the eulogistic title "divine" and identifies his first philosophy with theology, and so makes this kind of inquiry "superior" to all others, because it deals with the "highest of existing things." While he did not himself seek for this higher or supreme real in time, but rather located it, in its fullness of reality, just beyond space, this identification of existence as such with the divine led to such an identification the moment theology became supremely interested in "creation." But unless one approaches the study of the most general traits of the matter of scientific inquiry with theological presuppositions, there is, of course, no ground for the application to them of eulogistic predicates. There is no ground for thinking that they are any better or any worse, any higher or any lower, than other traits, or that any peculiar dignity attaches to a study of them.

clusion that—given an undifferentiated universe at the start—only one course of evolution can ever have been possible. Laplace long ago perceived this consequence of the mechanistic view of nature, and the inevitability of his conclusion has never been seriously disputed by scientific men. Nevertheless, this is a very strange result, and to many has seemed a *reductio ad absurdum* of the scientific view as applied to the whole of nature.

Note that the inevitable conclusion as to the predetermined course of evolution and the apparent incredibility of the conclusion both depend upon the premise "given an undifferentiated universe at the start." Now this is precisely a premise which a scientific view can not admit, for science deals with any particular existence only by tracing its occurrence to a plurality of prior changing interacting things. Any Laplacean formula would, in any case, be a formula for the structure of *some* existence *in* the world, not for the world as a "whole." The scientific grounds which make it impossible to take the world *en masse* at the present time and to give a comprehensive formula for it in its entirety apply even more strongly, if possible, to some earlier state of affairs. For such a formula can be reached only by tracing back a specific present phenomenon to its specific antecedents.

A curious illusion exists as to formulae for the ancient states of nature. It is frequently assumed that they denote not merely some absolute original (which is impossible), but also one from which later events unroll in a mathematically predetermined fashion. We seem to be passing in a one-sided way from the earlier to the later. The illusion vanishes when we ask where the formula came from. How was it obtained? Evidently, by beginning with some present existence and tracing its earlier course, till at some time (relevant to the object of the inquiry) we stop and condense the main features of the course into a formula for the structure of the state of things at the date where we stop. Instead of really deducing or deriving the course of subsequent events from an original state, we are simply taking out of a formula the traits which we have put into it on the basis of knowledge of subsequent events. Let the present state be anything you please, as different as may be from what is actually found, and it will still be true that we could (theoretically) construct a comprehensive formula for its earlier estate. In short, as a matter of fact, a Laplacean formula merely summarizes what the actual course of events has been with respect to some selected features. How then can it be said to describe an original state of nature in virtue of which just such and such things have necessarily happened? A statement that the world is thus and so can not be tortured into a statement of how and why it must be as it is. The account of how a thing came to be as it is always starts and comes back to the fact that it *is* thus and so. How then can this fact be derived according to some law of predestination from the consideration of its own prior history? For, I repeat, this history is *its* history.[3]

This discussion, however, oversimplifies matters. It overlooks the extent to which inference as to a prior state of affairs is dependent upon the diversity and complexity of what is now observed. We should be in a hard case in trying to fix upon the structure of the Latin language if our sole datum were, say, the French language. As matter of fact, in considering the growth of the French tongue we have other Romance languages to fall back upon. Above all, we have independent evidence as to the characteristics of Latin speech. If we had not, we should be reasoning in a circle. Science is rightly suspicious of accounts of things in terms of a hypothesis for whose existence nothing can be alleged save that if it existed it would or might account for something which is actually found. Independent evidence of the existence of such an object is required. This consideration has an interesting application to the question in hand. It brings out clearly the absurdity involved in supposing that any formula, of the Laplacean type, about some earlier state of existence, however comprehensive, is comprehensive enough to cover the whole scope of existence of that earlier time.

Let us suppose the formula to be descriptive of a primitive state of the solar system. Not only must it start from and be framed in terms of what *now* exists, but the present datum must be larger than the existing solar system if we are to escape reasoning in a circle. In such cosmological constructions, astronomers and geologists rely upon observation of

3. Compare Woodbridge, "Evolution," *Philosophical Review*, Vol. XXI, page 137.

what is going on outside of the solar system. Without such
data, the inquiry would be hopelessly crippled. The stellar
field now presents, presumably, systems in all stages of formation. Is there any reason for supposing that a like state of
affairs did not present itself at any and every prior time?
Whatever formula is arrived at for the beginning of our
present solar system describes, therefore, only one structure
existing amid a vaster complex. A state of things adequately
and inclusively described by the formula would be, by conception, a state of things in which nothing could happen. To
get change we have to assume other structures which interact
with it, existences not covered by the formula.

As a matter of fact, the conception of a solar system
seems to have exercised an hypnotic influence upon Newton's successors. The gathering together of sun, planets and
their satellites, etc., into a system which might be treated as
an individual having its own history was a wonderful achievement, and it impressed men's imaginations. It served for the
time as a kind of symbol of the "universe." But as compared
with the entire stellar field, the solar system is, after all, only
a "right little, tight little island." Yet unless its complex context be ignored the idea of "an undifferentiated universe"
which, by some immanent potential force, determined everything which has happened since, could hardly arise.[4] That
the French language did not evolve out of Latin because of
some immanent causality in the latter we have already noted.
It is equally true that the contact and interaction of those
speaking Latin with those speaking barbaric tongues were
not due to the fact that they spoke Latin, but to independent
variables. Internal diversity is as much a necessity as something externally heterogeneous.[5]

The consideration throws light, I think, upon the mean-

4. One who turns to Spencer's chapter on the "Instability of the
Homogeneous" will perceive that his proof of its instability consists in showing that it was really already heterogeneous.
5. Some contemporary metaphysical theories attempt to start from
pure "simple" entities and then refer change exclusively to "com-
plexes." This overlooks the fact that without internal diversification in the alleged simple entity, a complex entity would no
more exhibit change than a simple one. The history of the
doctrine of atoms is instinctive. Such a metaphysics transgresses
the conditions of intelligent inquiry in exactly the same way as
the metaphysics of ultimate origins.

ing of potentiality with reference to any state of things. We never apply the term except where there *is* change or a process of becoming. But we have an unfortunate tendency to conceive a fixed state of affairs and then appeal to a latent or potential something or other to effect change. But in reality the term refers to a characteristic of change. Anything changing might be said to exhibit potentiality with respect to two facts: first, that the change exhibits (in connection with interaction with new elements in its surroundings) qualities it did not show till it was exposed to them and, secondly, that the changes in which these qualities are shown run a certain course. To say that an apple has the potentiality of decay does not mean that it has latent or implicit within it a causal principle which will some time inevitably display itself in producing decay, but that its existing changes (in interaction with its surroundings) will take the form of decay, *if* they are exposed or subjected to certain conditions not now operating upon them. Potentiality thus signifies a certain limitation of present powers, due to the limited number of conditions with which they are in interaction plus the fact of the manifestation of new powers under different conditions. To generalize the idea, we have to add the fact that the very changes now going on have a tendency to expose the thing in question to these different conditions which will call out new modes of behavior, in other words, further changes of a different kind. Potentiality thus implies not merely diversity, but a progressively increasing diversification of a specific thing in a particular direction. So far is it from denoting a causal force immanent within a homogeneous something and leading it to change.

We may say then that an earlier condition of our earth was potential with life and mind. But this means that it was changing in a certain way and direction. Starting where we must start, with the present, the fact or organization shows that the world is of a certain kind. In spots, it *has* organization. Reference to the evolution of this organization out of an earlier world in which *such* organization was not found means something about that earlier condition—it means that it was characterized by a change having direction—that is, in the direction of vital and intelligent organization. I do not see that this justifies the conclusion that that earlier world was biocentric or vitalistic or psychic. Yet two conclusions seem to follow. One is negative. The fact that it is possible and desirable to state the processes of an organized being in chemico-physical terms does not eliminate, but rather takes for granted whatever peculiar features living beings have. It does not imply that the distinguishing features of living and thinking beings are to be explained away by resolution into the features found in non-living things. It is the *occurrence* of these peculiar features which is stated in physico-chemical terms. And, as we have already seen, the attempt to give an account of any occurrence involves the genuine and irreducible existence of the thing dealt with. A statement of the mechanism of vital and thinking creatures is a statement of *their* mechanism; an account of their production is an account of *their* production. To give such an account does not prove whether the existence in question is a good thing or a bad thing, but it proves nothing at all if it puts in doubt the specific existence of the subject-matter investigated.

The positive point is that the evolution of living and thinking beings out of a state of things in which life and thought were not found is a fact which must be recognized in any metaphysical inquiry into the irreducible traits of the world. For evolution appears to be just one of the irreducible traits. In other words, it is a fact to be reckoned with in considering the traits of diversity, interaction, and change which have been enumerated as among the traits taken for granted in all scientific subject-matter. If everything which is, is a changing thing, the evolution of life and mind indicates the nature of the changes of physico-chemical things and therefore something about those things. It indicates that as purely physical, they are still limited in their interactions; and that as they are brought into more and complex interactions they exhibit capacities not to be found in an exclusively mechanical world. To say, accordingly, that the existence of vital, intellectual, and social organization makes impossible a purely mechanistic metaphysics is to say something which the situation calls for. But it does not signify that the world "as a whole" is vital or sentient or intelligent. It is a remark of the same order as the statement that one is not adequately acquainted with water or iron until he has found it operating under a variety of different conditions, and hence a scientific doctrine which regards iron as essentially hard or water as essentially liquid is inadequate. Without a doctrine of evolution we might be able to say, not that matter *caused* life, but that matter under certain conditions of highly complicated and intensified interaction is living. With the doctrine of evolution, we can add to this statement that the interactions and changes of matter are themselves of a kind to bring about that complex and intensified interaction which is life. The doctrine of evolution implies that this holds good of any matter, irrespective of its date, for it is not the matter of 1915, as caused by matter that has now ceased to be, which lives. The matter which was active ten million years ago now lives: this is a feature of the matter of ten million years ago.

I am, however, getting beyond my main point. I am not concerned to develop a metaphysics; but simply to indicate one way of conceiving the problem of metaphysical inquiry as distinct from that of the special sciences, a way which settles upon the more ultimate traits of the world as defining its subject-matter, but which frees these traits from confusion with ultimate origins and ultimate ends—that is, from questions of creation and eschatology. The chief significance of evolution with reference to such an inquiry seems to be to indicate that while metaphysics takes the world irrespective of any particular time, yet time itself, or genuine change in a specific direction, is itself one of the ultimate traits of the world irrespective of date.

THE LOGIC OF JUDGMENTS OF PRACTICE

I. Their Nature

In introducing the discussion, I shall first say a word to avoid possible misunderstandings. It may be objected that such a term as "practical judgment" is misleading; that the term "practical judgment" is a misnomer, and a dangerous one, since all judgments by their very nature are intellectual or theoretical. Consequently, there is a danger that the term will lead us to treat as judgment and knowledge something which is not really knowledge at all and thus start us on the road which ends in mysticism or obscurantism. All this is admitted. I do not mean by practical judgment a type of judgment having a different organ and source from other judgments. I mean simply a kind of judgment having a specific type of subject-matter. Propositions exist relating to *agenda* —to things to do or be done, judgments of a situation demanding action. There are, for example, propositions of the form: M. N. should do thus and so; it is better, wiser, more prudent, right, advisable, opportune, expedient, etc., to act thus and so. And this is the type of judgment I denote practical.

It may also be objected that this type of subject-matter is not distinctive; that there is no ground for marking it off from judgments of the form *SP*, or *mRn*. I am willing, again, to admit that such may turn out to be the fact. But meanwhile the *prima-facie* difference is worth considering, if only for the sake of reaching a conclusion as to whether or no there is a kind of subject-matter so distinctive as to imply a distinctive logical form. To assume in advance that the subject-matter of practical judgments *must* be reducible

[First published in *Journal of Philosophy, Psychology and Scientific Methods* 12 (1915): 505–23, 533–43. Revised and reprinted in *Essays in Experimental Logic* (Chicago: University of Chicago Press, 1916), pp. 335–442.]

to the form *SP* or *mRn* is assuredly as gratuitous as the contrary assumption. It begs one of the most important questions about the world which can be asked: the nature of time. Moreover, current discussion exhibits, if not a complete void, at least a decided lacuna as to propositions of this type. Mr. Russell has recently said that of the two parts of logic the first enumerates or inventories the different kinds or forms of propositions.[1] It is noticeable that he does not even mention this kind as a possible kind. Yet it is conceivable that this omission seriously compromises the discussion of other kinds.

Additional specimens of practical judgments may be given: He had better consult a physician; it would not be advisable for you to invest in those bonds; the United States should either modify its Monroe Doctrine or else make more efficient military preparations; this is a good time to build a house; if I do that I shall be doing wrong, etc. It is silly to dwell upon the practical importance of judgments of this sort, but not wholly silly to say that their practical importance arouses suspicion as to the grounds of their neglect in discussion of logical forms in general. Regarding them, we may say:

1. Their subject-matter implies an incomplete situation. This incompleteness is not psychical. Something is "there," but what is there does not constitute the entire objective situation. *As* there, it requires something else. Only after this something else has been supplied will the given coincide with the full subject-matter. This consideration has an important bearing upon the conception of the indeterminate and contingent. It is sometimes assumed (both by adherents and by opponents) that the validity of these notions entails that the *given* is itself indeterminate—which appears to be nonsense. The logical implication is that of a subject-matter as yet *unterminated*, unfinished, or not wholly given. The implication is of future things. Moreover, the incompleteness is not personal. I mean by this that the situation is not confined *within* the one making the judgment; the practical judgment is neither exclusively nor primarily about one's self. On the

1. *Scientific Method in Philosophy*, p. 57.

contrary, it is a judgment about one's self only as it is a judgment about the situation in which one is included, and in which a multitude of other factors external to self are included. The contrary assumption is so constantly made about moral judgments that this statement must appear dogmatic. But surely the *prima-facie* case is that when I judge that I should not give money to the street beggar I am judging the nature of an objective situation, and that the conclusion about myself is governed by the proposition about the situation in which I happen to be included. The full, complex proposition includes the beggar, social conditions and consequences, a charity organization society, etc., on exactly the same footing as it contains myself. Aside from the fact that it seems impossible to defend the "objectivity" of moral propositions on any other ground, we may at least point to the fact that judgments of policy, whether made about ourselves or some other agent, are certainly judgments of a *situation* which is temporarily unfinished. "Now is a good time for me to buy certain railway bonds" is a judgment about myself only because it is primarily a judgment about hundreds of factors wholly external to myself. If the genuine existence of such propositions be admitted, the only question about moral judgments is whether or no they are cases of practical judgments as the latter have been defined—a question of utmost importance for moral theory, but not of crucial import for our logical discussion.

2. Their subject-matter implies that the proposition is itself a factor in the completion of the situation, carrying it forward to its conclusion. According as the judgment is that this or that should be done, the situation will, when completed, have this or that subject-matter. The proposition that it is well to do this is a proposition to treat the given in a certain way. Since the way is established by the proposition, the proposition is *a* determining factor in the outcome. As a proposition about the supplementation of the given, it is a factor *in* the supplementation—and this not as an extraneous matter, something subsequent to the proposition, but in its own logical force. Here is found, *prima-facie* at least, a marked distinction of the practical proposition from descriptive and narrative propositions, from the familiar *SP* propo-

sitions and from those of pure mathematics. The latter imply that the proposition does not enter into the constitution of the subject-matter of the proposition. There also is a distinction from another kind of contingent proposition, namely, that which has the form: "He has started for your house"; "The house is still burning"; "It will probably rain." The unfinishedness of the given is implied in these propositions, but it is not implied that the proposition is a factor in determining their completion.

3. The subject-matter implies that it makes a difference how the given is terminated: that one outcome is better than another, and that the proposition is to be a factor in securing (as far as may be) the better. In other words, there is something objectively at stake in the forming of the proposition. A right or wrong *descriptive* judgment (a judgment confined to the given, whether temporal, spatial, or subsistent) does not affect its subject-matter; it does not help or hinder its development, for by hypothesis it has no development. But a practical proposition affects the subject-matter for better or worse, for it is a judgment as to the condition (the thing to be done) of the existence of the complete subject-matter.[2]

4. A practical proposition is binary. It is a judgment that the given is to be treated in a specified way; it is also a judgment that the given admits of such treatment, that it admits of a specified objective termination. It is a judgment, at the same stroke, of end—the result to be brought about—and of means. Ethical theories which disconnect the discussion of ends—as so many of them do—from determination of means, thereby take discussion of ends out of the region of judgment. If there be such ends, they have no intellectual status.

To judge that I should see a physician implies that the given elements of the situation should be completed in a

2. The analytic realists have shown a peculiar disinclination to discuss the nature of future consequences as terms of propositions. They certainly are not identical with the mental act of referring to them; they are "objective" to it. Do they, therefore, already subsist in some realm of subsistence? Or is subsistence but a name for the fact of logical reference, leaving the determination of the meaning of "subsistence" dependent upon a determination of the meaning of "logical"? More generally, what is the position of analytic realism about the future?

specific way and also that they afford the conditions which make the proposed completion practicable. The proposition concerns both resources and obstacles—intellectual determination of elements lying in the way of, say, proper vigor, and of elements which can be utilized to get around or surmount these obstacles. The judgment regarding the need of a physician implies the existence of hindrances in the pursuit of the normal occupations of life, but it equally implies the existence of positive factors which may be set in motion to surmount the hindrances and reinstate normal pursuits.

It is worth while to call attention to the reciprocal character of the practical judgment in its bearing upon the statement of means. From the side of the end, the reciprocal nature locates and condemns utopianism and romanticism: what is sometimes called idealism. From the side of means, it locates and condemns materialism and predeterminism: what is sometimes called mechanism. By materialism I mean the conception that the given contains exhaustively the entire subject-matter of practical judgment: that the facts in their givenness are all "there is to it." The given is undoubtedly just what it is; it is determinate throughout. But it is the given *of* something to be done. The survey and inventory of present conditions (of facts) are not something complete in themselves; they exist for the sake of an intelligent determination of what is to be done, of what is required to complete the given. To conceive the given in any such way, then, as to imply that it negates in its given character the possibility of any doing, of any modification, is self-contradictory. As a part of a practical judgment, the discovery that a man is suffering from an illness is not a discovery that he must suffer, or that the subsequent course of events is determined by his illness; it is the indication of a needed and a possible course by which to restore health. Even the discovery that the illness is hopeless falls within this principle. It is an indication not to waste time and money on certain fruitless endeavors, to prepare affairs with respect to death, etc. It is also an indication of search for conditions which will render in the future similar cases remediable, not hopeless. The whole case for the genuineness of practical judgments stands or falls with this principle. It is open to question. But decision as to its validity must rest upon empirical evidence. It cannot be ruled out of court by a dialectic development of the implications of propositions about what is already given or what has already happened. That is, its invalidity cannot be deduced from an assertion that the character of the scientific judgment as a discovery and statement of what is forbids it, much less from an analysis of mathematical propositions. For this method only begs the question. Unless the facts are complicated by the surreptitious introduction of some preconception, the *prima-facie* empirical case is that the scientific judgment—the determinate diagnosis—favors instead of forbidding the doctrine of a possibility of change of the given. To overthrow this presumption means, I repeat, to discover specific evidence which makes it impossible. And in view of the immense body of empirical evidence showing that we add to control of what is given (the subject-matter of scientific judgment) by means of scientific judgment, the likelihood of any such discovery seems slight.

These considerations throw light upon the proper meaning of (practical) idealism and of mechanism. Idealism in action does not seem to be anything except an explicit recognition of just the implications we have been considering. It signifies a recognition that the given is given *as* obstacles to one course of active development or completion and *as* resources for another course by which development of the situation directly blocked may be indirectly secured. It is not a blind instinct of hopefulness or that miscellaneous obscurantist emotionalism often called optimism, any more than it is utopianism. It is recognition of the increased liberation and redirection of the course of events achieved through accurate discovery. Or, more specifically, it is this recognition operating as a ruling motive in extending the work of discovery and utilizing its results.

"Mechanism" means the reciprocal recognition on the side of means. It is the recognition of the import, within the practical judgment, of the given, of fact, in its determinate character. The facts in their isolation, taken as complete in themselves, are not mechanistic. At most, they just are, and that is the end of them. They are mechanistic as indicating the mechanism, the means, of accomplishing the possibilities which they indicate. Apart from a forward look (the anticipation of the future movement of affairs) mechanism is a meaningless conception. There is no sense in applying the conception to a finished world, to any scene which is simply and only done with. Propositions regarding a past world, just as past (not as furnishing the conditions of what is to be done), might be complete and accurate, but they would be of the nature of a complex catalogue. To introduce, in addition, the conception of mechanism is to introduce the implication of possibilities of future accomplishment.[3]

5. The judgment of what is to be done implies, as we have just seen, a statement of what the given facts of the situation are, taken as indications of the course to pursue and of the means to be employed in its pursuit. Such a statement demands accuracy. Completeness is not so much an additional requirement as it is a condition of accuracy. For accuracy depends fundamentally upon relevancy to the determination of what is to be done. Completeness does not mean exhaustiveness *per se*, but adequacy as respects end and its means. To include too much, or what is irrelevant, is a violation of the demand for accuracy quite as well as to leave out—to fail to discover—what is important.

Clear recognition of this fact will enable one to avoid certain dialectic confusions. It has been argued that a judgment of given existence, or fact, cannot be hypothetical; that factuality and hypothetical character are contradictions in

---

3. Supposing the question to be that of some molten state of the earth in past geologic ages. Taken as the complete subject-matter of a proposition—or science—the facts discovered cannot be regarded as causative of, or a mechanism of, the appearance of life. For by definition they form a closed system; to introduce reference to a future event is to deny the definition. Contrariwise, a statement of that past condition of the earth as a mechanical condition of the later emergence of life means that that past stage is taken not merely as past, but as in process of transition to its future, as in process of alteration in the direction of life. Change in this direction is an integral part of a statement of the early stage of the earth's history. A purely geologic statement may be quite accurate in its own universe of discourse and yet quite incomplete and hence inaccurate in another universe of discourse. That is to say, a geologist's propositions may accurately set forth a prior state of things, while ignoring any reference to a later state entailed by them. But a would-be philosophy may not ignore the implied future.

terms. They would be if the two qualifications were used in the same respect. But they are not. The hypothesis is that the facts which constitute the terms of the proposition of the given are relevant and adequate for the purpose in hand—the determination of a possibility to be accomplished in action. The data may be as factual, as absolute as you please, and yet in no way guarantee that they are the data *of* this particular judgment. Suppose the thing to be done is the formation of a prediction regarding the return of a comet. The prime difficulty is not in making observations, or in the mathematical calculations based upon them—difficult as these things may be. It is making sure that we have taken as data the observations really implicated in the doing rightly of this particular thing: that we have not left out something which is relevant or included something which has nothing to do with the further movement of the comet. Darwin's hypothesis of natural selection does not stand or fall with the correctness of his propositions regarding breeding of animals in domestication. The facts of artificial selection may be as stated—in themselves there may be nothing hypothetical about them. But their bearing upon the origin of species *is* a hypothesis. Logically, any factual proposition is a hypothetical proposition when it is made the basis of any inference.

6. The bearing of this remark upon the nature of the truth of practical judgments (including the judgment of what is given) is obvious. Their truth or falsity is constituted by the issue. The determination of end-means (constituting the terms and relations of the practical proposition) is hypothetical until the course of action indicated has been tried. The event or issue of such action *is* the truth or falsity of the judgment. This is an immediate conclusion from the fact that only the issue gives the complete subject-matter. In this case, at least, verification and truth completely coincide—unless there is some serious error in the prior analysis.

This completes the account, preliminary to a consideration of other matters. But the account suggests another and independent question with respect to which I shall make an excursus. How far is it possible and legitimate to extend or generalize the results reached to apply to all propositions of facts? That is to say, is it possible and legitimate to treat all

scientific or descriptive statements of matters of fact as implying, indirectly if not directly, something to be done, future
possibilities to be realized in action? The question as to
legitimacy is too complicated to be discussed in an incidental
way. But it cannot be denied that there is a possibility of such
application, nor that the possibility is worth careful examination. We may frame at least a hypothesis that all judgments
of fact have reference to a determination of courses of action
to be tried and to the discovery of means for their realization.
In the sense already explained all propositions which state
discoveries or ascertainments, all categorical propositions,
would be hypothetical, and their truth would coincide with
their tested consequences effected by intelligent action.

This theory may be called pragmatism. But it is a type of
pragmatism quite free from dependence upon a voluntaristic
psychology. It is not complicated by reference to emotional
satisfactions or the play of desires.

I am not arguing the point. But possibly critics of pragmatism would get a new light upon its meaning were they to
set out with an analysis of ordinary practical judgments and
then proceed to consider the bearing of its result upon judgments of facts and essences. Mr. Bertrand Russell has remarked[4] that pragmatism originated as a theory about the
truth of theories, but ignored the "truths of fact" upon which
theories rest and by which they are tested. I am not concerned
to question this so far as the origin of pragmatism is concerned. Philosophy, at least, has been mainly a matter of
theories; and Mr. James was conscientious enough to be
troubled about the way in which the meaning of such theories
is to be settled and the way in which they are to be tested. His
pragmatism was in effect (as Mr. Russell recognizes) a statement of the need of applying to philosophic theories the same
kinds of test as are used in the theories of the inductive
sciences. But this does not preclude the application of a like
method to dealing with so-called "truths of fact." Facts may
be facts, and yet not be the facts *of* the inquiry in hand. In
all scientific inquiry, however, to call them facts or data or
truths of fact signifies that they are taken as the *relevant*

4. *Philosophical Essays*, pp. 104, 105.

facts of the inference to be made. *If* (as this would seem to indicate) they are then implicated, however indirectly, in a proposition about what is to be done, they are themselves theoretical in logical quality. Accuracy of statement and correctness of reasoning would then be factors in truth, but so also would be verification. Truth would be a triadic relation, but of a different sort from that expounded by Mr. Russell. For accuracy and correctness would both be functions of verifiability.

II. *Judgments of Value*

I

It is my purpose to apply the conclusions previously drawn as to the implications of practical judgment to the subject of judgments of value. First, I shall try to clear away some sources of misunderstanding.

Unfortunately, however, there is a deep-seated ambiguity which makes it difficult to dismiss the matter of value summarily. The *experience* of a good and the *judgment* that something is a value of a certain kind and amount have been almost inextricably confused. The confusion has a long history. It is found in mediaeval thought; it is revived by Descartes; recent psychology has given it a new career. The senses were regarded as modes of knowledge of greater or less adequacy, and the feelings were regarded as modes of sense, and hence as modes of cognitive apprehension. Descartes was interested in showing, for scientific purposes, that the senses are not organs of apprehending the qualities of bodies as such, but only of apprehending their relation to the well-being of the sentient organism. Sensations of pleasure and pain, along with those of hunger, thirst, etc., most easily lent themselves to this treatment; colors, tones, etc., were then assimilated. Of them all he says: "These perceptions of sense have been placed within me by nature for the purpose of *signifying* what things are beneficial or harmful."[5] Thus it was possible to identify the real properties of bodies with their geometrical

5. *Sixth Meditation.*

ones, without exposing himself to the conclusion that God (or nature) deceives us in the perception of color, sound, etc. These perceptions are only intended to teach us what things to pursue and avoid, and as *such* apprehensions they are adequate. His identification of any and every experience of good with a judgment or cognitive apprehension is clear in the following words: "When we are given news the mind first judges of it and if it is good it rejoices."[6]

This is a survival of the scholastic psychology of the *vis aestimativa*. Lotze's theory that the emotions, as involving pleasure and pain, are organs of value-judgments, or, in more recent terminology, that they are cognitive appreciations of worth (corresponding to immediate apprehensions of sensory qualities) presents the same tradition in a new terminology.

As against all this, the present paper takes its stand with the position stated by Hume in the following words: "A passion is an original existence, or, if you will, modification of existence; and contains not any representative quality, which renders it a copy of any other existence or modification. When I am angry I am actually possest with the passion, and in that emotion have no more a reference to any other object, than when I am thirsty, or sick, or more than five feet high."[7] In so doing, I may seem to some to be begging the question at issue. But such is surely the *prima-facie* fact of the matter. Only a prior dogma to the effect that every conscious experience *is*, *ipso facto*, a form of cognition leads to any obscuration of the fact, and the burden of proof is upon those who uphold the dogma.[8]

6. *Principles of Philosophy,* p. 90.
7. *Treatise of Human Nature,* Part Three, sec. 3.
8. It is perhaps poor tactics on my part to complicate this matter with anything else. But it is evident that "passions" and pains and pleasures may be used as *evidences* of something beyond themselves (as may the fact of being more than five feet high) and so get a representative or cognitive status. Is there not also a *prima-facie* presumption that all sensory qualities are of themselves bare existences or occurrences without cognitive pretension, and that they acquire the latter status as signs or evidence of something else? Epistemological idealists or realists who admit the non-cognitive character of pleasure and pain would seem to be under special obligations carefully to consider the thesis of the non-cognitive nature of all sensory qualities except as they are employed as indications or indexes of some other thing. This recognition frees logic from the epistemological discussion of secondary qualities.

A further word upon "appreciation" seems specially called for in view of the currency of the doctrine that "appreciation" is a peculiar kind of knowledge, or cognitive revelation of reality: peculiar in having a distinct type of reality for its object and in having for its organ a peculiar mental condition differing from the intelligence of every-day knowledge and of science. Actually, there do not seem to be any grounds for regarding appreciation as anything but an intentionally enhanced or intensified experience of an object. Its opposite is not descriptive or explanatory knowledge, but *de*preciation—a degraded realization of an object. A man may climb a mountain to get a better realization of a landscape; he may travel to Greece to get a realization of the Parthenon more full than that which he has had from pictures. Intelligence, knowledge, may be involved in the steps taken to get the enhanced experience, but that does not make the landscape or the Parthenon as fully savored a cognitive object. So the fullness of a musical experience may depend upon prior critical analysis, but that does not necessarily make the hearing of music a kind of non-analytic cognitive act. Either appreciation means just an intensified experience, or it means a kind of criticism, and then it falls within the sphere of ordinary judgment, differing in being applied to a work of art instead of to some other subject-matter. The same mode of analysis may be applied to the older but cognate term "intuition." The terms "acquaintance" and "familiarity" and "recognition" (acknowledgment) are full of like pitfalls of ambiguity.

In contemporary discussion of value-judgments, however, appreciation is a peculiarly treacherous term. It is first asserted (or assumed) that all experiences of good are modes of knowing: that good is a term of a proposition. Then when experience forces home the immense difference between evaluation as a critical process (a process of inquiry for the determination of a good precisely similar to that which is undertaken in science in the determination of the nature of an event) and ordinary experience of good and evil, appeal is made to the difference between direct apprehension and indirect or inferential knowledge, and "appreciation" is called in to play the convenient role of an immediate cognitive apprehension. Thus a second error is used to cover up and protect a primary one. To savor a thing fully—as Arnold Bennett's heroines are wont to do—is no more a knowing than is the chance savoring which arises when things smelled are found good, or than is being angry or thirsty or more than five feet high. All the language which we can employ is charged with a force acquired through reflection. Even when I speak of a direct experience of a good or bad, one is only too likely to read in traits characterizing a thing which is found in consequence of thinking to be good; one has to use language simply to stimulate a recourse to a direct experiencing in which language is not depended upon. If one is willing to make such an imaginative excursion—no one can be compelled—he will note that *finding* a thing good apart from reflective judgment means simply treating the thing in a certain way, hanging on to it, dwelling upon it, welcoming it and acting to perpetuate its presence, taking delight in it. It is a way of behaving toward it, a mode of organic reaction. A psychologist may, indeed, bring in the emotions, but if his contribution is relevant it will be because the emotions which figure in his account are just part of the primary organic reaction to the object. In contrary fashion, to find a thing bad (in a direct experience as distinct from the result of a reflective examination) is to be moved to reject it, to try to get away from it, to destroy or at least to displace it. It connotes not an act of apprehension but an act of repugning, of repelling. To term the thing good or evil is to state the fact (noted in recollection) that it was actually involved in a situation of organic acceptance or rejection, with whatever qualities specifically characterize the act.

All this is said because I am convinced that contemporary discussion of values and valuation suffers from confusion of the two radically different attitudes—that of direct, active, non-cognitive experience of goods and bads and that of valuation, the latter being simply a mode of judgment like any other form of judgment, differing in that its subject-matter happens to be a good or a bad instead of a horse or planet or curve. But unfortunately for discussions, "to value" means two radically different things: to prize and appraise; to esteem and to estimate: to find good in the sense described above, and to judge it to be good, to *know* it as good. I call them radically different because to prize names a practical, non-intellectual attitude, and to appraise names a judgment. That men love and hold things dear, that they cherish and care for some things, and neglect and contemn other things, is an undoubted fact. To call these things values is just to repeat that they are loved and cherished; it is not to give a reason for their being loved and cherished. To call them values and then import into them the traits of objects of valuation; or to import into values, meaning valuated objects, the traits which things possess as held dear, is to confuse the theory of judgments of value past all remedy.

And before coming to the more technical discussion, the currency of the confusion and the bad result consequences may justify dwelling upon the matter. The distinction may be compared to that between eating something and investigating the food properties of the thing eaten. A man eats something; it may be said that his very eating implies that he *took* it to be food, that he judged it, or regarded it cognitively, and that the question is just whether he judged truly or made a false proposition. Now if anybody will condescend to a concrete experience he will perceive how often a man eats *without* thinking; that he puts into his mouth what is set before him from habit, as an infant does from instinct. An onlooker or anyone who reflects is justified in saying that he *acts as if* he judged the material to be food. He is not justified in saying that any judgment or intellectual determination has entered in. He has acted; he has behaved toward something as food: that is only to say that he has put it in his mouth and swallowed it instead of spewing it forth. The object may then be called food. But this does not mean either that it *is* food (namely, digestible and nourishing material) or that the eater judged it to be food and so formed a proposition which is true or false. The proposition would arise only in case he is in some doubt, or if he reflects that in spite of his immediate attitude of aversion the thing is wholesome and his system needs recuperation, etc. Or later, if the man is ill, a physician may inquire what he ate, and pronounce that something not food at all, but poison.

In the illustration employed, there is no danger of any harm arising from using the retroactive term "food"; there is no likelihood of confusing the two senses "actually eaten" and "nourishing article." But with the terms "value" and "good" there is a standing danger of just such a confusion. Overlooking the fact that good and bad as *reasonable* terms involve a *relationship to other things* (exactly similar to that implied in calling a particular article food or poison), we suppose that when we are reflecting upon or inquiring into the good or value of some act or object, we are dealing with something as simple, as self-enclosed, as the simple act of immediate prizing or welcoming or cherishing performed without rhyme or reason, from instinct or habit. In truth just as determining a thing *to be* food means considering its relations to digestive organs, to its distribution and ultimate destination in the system, so determining a thing found good (namely, treated in a certain way) *to be* good means precisely ceasing to look at it as a direct, self-sufficient thing and considering it in its consequences—that is, in its relations to a large set of other things. If the man in eating consciously implies that what he eats is food, he anticipates or predicts certain consequences, with more or less adequate grounds for so doing. He passes a judgment or apprehends or knows— truly or falsely. So a man may not only enjoy a thing, but he may judge the thing enjoyed to be good, to be a value. But in so doing he is going beyond the thing immediately present and making an inference to other things, which, he implies, are connected with it. The thing taken into the mouth and stomach *has* consequences whether a man thinks of them or not. But he does not *know* the thing he eats—he does not make it a term of a certain character—unless he thinks of the consequences and connects them with the thing he eats. If he just stops and says "Oh, how good this is," he is not saying anything about the object except the fact that he enjoys eating it. We may if we choose regard this exclamation as a reflection or judgment. But if it is intellectual, it is asserted for the sake of enhancing the enjoyment; it is a means to an end. A very hungry man will generally satisfy his appetite to some extent before he indulges in even such rudimentary propositions.[9]

9. To readers who have grasped the thought of my argument, it may not be meaningless to say that the typical idealistic fallacy is to import into the direct experience the results of the intel-

II

But we must return to a placing of our problem in this context. My theme is that a judgment of value is simply a case of a practical judgment, a judgment about the doing of something. This conflicts with the assumption that it is a judgment about a particular kind of existence independent of action, concerning which the main problem is whether it is subjective or objective. It conflicts with every tendency to make the determination of the right or wrong course of action (whether in morals, technology, or scientific inquiry) dependent upon an independent determination of some ghostly things called value-objects—whether their ghostly character is attributed to their existing in some transcendental eternal realm or in some realm called states of mind. It asserts that value-objects mean simply objects as judged to possess a certain *force* within a situation temporally developing toward a determinate result. To *find* a thing good is, I repeat, to attribute or impute nothing to it. It is just to do something to it. But to consider *whether* it is good and how good it is, is to ask how it, *as if acted upon*, will operate in promoting a course of action.

Hence the great contrast which may exist between a good or an immediate experience and an evaluated or judged good. The rain may be most uncomfortable (just *be* it, as a man is more than five feet tall) and yet be "good" for growing crops—that is, favor or promote their movement in a given direction. This does not mean that two contrasting judgments of value are passed. It means that *no* judgment has yet taken place. If, however, I am moved to pass a value-judgment I should probably say that in spite of the disagreeableness of getting wet, the shower *is* a good thing. I am now judging it as a *means* in two contrasting situations, as a means with

lectual or reflective examination, while that of realism is to treat the reflective operation as dealing with precisely the same subject-matter as the original act was concerned with—taking the good of "reason" and the good of immediate behavior to be the same sort of things. And both fallacies will result from any assimilation of two different acts to one another through giving them both the title "knowledge," and hence treating the difference between them as simply the difference between a direct apprehension and a mediated one.

respect to two ends. I compare my discomfort as a *consequence* of the rain with the prospective crops as another consequence, and say "let the latter consequence be." I identify myself as agent with it, rather than with the immediate discomfort of the wetting. It is quite true that in this case I cannot do anything about it; my identification is, so to speak, sentimental rather than practical so far as stopping the rain or growing the crops is concerned. But in effect it is an assertion that one would not on account of the discomfort of the rain stop it; that one would, if one could, encourage its continuance. Go it, rain, one says.

The specific intervention of action is obvious enough in plenty of other cases. It occurs to me that this agreeable "food" which I am eating isn't a food for me; it brings on indigestion. It functions no longer as an *immediate* good; as something to be accepted. If I continue eating, it will be after I have deliberated. I have considered it as a means to two conflicting possible consequences, the present enjoyment of eating and the later state of health. One or other is possible, not both—though of course I may "solve" the problem by persuading myself that in this instance they are congruent. The value-object now means thing judged to be a means of procuring this or that end. As prizing, esteeming, holding dear denote ways of acting, so valuing denotes a passing judgment upon such acts with reference to their connection with other acts, or with respect to the continuum of behavior in which they fall. Valuation means change of mode of behavior from direct acceptance and welcoming to doubting and looking into—acts which involve postponement of direct (or so-called overt) action and which imply a future act having a different *meaning* from that just now occurring—for even if one decides to continue in the previous act its meaning-content is different when it is chosen after reflective examination.

A practical judgment has been defined as a judgment of what to do, or what is to be done: a judgment respecting the future termination of an incomplete and in so far indeterminate situation. To say that judgments of value fall within this field is to say two things: one, that the judgment of value is never complete in itself, but always in behalf of determining what is to be done; the other, that judgments of value (as distinct from the direct experience of something as good) imply that value is not anything previously given, but is something to be given by future action, itself conditioned upon (varying with) the judgment. This statement may appear to contradict the recent assertion that a value-object for knowledge means one investigated as a means to competing ends. For such a means it already is; the lobster *will* give me present enjoyment and future indigestion *if* I eat it. But as long as I judge, *value* is indeterminate. The question is not what the thing will do—I may be quite clear about that: it is whether to perform the act which will actualize its potentiality. What will I have the situation *become* as between alternatives? And that means what force shall the thing as means be given? Shall I take it as means to present enjoyment, or as a (negative) condition of future health? When its status in these respects is determined, its value is determined; judgment ceases, action goes on.

Practical judgments do not therefore primarily concern themselves with the value of *objects*; but with the course of action demanded to carry an incomplete situation to its fulfilment. The adequate control of such judgments may, however, be facilitated by judgment of the worth of objects which enter as ends and means into the action contemplated. For example, my primary (and ultimate) judgment has to do, say, with buying a suit of clothes: whether to buy and, if so, what? The question is of better and worse with respect to alternative courses of action, not with respect to various objects. But the judgment will be a judgment (and not a chance reaction) in the degree in which it takes for its intervening subject-matter the value-status of various objects. What are the prices of given suits? What are their styles in respect to current fashion? How do their patterns compare? What about their durability? How about their respective adaptability to the chief wearing use I have in mind? Relative, or comparative, durability, cheapness, suitability, style, aesthetic attractiveness constitute value traits. They are traits of objects not *per se*, but *as entering into a possible and foreseen completing of the situation*. Their value is their force in precisely this function. The decision of better and worse is the determination of their respective capacities and intensities *in this regard*. Apart from their status in this office, they have no traits of value for knowledge. A determination of better value as found in some one suit is equivalent to (has the force of) a decision as to what it is better to do. It provided the lacking stimulus so that action occurs, or passes from its indeterminate-indecisive-state into decision.

Reference to the terms "subjective" and "objective" will, perhaps, raise a cloud of ambiguities. But for this very reason it may be worth while to point out the ambiguous nature of the term objective as applied to valuations. Objective may be identified, quite erroneously, with qualities existing outside of and independently of the situation in which a decision as to a future course of action has to be reached. Or, objective may denote the status of qualities of an object *in respect* to the situation to be completed through judgment. Independently of the situation requiring practical judgment, clothes already have a given price, durability, pattern, etc. These traits are not affected by the judgment. They exist; they are given. But as given they are *not* determinate values. They are not *objects of* valuation; they are *data for* a valuation. We may have to take pains to discover that these given qualities are, but their discovery is in order that there may be a subsequent judgment of value. Were they already definite values, they would not be estimated; they would be stimuli to direct response. If a man had already decided that cheapness constituted value, he would simply take the cheapest suit offered. What he judges is the value of cheapness, and this depends upon its weight or importance in the situation requiring action, as compared with durability, style, adaptability, etc. Discovery of shoddy would not affect the *de facto* durability of the goods, but it would affect the value of cheapness— that is, *the weight assigned that trait in influencing judgment* —which it would not do, if cheapness already had a definite value. A value, in short, means a *consideration*, and a consideration does not mean an existence merely, but an existence having a claim upon judgment. Value judged is not existential quality noted, but is the influence attached by judgment to a given existential quality in determining judgment.

The conclusion is not that value is subjective, but that it is practical. The situation in which judgment of value is required is not mental, much less fanciful. I can but think that much of the recent discussion of the objectivity of value and of value-judgments rests upon a false psychological theory. It rests upon giving certain terms meanings that flow from an introspective psychology which accepts a realm of purely private states of consciousness, private not in a social sense (a sense implying courtesy or mayhap secrecy toward others), but existential independence and separateness. To refer value to choice or desire, for example, is in that case to say that value is subjectively conditioned. Quite otherwise, if we have steered clear from such a psychology. Choice, decision, means primarily a certain act, a piece of behavior on the part of a particular thing. That a horse chooses to eat hay means only that it eats hay; that the man chooses to steal means (at least) that he tries to steal. This trial may come, however, *after* an intervening act of reflection. It then has a certain intellectual or cognitive quality. But it may mean simply the bare fact of an action which is retrospectively called a choice: as a man, in spite of all temptation to belong to another nation, chooses to be born an Englishman, which, if it has any sense at all, signifies a choice to continue in a line adopted without choice. Taken in this latter sense (in which case, terms like choice and desire refer to ways of behavior), their use is only a specification of the general doctrine that all valuation has to do with the determination of a course of action. Choice, preference, is originally only a bias in a given direction, a bias which is no more subjective or psychical than is the fact that a ball thrown is swerving in a particular direction rather than in some other curve. It is just a name for the differential character of the action. But let continuance in a certain line of action become questionable, let, that is to say, it be regarded as a means to a future consequence, which consequence has alternatives, and then choice gets a logical or intellectual sense; a *mental* status if the term "mental" is reserved for acts having this intellectualized quality. Choice still means the fixing of a course of action; it means at least a *set* to be released as soon as physically possible. Otherwise man has not chosen, but has quieted himself into a belief that he has chosen in order to relieve himself of the strain of suspense.

Exactly the same analysis applies to desire. Diverse anticipated ends may provoke divided and competing present reactions; the organism may be torn between different courses, each interfering with the completion of the other. This intra-organic pulling and hauling, this strife of active tendencies, is a genuine phenomenon. The pull in a given direction measures the immediate hold of an anticipated termination or end upon us, as compared with that of some other. If one asked after the mechanism of the valuing process, I have no doubt that the answer would be in terms of desires thus conceived. But unless everything relating to the activity of a highly organized being is to be denominated subjective, I see no ground for calling it subjective. So far as I can make out, the emphasis upon a psychological treatment of value and valuation in a subjective sense is but a highly awkward and negative way of maintaining a positive truth: that value and valuation fall within the universe of *action*: that as welcoming, accepting, is an act, so valuation is a present act determining an act *to be* done, a present act taking place because the future act is uncertain and incomplete.

It does follow from this fact that valuation is not simply a *recognition* of the force or efficiency of a means with respect to continuing a process. For unless there is *question* about its continuation, about its termination, valuation will not occur. And there is no question save where activity is hesitant in direction because of conflict within it. Metaphorically we may say that rain is good to lay the dust, identifying force or efficiency with value. I do not believe that valuations occur and values are brought into being save in a continuing situation where things have potency for carrying forward processes. There is a close relationship between prevailing, valiancy, valency, and value. But the term "value" is not a mere reduplication of the term "efficiency": it adds something. When we are moving toward a result and at the same time are stimulated to move toward something else which is incompatible with it (as in the case of the lobster as a cause of both enjoyment and indigestion), a thing has a dual potency. Not until the end has been established is the value of the lobster settled, although there need be no doubt about its efficiencies. As was pointed out earlier, the practical judgment determines means and end at the same time. How then can value be given, as efficiency is given, until the end is chosen? The rain is (metaphorically) valuable for laying dust. Whether it is valuable for us to have the dust laid—and if so, how valuable—we shall never know until some activity of our own which is a factor in dust-laying comes into conflict with an incompatible activity. Its value is its force, indeed, but it is its force in moving us to one end *rather* than to another. Not every potency, in other words, but potency with the specific qualification of falling within judgment about future action, means value or valuable thing. Consequently there is no value save in situations where desires and the need of deliberation in order to choose are found, and yet this fact gives no excuse for regarding desire and deliberation and decision as subjective phenomena.

To use an Irish bull, as long as a man *knows* what he desires there is no desire; there is movement or endeavor in a given direction. Desire is desires, and simultaneous desires are incompatible; they mark, as we have noted, competing activities, movements in directions, which cannot both be extended. Reflection is a process of finding out what we want, what, as we say, we *really* want, and this means the formation of new desire, a new direction of action. In this process, things *get* values—something they did not possess before, although they had their efficiencies.

At whatever risk of shock, this doctrine should be exposed in all its nakedness. To judge value is to engage in instituting a determinate value where none is given. It is not necessary that antecedently given values should be the data of the valuation; and where they are given data they are only terms in the determination of a not yet existing value. When a man is ill and after deliberation concludes that it be well to see a doctor, the doctor doubtless exists antecedently. But it is not the doctor who is judged to be the good of the situation, but the *seeing* of the doctor: a thing which, by description, exists only because of an act dependent upon

a judgment. Nor is the health the man antecedently possessed (or which somebody has) the thing which he judges
to be a value; the thing judged to be a value is the restoring
of health—something by description not yet existing. The
results flowing from his past health will doubtless influence
him in reaching his judgment that it will be a good to have
restored health, but they do not constitute the good which
forms his subject-matter and object of his judgment. He may
judge that they *were* good without judging that they are now
good, for to be judged now good means to be judged to be the
object of a course of action still to be undertaken. And to
judge that they were good (as distinct from merely recalling
certain benefits which accrued from health) is to judge that
if the situation had required a reflective determination of a
course of action one would have judged health an existence
to be attained or preserved by action. There are dialectic
difficulties which may be raised about judgments of this sort.
For they imply the seeming paradox of a judgment whose
proper subject-matter is its own determinate formation. But
nothing is gained by obscuring the fact that such is the
nature of the practical judgment: it is a judgment of what
and how to judge—of the weight to be assigned to various
factors in the determination of judgment. It would be interesting to inquire into the question whether this peculiarity
may not throw light upon the nature of "consciousness," but
into that field we cannot now go.

III

From what has been said, it immediately follows, of
course, that a determinate value is instituted as a decisive
factor with respect to what is to be done. Wherever a determinate good exists, there is an adequate stimulus to action
and no judgment of what is to be done or of the value of an
object is called for. It is frequently assumed, however, that
valuation is a process of applying some fixed or determinate
value to the various competing goods of a situation; that
valuation implies a prior standard of value and consists in
comparing various goods with the standard as the supreme
value. This assumption requires examination. If it is sound,
it deprives the position which has been taken of any validity.

For it renders the judgment of what to do a matter of applying a value existing ready-made, instead of making—as we have done—the valuation a determination within the practical judgment. The argument would run this way: Every practical judgment depends upon a judgment of the value of the end to be attained; this end may be such only proximately, but that implies something else judged to be good, and so, logically, till we have arrived at the judgment of a supreme good, a final end or *summum bonum*. If this statement correctly describes the state of the case, there can be no doubt that a practical judgment depends upon a prior recognition of value; consequently, the hypothesis upon which we have been proceeding reverses the actual facts.

The first thing by way of critical comment is to point out the ambiguity in the term "end." I should like to fall back upon what was said earlier about the thoroughly reciprocal character of means and end in the practical judgment. If this be admitted, it is also admitted that only by a judgment of means—things having value in the carrying of an indeterminate situation to a completion—is the end determinately made out in judgment. But I fear I cannot count upon this as granted. So I will point out that "end" may mean either the *de facto* limit to judgment, which by definition does not enter into judgment at all, or it may mean the last and completing object of judgment, the conception of that object in which a transitive incompletely given situation would come to rest. Of end in the first sense, it is to be said that it is not a value at all; of end in the second sense, that it is identical with a finale of the kind we have just been discussing or that it is determined in judgment, not a value given by which to control the judgment. It may be asserted that in the illustration used some typical suit of clothes is the value which affords the standard of valuation of all the suits which are offered to the buyer; that he passes judgment on their value as compared with the standard suit as an end and supreme value. This statement brings out the ambiguity just referred to. The need of something to wear is the *stimulus* to the judgment of the value of suits offered, and possession of a suit puts an end *to* judgment. It is an end *of* judgment in the objective, not in the possessive, sense of the preposition "of"; it is an end not in the sense of aim, but in the sense of a terminating limit. When possession begins, judgment has already ceased. And if argument *ad verucundiam* has any weight I may point out that this is the doctrine of Aristotle when he says we never deliberate about ends, but only about means. That is to say, in all deliberation (or practical judgment or inquiry) there is always something outside of judgment which fixes its beginning and end or terminus. And I would add that, according to Aristotle, deliberation always ceases when we have come to the "first link in the chain of causes, which is last in the order of discovery," and this means "when we have traced back the chain of causes [means] to ourselves." In other words, the last end-in-view is always that which operates as the direct or immediate means of setting our own powers in operation. The end-in-view upon which judgment of action settles down is simply the adequate or complete means to the doing of something.

We do deliberate, however, about *aims*, about ends-in-view—a fact which shows their radically different nature from ends as limits to deliberation. The aim in the present instance is not the suit of clothes, but the *getting of a proper* suit. That is what is precisely estimated or valuated; and I think I may claim to have shown that the determination of this aim is identical with the determination of the value of a suit through comparison of the values of cheapness, durability, style, pattern of different suits offered. Value is not determined by comparing various suits with an ideal model, but by comparing various suits with respect to cheapness, durability, adaptability *with one another*—involving, of course, reference also to length of purse, suits already possessed, etc., and other specific elements in the situation which demands that something be done. The purchaser may, of course, have settled upon something which serves as a model before he goes to buy; but that only means that his judging has been done beforehand; the model does not then function in judgment, but in his act as stimulus to immediate action. And there is a consideration here involved of the utmost importance as to practical judgments of the moral type: The more completely the notion of the model is formed outside and irrespective of the specific conditions which the situation of action presents, the less intelligent is the act. Most men might have their ideals of the model changed somewhat in the face of the actual offering, even in the case of buying clothes. The man who is not accessible to such change in the case of moral situations has ceased to be a moral agent and become a reacting machine. In short, the standard of valuation is formed in the process of practical judgment or valuation. It is not something taken from outside and applied within it—such application means there is no judgment.

IV

Nothing has been said thus far about a standard. Yet the conception of a standard, or a measure, is so closely connected with valuation that its consideration affords a test of the conclusions reached. It must be admitted that the concepts of the nature of a standard pointed to by the course of the prior discussion is not in conformity with current conceptions. For the argument points to a standard which is determined within the process of valuation, not outside of it, and hence not capable of being employed ready-made, therefore, to settle the valuing process. To many persons, this will seem absurd to the point of self-contradiction. The prevailing conception, however, has been adopted without examination; it is a preconception. If accepted, it deprives judgment and knowledge of all significant import in connection with moral action. If the standard is already given, all that remains is its mechanical application to the case in hand—as one would apply a yard rule to dry-goods. Genuine moral uncertainty is then impossible; where it seems to exist, it is only a name for a moral unwillingness, due to inherent viciousness, to recognize and apply the rules already made and provided, or else for a moral corruption which has enfeebled man's power of moral apprehension. When the doctrine of standards prior to and independent of moral judgments is accompanied by these other doctrines of original sin and corruption, one must respect the thoroughgoing logic of the doctrine. Such is not, however, the case with the modern theories which make the same assumption of standards preceding instead of resulting

from moral judgments, and which ignore the question of uncertainty and error in their apprehension. Such considerations do not, indeed, decide anything, but they may serve to
get a more unprejudiced hearing for a hypothesis which runs
counter to current theories, since it but formulates the trend
of current practices in their increasing tendency to make the
act of intelligence the central factor in morals.

Let us, accordingly, consider the alternatives to regarding the standard of value as something evolved in the process
of reflective valuation. How can such a standard be known?
Either by an a priori method of intuition, or by abstraction
from prior cases. The latter conception throws us into the
arms of hedonism. For the hedonistic theory of the standard
of value derives its logical efficiency from the consideration
that the notion of a prior and fixed standard (one which is
not determined within the situation by reflection) forces us
back upon antecedent irreducible pleasures and pains which
alone are values definite and certain enough to supply
standards. They alone are simple enough to be independent
and ultimate. The apparently common-sense alternative
would be to take the "value" of prior situations *in toto*, say,
the value of an act of kindness to a sufferer. But any such
good is a function of the total unanalyzed situation; it has,
consequently, no application to a new situation unless the
new exactly repeats the old one. Only when the "good" is
resolved into simple and unalterable units, in terms of which
old situations can be equated to new ones on the basis of the
number of units contained, can an unambiguous standard
be found.

The logic is unimpeachable, and points to irreducible
pleasures and pains as the standard of valuation. The difficulty is not in the logic but in empirical facts, facts which
verify our prior contention. Conceding, for the sake of argument, that there are definite existences such as are called
pleasures and pains, they are *not* value-objects, but are only
things to be valued. Exactly the same pleasure or pain, as an
existence, has different values at different times according to
the way in which it is judged. What is the value of the
pleasure of eating the lobster as compared with the pains of
indigestion? The rule tells us, of course, to break up the

pleasure and pain into elementary units and count.[10] Such ultimate simple units seem, however, to be about as much within the reach of ordinary knowledge as atoms or electrons are within the grasp of the man of the street. Their resemblance to the ultimate, neutral units which analytic psychologists have postulated as a methodological necessity is evident. Since the value of even such a definite entity as a toothache varies according to the organization constructed and presented in reflection, it is clear that ordinary empirical pleasures and pains are highly complex.

This difficulty, however, may be waived. We may even waive the fact that a theory which set out to be ultra-empirical is now enmeshed in the need for making empirical facts meet dialectical requirements. Another difficulty is too insuperable to be waived. In any case the quantity of elementary existences which constitutes the criterion of measurement is dependent upon the very judgment which is assumed to be regulated by it. The standard of valuation is the units which will *result* from an act; they are future consequences. Now the character of the agent judging is one of the conditions of the production of these consequences. A callous person not only will not foresee certain consequences, and will not be able to give them proper weight, but he does not afford the same condition of their occurrence which is constituted by a sensitive man. It is quite possible to employ judgment so as to produce acts which will increase this organic callousness. The analytic conception of the

10. Analytic realism ought to be favorable to such a hedonism; the fact that present-day analytic realists are not favorable would seem to indicate that they have not taken their logic seriously enough, but have been restrained, by practical motives, from applying it thoroughly. To say that the moral life presents a high degree of organization and integration is to say something which is true, but is also to say something which by the analytic logic calls for its resolution into ultimate and independent simples. Unless they accept the pleasures and pains of Bentham as such ultimates, they are bound to present acceptable substitutes. But here they tend to shift their logic and to make the fulfilment of some *organization* (variously defined) the standard good. Consistency would then admit the hypothesis that in *all* cases an eventual organization rather than antecedent simples supplies the standard of knowledge. Meanwhile the term "fulfilment" (or any similar term) stands as an acknowledgment that the organization in question is not something ontologically prior but is one yet to be achieved.

moral criterion provides—logically—for deliberate blunting
of susceptibilities. If the matter at issue is simply one of
number of units of pleasure over pain, arrange matters so
that certain pains will not, as matter of fact, be felt. While
this result may be achieved by manipulation of extra-
organic conditions, it may also be effected by rendering the
organism insensitive. Persistence in a course which in the
short run yields uneasiness and sympathetic pangs will in
the long run eliminate these pains and leave a net pleasure
balance.

This is a time-honored criticism of hedonism. My
present concern with it is purely logical. It shows that the
attempt to bring over from past objects the elements of a
standard for valuing future consequences is a hopeless one.
The express object of a valuation-judgment is to release
factors which, being new, cannot be measured on the basis
of the past alone. This discussion of the analytic logic as
applied in morals would, however, probably not be worth
while did it not serve to throw into relief the significance of
any appeal to fulfilment of a system or organization as *the*
moral good—the standard. Such an appeal, if it is wary, is
an appeal to the present situation as *undergoing that reorganization that will confer upon it the unification which
it lacks*; to organization as something to be brought about,
to be made. And it is clear that this appeal meets all the
specifications of judgments of practice as they have been
described. The organization which is to be fulfilled through
action is an organization which, at the time of judging, is
present in conception, in idea—in, that is, reflective inquiry
as a phase of reorganizing activity. And since its presence
in conception is both a condition of the organization aimed
at *and* a function of the adequacy of the reflective inquiry,
it is evident that there is here a confirmation of our statement that the practical judgment is a judgment of what and
how to judge as an integral part of the completion of an
incomplete temporal situation. More specifically, it also appears that the standard is a rule for conducting inquiry to
its completion: it is a counsel to make examination of the
operative factors complete, a warning against suppressing
recognition of any of them. However a man may impose

upon himself or upon others, a man's real measure of value is exhibited in what he *does*, not in what he consciously thinks or says. For the doing is the *actual* choice. It is the completed reflection.

It is comparatively easy at the present time in moral theory to slam both hedonism and apriorism. It is not so easy to see the logical implications of the alternative to them. The conception of an organization of interests or tendencies is often treated as if it were a conception which is definite in subject-matter as well as clear-cut in form. It is taken not as a rule for procedure in inquiry, a direction and a warning (which it is), but as something all of whose constituents are already given for *knowledge*, even though not given in fact. The act of fulfilling or realizing must then be treated as devoid of intellectual import. It is a mere doing, not a learning and a testing. But how can a situation which is incomplete in fact be completely known until it *is* complete? Short of the fulfilment of a conceived organization, how can the conception of the proposed organization be anything more than a working hypothesis, a method of treating the given elements in order to see what happens? Does not every notion which implies the possibility of an apprehension of knowledge of the end to be reached[11] also imply either an a priori revelation of the nature of that end, or else that organization is nothing but a whole composed of elementary parts already given—the logic of hedonism?

The logic of subsumption in the physical sciences meant that a given state of things could be compared with a ready-made concept as a model—the phenomena of the heavens with the implications of, say, the circle. The methods of experimental science broke down this notion; they substituted for an alleged regulative model a formula which was the integrated function of the particular phenomena themselves, a formula to be used as a method of further observa-

---

11. It must not be overlooked that a mere reminder of an end previously settled upon may operate as a sufficient stimulus to action. It is probably this act of calling the end to mind which the realist confuses with knowledge, and therefore terms apprehension. But there is nothing cognitive about it, any more than there is in pressing a button to give the signal for an act already decided upon.

tions and experiments and thereby tested and developed. The unwillingness to believe that, in a similar fashion, moral standards or models can be trusted to develop out of the specific situations of action shows how little the general logical force of the method of science has been grasped. Physical knowledge did not as matter of fact advance till the dogma of models or forms as standards of knowledge had been ousted. Yet we hang tenaciously to a like doctrine in morals for fear of moral chaos. It once seemed to be impossible that the disordered phenomena of perception could generate a knowledge of law and order; it was supposed that independent principles of order must be supplied and the phenomena measured by approach to or deviation from the fixed models. The ordinary conception of a standard in practical affairs is a precise analogue. Physical knowledge started on a secure career when men had courage to start from the irregular scene and to treat the suggestions to which it gave rise as methods for instituting new observations and experiences. Acting upon the suggested conceptions they analyzed, extended, and ordered phenomena and thus made improved conceptions—methods of inquiry—possible. It is reasonable to believe that what holds moral knowledge back is above all the conception that there are standards of good given to knowledge apart from the work of reflection in constructing methods of action. As the bringer of bad news gets a bad name, being made to share in the production of the evil which he reports, so honest acknowledgment of the uncertainty of the moral situation and of the hypothetical character of all rules of moral mensuration prior to acting upon them is treated as if it originated the uncertainty and created the skepticism.

It may be contended, however, that all this does not justify the earlier statement that the limiting situation which occasions and cuts off judgment is not itself a value. Why, it will be asked, does a man buy a suit of clothes unless that is a value, or at least a proximate means to a further value? The answer is short and simple: Because he has to; because the situation in which he lives demands it. The answer probably seems too summary. But it may suggest that while a man lives, he never is called upon to judge whether he shall act, but simply *how* he shall act. A decision not to act is a decision to act in a certain way; it is never a judgment not to act, unqualifiedly. It is a judgment to do something else—to wait, for example. A judgment that the best thing to do is to retire from active life, to become a Simon Stylites, is a judgment to act in a certain way, conditioned upon the necessity that, irrespective of judging, a man will have to act somehow anyway. A decision to commit suicide is not a decision to be dead; it is a decision to perform a certain act. The act may depend upon reaching the conclusion that life is not worth living. But as a judgment, this is a conclusion to act in a way to terminate the possibility of further situations requiring judgment and action. And it does not imply that a judgment about life as a supreme value and standard underlies all judgments as to how to live. More specifically, it is not a judgment upon the value of life *per se*, but a judgment that one does not find at hand the specific means of making life worth while. As an act to be done, it falls within and assumes life. As a judgment upon the value of life, by definition it evades the issue. No one ever influenced a person considering committing suicide by arguments concerning the value of life, but only by suggesting or supplying conditions and means which make life worth living; in other words, by furnishing *direct* stimuli to living.

However, I fear that all this argument may only obscure a point obvious without argument, namely, that all deliberation upon what to do is concerned with the completion and determination of a situation in some respect incomplete and so indeterminate. Every such situation is specific; it is not *merely* incomplete; the incompleteness is *of* a specific situation. Hence the situation sets limits to the reflective process; what is judged has reference to it and that which limits never is judged in the particular situation in which it is limiting. Now we have in ordinary speech a word which expresses the nature of the conditions which limit the judgments of value. It is the word "invaluable." The word does not mean something of supreme value as compared with other things any more than it means something of zero value. It means something out of the scope of valuation— something out of the range of judgment; whatever in the situation at hand is not and cannot be any part of the subject-matter of judgment and which yet instigates and cuts short the judgment. It means, in short, that judgment at some point runs against the brute act of holding something dear as its limit.

V

The statement that values are determined in the process of judgment of what to do (that is, in situations where preference depends upon reflection upon the conditions and possibilities of a situation requiring action) will be met by the objection that our practical deliberations usually assume precedent specific values and also a certain order or grade among them. There is a sense in which I am not concerned to deny this. Our deliberate choices go on in situations more or less like those in which we have previously chosen. When deliberation has reached a valuation, and action has confirmed or verified the conclusion, the result remains. Situations overlap. The m which is judged better than n in one situation is found worse than l in another, and so on; thus a certain order of precedence is established. And we have to broaden the field to cover the habitual order of reflective preferences in the community to which we belong. The valu-eds or valuables thus constituted present themselves as facts in subsequent situations. Moreover, by the same kind of operation, the dominating objects of past valuations present themselves as standardized values.

But we have to note that such value-standards are only presumptive. Their status depends, on one hand, upon the extent in which the present situation is like the past. In a progressive or rapidly altering social life, the presumption of identical present value is weakened. And while it would be foolish not to avail one's self of the assistance in present valuations of the valuables established in other situations, we have to remember that habit operates to make us overlook differences and presume identity where it does not exist —to the misleading of judgment. On the other hand, the contributory worth of past determinations of value is dependent upon the extent in which *they* were critically made; especially upon the extent in which the consequences brought about through acting upon them have been carefully noted. In other words, the presumptive force of a past value in present judgment depends upon the pains taken with its verification.

In any case, so far as judgment takes place (instead of the reminiscence of a prior good operating as a direct stimulus to present action) all valuation is in some degree a revaluation. Nietzsche would probably not have made so much of a sensation, but he would have been within the limits of wisdom, if he had confined himself to the assertion that all judgment, in the degree in which it is critically intelligent, is a transvaluation of prior values. I cannot escape recognition that any allusion to modification or transformation of an object through judgment arouses partisan suspicion and hostility. To many it appears to be a survival of an idealistic epistemology. But I see only three alternatives. Either there are no practical judgments—as judgments they are wholly illusory; or the future is bound to be but a repetition of the past or a reproduction of something eternally existent in some transcendent realm (which is the same thing logically),[12] or the object of a practical judgment is some change, some alteration, to be brought about in the given, the nature of the change depending upon the judgment and yet constituting its subject-matter. Unless the epistemological realist accepts one of the two first alternatives, he seems bound, in accepting the third, to admit not merely that practical judgments make a difference in things as an after-effect (this he seems ready enough to admit), but that the import and validity of judgments is a matter of the difference thus made. One may, of course, hold that this is just what marks the distinction of the practical judg-

12. Upholders of this view generally disguise the assumption of repetition by the notion that what is judged is progress in the direction of approximation to an eternal value. But as matter of fact, progress is never judged (as I have had repeated occasion to point out) by reference to a transcendent eternal value, but in reference to the success of the end-in-view in meeting the needs and conditions of the specific situation—a surrender of the doctrine in favor of the one set forth in the text. Logically, the notion of progress as approximation has no place. The thesis should read that we always try to repeat a given value, but always fail as a matter of fact. And constant failure is a queer name for progress.

ment from the scientific judgment. But one who admits this fact as respects a practical judgment can no longer claim that it is fatal to the very idea of judgment to suppose that its proper object is some difference to be brought about in things, and that the truth of the judgment is constituted by the differences in consequences actually made. And a logical realist who takes seriously the notion that moral good is a fulfilment of an organization or integration must admit that any proposition about such an object is prospective (for it is something *to be* attained through action), and that the proposition is made for the sake of furthering the fulfilment. Let one start at this point and carry back the conception into a consideration of other kinds of propositions, and one will have, I think, the readiest means of apprehending the intent of the theory that all propositions are but the propoundings of possible knowledge, not knowledge itself. For unless one marks off the judgment of good from other judgment by means of an arbitrary division of the organism from the environment, or of the subjective from the objective, no ground for any sharp line of division in the propositional-continuum will appear.

But (to obviate misunderstanding) this does not mean that some psychic state or act makes the difference in things. In the first place, the subject-matter of the judgment is a change to be brought about; and, in the second place, this subject-matter does not become an *object* until the judgment has issued in act. It is the act which makes the difference, but nevertheless the act is but the complete object of judgment and the judgment is complete as a judgment only in the act. The anti-pragmatists have been asked (notably by Professor A. W. Moore) how they sharply distinguish between judgment—or knowledge—and act and yet freely admit and insist that knowledge makes a difference in action and hence in existence. This is the crux of the whole matter. And it is a logical question. It is not a query (as it seems to have been considered) as to how the mental can influence a physical thing like action—a variant of the old question of how the mind affects the body. On the contrary, the implication is that the relation of knowledge to action becomes a problem of the action of a mental (or logical) entity upon a physical one only when the logical import of judgment has been misconceived. The positive contention is that the realm of logical propositions presents in a realm of *possibility* the specific rearrangement of things which overt action presents in actuality. Hence the passage of a proposition into action is not a miracle, but the realization of its own character— its own meaning as logical. I do not profess, of course, to have shown that such is the case for *all* propositions; that is a matter which I have not discussed. But in showing the tenability of the hypothesis that practical judgments are of that nature, I have at least ruled out any purely dialectic proof that the *nature* of knowledge as such forbids enter- taining the hypothesis that the import—indirect if not direct —of all logical propositions is some difference to be brought about. The road is at least cleared for a more unprejudiced consideration of this hypothesis on its own merits.

III. Sense Perception as Knowledge

I mentioned incidentally in the first section that it is conceivable that failure to give adequate consideration to practical judgments may have a compromising effect upon the consideration of other types. I now intend to develop this remark with regard to sense perception as a form of knowledge. The topic is so bound up with a multitude of perplexing psychological and epistemological traditions that I have first to make it reasonably clear what it is and what it is not which I propose to discuss. I endeavored in an earlier series of papers[13] to point out that the question of the *ma- terial* of sense perception is not, as such, a problem of the theory of knowledge at all, but simply a problem of the occurrence of a certain material—a problem of causal condi- tions and consequences. That is to say, the problem pre- sented by an image[14] of a bent stick, or by a dream, or by "secondary" sensory qualities is properly a problem of physics

---

13. See IX and X, "Naïve Realism *vs.* Presentative Realism and Epistemological Realism: The Alleged Ubiquity of the Knowledge Relation" in *Essays in Experimental Logic* [*Middle Works* 6: 103–22].
14. I use the term "image" in the sense of optics, not of psychology.

—of conditions of occurrence, and not of logic, of truth or falsity, fact or fiction. That the existence of a red *quale* is dependent upon disturbances of a certain velocity of a medium in connection with certain changes of the organism is not to be confused with the notion that red is a way of knowing, in some more or less adequate fashion, some more "real" object or else of knowing itself. The fact of causation —or functional dependence—no more makes the *quale* an "appearance" to the mind of something more real than itself or of itself than it makes bubbles on the water a real fish transferred by some cognitive distortion into a region of appearance. With a little stretching we may use the term appearance in either case, but the term only means that the red *quale* or the water-bubble is an *obvious* or conspicuous thing from which we infer something else not so obvious.

This position thus freely resumed here needs to be adequately guarded on all sides. It implies that the question of the existence or presence of the *subject-matter* of even a complex sense perception may be treated as a question of physics. It also implies that the *existence* of a sense perception may be treated as a problem of physics. But the position is not that *all* the problems of sense perception are thereby exhausted. There is still, on the contrary, the problem of the cognitive status of sense perception. So far from denying this fact, I mean rather to emphasize it in holding that this knowledge aspect is not to be identified—as it has been in both realistic and idealistic epistemologies—with the simple *occurrence* of presented subject-matter and with the *occurrence* of a perceptive act. It is often stated, for example, that primitive sense objects when they are stripped of all inferential material cannot possibly be false—but with the implication that they, therefore, must be true. Well, I meant to go this statement one better—to state that they are neither true nor false—that is, that the distinction of true-or-false is as irrelevant and inapplicable as to any other existence, as it is, say, to being more than five feet high or having a low blood pressure. This position when taken leaves over the question of sense perception as knowledge, as capable of truth or falsity. It is this question, then, which I intend to discuss in this paper.

I

My first point is that some sense perceptions, at least (as matter of fact the great bulk of them), are without any doubt forms of practical judgment—or, more accurately, are terms in practical judgments as propositions of what to do. When in walking down a street I see a sign on the lamp-post at the corner, I assuredly see a sign. Now in ordinary context (I do not say always or necessarily) this is a sign of what to do—to continue walking or to turn. The other term of the proposition may not be stated or it may be; it is probably more often tacit. Of course, I have taken the case of the sign purposely. But the case may be extended. The lamp-post as perceived is to a lamp-lighter a sign of something else than a turn, but still a sign of something to be done. To another man, it may be a sign of a possible support. I am anxious not to force the scope of cases of this class beyond what would be accepted by an unbiased person, but I wish to point out that certain features of the perceived object, as a cognitive term, which do not seem at first sight to fall within this conception of the object, as, an intellectual sign of what to do, turn out upon analysis to be covered by it. It may be said, for example, that our supposed pedestrian perceives much besides that which serves as evidence of the thing to be done. He perceives the lamp-*post*, for example, and possibly the carbons of the arc. And these assuredly do not enter into the indication of what to do or how to do it.

The reply is threefold. In the first place, it is easy—and usual—to read back into the sense perception more than was actually in it. It is easy to *recall* the familiar features of the lamp-post; it is practically impossible—or at least very unusual—to recall what was actually perceived. So we read the former into the latter. The *tendency* is for actual perception to limit itself to the minimum which will serve as sign. But, in the second place, since it is never wholly so limited, since there is always a surplusage of perceived object, the fact stated in the objection is admitted. But it is precisely this surplusage which has not *cognitive* status. It does not serve as a sign, but neither is it *known*, or a term in knowledge. A child, walking by his father's side, with no aim and hence no reason for securing indications of what to do, will probably see more in his idle curiosity than his parent. He will have more presented material. But this does not mean that he is making more propositions, but only that he is getting more material for possible propositions. It means, in short, that he is in an aesthetic attitude of realization rather than in a cognitive attitude. But even the most economical observer has some aesthetic, non-cognitive surplusage.[15] In the third place, surplusage is necessary for the operation of the signifying function. Independently of the fact that surplusage may be required to render the sign specific, action is free (its variation is under control) in the degree in which *alternatives* are present. The pedestrian has probably the two alternatives in mind: to go straight on or to turn. The perceived object might indicate to him another alternative—to stop and inquire of a passer-by. And, as is obvious in a more complicated case, it is the extent of the perceived object which both multiplies alternative ways of acting and gives the grounds for selecting among them. A physician, for example, deliberately avoids such hard-and-fast alternatives as have been postulated in our instance. He does not observe simply to get an indication of whether the man is well or ill, but, in order to determine what to do, he extends his explorations over a wide field. Much of his perceived object field is immaterial to what he finally does; that is, does not serve as sign. But it is all relevant to *judging* what he is to do. Sense perception as a term in practical judgment *must* include more than the element which finally serves as sign. If it did not, there would be no perception, but only a direct stimulus to action.[16]

15. That something of the cognitive, something of the sign or term function, enters in as a catalyzer, so to speak, in even the most aesthetic experiences, seems to be altogether probable, but that question it is not necessary to raise here.

16. The superstition that whatever influences the action of a conscious being must be an unconscious sensation or perception, if it is not a conscious one, should be summarily dismissed. We are active beings from the start and are naturally, wholly apart from consciousness, engaged in redirecting our action in response to changes in our surroundings. *Alternative* possibilities, and hence an indeterminate situation, change direct response into a response mediated by a perception as a sign of possibilities, that is, a physiological stimulus into a perceived quality: a sensory datum.

The conclusion that such perceptions as we have been considering are terms in an inference is to be carefully discriminated from the loose statement that sense perceptions are unconscious inferences. There is a great difference between saying that the perception of a shape affords an indication for an inference and saying that the perception of shape is itself an inference. That definite shapes would not be perceived, were it not for neural changes brought about in prior inferences, is a possibility; it may be, for aught I know, an ascertained fact. Such telescoping of a perceived object with the object inferred from it may be a constant function; but in any case the telescoping is not a matter of a present inference going on unconsciously, but is the result of an organic modification which has occurred in consequence of prior inferences. In similar fashion, to say that to see a table is to get an indication of something to write on is in no way to say that the perception of a table is an inference from sensory data. To say that certain earlier perceived objects not having as perceived the character of a table have now "fused" with the results of inferences drawn from them is not to say that the perception of the table is now an inference. Suppose we say that the first perception was of colored patches; that we inferred from this the possibility of reaching and touching, and that on performing these acts we secured certain qualities of hardness, smoothness, etc., and that these are now all fused with the color-patches. At most this only signifies that certain *previously* inferred qualities have now become consolidated with qualities from which they were formerly inferred. And such fusion or consolidation is precisely *not inference*. As matter of fact, such "fusion" of qualities, given and *formerly* inferred, is but a matter of speaking. What has really happened is that *brain* processes which formerly happened successively now happen simultaneously. What we are dealing with is not a fact of cognition, but a fact of the organic conditions of the occurrence of an act of perception.

Let us apply the results to the question of sense "illusions." The bent reed in the water comes naturally to mind. Purely physical considerations account for the refraction of the light which produces an optical image of a bent stick.

This has nothing to do with knowledge or with sense perception—with seeing. It is simply and wholly a matter of the
properties of light and a lens. Such refractions are constantly
produced without our noting them. In the past, however,
light refracted and unrefracted has been a constant stimulus
to responsive actions. It is a matter of the native constitution
of the organism that light stimulates the eyes to follow and
the arms to reach and the hands to clutch and handle. As a
consequence, certain arrangements of reflected and refracted
light have become a sign to perform certain specific acts of
handling and touching. As a rule, stimuli and reactions occur
in an approximately homogeneous medium—the air. The
system of signs or indexes of action set up has been based
upon this fact and accommodated to it. A habit or bias in
favor of a certain kind of inference has been set up. We
infer from a bent ray of light that the hand, in touching the
reflecting object, will, at a certain point, have to change its
direction. This habit is carried over to a medium in which
the conclusion does not hold. Instead of saying that light is
bent—which it is—we *infer* that the stick is bent: we infer
that the hand could not protract a straight course in handling
the object. But an expert fisherman never makes such an
error in spearing fish. Reacting in media of different re-
fractive capacities, he bases his signs and inferences upon
the conditions and results of his media. I see no difference
between these cases and that of a man who can read his own
tongue. He sees the word "pain" and infers it means a certain
physical discomfort. As matter of fact, the thing perceived
exists in an unfamiliar medium and signifies bread. To the
one accustomed to the French language the right inference
occurs.[17] There is neither error nor truth in the optical image:
It just exists physically. But we take it for something else,
we behave to it as if it were something else. We *mis*-take it.

II

So far as I can see, the pronounced tendency to regard
the perceived object as itself the object of a peculiar kind of
knowledge instead of as a term in knowledge of the practical

17. Compare Woodbridge, *Journal of Philosophy, Psychology and
Scientific Methods*, X, 5.

kind has two causes. One is the confirmed habit of neglecting the wide scope and import of practical judgments. This leads to overlooking the responsive act as the other term indicated by the perception, and to taking the perceived object as the whole of the situation just by itself. The other cause is the fact that because perceived objects are constantly employed as evidence of what is to be done—or how to do something —they themselves become the objects of prolonged and careful scrutiny. We pass naturally and inevitably from recognition to *observation*. Inference will usually take care of itself if the datum is properly determined. At the present day, a skilled physician will have little difficulty in inferring typhoid instead of malaria from certain symptoms provided he can make certain observations—that is, secure certain data from which to infer. The labor of intelligence is thus transferred from inference to the determination of data, the data being determined, however, in the interests of inference and as parts of an inference.

At this point, a significant complication enters in. The ordinary assumption in the discussion of the relation of perceived objects to knowledge is that "the" object—the real object—of knowledge in perception is the thing which *caused* the qualities which are given. It is assumed, that is, that the other term of a proposition in which a sense datum is one term must be the thing which produced it. Since this producing object does not for the most part appear in ordinary sense perception, we have on our hands perception as an epistemological problem—the relation of an appearance to some reality which it, somehow, conceals rather than indicates. Hence also the difficulties of "reconciling" scientific knowledge in physics where these causes are the terms of the propositions with "empirical" or sense perception knowledge where they do not even appear. Here is where the primary advantage of recognizing that ordinary sense perceptions are forms of practical judgment comes in. In practical judgments, the other term is as open and above board as is the sensory quality: it is the thing to be done, the response to be selected. To borrow an illustration of Professor Woodbridge's: A certain sound indicates to the mother that her baby needs attention. If she turns out to be in error, it is not because sound ought to mean so many vibrations of the air, and as matter of fact doesn't even suggest air vibrations, but because there is wrong inference as to the act to be performed.

I imagine that if error never occurred in inferences of this practical sort the human race would have gone on quite contented with them. However that may be, errors *do* occur and the endeavor to control inference as to consequences (so as to reduce their likelihood of error) leads to propositions where the knowledge-object of the perceived thing is not something to be done, but the cause which produced it. The mother finds her baby peacefully sleeping and says the baby didn't *make* the noise. She investigates and decides a swinging door *made* it. Instead of inferring a consequence, she infers a cause. If she had identified the noise in the first place, she would have concluded that the hinges needed oiling.

Now where does the argument stand? The proper control of inference in specific cases is found (*a*) to lie in the proper identification of the datum. If the perception is of a certain kind, the inference takes place as a matter of course; or else inference can be suspended until more adequate data are found, and thus error is avoided even if truth be not found. Furthermore (*b*) it is discovered that the most effective way of identifying datum (and securing adequate data) is by inference to its cause. The mother stops short with the baby and the door as causes. But the same motives which made her transfer her inference from consequences to conditions are the motives which lead others to inferring from sounds to vibrations of air. Hence our scientific propositions about sensory data. They are not, as such, about things to do, but about things which have been done, have happened—"facts." But they have reference, nevertheless, to inferences regarding consequences to be effected. They are the means of securing data which will prevent errors which would otherwise occur, and which facilitate an entirely new crop of inferences as to possibilities—means and ends—of action. That scientific men should be conscious of this reference or even interested in it is not at all necessary, for I am talking about the logic of propositions, not about biography or psychology. If I reverted to psychology, it would be to point out that there is no reason in the world why the practical activity of some men should not be predominantly directed into the pursuits connected with discovery. The extent in which they actually are so directed depends upon social conditions.

III

We are brought to a consideration of the notion of "primitive" sense data. It was long customary to treat the attempt to define true knowledge in terms derived from sense data as a confusion of psychology—or the history of the growth of knowledge—with logic, the theory of the character of knowledge as knowledge. As matter of fact, there *is* confusion, but in the opposite direction. The attempt involved a confusion of logic with psychology—that is, it treated a phase of the technique of inference as if it were a natural history of the growth of ideas and beliefs.

The chief source of error in ordinary inference is an unrecognized complexity of data. Perception which is not experimentally controlled fails to present sufficiently wide data to secure differentia of possible inferences, and it fails to present, even in what is given, lines of cleavage which are important for proper inference. This is only an elaborate way of saying what scientific inquiry has made clear, that, for purposes of inference as to conditions of production of what is present, *ordinary* sense perception is too narrow, too confused, too vivid as to some *quales* and too blurred as to some others. Let us confine our attention for the moment to confusion. It has often been pointed out that sense qualities being just what they are, it is illegitimate to introduce such notions as obscurity or confusion into them: a slightly illuminated color is just as irretrievably what it is, as clearly itself, as an object in the broad glare of noon day. But the case stands otherwise when the *quale* is taken as a datum for inference. It is not so easy to identify a perceived object *for purposes of inference* in the dusk as in bright light. From the standpoint of an inference to be effected, the confusion is the same as an unjustifiable simplification. This oversimplification has the effect of making the *quale*, as a term

of inference, ambiguous. To infer from it is to subject ourselves to the danger of all fallacies of ambiguity which are
expounded in the text-books. The remedy is clearly the resolution, by experimental means, of what seems to be a simple
datum into its "elements." This is a case of analysis; it differs
from other modes of analysis only in the subject-matter upon
which it is directed, viz., something which had been previously accepted as a simple whole. The result of this analysis
is the existence as objects of perception of isolated qualities
like the colors of the spectrum scientifically determined, the
tones of the scale in all their varying intensities, etc., in
short, the "sensations" or sense qualities of contemporary
psychology text-books or the "simple ideas" of sensation of
Locke or the "objects of sense" of Russell. They are the
material of sense perception discriminated for the purpose
of better inferences.

Note that these simple data or elements are not original,
psychologically or historically; they are *logical* primitives—
that is, irreducible for purposes of inference. They are simply
the most unambiguous and best defined objects of perception
which can be secured to serve as *signs*. They are experimentally determined, with great art, precisely because the
naturally given, the customary, objects in perception have
been ambiguous or confused terms in inference. Hence they
are replaced, through experimental means involving the use
of wide scientific knowledge deductively employed, by simpler sense objects. Stated in current phraseology, "sensations" (i.e., qualities present to sense) are not the elements
out of which perceptions are composed, constituted, or constructed; they are the finest, most carefully discriminated
objects of perception. We do not first perceive a single,
thoroughly defined shade, a tint and hue of red; its perception is the last refinement of observation. Such things are
the limits of perception, but they are final, not initial, limits.
They are what is perceived to be given under the most
favorable possible conditions; conditions, moreover, which
do not present themselves accidentally, but which have to
be intentionally and experimentally established, and detection of which exacts the use of a vast body of scientific
propositions.

I hope it is now evident what was meant by saying that current logic presents us not with a confusion of psychology with logic, but with a wholesale mistaking of logical determinations for facts of psychology. The confusion was begun by Locke—or rather made completely current through the enormous influence exercised by Locke—and some reference to Locke may be of aid in clearing up the point. Locke's conception of knowledge was logical, not psychological. He meant by knowledge thoroughly justified beliefs or propositions, "certainty," and carefully distinguished it from what passed current as knowledge at a given time. The latter he called "assent," opinion, belief, or judgment. Moreover, his interest in the latter was logical. He was after an art of controlling the proper degree of assent to be given in matters of probability. In short, his sole aim was to determine certainty where certainty is possible and to determine the due degree of probability in the much vaster range of cases where only probability is attainable. A natural history of the growth of "knowledge" in the sense of what happens to pass for knowledge was the last of his interests. But he was completely under the domination of the ruling idea of his time: namely, that *Nature* is the norm of truth. Now the earliest period of human life presents the "work of nature" in its pure and unadulterated form. The normal is the original, and the original is the normative. Nature is both beneficent and truthful in its work; it retains all the properties of the Supreme Being whose vice-regent it is. To get the logical ultimates we have only, therefore, to get back to the natural primitives. Under the influence of such deistic ideas, Locke writes a mythology of the history of knowledge, starting from clear and distinct meanings, each simple, well-defined, sharply and unambiguously just what it is on its face, without concealments and complications, and proceeds by "natural" compoundings up to the store of complex ideas, and to the perception of simple relations of agreement among ideas: a perception always certain if the ideas are simple, and always controllable in the case of complex ideas if we consider the simple ideas and their compoundings. Thus he established the habit of taking logical discriminations as historical or psychological primitives—as "sources" of beliefs and knowledge instead of as checks upon inference and as means of knowing.

I hope reference to Locke will not make him a scapegoat. I should not have mentioned him if it were not that this way of looking at things found its way over into orthodox psychology and then back again into the foundations of logical theory. It may be said to be the stock in trade of the school of empiricist logicians, and (what is even more important) of the other schools of logic whenever they are dealing with propositions of perception and observation: *vide* Russell's trusting confidence in "atomic" propositions as psychological primitives. It led to the supposition that there is a kind of *knowledge* or simple apprehension (or sense acquaintance) implying no inference and yet basic to inference. Note, if you please, the multitude of problems generated by thinking of whatever is present in experience (as sensory qualities are present) as if it were, intrinsically and apart from the use made of it, subject-matter of knowledge.

a) The mind-body problem becomes an integral part of the problem of knowledge. Sense organs, neurones, and neuronic connections are certainly involved in the occurrence of a sense quality. If the occurrence of the latter is in and of itself a mode of knowledge, it becomes a matter of utmost importance to determine just how the sense organs take part in it. If one is an idealist he responds with joy to any intimation that the "process of apprehension" (that is, speaking truly, the physical conditions of the occurrence of the sensory datum) transforms the extra-organic stimulus: the alteration is testimony somehow to the constitutive nature of mind! But if he is a realist he conceives himself under obligation to show that the external stimulus is transmitted without any alteration and is apprehended just as it is; color must be shown to be simply, after all, a compacting of vibrations—or else the validity of knowledge is impugned! Recognize that knowledge is something *about* the color, whether about its conditions or causes or consequences or whatever and that we don't have to identify color itself with a mode of knowing, and the situation changes. We know a color when we understand, just as we know a thunder-storm when we understand. More generally speaking, the relation of brain-change to consciousness is thought to be an essential part of the problem of knowledge. But if the brain is involved in knowing simply as part of the mechanism of acting, as the mechanism for coordinating partial and competing stimuli into a single scheme of response, as part of the mechanism of actual experimental inquiry, there is no miracle about the participation of the brain in knowing. One might as well make a problem of the fact that it takes a hammer to drive a nail and takes a hand to hold the hammer as to make a problem out of the fact that it also requires a physical structure to discover and to adapt the particular acts of holding and striking which are needed.

b) The propositions of physical science are not found among the data of apprehension. Mathematical propositions may be disposed of by making them purely a priori; propositions about sense objects by making them purely a posteriori.[18] But physical propositions, such as make up physics, chemistry, biology, to say nothing of propositions of history, anthropology, and society, are neither one nor the other. I cannot state the case better than Mr. Russell has stated it, although, I am bound to add, the stating did not arouse in Mr. Russell any suspicion of the premises with which he was operating. "Men of science, for the most part, are willing to condemn immediate data as 'merely subjective,' while yet maintaining the truth of the physics inferred from those data. But such an attitude, though it may be *capable* of justification, obviously stands in need of it; and the only justification possible must be one which exhibits matter as a logical construction from sense data. . . . It is therefore necessary to find some way of bridging the gulf between the world of physics and the world of sense."[19] I do not see how anyone familiar with the two-world schemes which have played such a part in the history of humanity can read this statement without depression. And if it occurred to one that the sole generating condition of *these* two worlds is the assumption that sense objects are modes of apprehension or knowledge (are so intrinsically and not in the use made of

18. See Russell, *Scientific Method in Philosophy*, p. 53.
19. *Ibid.*, p. 101.

them), he might think it a small price to pay to inquire into the standing of this assumption. For it was precisely the fact that sense perception and physical science appeared historically (in the seventeenth century) as rival modes of knowing the same world which led to the conception of sense objects as "subjective"—since they were so different from the objects of science. Unless sense and science had both first been thought of as modes of knowing and then as modes of knowing the same things, there would not have been the slightest reason for regarding immediate data as "merely subjective." They would have been natural phenomena, like any other. That they are phenomena which involve the interaction of an organism with other things is just an important discovery about them, as is also a discovery about starch in plants.

Physical science is the *knowledge* of the world by their means. It is a rival, not of them, but of the medley of prior dogmas, superstitions, and chance opinions about the world —a medley which grew up and flourished precisely because of absence of a will to explore and of a technique for detecting unambiguous data. That Mr. Russell, who is a professed realist, can do no better with the problem (once committed to the notion that sense objects are of themselves *objects* of knowledge) than to hold that although the world of physics is not a legitimate inference from sense data, it is a permissible logical construction from them—permissible in that it involves no logical inconsistencies—suggests that the pragmatic difference between idealist and realist—of this type— is not very great. From necessary ideal constructions to permissible logical constructions involves considerable difference in technique but no perceptible practical difference. And the point of this family likeness is that both views spring from regarding sense perception and science as ways of knowing the same objects, and hence as rivals until some scheme of conciliation has been devised.

c) It is but a variant of this problem to pass to what may be called either the ego-centric predicament or the private-public problem. Sense data differ from individual to individual. If they are recognized to be natural events, this variation is no more significant than any change depending upon variation of generating conditions. One does not expect two lumps of wax at different distances from a hot body to be affected exactly alike; the upsetting thing would be if they were. Neither does one expect cast-iron to react exactly as does steel. That organisms, because of different positions or different internal structures, should introduce differences in the phenomena which they respectively have a share in producing is a fact of the same nature. But make the sense qualities thus produced not natural events (which may then be made either objects of inquiry or means of inquiry into something else) but modes of knowing, and every such deviation marks a departure from true knowing: it constitutes an anomaly. Taken *en masse* the deviations are so marked as to lead to the conclusion (even on the part of a realist like Mr. Russell) that they constitute a world of private existences, which, however, may be correlated without logical inconsistency with other such worlds. Not all realists are Leibnizian monadists as is Mr. Russell; I do not wish to leave the impression that all come to just this solution. But all who regard sense data as apprehensions have on their hands in some form the problem of the seemingly distorting action exercised by the individual knower upon a public or common thing known or believed in.

IV

I am not trying to discuss or solve these problems. On the contrary, I am trying to show that these problems exist only because of the identification of a datum determined with reference to control of inference with a self-sufficient knowledge-object. As against this assumption I point to the following facts. What is actually given as matter of empirical fact may be indefinitely complicated and diffused. As empirically existent, perceived objects never constitute the whole scope of the given; they have a context of indefinite extent in which they are set. To control inference it is necessary to analyze this complex situation—to determine what is data for inference and what is irrelevant. This analysis involves discriminative resolution into more ultimate simples. The resources of experimentation, all sorts of microscopic, telescopic, and registering apparatus, are called in to perform that analysis. As a result we differentiate not merely visual data from auditory—a discrimination effected by experiments within the reach of everybody—but a vast multitude of visual and auditory data. Physics and physiology and anatomy all play a part in the analysis. We even carry the analysis to the point of regarding, say, a color as a self-included object unreferred to any other object. We may avoid a false inference by conceiving it, not as a quality of any object, but as merely a product of a nervous stimulation and reaction. Instead of referring it to a ribbon or piece of paper we may refer it to the organism. But this is only as a part of the technique of suspended inference. We avoid some habitual inference in order to make a more careful inference.

Thus we escape, by a straightening out of our logic (by avoiding erecting a system of logical distinctions and checks into a mythological natural history), the epistemological problems. We also avoid the contradiction which haunts every epistemological scheme so far propounded. As matter of fact every proposition regarding what is "given" to sensation or perception is dependent upon the assumption of a vast amount of scientific knowledge which is the result of a multitude of prior analyses, verifications, and inferences. What a combination of Tantalus and Sisyphus we get when we fancy that we have cleared the slate of all these material implications, fancy that we have really started with simple and independent givens, and then try to show how from these original givens we can arrive at the very knowledge which we have all the time employed in the discovery and fixation of the simple sense data![20]

IV. Science as a Practical Art

No one will deny that, as seen from one angle, science is a pursuit, an enterprise—a mode of practice. It is at least that, no matter how much more or else it is. In course of the practice of knowing distinctive practical judgments will then naturally be made. Especially does this hold good when

---

20. See the essay on *The Existence of the World as a Logical Problem* [this volume, pp. 83–97].

an intellectual class is developed, when there is a body of persons working at knowing as another body is working at farming or engineering. Moreover, the instrumentalities of this inquiring class gain in importance for all classes in the degree in which it is realized that success in the conduct of the practice of farming or engineering or medicine depends upon use of the successes achieved in the business of knowing. The importance of the latter is thrown into relief from another angle if we consider the enterprises, like diplomacy, politics, and, to a considerable extent, morals, which do not acknowledge a thoroughgoing and constant dependence upon the practice of science. As Hobbes was wont to say, the advantages of a science of morals are most obvious in the evils which we suffer from its lack.

To say that something is to be learned, is to be found out, is to be ascertained or proved or believed, is to say that something is to be done. Every such proposition in the concrete is a practical proposition. Every such proposition of inquiry, discovery and testing will have then the traits assigned to the class of practical propositions. They imply an incomplete situation going forward to completion, and the proposition as a specific organ of carrying on the movement. I have not the intention of dwelling at length upon this theme. I wish to raise in as definite and emphatic a way as possible a certain question. Suppose that the propositions arising within the *practice* of knowing and functioning as agencies in its conduct could be shown to present all the distinctions and relations characteristic of the subject-matter of logic: what would be the conclusion? To an unbiased mind the question probably answers itself: All purely logical terms and propositions fall within the scope of the class of propositions of inquiry as a special form of propositions of practice. My further remarks are not aimed at *proving* that the case accords with the hypothesis propounded, but are intended to procure hospitality for the hypothesis.

If thinking is the art by which knowledge is practiced, then the materials with which thinking deals may be supposed, by analogy with the other arts, to take on in consequence special shapes. The man who is making a boat will give wood a form which it did not have, in order that it may

serve the purposes to which it is to be put. Thinking may
then be supposed to give its material the form which will
make it amenable to its purpose—attaining knowledge, or, as
it is ordinarily put, going from the unknown to the known.
That physical analysis and synthesis are included in the
processes of investigation of natural objects makes them a
part of the practice of knowing. And it makes any general
traits which result in consequence of such treatment characters of *objects as they are involved in knowledge-getting.*
That is to say, if there are any features which natural existences assume in order that inference may be more fertile
and more safe than it would otherwise be, those features
correspond to the special traits which would be given to
wood in process of constructing a boat. They are manufactured, without being any worse because of it. The question which I raised in the last paragraph may then be restated in this fashion: Are there such features? If there are,
are they like those characters which books on logic talk
about?

Comparison with language may help us. Language—I
confine myself for convenience to spoken language—consists
of sounds. But it does not consist simply of those sounds
which issue from the human organs prior to the attempt to
communicate. It has been said that an American baby before
talking makes almost every sound found in any language.
But elimination takes place. And so does intensification.
Certain sounds originally slurred over are made prominent;
the baby has to work for them and the work is one which
he neither undertakes nor accomplishes except under the
incitation of others. Language is chiefly marked off, however,
by articulation; by the arrangement of what is selected into
an orderly sequence of vowels and consonants with certain
rules of stress, etc. It may fairly be said that speech is a
manufactured article: it consists of natural ebullitions of
sound which have been shaped for the sake of being effective
instrumentalities of a purpose. For the most part the making
has gone on under the stress of the necessities of communication with little deliberate control. Works on phonetics, dic-
tionaries, grammars, rhetorics, etc., mark some participation
of deliberate intention in the process of manufacture. If we

bring written language into the account, we should find the conscious factor extended somewhat. But making, shaping for an end, there is, whether with or without conscious control.

Now while there is something in the antecedent properties of sound which enters into the determination of speech, the *worth* of speech is in no way measured by faithfulness to these antecedent properties. It is measured only by its efficiency and economy in realizing the special results for which it is constructed. Written language need not look like sounds any more than sounds look like objects. It must *represent* articulate sounds, but faithful representation is wholly a matter of carrying the mind to the same outcome, of exercising the same function, not of resemblance or copying. Original structure *limits* what may be made out of anything: one cannot (at least at present) make a silk purse out of pigs' bristles. But this conditioning relationship is very different from one in which the antecedent existences are a model or prototype to which the consequent must be servilely faithful. The boatmaker must take account of the grain and strength of his wood. To take account of, to reckon with, is a very different matter, however, from repetition or literal loyalty. The measure is found in the consequences for which existences are used.

I wish, of course, to suggest that logical traits are just features of original existences as they have been worked over for use in inference, as the traits of manufactured articles are qualities of crude materials modified for specific purposes. Upon the whole, past theories have vibrated between treating logical traits as "subjective," something resident in "mind" (mind being thought of as an immaterial or psychical existence independent of natural things and events), and ascribing ontological pre-existence to them. Thus far in the history of thought, each method has flourished awhile and then called out a reaction to its opposite. The reification (I use the word here without prejudice) of logical traits has taken both an Idealistic form (because of emphasis upon their spiritual or ideal nature and stuff) and a Realistic one, due to emphasis upon their immediate apprehension and givenness. That mathematics have been from

Plato to Descartes and contemporary analytic realism the
great provocative of Realistic Idealisms is a familiar fact.
The hypothesis here propounded is a *via media*. What has
been overlooked is the reality and importance of art and its
works. The tools and works of art are neither mental, subjective things, nor are they antecedent entities like crude or
raw material. They are the latter shaped for a purpose. It
is impossible to overstate their objectivity from the standpoint of their existence and their efficacy within the operations in question; nor their objectivity in the sense of their
dependence upon prior natural existences whose traits have
to be taken account of, or reckoned with, by the operations
of art. In the case of the art of inference, the art securely
of going from the given to the absent, the dependence of
mind upon inference, the fact that wherever inference occurs we have a conscious agent—one who recognizes, plans,
invents, seeks out, deliberates, anticipates, and who, reacting to anticipations, fears, hates, desires, etc.—explains the
theories which, because of misconception of the nature of
mind and consciousness, have labeled logical distinctions
psychical and subjective. In short, the theory shows why
logical features have been made into ontological entities and
into mental states.

To elaborate this thesis would be to repeat what has
been said in all the essays of this volume. I wish only to call
attention to certain considerations which may focus other
discussions upon this hypothesis.

1. The existence of inference is a fact, a fact as certain
and unquestioned as the existence of eyes or ears or the
growth of plants, or the circulation of the blood. One ob-
serves it taking place everywhere where human beings exist.
A student of the history of man finds that history is composed of beliefs, institutions, and customs which are inexplicable without acts of inference. This fact of inference
is as much a datum—a hard fact—for logical theory as any
sensory quality whatsoever. It is something men do as they
walk, chew, or jump. There is nothing a priori or ideological
about it. It is just a brute empirically observable event.

2. Its importance is almost as conspicuous as its existence. Every act of human life, not springing from instinct

or mechanical habit, contains it; most habits are dependent upon some amount of it for their formation, as they are dependent upon it for their readaptation to novel circumstances. From the humblest act of daily life to the most intricate calculations of science and the determination and execution of social, legal, and political policies, things are used as signs, indications, or evidence from which one proceeds to something else not yet directly given.

3. The act of inferring takes place naturally, i.e., without intention. It is at first something we do, not something which we *mean* to do. We do it as we breathe or walk or gesture. Only after it is done do we notice it and reflect upon it—and the great mass of men no more reflect upon it after its occurrence than they reflect upon the process of walking and try to discover its conditions and mechanism. To say that an individual, an animal organism, a man or a woman performs the acts is to say something capable of direct proof through appeal to observation; to say that something called mind, or consciousness does it is itself to employ inference and dubious inference. The fact of inference is much surer, in other words, than that of a particular inference, such as that to something called reason or consciousness, in connection with it; save as mind is but another word for the fact of inference, in which case of course it cannot be referred to as its cause, source, or author. Moreover, by all principles of science, inference cannot be referred to mind or consciousness as its condition, unless there is *independent* proof of the existence of that mind to which it is referred. *Prima-facie* we are conscious or aware *of* inference precisely as we are of anything else, not by introspection of something within the very consciousness which is supposed to be its source, but by observation of something taking place in the world—as we are conscious of walking *after* we have walked. After it has been done naturally—or "unconsciously"—it may be done "consciously," that is, with intent or on purpose. But this means that it is done *with* consciousness (whatever consciousness may be discovered to mean), not that it is done *by* consciousness. Now if other natural events characteristic only (so far as can be ascertained) of highly organized beings are marked by unique or

by distinctive traits, there is good ground for the assumption
that inference will be so marked. As we do not find the circulation of blood or the stimulation of nerves in a stone, and as
we expect as a matter of course to find peculiar conditions,
qualities, and consequences in the being where such operations occur, so we do not find the act of inference in a stone,
and we expect peculiar conditions, qualities, and consequences in whatever beings perform the act. Unless, in other
words, all the ordinary canons of inquiry are suspended,
inference is not an isolated nor a merely formal event. As
against the latter, it has its own distinctive structure and
properties; as against the former, it has specific generating
conditions and specific results.

4. Possibly all this seems too obvious for mention. But
there is often a virtual conspiracy in philosophy, not to mention obvious things nor to dwell upon them: otherwise remote
speculations might be brought to a sudden halt. The point of
these commonplaces resides in the push they may give anyone to engage in a search for *distinctive features in the act of
inference.* The search may perhaps be best initiated by noting
the seeming inconsistency between what has been said about
inference as an art and inference as a natural, unpremedi-
tated occurrence. The obvious function of spontaneous inference is to bring before an agent absent considerations
to which he may respond as he otherwise responds to the
stimulating force of the given situation. To infer rain is to
enable one to behave *now* as given conditions would not
otherwise enable him to conduct himself. This instigation to
behave toward the remote in space or time is the primary
trait of the inferential act; descriptively speaking, the act
consists in taking up an attitude of response to an absent
thing as if it were present. But just because the thing is
absent, the attitude taken may be either irrelevant and positively harmful or extremely pertinent and advantageous. We
may infer rain when rain is not going to happen, and acting
upon the inference be worse off than if there had been no
inference. Or we may make preparations, which we would
not otherwise have made; the rain may come, and the inference save our lives—as the ark saved Noah. Inference
brings, in short, truth and falsity into the world, just as def-

initely as the circulation of the blood brings its distinctive consequences, both advantages and liabilities, into the world, or as the existence of banking brings with it consequences of business extension and of bankruptcy not previously existent. If the reader objects to the introduction of the terms "truth" and "falsity," I am perfectly willing to leave the choice of words to him, provided the fact is recognized that through inference men are capable of a kind of success and exposed to a kind of failure not otherwise possible: dependent upon the fact that inference takes absent things as being in a certain real continuum with present things, so that our attitude toward the latter is bound up with our reaction to the former as parts of the same situation. And in any event, I wish to protest against a possible objection to the introduction of the terms "false" and "true." It may be said that inference is not responsible for the occurrence of errors and truths, because these accompany simple apprehensions where there is no inference: as when I see a snake which isn't there—or any other case which may appear to the objector to afford an illustration of his point. The objection illustrates my point. To affirm a snake is to affirm potentialities going beyond what is actually given; it says that what is given is *going* to do something—the doing characteristic of a snake, so that we are to react to the given as to a snake. Or if we take the case of a face in the cloud recognized as a fantasy, then (to say nothing of "in the cloud" which involves reference beyond the given) "fantasy," "dream," equally means a reference to objects and considerations *not* given as the actual datum is given.

We have not got very far with our question of distinctive, unique traits called into existence by inference, but we have got far enough to have light upon what is called the "transcendence" of knowledge. All inference is a *going beyond* the assuredly present to an absent. Hence it is a more or less precarious journey. It is transcending limits of security of immediate response. The stone which reacts only to stimuli of the present, not of the future, cannot make the mistakes which a being reacting to a future taken to be connected with the present is sure to make. But it is important to note just what this transcendence consists in. It has nothing to do with transcending mental states to arrive at an external object. *It is behaving to the given situation as involving something not given.* It is Robinson Crusoe going from a seen foot to an unseen man, not from a mental state to something unmental.

5. The mistakes and failures resulting from inference constitute the ground for transition from natural spontaneous performance to a technique or deliberate art of inference. There is something humorous about the discussion of the problem of error as if it were a rare or exceptional thing —an anomaly—when the barest glance at human history shows that mistakes have been the rule, and that truth lies at the bottom of a well. As to inferences bound up with barely keeping alive, man has had to effect a considerable balance of good guesses over bad. Aside from this somewhat narrow field, the original appearance of inference upon the scene probably added to the interest of life rather than to its efficiency. If the classic definition of man as a rational animal means simply an inferring or guessing animal, it applies to the natural man, for it allows for the guesses being mostly wrong. If it is used with its customary eulogistic connotations, it applies only to man chastened to the use of a hardly won and toilsome art. If it alleges that man has any natural preference for a reasonable inference or that the rationality of an inference is a measure of its hold upon him, it is grotesquely wrong. To propagate this error is to encourage man in his most baleful illusion, and to postpone the day of an effective and widespread adoption of a perfected art of knowing.

Summarily put, the waste and loss consequent upon the natural happening of inference led man, slowly and grudgingly, to the adoption of safeguards in its performance. In some part, the scope of which is easily exaggerated, man has come to attribute many of the ills from which he suffers to his own premature, inept, and unguarded performing of inference, instead of to fate, bad luck, and accident. In some things, and to some extent in all things, he has invented and perfected an art of inquiry: a system of checks and tests to be used before the conclusion of inference is categorically affirmed. Its nature has been considered in many other places in these pages, but it may prove instructive to restate it in this context.

a) Nothing is less adapted to a successful accomplishing of an inference than the subject-matter from which it ordinarily fares forth. That subject-matter is a nest of obscurities and ambiguities. The ordinary warnings against trusting to imagination, the bad name which has come intellectually to attach to fancy, are evidences that anything may suggest anything. Regarding most of the important happenings in life no inference has been too extravagant to obtain followers and influence action, because subject-matter was so variegated and complex that any objects which it suggested had a *prima-facie* plausibility. That every advance in knowledge has been effected by using agencies which break up a complex subject-matter into independent variables (from each of which a distinct inference may be drawn), and by attacking each one of these things by every conceivable tool for further resolution so as to make sure we are dealing with something so simple as to be unambiguous, is the report of the history of science. It is sometimes held that knowledge comes ultimately to a necessity of belief, or acceptance, which is the equivalent of an incapacity to think otherwise than so and so. Well, even in the case of such an apparently simple "self-evident" thing as a red, this inability, if it is worth anything, is a residuum from experimental analysis. We do not believe in the thing as red (whenever there is a need of scientific testing) till we have exhausted all kinds of active attack and find the red still resisting and persisting. Ordinarily we move the head; we shade the eyes; we turn the thing over; we take it to a different light. The use of lens, prism, or whatever device, is simply carrying farther the use of like methods as of physical resolution. Whatever endures all these active (not mental) attacks, we accept—pending invention of more effective weapons. To make sure that a given fact *is* just and such a shade of red is, one may say, a final triumph of scientific method. To turn around and treat it as something naturally or psychologically given is a monstrous superstition.

When assured, such a simple datum is for the sake of guarding the act of inference. Color may mean a lot of things; any red may mean a lot of things; such things are ambiguous; they afford unreliable evidence or signs. To get the color down to the last touch of possible discrimination is to limit its range of testimony; ideally, it is to secure a voice which says but one thing and says that unmistakably. Its simplicity is not identical with isolation, but with *specified* relationship. Thus the hard "facts," the brute data, the simple qualities or ideas, the sense elements of traditional and of contemporary logic, get placed and identified within the art of controlling inference. The allied terms "self-evident," "sensory truths," "simple apprehensions" have their meanings unambiguously determined in this same context; while apart from it they are the source of all kinds of error. They are no longer notions to conjure with. They express the last results attainable by present physical methods of discriminative analysis employed in the search for dependable data for inference. Improve the physical means of experimentation, improve the microscope or the registering apparatus or the chemical reagent, and they may be replaced tomorrow by new, simple apprehensions of simple and ultimate data.

b) Natural or spontaneous inference depends very largely upon the habits of the individual in whom inferring takes place. These habits depend in turn very largely upon the customs of the social group in which he has been brought up. An eclipse suggests very different things according to the rites, ceremonies, legends, traditions, etc., of the group to which the spectator belongs. The average layman in a civilized group may have no more personal science than an Australian Bushman, but the legends which determine his reactions are different. His inference is better, neither because of superior intellectual capacity, nor because of more careful personal methods of knowing, but because his instruction has been superior. The instruction of a scientific inquirer in the best scientific knowledge of his day is just as much a part of the control (or art) of inference as is the technique of observational analysis which he uses. As the bulk of prior ascertainments increases, the tendency is to identify this stock of learning, this store of achieved truth, with knowledge. There is no objection to this identification

save as it leads the logician or epistemologist to ignore that
which *made* it "knowledge" (that which gives it a right to
the title), and as a consequence to fall into two errors: one,
overlooking its function in the guidance and handling of
future inferences; the other, confusing the mere act of
reference to what is known (known so far as it has accrued
from prior tested inquiries) with knowing. To remind myself of what is known as to the topic with which I am dealing is an indispensable performance, but to call this reminder "knowing" (as the presentative realist usually does)
is to confuse a psychological event with a logical achievement. It is from misconception of this act of reminding one's
self of what is known, as a check in some actual inquiry,
that arise most of the fallacies about simple acquaintance,
mere apprehension, etc.—the fallacies which eliminate inquiry and inferring from knowledge.

   c) The art of inference gives rise to specific features
characterizing the *inferred* thing. The natural man reacts to
the suggested thing as he would to something present. That
is, he tends to accept it uncritically. The man called up by
the footprint on the sand is just as real a man as the footprint is a real footprint. It is a *man,* not the idea of a man,
which is indicated. What a thing means is another *thing*;
it doesn't mean a meaning. The only difference is that the
thing indicated is farther off, or more concealed, and hence
(probably) more mysterious, more powerful and awesome,
on that account. The man indicated to Crusoe by the foot-
prints was like a man of menacing powers seen at a distance
through a telescope. Things naturally inferred are accepted,
in other words, by the natural man on altogether too realistic
a basis for adequate control; they impose themselves too directly and irretrievably. There are no alternatives save either
acceptance or rejection *in toto.* What is needed for control is
some device by which they can be treated for just what they
are, namely, *inferred* objects which, however assured as
objects of *prior* experiences, are uncertain as to their existence in connection with the object from which present inference sets out. While more careful inspection of the given
object—to see if it be really a footprint, how fresh, etc.—
may do much for safe-guarding inference; and while forays

into whatever else is known may help, there is still need for something else. We need some method of freely examining and handling the object in its status as an inferred object. This means some way of detaching it, as it were, from the particular act of inference in which it presents itself. Without some such detachment, Crusoe can never get into a free and effective relation with the man indicated by the footprint. He can only, so to speak, go on repeating, with continuously increasing fright, "There's a man about, there's a man about." The "man" needs to be treated, not as man, but as something having a merely inferred and hence potential status; as a meaning or thought, or "idea." There is a great difference between meaning and *a* meaning. Meaning is simply a function of the situation: this thing means that thing: meaning is this relationship. A meaning is something quite different; it is not a function, but a specific entity, a peculiar thing, namely the man *as* suggested.

Words are the great instrument of translating a relation of inference existing between two things into a new kind of thing which can be operated with on its own account; the term of discourse or reflection is the solution of the requirement for greater flexibility and liberation. Let me repeat: Crusoe's inquiry can play freely around and about the man inferred from the footprint only as he can, so to say, get away from the immediate suggestive force of the footprint. As it originally stands, the man suggested is on the same coercive level as the suggestive footprint. They are related, tied together. But a gesture, a sound, may be used as a *substitute* for the thing inferred. It exists independently of the footprint and may therefore be thought about and ideally experimented with irrespective of the footprint. It at once preserves the meaning-force of the situation and detaches it from the immediacy of the situation. It is *a* meaning, an idea.

Here we have, I submit, the explanation of notions, forms, essences, terms, subsistences, ideas, meanings, etc. They are surrogates of the objects of inference of such a character that they may be elaborated and manipulated exactly as primary things may be, so far as inference is concerned. They can be brought into relation with one another, quite irrespective of the things which originally suggested them. Without such free play reflective inquiry is mockery, and control of inference an impossibility. When a speck of light suggests to the astronomer a comet, he would have nothing to do but either to accept the inferred object as a real one, or to reject it as a mere fancy unless he could treat "comet" for the time being not as a thing at all, but as a meaning, a conception; a meaning having, moreover, by connection with other meanings, implications—meanings consequent from it. Unless a meaning is an inferred object, detached and fixed as a term capable of independent development, what sort of a ghostly Being is it? Except on the basis stated, what is the transition from the function of meaning to *a* meaning as an entity in reasoning? And, once more, unless there is such a transition, is reasoning possible?

Cats have claws and teeth and fur. They do not have implications. No physical thing has implications. The *term* "cat" has implications. How can this difference be explained? On the ground that we cannot use the "cat" object inferred from given indications in such a way as will test the inference and make it fruitful, helpful, unless we can detach it from its existential dependence upon the particular things which suggest it. We need to know what a cat would be *if* it were there; what other things would also be indicated if the cat is really indicated. We therefore create a *new* object: we take something to stand for the cat-in-its-status-as-inferred in contrast with the cat as a live thing. A sound or a visible mark is the ordinary mechanism for producing such a new object. Whatever the physical means employed, we now have a new object; a term, a meaning, a notion, an essence, a form or species, according to the terminology which may be in vogue. It is as much a specific existence as any sound or mark is. But it is a mark which notes, concentrates, and records an outcome of an inference which is not yet accepted and affirmed. That is to say, it designates an object which is *not yet* to be reacted to as one reacts to the given stimulus, but which is an object of further examination and inquiry, a medium of a postponed conclusion and of investigation continued till better grounds for affirming an object (making a definite, unified response) are given. *A term is an object so far as that object is undergoing shaping in a directed act of inquiry.* It may be called a possible object or a hypothetical object. Such objects do not walk or bite or scratch, but they are nevertheless actually present as the vital agencies of reflection. If we but forget where they live and operate—within the event of controlled inference—we have on our hands all the mysteries of the double world of existence and essence, particular and universal, thing and idea, ordinary life and science. For the world of science, especially of mathematical science, is the world of considerations which have approved themselves to be effectively regulative of the operations of inference. It is easier to wash with ordinary water than with H_2O, and there is a marked difference between falling off a building and $\frac{1}{2}gt^2$. But H_2O and $\frac{1}{2}gt^2$ are as potent for the distinctive act of inference—as genuine and distinctive an act as washing the hands or rolling down hill —as ordinary water and falling are impotent.

Scientific men can handle these things-of-inference precisely as the blacksmith handles his tools. They are not thoughts as they are ordinarily used, not even in the logical sense of thought. They are rather things whose manipulation (as the blacksmith manipulates his tools) yield knowledge— or methods of knowledge—with a minimum of recourse to thinking and a maximum of efficiency. When one considers the importance of the enterprise of knowledge, it is not surprising that appropriate tools have been devised for carrying it on, and that these tools have no prototypes in pre-existent materials. They are real objects, but they are just the real objects which they are and not some other objects.

V. *Theory and Practice*

Our last paragraphs have touched upon the nature of science. They contain, by way of intimation, an explanation of the distance which lies between the things of daily intercourse and the terms of science. Controlled inference is science, and science is, accordingly, a highly specialized industry. It is such a specialized mode of practice that it does not appear to be a mode of practice at all. This high specialization is part of the reason for the current antithesis of theory and practice, knowledge and conduct, the other part being the survival of the ancient conception of knowledge as intuitive and dialectical—the conception which is set forth in the Aristotelian logic.

Starting from the hypothesis that the art of controlled inference requires for its efficient exercise specially adapted entities, it follows that the various sciences are the various forms which the industry of controlled inquiry assumes. It follows that the conceptions and formulations of the sciences —physical and mathematical—concern things which have been reshaped in view of the exigencies of regulated and fertile inference. To get things into the estate where such inference is practicable, many qualities of the water and air, cats and dogs, stones and stars, of daily intercourse with the world have been dropped or depressed. Much that was trivial or remote has been elevated and exaggerated. Neither the omissions nor the accentuations are arbitrary. They are purposeful. They represent the changes in the things of ordinary life which are needed to safeguard the important business of inference.

There is then a great difference between the entities of science and the things of daily life. This may be fully acknowledged. But unless the admission is accompanied by an ignoring of the function of inference, it creates no problem of conciliation, no need of apologizing for either one or the other. It generates no problem of the real and the apparent. The "real" or "true" objects of science are those which best fulfil the demands of secure and fertile inference. To arrive at them is such a difficult operation, there are so many specious candidates clamoring for the office, that it is no wonder that when the objects suitable for inference are constituted, they tend to impose themselves as *the* real objects, in comparison with which the things of ordinary life are but impressions made upon us (according to much modern thought), or defective samples of Being—according to much of ancient thought. But one has only to note that their genuinely characteristic feature is fitness for the aims of inference to awaken from the nightmare of all such problems. They differ from the things of the common world of action and association as the means and ends of one occupation differ from those of another. The difference is not that which exists between reality and appearance, but is that between the subject-matter of crude occupations and of a highly specialized and difficult art, upon the success of which (so it is discovered) the progress of other occupations ultimately depends.

The entities of science are not only *from* the scientist; they are also *for* him. They express, that is, not only the outcome of reflective inquiries, but express them in the particular form in which they can enter most directly and efficiently into subsequent inquiries. The fact that they are sustained within the universe of inquiry accounts for their remoteness from the things of daily life, the latter being promptly precipitated out of suspense in such solutions. That most of the immediate qualities of things (including the so-called secondary qualities) are dropped signifies that such qualities have not turned out to be fruitful for inference. That mathematical, mechanical, and "primary" distinctions and relations have come to constitute the proper subject-matter of science signifies that they represent such qualities of original things as are most manipular for knowledge-getting or assured and extensive inference. Consider what a hard time the scientific man had in getting away from other qualities, and how the more immediate qualities have been pressed upon him from all quarters, and it is not surprising that he inclines to think of the intellectually useful properties as alone "real" and to relegate all others to a quasi-illusory field. But his victory is now sufficiently achieved so that this tension may well relax; it may be acknowledged that the difference between scientific entities and ordinary things is one of function, the former being selected and arranged for the successful conduct of inferential knowings.

I conclude with an attempt to show how bootless the ordinary antithesis between knowledge (or theory) and practice becomes when we recognize that it really involves only a contrast between the kinds of judgments appropriate to ordinary modes of practice and those appropriate to the specialized industry of knowledge-getting.

It is not true that to insist that scientific propositions

fall within the domain of practice is to depreciate them. On its face, the insistence means simply that all knowledge involves experimentation, with whatever appliances are suited to the problem in hand, of an active and physical type. Instead of this doctrine leading to a low estimate of knowledge, the contrary is the case. This art of experimental thinking turns out to give the key to the control and development of other modes of practice. I have touched elsewhere in these essays upon the way in which knowledge is the instrument of regulation of our human undertakings, and I have also pointed out that intrinsic increments of meaning accrue in consequence of thinking. I wish here to point out how that mode of practice which is called theorizing emancipates experience—how it makes for steady progress. No matter how much specialized skill improves, we are restricted in the degree in which our ends remain constant or fixed. Significant progress, progress which is more than technical, depends upon ability to foresee new and different results and to arrange conditions for their effectuation. Science is the instrument of increasing our technique in attaining results already known and cherished. More important yet, it is the method of emancipating us from enslavement to customary ends, the ends established in the past.

Let me borrow from political philosophy a kind of caricature of the facts. As social philosophers used to say that the state came into existence when individuals agreed to surrender some of their native personal rights for the sake of getting the advantages of non-interference and aid from others who made a like surrender, so we might say that science began when men gave up the claim to form the structure of knowledge each from himself as a centre and measure of meaning—when there was an agreement to take an impersonal standpoint. Non-scientific modes of practice, left to their natural growth, represent, in other words, arrangements of objects which cluster about the self, and which are closely tied down to the habits of the self. Science or theory means a system of objects detached from any particular personal standpoint, and therefore available for any and every possible personal standpoint. Even the exigencies of ordinary social life require a slight amount of such detachment or abstraction. I must neglect my own peculiar ends enough to take some account of my neighbor if I am going to be intelligible to him. I must at least find common ground. Science systematizes and indefinitely extends this principle. It takes its stand, not with what is common with some particular neighbor living at this especial date in this particular village, but with any possible neighbor in the wide stretches of time and space. And it does so by the mere fact that it is continually reshaping its peculiar objects with an eye single to availability in inference. The more abstract, the more impersonal, the more impartially objective are *its* objects, the greater the variety and scope of inference made possible. Every street of experience which is laid out by science has its tracks for transportation, and every line issues transfer checks to every other line. You and I may keep running in certain particular ruts, but conditions are provided for somebody else to foresee—or infer—new combinations and new results. The depersonalizing of the things of everyday practice becomes the chief agency of their repersonalizing in new and more fruitful modes of practice. The paradox of theory and practice is that theory is with respect to all other modes of practice the most practical of all things, and the more impartial and impersonal it is, the more truly practical it is. And this is the sole paradox.

But lest the man of science, the man of dominantly reflective habits, be puffed up with his own conceits, he must bear in mind that practical application—that is, experiment—is a condition of his own calling, that it is indispensable to the institution of knowledge or truth. Consequently, in order that he keep his own balance, it is needed that his findings be everywhere applied. The more their application is confined within his own special calling, the less meaning do the conceptions possess, and the more exposed they are to error. The widest possible range of application is the means of the deepest verification. As long as the specialist hugs his own results they are vague in meaning and unsafe in content. That individuals in every branch of human endeavor should be experimentalists engaged in testing the findings of the theorist is the sole final guarantee for the sanity of the theorist.

THE EXISTENCE OF THE WORLD AS A LOGICAL PROBLEM

Of the two parts of this paper the first is a study in formal analysis. It attempts to show that there is no problem, logically speaking, of the existence of an external world. Its point is to show that the very attempt to state the problem involves a self-contradiction: that the terms cannot be stated so as to generate a problem without assuming what is professedly brought into question. The second part is a summary endeavor to state the actual question which has given rise to the unreal problem and the conditions which have led to its being misconstrued. So far as subject-matter is concerned, it supplements the first part; but the argument of the first part in no way depends upon anything said in the second. The latter may be false and its falsity have no implications for the first.

I

There are many ways of stating the problem of the existence of an external world. I shall make that of Mr. Bertrand Russell the basis of my examinations, as it is set forth in his recent book *Our Knowledge of the External World as a Field for Scientific Method in Philosophy*. I do this both because his statement is one recently made in a book of commanding importance, and because it seems to me to be a more careful statement than most of those in vogue. If my point can be made out for his statement, it will apply, *a fortiori*, to other statements. Even if there be those to whom this does not seem to be the case, it will be admitted

[First published with the title "The Existence of the World as a Problem" in *Philosophical Review* 24 (1915): 357–70. Revised and reprinted in *Essays in Experimental Logic* (Chicago: University of Chicago Press, 1916), pp. 281–302.]

that my analysis must begin somewhere. I cannot take the space to repeat the analysis in application to differing modes of statement with a view to showing that the method employed will yield like results in all cases. But I take the liberty of throwing the burden upon the reader and asking him to show cause why it does not so apply.

After rejecting certain familiar formulations of the question because they employ the not easily definable notions of the self and independence, Mr. Russell makes the following formulation: Can we "know that objects of sense . . . exist at times when we are not perceiving them?" (p. 75). Or, in another mode of statement: "Can the existence of anything other than our own[1] hard data be inferred from the existence of those data?" (pp. 73 and 83).

I shall try to show that identification of the "data of sense" as the sort of term which will generate the problem involves an affirmative answer to the question—that it must have been answered in the affirmative before the question can be asked. And this, I take it, is to say that it is not a question at all. A point of departure may be found in the following passage: "I think it must be admitted as probable that the immediate objects of sense depend for their existence upon physiological conditions in ourselves, and that, for example, the coloured surfaces which we see cease to exist when we shut our eyes" (p. 64). I have not quoted the passage for the sake of gaining an easy victory by pointing out that this statement involves the existence of physiological conditions. For Mr. Russell himself affirms that fact. As he points out, such arguments assume precisely the "common-sense world of stable objects" professedly put in doubt (p. 83). My purpose is to ask what justification there is for calling immediate data "objects of sense." Statements of this type always call color visual, sound auditory, and so on. If it were merely a matter of making certain admissions for the sake of being able to play a certain game, there would be no objection. But if we are concerned with a matter of serious

---

1. I shall pass over the terms "our own" so far as specific reference is concerned, but the method employed applies equally to them. Who are the "we" and what does "own" mean, and how is ownership established?

analysis, one is bound to ask, Whence come these adjectives? That color is visual in the sense of being an object of vision is certainly admitted in the common-sense world, but this is the world we have left. That color is visual is a proposition about color and it is a proposition which color itself does not utter. Visible or visual color is already a "synthetic" proposition, not a term nor an analysis of a single term. That color is seen, or is visible, I do not call in question; but I insist that fact already assumes an answer to the question which Mr. Russell has put. It presupposes existence beyond the color itself. To call the color a "sensory" object involves another assumption of the same kind but even more complex—involving, that is, even more existence beyond the color.

I see no reply to this statement except to urge that the terms "visual" and "sensory" as applied to the object are pieces of verbal supererogation having no force in the statement. This supposititious answer brings the matter to a focus. Is it possible to institute even a preliminary disparaging contrast between immediate objects and a world external to them unless the term "sensory" has a definite effect upon the meaning assigned to immediate data or objects? Before taking up this question, I shall, however, call attention to another implication of the passage quoted. It appears to be implied that existence of color and "being seen" are equivalent terms. At all events, in similar arguments the identification is frequently made. But by description all that is required for the existence of color is certain physiological conditions. They may be present and color exist and yet not be seen. Things constantly act upon the optical apparatus in a way which fulfills the conditions of the existence of color without color being seen. This statement does not involve any dubious psychology about an act of attention. I only mean that the argument implies over and above the existence of color something called seeing or perceiving—noting is perhaps a convenient neutral term. And this clearly involves an assumption of something beyond the existence of the datum—and this datum is by definition an external world. Without this assumption the term "immediate" could not be introduced. Is the *object* immediate or is it the object of an immediate noting? If the latter, then the hard datum already stands in connection with something beyond itself.

And this brings us to a further point. The sense objects are repeatedly spoken of as "known." For example: "It is obvious that since the senses give knowledge of the latter kind [believed on their own account, without the support of any outside evidence] the immediate facts perceived by sight or touch or hearing do not need to be proved by argument but are completely self-evident" (p. 68). Again, they are spoken of as "facts of sense"[2] (p. 70), and as facts going along, for knowledge, with the laws of logic (p. 72). I do not know what belief or knowledge means here: nor do I understand what is meant by a *fact* being evidence for itself.[3] But obviously Mr. Russell knows, and knows their application to the sense object. And here is a further assumption of what, by definition, is a world external to the datum. Again, we have assumed in getting a question stated just what is professedly called into question. And the assumption is not made the less simple in that Mr. Russell has defined belief as a case of a triadic relation, and said that without the recognition of the three-term relation the difference between perception and belief is inexplicable (p. 50).

We come to the question passed over. Can such terms as "visual," "sensory," be neglected without modifying the force of the question—that is, without affecting the implications which give it the force of a problem? Can we "know that objects of sense, or very similar objects, exist at times when we are not perceiving them? Secondly, if this cannot be known, can we know that other objects, inferable from objects of sense but not necessarily resembling them, exist

2. Contrast the statement: "When I speak of a fact, I do not mean one of the simple things of the world, I mean that a certain thing has a certain quality, or that certain things have a certain relation" (p. 51).

3. In view of the assumption, shared by Mr. Russell, that there is such a thing as non-inferential knowledge, the conception that a thing offers evidence for itself needs analysis. Self-evidence is merely a convenient term for disguising the difference between the indubitably given and the believed in. Hypotheses, for example, are self-evident sometimes, that is, obviously present for just what they are, but they are still hypotheses, and to offer their self-evident character as "evidence" would expose one to ridicule. Meanings may be self-evident (the Cartesian "clear and distinct") and truth dubious.

either when we are perceiving the objects of sense or at any other time?" (p. 75).

I think a little reflection will make it clear that without the limitation of the term "perceiving" by the term "sense" no *problem* as to existence *at other times* can possibly arise. For neither (*a*) reference to time nor (*b*) limitation to a particular time is given either in the fact of existence of color or of perceiving color. Mr. Russell, for example, makes allusion to "a patch of colour which is momentarily seen" (p. 76). This is the sort of thing that may pass without challenge in the common-sense world, but hardly in an analysis which professes to call that world in question. Mr. Russell makes the allusion in connection with discriminating between sensation as signifying "the mental event of our being aware" and the sensation as object of which we are aware— the sense object. He can hardly be guilty, then, in the immediate context, of proceeding to identify the momentariness of the event with the momentariness of the object. There must be some grounds for assuming the temporal quality of the object—and that "immediateness" belongs to it in any other way than as an object of immediate seeing. What are these grounds?

How is it, moreover, that even the act of being aware is describable as "momentary"? I know of no way of so identifying it except by discovering that it is delimited in a time continuum. And if this be the case, it is surely superfluous to bother about *inference* to "other times." They are assumed in stating the question—which thus turns out again to be no question. It may be only a trivial matter that Mr. Russell speaks of "that patch of colour which is momentarily seen when we *look at the table*" (p. 76, italics mine). I would not attach undue importance to such phrases. But the frequency with which they present themselves in discussions of this type suggests the question whether as matter of fact "the patch of color" is not determined by reference to an object— the table—and not vice-versa. As we shall see later, there is good ground for thinking that Mr. Russell is really engaged, not in bringing into question the existence of an object beyond the datum, but in *re*defining the nature of an object, and that the reference to the patch of color as something more primitive than the table is really relevant to this reconstruction of traditional metaphysics. In other words, it is relevant to defining an object as a constant correlation of variations in qualities, instead of defining it as a substance in which attributes inhere—or a subject of predicates.

a) If anything is an eternal essence, it is surely such a thing as color taken by itself, as by definition it must be taken in the statement of the question by Mr. Russell. Anything more simple, timeless, and absolute than a red can hardly be thought of. One might question the eternal character of the received statement of, say, the law of gravitation on the ground that it is so complex that it may depend upon conditions not yet discovered and the discovery of which would involve an alteration in the statement. If 2 plus 2 equal 4 be taken as an isolated statement, it might be conceived to depend upon hidden conditions and to be alterable with them. But by conception we are dealing in the case of the colored surface with an ultimate, simple datum. It can have no implications beyond itself, no concealed dependencies. How then can its existence, even if its perception be but momentary, raise a question of "other times" at all?

b) Suppose a perceived blue surface to be replaced by a perceived red surface—and it will be conceded that the change, or replacement, is also perceived. There is still no ground for a belief in the temporally limited duration of either the red or the blue surface. Anything that leads to this conclusion would lead to the conclusion that the number two ceases when we turn to think of an atom. There is no way then of escaping the conclusion that the adjective "sense" in the term "sense object" is not taken innocently. It is taken as qualifying (for the purposes of statement of the problem) the nature of the object. Aside from reference to the momentariness of the *mental* event—a reference which is expressly ruled out—there is no way of introducing delimited temporal existence into the object save by reference to one and the same object which is perceived at different times to have different qualities. If the same object—however object be defined—is perceived to be of one color at one time and of another color at another time, then as a matter of course the color-datum of either the earlier or later time is identified as of transitory duration. But equally, of course, there is no question of *inference* to "other times." Other times have already been used to describe, define, and delimit *this* (brief) time. A moderate amount of unbiased reflection will, I am confident, convince anyone that apart from a reference to the same existence, perduring through different times while changing in *some* respect, no temporal delimitation of the existence of such a thing as sound or color can be made. Even Plato never doubted the eternal nature of red; he only argued from the fact that a *thing* is red at one time and blue at another to the unstable, and hence phenomenal, character of the *thing*. Or, put in a different way, we can know that a red is a momentary or transitory existence only if we know of other things which determine its beginning and cessation.

Mr. Russell gives a specific illustration of what he takes to be the correct way of stating the question in an account of what, in the common-sense universe of discourse, would be termed walking around a table. If we exclude considerations to which we have (apart from assuming just the things which are doubtful) no right, the datum turns out to be something to be stated as follows: "What is really known[4] is a correlation of muscular and other bodily sensations with changes in visual sensations" (p. 77). By "sensations" must be meant sensible objects, not mental events. This statement repeats the point already dealt with: "muscular," "visual," and "other bodily" are all terms which are indispensable and which also assume the very thing professedly brought into question: the external world as that was defined. "Really known" assumes both noting and belief, with whatever complex implications they may involve—implications which, for all that appears to the contrary, may be indefinitely complex, and which, by Mr. Russell's own statement, involve relationship to at least two other terms besides the datum. But in addition there appears the new term "correlation." I cannot avoid the conclusion that this term involves an *explicit* acknowledgment of the external world.

---

4. "Really known" is an ambiguous term. It may signify *understood,* or it may signify known to be *there* or *given.* Either meaning implies reference beyond.

Note, in the first place, that the correlation in question is not simple: it is three-fold, being a correlation of correlations. The "changes in visual sensations" (objects) must be correlated in a temporal continuum; the "muscular and other bodily sensations" (objects) must also constitute a connected series. One set of changes belongs to the serial class "visual"; the other set to the serial class "muscular." And these two classes sustain a point-to-point correspondence to each other—they are correlated.

I am not raising the old question of how such complex correlations can be said to be either "given" or "known" in sense, though it is worth a passing notice that it was on account of this sort of phenomenon that Kant postulated his threefold intellectual synthesis of apprehension, reproduction, and recognition in conception; and that it is upon the basis of necessity for such correlations that the rationalists have always criticized sensationalist empiricism. Personally I agree that temporal and spatial qualities are quite as much given in experience as are particulars—in fact, as I have been trying to show, particulars can be identified *as* particulars only in a relational complex. My point is rather (i) that any such given is already precisely what is meant by the "world"; and (ii) that such a highly specified correlation as Mr. Russell here sets forth is in no case a psychological, or historical, primitive, but is a *logical* primitive arrived at by an analysis of an empirical complex.

(i) The statement involves the assumption of two temporal "spreads" which, moreover, are determinately specified as to their constituent elements and as to their order. And these sustain to each other a correlation, element to element. The elements, moreover, are all specifically qualitative and some of them, at least, are spatial. How this differs from the external world of common sense I am totally unable to see. It may not be a very big external world, but having begged a small external world, I do not see why one should be too squeamish about extending it over the edges. The reply, I suppose, is that this complex defined and ordered object is by conception the object of a single perception, so that the question remains as to the possibility of inferring from it to something beyond.[5] But the reply only throws us back upon the point previously made. A particular or single event of perceptual awareness can be *determined* as to its ingredients and structure only in a continuum of objects. That is, the series of changes in color and shape can be determined as just such and such an ordered series of specific elements, with a determinate beginning and end, only in respect to a temporal continuum of things anteceding and succeeding. Moreover, the determination involves an analysis which disentangles qualities and shapes from contemporaneously given objects which are irrelevant. In a word, Mr. Russell's object already extends beyond itself; it already belongs to a larger world.

(ii) A sensible object which can be described as a correlation of an ordered series of shapes and colors with an ordered series of muscular and other bodily objects presents a definition of an object, not a psychological datum. What is stated is the definition of an object, of any object in the world. Barring ambiguities[6] in the terms "muscular" and "bodily," it seems to be an excellent definition. But good definition or poor, it states what a datum is *known* to be as an object in a known system; viz., definite correlations of

5. The reply implies that the exhaustive, all-at-once perception of the entire universe assumed by some idealistic writers does not involve any external world. I do not make this remark for the sake of identifying myself with this school of thinkers, but to suggest that the limited character of empirical data is what occasions inference. But it is a fallacy to suppose that the nature of the limitations is psychologically given. On the contrary, they have to be determined by descriptive identifications which involve reference to the more extensive world. Hence no matter how "self-evident" the existence of the data may be, it is never self-evident that they are rightly delimited with respect to the specific inference in process of making.

6. The ambiguities reside in the possibility of treating the "muscular and other bodily sensations" as meaning something other than data of motion and corporealness—however these be defined. Muscular sensation may be an awareness of motion of the muscles, but the phrase "of the muscles" does not alter the nature of motion as motion; it only specifies *what* motion is involved. And the long controversy about the existence of immediate "muscular sensations" testifies to what a complex cognitive determination we are here dealing with. Anatomical directions and long experimentation were required to answer the question. Were they psychologically primitive data no such questions could ever have arisen.

specified and ordered elements. As a definition, it is general. It is not made from the standpoint of any particular percipient. It says: *If* there be any percipient at a specified position in a space continuum, *then* the object may be perceived as such and such. And this implies that a percipient at any *other* position in the space continuum can deduce from the known system of correlations just what the series of shapes and colors will be from another position. For, as we have seen, the correlation of the series of changes of shape assumes a spatial continuum; hence one perspective projection may be correlated with that of any position in the continuum.

I have no direct concern with Mr. Russell's solution of his problem. But if the prior analysis is correct, one may anticipate in advance that it will consist simply in making explicit the assumptions which have tacitly been made in stating the problem—subject to the conditions involved in failure to recognize that they have been made. And I think an analytic reading of the solution will bear out the following statement. His various "peculiar," "private" points of view and their perspectives are nothing but names for the positions and projectional perspectives of the ordinary space of the public worlds. Their correlation by likeness is nothing but the explicit recognition that they are all defined and located, from the start, in one common spatial continuum. One quotation must suffice. "If two men are sitting in a room, two somewhat similar worlds are perceived by them; if a third man enters and sits between them, a third world, intermediate between the two others, begins to be perceived" (pp. 87–88). Pray what is this room and what defines the position (standpoint and perspective) of the two men and the standpoint "intermediate" between them? If the room and all the positions and perspectives which they determine are only within, say, Mr. Russell's private world, that private world is interestingly complex, but it gives only the original problem over again, not a "solution" of it. It is a long way from likenesses *within* a private world to likenesses *between* private worlds. And if the worlds are all private, pray who judges their likeness or unlikeness? This sort of thing makes one conclude that Mr. Russell's actual procedure is the reverse of his professed one. He really starts with one room as a spatial continuum within which different positions and projections are determined, and which are readily correlated with one another just because they are projections from positions within one and the same space-room. Having employed this, he, then, can assign different positions to different percipients and institute a comparison between what each perceives and pass upon the extent of the likeness which exists between them.

What is the bearing of this account upon the "empirical datum"? Just this: The correlation of correlative series of changes which defines the object of sense perception is in no sense an original historic or psychologic datum. It signifies the result of an analysis of the usual crude empirical data, and an analysis which is made possible only by a very complex knowledge of the world. It marks not a primitive psychologic datum but an outcome, a limit, of analysis of a vast amount of empirical objects. The definition of an object as a correlation of various sub-correlations of changes represents a great advance—so it seems to me—over the definition of an object as a number of adjectives stuck into a substantive; but it represents an improved definition made possible by the advance of scientific knowledge about the common-sense world. It is a definition not only wholly independent of the context in which Mr. Russell arrives at it, but is one which (once more and finally) assumes extensive and accurate knowledge of just the world professedly called into question.

II

I have come to the point of transition to the other part of my paper. A formal analysis is necessarily dialectical in character. As an empiricist I share in the dissatisfaction which even the most correct dialectical discussion is likely to arouse when brought to bear on matters of fact. I do not doubt that readers will feel that some *fact* of an important character in Mr. Russell's statement has been left untouched by the previous analysis—even upon the supposition that the criticisms are just. Particularly will it be felt, I think, that psychology affords to his statement of the problem a support of fact not affected by any logical treatment. For this reason I append a summary statement as to the facts which are mis-construed by any statement which makes the existence of the world problematic.

I do not believe a psychologist would go as far as to admit that a definite correlation of elements as specific and ordered as that of Mr. Russell's statement is a primitive psychological datum. Many would doubtless hold that patches of colored extensity, sounds, kinesthetic qualities, etc., are psychologically much more primitive than, say, a table, to say nothing of a group of objects in space or a series of events in time; they would say, accordingly, that there is a real problem as to how we infer or construct the latter on the basis of the former. At the same time, I do not believe that they would deny that their own knowledge of the existence and nature of the ultimate and irreducible qualities of sense is the product of a long, careful, and elaborate anal-ysis to which the sciences of physiology, anatomy, and con-trolled processes of experimental observation have contrib-uted. The ordinary method of reconciling these two seem-ingly inconsistent positions is to assume that the original sensible data of experience, as they occurred in infancy, have been overlaid by all kinds of associations and inferential constructions so that it is now a work of intellectual art to recover them in their innocent purity.

Now I might urge that as matter of fact the reconstruc-tion of the experience of infancy is itself an inference from present experience of an objective world, and hence cannot be employed to make a problem out of the knowledge of the existence of that world. But such a retort involves just the dialectic excursus which I am here anxious to avoid. I am on matter-of-fact ground when I point out that the assump-tion that even infancy begins with such highly discriminated particulars as those enumerated is not only highly dubious but has been challenged by eminent psychologists. According to Mr. James, for example, the original datum is large but confused, and specific sensible qualities represent the result of discriminations. In this case, the elementary data, in-stead of being primitive empirical data, are the last terms, the limits, of the discriminations we have been able to make. That knowledge grows from a confusedly experienced external world to a world experienced as ordered and specified would then be the teaching of psychological science, but at no point would the mind be confronted with the problem of inferring a world. Into the arguments in behalf of such a psychology of original experience I shall not go, beyond pointing out the extreme improbability (in view of what is known about instincts and about the nervous system) that the starting point is a quality corresponding to the functioning of a single sense-organ, much less of a single neuronic unit of a sense-organ. If one adds, as a hypothesis, that even the most rudimentary conscious experience contains within itself the element of suggestion or expectation, it will be granted that the object of conscious experience even with an infant is homogeneous with the world of the adult. One may be unwilling to concede the hypothesis. But no one can deny that inference from one thing to another is itself an empirical event, and that just as soon as such inference occurs, even in the simplest form of anticipation and prevision, a world exists like in kind to that of the adult.

I cannot think that it is a trivial coincidence that psychological analysis of sense perception came into existence along with that method of experimentally controlled observation which marks the beginning of modern science. Modern science did not begin with discovery of any new kind of inference. It began with the recognition of the need of different data if inference is to proceed safely. It was contended that starting with the ordinary—or customary—objects of perception hopelessly compromised in advance the work of inference and classification. Hence the demand for an experimental resolution of the common-sense objects in order to get data less ambiguous, more minute, and more extensive. Increasing knowledge of the structure of the nervous system fell in with increased knowledge of other objects to make possible a discrimination of specific qualities in all their diversity; it brought to light that habits, individual and social (through influence on the formation of individual habits), were large factors in determining the accepted or current system of objects. It was brought to light, in other words, that factors of chance, habit, and other non-rational factors were greater influences than intellectual inquiry in determining what men currently believed about the world. What psychological analysis contributed was, then, *not* primitive historic data out of which a world had somehow to be extracted, but an analysis of the world, which had been previously thought of and believed in, into data making possible better inferences and beliefs about the world. Analysis of the influences customarily determining belief and inference was a powerful force in the movement to improve knowledge of the world.

This statement of matters of fact bears out, it will be observed, the conclusions of the dialectical analysis. That brought out the fact that the ultimate and elementary data of sense perception are identified and described as limiting elements in a complex world. What is now added is that such an identification of elements marks a significant addition to the resources of the technique of inquiry devoted to improving knowledge of the world. When these data are isolated from their logical status and office, they are inevitably treated as self-sufficient, and they leave upon our hands the insoluble, because self-contradictory, problem of deriving from them the world of common sense and science. Taken for what they really are, they are elements detected *in* the world and serving to guide and check our inferences about it. They are never self-enclosed particulars; they are always —even as crudely given—connected with other things in experience. But analysis gets them in the form where they are keys to much more significant relations. In short, the particulars of perception, taken as complete and independent, make nonsense. Taken as objects discriminated for the purposes of improving, reorganizing, and testing knowledge of the world they are invaluable assets. The material fallacy lying behind the formal fallacy which the first part of this paper noted is the failure to recognize that what is doubtful is not the existence of the world but the validity of certain customary yet inferential beliefs about things in it. It is not the common-sense *world* which is doubtful, or which is inferential, but *common sense* as a complex of beliefs about specific things and relations *in* the world. Hence never in any actual procedure of inquiry do we throw the existence of the world into doubt, nor can we do so without self-contradiction. We doubt some received piece of "knowledge" about some specific thing of that world, and then set to work, as best we can, to rectify it. The contribution of psychological science to determining unambiguous data and eliminating the irrelevant influences of passion and habit which control the inferences of common sense is an important aid in the technique of such rectifications.

INTRODUCTORY ADDRESS TO THE AMERICAN ASSOCIATION OF UNIVERSITY PROFESSORS

In calling this meeting to order, I wish first to say a few words about the services performed by the committee on organization—and I am sure none of them will think it invidious if I refer particularly to the work of the secretary, Professor Lovejoy, who has borne the heat and labor of the day more than any one else. All of its members are busy men and the work they have done is a labor of love. It is but fair to them that it should be known to all that their labors, continued for over a year, have been singularly free from a disposition on the part of any one to push a particular scheme or ride a particular hobby. If any one, perchance, has come here to-day with a fear that something is to be sprung upon the meeting, or that the committee has, as the saying goes, something up its sleeve, pray let him disabuse himself of the idea. The committee has tried to do nothing more than had to be done to bring together a representative body, without reference to factions or sections; to get matters into shape to facilitate discussion and economize time.

Doubtless we have made mistakes. But they are only such as are incident to getting a large enterprise under way, especially considering the lack of authoritative precedents to follow, and the lack of such clerical and other machinery as the organization itself will bring into being. The committee found itself between the Scylla of doing nothing definite and the Charybdis of doing so much as to forestall action that ought to be taken only by the organization itself. So it thought its main effort should be to collect representative opinions and to secure the adhesion of a body of men large enough to represent different types of institutions, different lines of work and different sections of the country. Each

[Delivered at the organizational meeting of the American Association of University Professors, 1 January 1915, and first published in *Science*, n.s. 41 (1915): 147–51.]

member of the committee was asked to prepare two lists of names; one of men of full professorial rank in his own institution, and the other of men (of like grade) in his own subject, irrespective of institutional connection. Then these two lists were combined so as to include names found on either. To simplify the work, invitations were not sent to men in institutions represented by less than five names.

You will readily see that there was no available way for standardizing the basis of selection employed by the more than thirty men on the committee. Hence it is not only probable that there are omissions of teachers who should have been asked, but that there is inequity of distribution among different institutions and branches of learning. But I am sure that there is no inequality which can not readily be straightened out in the workings of the association itself. It should also be stated that the draft of a constitution to be submitted has not, for lack of time and because of the wide geographical distribution of the men on the committee, been authorized by the committee as a whole. This is hardly to be regretted for it reserves for each member complete freedom of action, and emphasizes the point that the chief object of its preparation is not to supply an ideal or final draft, but a definite basis for discussions to bring out and register the will of the meeting. At the same time it should be said that the draft does not represent so much the wishes of the members of the subcommittee personally as the preponderant drift of the opinions expressed in letters in reply to the circulars sent out.

As much as this I should probably have felt like saying in any case. But the committee has asked me also to speak upon the reasons for calling this assembly together. What is the proposed association for? Any proposal to increase the existing number of associations, meetings, etc., assumes a serious responsibility. The burden of proof is upon it.

We are in a period of intense and rapid growth of higher education. No minister of public education controls the growth; there is no common educational legislature to discuss and decide its proper course; no single tribunal to which moot questions may be brought. There are not even long-established traditions to guide the expansive growth. Whatever unity is found is due to the pressure of like needs, the influence of institutional imitation and rivalry, and to informal exchange of experience and ideas. These methods have accomplished great things. Within almost a single generation our higher education has undergone a transformation amounting to a revolution. And I venture to say that, in spite of the deficiencies we so freely deplore, no country has at any time accomplished more in the same number of years.

But have we not come to a time when more can be achieved by taking thought together? In the future, as in the past, progress will depend upon local efforts in response to local needs and resources. We have the advantages as well as the disadvantages of the lack of the European system of centralized control. So much the more reason for the existence of a central body of teachers, which, lacking official and administrative power, will express the opinion of the profession where it exists and foster its formation where it does not exist. I am a great believer in the power of public opinion. In this country nothing stands against it. But to act, it must exist. To act wisely, it must be intelligently formed. To be intelligently formed, it must be the result of deliberate inquiry and discussion. It can not be developed in corners here and there; it can not be the voice of a few, however wise. It must be formed democratically; that is, cooperatively. All interests, however humble, must be heard; inquiry and conference must glean all the experiences available; decision must be based upon mutual consultation.

The need of a voluntary organization is the greater because of certain facts in the history of the American university. The rapid growth already referred to has occurred under a machinery designed for very different conditions. We are doing our educational work under methods of control developed decades ago, before anything like the existing type of university was thought of. Our official methods of fixing fundamental educational polity as well as of recruiting, appointing, promoting and dismissing teachers, are an inheritance from bygone conditions. Their lack of adaptation to the present situation is due not to sinister intent, but to the fact that they are a heritage from colonial days and provincial habits. The wonder is not that there is so much restlessness and friction, but that there is not more. A system inherently absurd in the present situation has been made workable because of the reasonableness and good will of the governors on one side and, even more, of the governed on the other.

All the more need, then, of ascertaining, precipitating in discussions and crystallizing in conclusions the educational experiences and aspirations of the scholars of the country. I confess myself unable to understand the temper of mind which anticipates the danger of what some term trades-unionism or of interference with constituted administrative authorities as a result of the formation of this organization. As to the latter: I know of few teachers who wish additional administrative work: most would be glad of relief from duties that do not seem exactly significant and that are time-consuming. But it is not expedient, in view of the trust committed to us, to maintain a state of affairs which makes difficult or impossible among college teachers the formation and expression of a public opinion based on ascertained facts. I can not imagine that existing authorities will not welcome the results of inquiries and discussion carried on by a truly representative body of teachers. To think otherwise is to dishonor both ourselves and them. The only thing which is undignified and intolerable is that teachers, individually or collectively, should indulge in carping criticism of boards of trustees when they have not thought it worth while to cultivate an enlightened educational polity among themselves nor found the means for making themselves heard. If we do not like the present situation we have nobody but ourselves to blame.

Let me add that I can think of nothing so well calculated to lift discussions of educational defects and possibilities from the plane of emotion to that of intelligence as the existence of a truly representative body of professors. The best way to put educational principles where they belong—in the atmosphere of scientific discussion—is to disentangle them from the local circumstances with which they so easily get bound up in a given institution. So to free them is already to have taken a step in their generalization. The very moment we free our perplexities from their local setting they perforce fall into a truer perspective. Passion, prejudice, partisanship, cowardice and truculence alike tend to be eliminated, and impartial and objective considerations to come to the front. The very existence of a recognized free forum of discussion with one's fellows gathered from all parts of the country will make for sanity and steadiness quite as much as for courage.

The fear that a "trade unionism" of spirit will be cultivated is ungrounded. I have great respect for trade unions and what they accomplish. Many of the questions which have been suggested for consideration by this body have their economic aspect. Since economic conditions seriously affect the efficiency and scope of our educational work, such topics are surely legitimate ones for inquiry and report. But the term trades unionism has been used to suggest a fear that we are likely to subordinate our proper educational activities to selfish and monetary considerations. I have never heard any one suggest such a danger for the American Bar Association or the American Medical Association. Pray, are the aims of college teachers less elevated? Or is it that our position is so much less assured that any organized association must take on such a color? Are we animated by a narrower or more sordid spirit? Is there anything in the history of our body which indicates materialism of spirit, or indeed anything but an idealism which lends itself to being imposed upon rather than to propaganda in behalf of narrow trade interests? Ladies and gentlemen, I resent such insinuations. I can not believe that we are fallen so low that association for the purpose of careful investigation and discussion of common educational interests can be interpreted by any right-minded person as a rebellious and mercenary organization. If we have so fallen, something immensely more radical than the formation of this organization is the indicated remedy.

A word upon the subject of the relation of the association to academic freedom may be in place, especially as it has been mistakenly stated in the public prints that this matter is the chief cause of the formation of this organization. I do not know any college teacher who does not believe that cases of infringement may arise. I do not know any who does not hold that such infringement, when it occurs, is an attack upon the integrity of our calling. But such cases are too rare to demand or even suggest the formation of an association like this. Existing learned societies are already disposed to deal with cases of infringement as they may come to light, and in my opinion it is a matter of detail rather than of principle whether they should be dealt with by such special bodies or by a more inclusive body like this. In any case, I am confident that the topic can not be more than an incident of the activities of the association in developing professional standards, standards which will be quite as scrupulous regarding the obligations imposed by freedom as jealous for the freedom itself. The existence of publicly recognized and enforced standards would tend almost automatically to protect the freedom of the individual and to secure institutions against its abuse.

In conclusion, let me say that proposing such an association as this is to my mind but proposing to apply to our common calling the standards and ideals to which we have been trained, each in his special line of work. In his own branch, each of us recognizes how little he can do by himself; how dependent his efforts are upon cooperation and reinforcement by the work of a multitude of others. Let us cultivate a like social sense of the wide educational interests we have in common; of our dependence upon one another as institutions and as teachers. In his own specialty, each of us recognizes the need of careful study of facts before coming to a conclusion. Shall we not require of ourselves a similar scientific spirit as we try to settle educational questions? A more intense consciousness of our common vocation, our common object and common destiny; and a more resolute desire to apply the methods of science, methods of inquiry and publicity, to our work in teaching—these are the things which call for the existence of organized effort. Surely we shall have the judgment, the courage and the self-sacrifice commensurate with reverence for our calling, which is none other than the discovery and diffusion of truth. No one has any illusions about what can be immediately accomplished. Let us therefore arm ourselves with patience and endurance in view of remoter issues. No one underestimates the practical difficulties in our way. But arming ourselves with the good will and mutual confidence our profession exacts of us, we shall go forward and overcome them.

ANNUAL ADDRESS OF THE PRESIDENT
TO THE AMERICAN ASSOCIATION OF
UNIVERSITY PROFESSORS

What I had to say of a general sort about the aims and work of an organization like ours, I was delivered of last year. In dealing with some of the specific and detailed matters which confront us, I am in danger of trenching upon the future discussions of the Association or forestalling the reports of some of its committees. But I am anxious to do what I can to set a precedent in favor of an annual address from the president of the year, and so shall run the risk: — at least so far as to submit to you a few notes which have recorded themselves in my mind in connection with the year's experience.

I think it may safely be said that this first year's experience shows that various fears expressed in advance as to the theory of our organization were ungrounded. But it also shows that the anticipations of many of us that the difficulties attending the operations of the Association are of a definitely practical nature had a basis. Take for example the matter of our place of our meeting. Certainly in itself this is a perfectly satisfactory place. But we cannot now be meeting in Washington without calling to mind, first, that the largest gathering of college teachers is assembled this week in Columbus; secondly, that plans had been made for our meeting there also; and, thirdly, that our western members have ground for complaint in the fact that we are assembling two years in succession on the Atlantic seaboard. There were, to the Council, adequate grounds for making the shift from Columbus to Washington. The fact that the report of the committee on academic tenure and academic freedom is the chief feature of this year's program, and that that committee was a joint committee with the three soci-

[Delivered before the American Association of University Professors, 31 December 1915, and first published in *Bulletin of the American Association of University Professors* 1 (1915): 9–13.]

eties concerned with the social sciences which meet this
year in Washington, was the controlling consideration. In
spite of its weight, the outcome is only the choice of the
less of two evils, and is sufficiently unsatisfactory to justify
laying stress on the difficulties connected with selection of
a proper place of meeting. It is not practicable to attempt
to assemble all the conventions and conferences of Convoca-
tion Week in one city. It may be questioned, however,
whether an arrangement might not be made, by cooperative
effort, by which the societies should at least all meet in the
same geographical section in a given year, so that after
their adjournment a place of meeting of our Association
might be found within reasonable proximity of most of
them. The matter is now complicated by the fact that the
American Association for the Advancement of Science will
presumably meet in the east next year, so that we have apparently to face the dilemma of either splitting off again
from the men in the natural sciences or still further giving
ground for complaint to our western members. This matter
is so intimately connected with the problems of getting at
our annual meeting a representative gathering that I make
no apology for calling it emphatically to your attention.
Our Council might well devote considerable time and effort
during the coming year to a solution of the difficulty, by
means of a common policy to be pursued in our specialistic
learned societies with respect to future meetings.

It is a natural transition from this topic to that of membership and of local chapters or associations.[1] This organization (like every other drawing its membership from our
entire territory) is between the danger represented by the
saying that what is everybody's business is nobody's, and
the danger, in the interests of efficiency, of so compact an
administrative management as to fail to secure the needed
representation of diverse local interests, or even as to arouse
such suspicions as would weaken confidence and alienate
loyalty. I shall not express my opinion on the matter of
local chapters, which will doubtless come before this meeting

1. The references to the topic of membership are omitted as the
Association authorized the appointment of a committee to deal
with this matter.

for action. But it is not out of place to say that we must devise some means of stimulating and securing local co-operation and trust. We require local interest and support to make sure of a permanent and attached membership, to make possible the prompt and wide securing of information on matters inquired into, and to distribute the burdens and rights incident to the work of the various committees of the Association, as well as to prevent the rise of any feeling that the affairs of the Association are in the hands of a clique. At the same time, the Association must remain a national Association, concerned with common and fundamental interests; it must not in any way entangle itself in local politics or controversies. I have no doubt that the collective wisdom of this body will be quite adequate to securing efficiency of operation along with full attention to individual and local opinions from every section of the country, and of building up a continuous policy without also building up an administrative machine.

In concluding I wish to say a word about the large place occupied in this year's program by the question of academic freedom in its relation to academic tenure. I have heard rumors of some criticism on this point. Some have expressed to me fear lest attention to individual grievances might crowd out attention to those general and constructive matters which are the Association's reason for existence. Let me say for the reassurance of any such that none of the officers of the Association, least of all those who have been overwhelmed by the duties incident to these investigations, regard this year's work as typical or even as wholly normal. The general report of the committee of fifteen was, indeed, definitely contemplated in the plan of the year's work. The investigations of particular cases were literally thrust upon us. To have failed to meet the demands would have been cowardly; it would have tended to destroy all confidence in the Association as anything more than a talking body. The question primarily involved was not whether the Council should authorize the investigation of this or that case, but whether the Association was to have legs and arms and be a working body. In short, as conditions shaped themselves for us, I personally feel that the work done on particular cases this year turned out to be of the most constructive sort which could have been undertaken. While a succession of incidents like those at Utah, Montana, Colorado and Pennsylvania was wholly unexpected (and, let it be hoped, never to be repeated), it may well be doubted whether any cut-and-dried, predetermined plan of "constructive" work would have been equally effective in shaking a multitude of things together and making an Association on paper into a working unity with a mind and movement of its own. Incidentally, the detailed information secured was of great assistance to the general committee in shaping its report on principles and its program of policy; while the improvements in rules as to appointment and dismissal since made in three of the institutions where inquiries have taken place are of themselves evidence of constructive work. I do not say that the existence and work of the society has been the sole or chief agency in effecting these improvements, but I will say that in my judgment it has had a sufficiently definite share in them to justify, apart from any other considerations, the first year's existence of this Association. The amount and quality of energy and the time spent upon these matters by our secretary and by the chairman of our committee of fifteen are such as to beggar thanks. These gentlemen and the others who have labored with them must find their reward not only in the increased prosperity of this Association in the future, but, above all, in the enhanced security and dignity of the scholar's calling throughout our country.

While the question of academic freedom and academic tenure has thus, unexpectedly, had the centre of the stage during the year, its consideration has not precluded the formation of investigating committees for other subjects. We hope, in fact, that what has been accomplished this year has cleared the way for other work. Three such inquiries are now in progress, dealing with the following subjects: "methods of appointment and promotion"; "the recruiting of the profession, and the effect thereon of the existing system of graduate fellowships and scholarships"; and "the limits of 'standardization' in higher education, with especial reference to the standardizing activities of extra-academic corporations." Without doubt the reports of these committees will form the substance of the discussions of our next year's meeting.

We met one year ago with mingled hopes and fears. We meet today with a record of things accomplished and a definite program of things yet to be undertaken—with fears allayed and hopes confirmed.

FACULTY SHARE IN UNIVERSITY CONTROL

My purpose in this paper is to suggest some of the reasons for giving the teaching body in universities a greater share in the control of university policies; and then to sketch a method by which this may most readily be brought about. I assume without argument that there is much dissatisfaction felt by most faculties at present, because so many important questions, educational directly and educational or administrative secondarily, are settled without their active participation; and that, after all allowances for weaknesses of human nature have been made, the essence of the feeling is justified. It is an undesirable anomaly that fundamental control should be vested in a body of trustees or regents having no immediate connection with the educational conduct of our institutions.

For convenience of discussion, control may be considered in four aspects. The first concerns the initiation of new developments, the founding of new schools or colleges within the university, or new lines of work involving a considerable expenditure of funds. So far as I am aware, this matter is almost universally reserved for the trustees in consultation with executive officers, faculties generally having no official knowledge until action has been taken. The second concerns action which modifies existing courses— conditions of entrance and graduation, etc. Here faculties generally have the initiative, but cases are not infrequent where trustees negate the action of a faculty or seriously alter its terms. The third has to do with appointments and dismissals. Here custom, if not constitutional legislation, leaves the first step in appointments with the faculty—not,

[Prepared on behalf of Columbia University by John Dewey and delivered by Cassius J. Keyser to the Association of American Universities, 27 August 1915. First published in *Journal of Proceedings and Addresses of the Seventeenth Annual Conference* (1915): 27–32.]

however, as a rule with the faculty as a body, but with the head of a department or the department as a whole in consultation with the president. In dismissals, the initiative is more frequently taken by the trustees than in appointments. Cases of discipline of students are generally left practically entirely with the faculty. Intervention by the trustees is usually regarded on all hands as an interference, and sometimes as a scandalous one. It is accordingly left out of account in the subsequent discussion, although it is reported that in an otherwise reputable New England college the governing board has recently decreed that no expulsions can be made except by its express action.

It is obvious—at least to the writer—that, while the desirable division between trustees and faculties is that the former should be trustees of funds and the latter the guardians of all educational interests, financial and educational matters overlap. Faculty legislation may involve the expenditures of funds, and the governing board may not have the funds at hand, or may have reasons for thinking that a better distribution of available funds may be made. I fancy that this is the reason why the initiation of new policies has been so generally monopolized by trustees. The monopoly is, however, a serious matter. Branching out in new lines of work when new funds are at hand encroaches on work already undertaken, if not directly, then by preventing expansions which otherwise might occur. Consequently faculties have a very direct interest in the matter. In the second place, when faculties have nothing to say in such affairs, when they are not kept officially informed of the existence of funds making new developments possible, and asked at least to suggest plans and measures, one of the chief motives to an intelligent interest in the affairs of the institution as a whole is left untouched. The most important business which could come before a faculty does not come before it. In consequence, faculty meetings are likely to be taken up largely with routine and perfunctory matters, and are attended in a perfunctory way which enlists neither interest, serious reflection upon fundamental educational questions, nor loyalty to the institution as a whole. I am convinced that a large part of the critical attitude of faculties toward the administration of the institutions to which they belong is due to the fact that, not having been taken into counsel in matters of chief importance, they feel that they are "out of it." The policies of the institution are not theirs; they have no particular responsibility for developing the plans they are expected to carry out. Even on the supposition that their criticisms are more or less ungrounded, the state of affairs is deplorable and remediable. If they knew the entire situation, with the reasons for actions taken, and the difficulties in the way of other plans (as they would if they were consulted before action was taken), grounds for suspicion and latent antagonism would be lacking. If they had a responsible share in the action, loyal cooperation would follow.

I know it is sometimes stated that university teachers are too impractical and too individualistic to be trusted to work together in such matters. They are even sometimes said to be intrinsically querulous and cranky. There is no doubt that highly specialized work develops an individualistic spirit. A colleague of mine once remarked to me that college teachers were the easiest men in the world to drive and the hardest to lead. There is no doubt that specialism tends to foster an interest in departmental matters at the expense of general educational interest—concern with the policies of the university as a whole. But these facts would seem to be good reasons for following a course which would counteract the tendencies instead of fostering them. And it is unjust to the men in question to permit such charges without asking how far the obnoxious qualities of impracticality and fault-finding have been generated by existing methods of university control. Grown men with a high degree of intellectual training and often with wide reputations in their special branches do not enjoy being treated as children. And when everything is boiled down, that is what a system comes to which puts ultimate control in the hands of a body of men of business, lawyers, clergymen, and politicians with no direct contact with education. It is wholly unfair to take a state of affairs where teachers are lacking in responsibility for the conduct of their institutions in fundamental points as a measure for what would happen if adequate responsibility were granted.

The reasons assigned for giving the faculty a greater share in the formulation of new departures and developments apply in their degree to the second point—the modification of existing policies. That a faculty should give months to the investigation and discussion of some educational topic only to have its decision turned down by a body of outsiders which happens to have legal authority is almost too absurd for serious discussion. As a principle of the conduct of higher education it would seem to belong in *Alice in Wonderland*. That faculties take it as a sign of distrust of their own competency, that they attribute it to ignorance, or to a casual opposition based upon the fact that such measures did not happen to exist when some influential trustee went to college, is not unnatural. It is not wholly surprising that they sometimes attribute it to the sinister influence of an administrative officer who, not having had his own way in faculty-meeting, more readily secures it in the privacy of a trustees' meeting. No doubt the faculties are sometimes wrong and the governing board sometimes right in these cases. But the reverse is also the case. And a complete concentration of responsibility in the hands of those directly engaged in educational work would tend to increase the wisdom of their action and their interest in correcting such mistakes as they would undoubtedly make from time to time. The suggestion made below for a standing conference committee would secure, moreover, the point of view of the trustees getting a hearing.

With respect to appointments, it is inevitable that trustees should leave them for the most part, save in the case of new departments or headships, to the faculty. The difficulty here is, I think, primarily in the fact that recommendations are made by a person interested in pushing a single department, or perhaps not enough interested to compete with more energetic and skilful persons. Of the remedy I have something to say below. Here I would only point out that since the recommendation is now usually made to the president, the latter is put in the difficult position of being a kind of final arbiter on the competing claims submitted to him. Consequently disappointments and complaints are visited upon him, although he is probably doing the best he can under the circumstances. I hope I do not exaggerate the

SPLITTING UP THE SCHOOL SYSTEM

Within the last few years the rich variety of pedagogical terminology has been added unto by the terms "unit" and "dual control." These terms have an interest for the average citizen far beyond that attaching to most of the words in the pedagogical vocabulary. The question which they partly raise and partly disguise is whether we shall continue to have a unified system of public education, or whether for all pupils over the age of fourteen it shall be split in two. Most of us have probably settled back in a conviction that the unity of the public-school system is the best guarantee we possess of a unifying agency to deal successfully with the diversified heterogeneity of our population. Knowledge of the location of the proposed line of cleavage is not adapted to reduce disquietude. The segregation proposed is to divide the children of the more well-to-do and cultured families of the community from those children who will presumably earn their living by working for wages in manual and commercial employments—chiefly the former. Many of us have been disturbed at the increasing tendency toward stratification of classes in this country. We have wondered if those European prophets were correct who have insistently foretold that the development of fixed classes in this country was only a question of time. Few have dreamed that the day was already at hand when responsible and influential persons would urge that the public-school system should recognize the separation as an accomplished fact, and adapt to it its machinery of administrative control, its courses of study and its methods of instruction in the public school.

The matter is not one of academic import. A bill providing for such division was introduced into the last session

[First published in *New Republic* 2 (1915): 283–84. For Charles P. Megan's response to this article, see this volume, pp. 471–72. Dewey's rejoinder to Megan also appears in this volume on pp. 416–17.]

of the legislature of the state of Illinois under the auspices of the Commercial Club of Chicago. Although it failed to pass, and although its principle has since been condemned by the state bankers' association, the state association of teachers and the state federation of labor, the proposal has been reintroduced in the present session with powerful backing. Independently of the particular kind of a division which the bill would bring about, it prepares the way, if it passes, for future separations. It was publicly stated and not denied that at the previous session every member of the legislature of the Roman Catholic faith received a letter from a superior dignitary of that church urging support of the bill. And why not? Here at least is a group of citizens already paying taxes for the support of the public schools and supporting from their own funds private schools. They have shown their faith by their works. And if commercial bodies and employers of labor can procure a state-supported system of schools in their own special behalf, what sound reasons can be urged against further administrative segregations in behalf of profound religious convictions? And if there are communities where Poles or Germans predominate or form a considerable fraction of the community, why should not another splitting occur to care for their special needs? These considerations may seem fanciful, but any one who is aware of the compelling force of the cumulative logic of events when once a movement gets headway will not dismiss them as idle.

The statement that the proposed movement is in behalf of the interests of employers of labor will meet with indignant denials—in many cases quite sincere. It is insisted that the division is in the interests of the large number of pupils who at present go out into wage-earning pursuits and to whom the existing system affords no adequate preparation. It is insisted that a greater industrial efficiency which can be assured only by systematized educational endeavor is required by the interests of the community as a whole. It is pointed out that workingmen as well as employers of labor are conjointly to constitute the special state and local boards who are to have charge of the state-aided trade schools for pupils above fourteen. All this is aside from the point. Measures have to be judged not on the basis of personal feelings animating the bosoms of those who propose them, but from the standpoint of their consequences when put in operation. And the issue at stake is not whether the existing school system shall be progressively reorganized and supplemented to care for social functions not adequately cared for in the past, but whether a sharp line of cleavage shall be drawn as respects administrative control, studies, methods and personal associations of pupils, between schools of the traditional literary type and schools of a trade-preparatory type.

The issue has been raised in a definite, clear-cut way. The sponsors for the bill have left no one in doubt. In support of the proposed division they have been profuse in attacks upon the existing school system, its directors and teachers. They have urged that vocational education cannot be secured under existing auspices; that the latter obstruct intelligent preparation for making a living and divert funds and measures to academic purposes, while its teachers vitiate whatever is undertaken by clothing it with cultural aims. What does this mean but that the forces which are even now effecting a readaptation of the traditional curriculum of the elementary and high school to meet the change of social conditions, are to be driven into a narrow channel, while the old curriculum is to be left frozen in its narrow form? The affair is the more serious because the intelligent and forceful changes already going on will, if the measure for splitting the schools goes into effect, be left high and dry for lack of pecuniary support.

The scope of the readaptation already in progress is not generally known. Chicago is obviously the city in Illinois which would be most directly influenced by the scheme. More than half of the pupils in the high schools of Chicago to-day are engaged in "vocational" work. There are industrial centres in twenty elementary schools; were there funds they would have been established in twenty-six more. There are four or five schools for workers in the apprenticeship trades and preparations for three more. Under unified control, the pupils are kept in constant personal association with youth not going into manual pursuits; the older type of school work is receiving constant stimulation and permeation. Technical subjects are taught by practical men and women whose horizon and methods are broadened by contact with wider educational interests, while the teachers in the more theoretical subjects are brought into living touch with problems and needs of modern life which in the isolated state they might readily ignore.

In short, a complete education system preserving the best in the old and redeeming the heritage by lively association with studies, methods and teachers representing newer social needs, is in active development. It is self-evident that under the divided plan either the public must meet the expense of a vast and costly duplication of buildings, equipment, teachers and administrative directors; or else the old schools will have to strip themselves of everything but the rudiments of a traditional bookish education; and the new schools confine themselves to a narrow trade preparation. That the latter will be ineffective for every industrial end except setting up a congested labor market in the skilled trades and a better grade of labor—at public expense—for employers to exploit, I have shown in previous articles.

All discussion of social matters tends to go under a mask of eulogistic question-begging epithets. Education is no exception. Such labels as "discipline" and "culture" have operated as fortresses to protect established habits from intelligent criticism and cross-examination. Now we have the inspiring term "vocational." Examined in the light of the details of the Illinois bill and of the arguments in its favor put forward by its representatives, vocational education is nothing but technical trade-training dignified with a high-sounding title. Ex-Superintendent Cooley, the authorized spokesman of the Chicago Commercial Club, says that the vocational schools are to provide "practical instruction in vocational lines for youths between fourteen and eighteen." That there may be no doubt as to what this means, he says that the vocational type of school has for its problem "the *direct* training in vocational life of the youth who *must* leave the ordinary school at fourteen." At a public discussion in Chicago, an official representative of the Commercial Club stated that "vocational education must be shaped to dovetail with the industry in which the group of pupils happen to be." It is no wonder that Mr. Cooley concludes that an efficient system of vocational education (as thus defined) "requires different methods of administration, different courses of study, different qualifications of teachers, different equipment" from those of the unified school system. No greater tribute has ever been paid to the existing school system, with all its faults. It is for the average citizen who retains his belief in democracy and in the duty of the public school to educate for a still better democracy, to decide whether the simple statement of the ground for the radical splitting up of the school system is not its own self-sufficient condemnation.

STATE OR CITY CONTROL OF SCHOOLS?

The morning newspapers of February twelfth reported briefly and with little comment a resolution which had just passed the Board of Estimate and Apportionment of the city of New York, looking to a considerable extension of its powers. The resolution provided for the preparation of a bill to be acted upon by the state legislature, giving the Board of Estimate the power to determine the number of all city officers and employees paid from the city treasury and to fix their salaries. The point of the proposed bill is that it applies to the employees of the counties, courts and Department of Education, whose salaries are not now fixed by the Board. The action was taken only after a more radical and drastic proposition, giving the Board the power to eliminate and modify departments and bureaus, had been lost—the mayor and controller, however, both voting for it. The purpose of the proposed bill is to secure a greater measure of self-government to the city in the fundamental matter of control of the budget. At the present time a very considerable portion of city expenditure is imposed upon the Board by mandatory statutes.

Those who believe that many of the evils of our municipal government are due to an absurd division of responsibility brought about by state-imposed regulations will wish well to this measure. With respect to the control of educational policy—which inevitably goes with control of the pursestrings—the measure is, however, more revolutionary than at first sight appears. The question of the relation of the Board of Education to the state on the one hand, and to the municipality on the other, is about the most vexatious and the most unsettled of all our administrative questions—which is saying a good deal. The theory and practice in our earlier history

[First published in *New Republic* 2 (1915): 178–80.]

was that the Board of Education was an independent corporation. In the earlier school charters the Board had not only plenary control of educational expenditures, but also power to fix the amount to be spent. While the principle has since been modified, it has been, in the words of the Court of Appeals, "the settled policy of the state, from an early date, to divorce the business of public education from all other municipal interests or business, and to take charge of it as a peculiar and separate function through agents of its own selection and immediately subject and responsive to its control."

It so happens that the city of New York is amply endowed with literature on the subject of municipal control of school expenditures. The Committee on School Inquiry—popularly known as the Hanus Survey—evolved two reports on this topic. The first, prepared by Professor E. C. Moore, now professor of education in Harvard University, was not acceptable to the Board of Estimate. Its official censorship resulted in this particular report getting more newspaper publicity than any other document of the whole inquiry. Professor Goodnow, now president of Johns Hopkins University, and Mr. Howe, now Commissioner of Immigration, then prepared another report which stands as the official document. Mr. Moore warmly espoused the theory embodied in the words of the Court cited above. It happened—happened is, I think, an unusually exact word in this case—that the present school charter of the city is loosely drawn and contains inconsistent provisions. This has led to considerable friction between the Board of Estimate and the Board of Education. The former felt that the latter was trying to evade proper recognition of its subordination in fiscal matters. The latter felt that the former was invading its own proper domain. In view of the inconsistent statements of the charter, an unprejudiced outsider would probably conclude that either would be right, according to whichever provision of the charter one should attach the most importance.

The weight of educational history and of past political policy was undoubtedly, however, on the side of the Board of Education. Approaching the matter from this side and influenced by educational considerations rather than by those

of city administration, Professor Moore took sides with the
Board of Education and against his employers, the Board of
Estimate. A former superintendent of schools in a Western
city where he had made a gallant fight for the integrity of
the educational system against the attacks of local politicians, he was especially sensitive to all the historic considerations which have made public education a ward of the state
rather than of the municipality. He concluded that by gradual usurpations the schools were becoming "almost as completely annexed to the City Hall as they would have been if
the proposed new charter had become the organic law of the
city."

Mr. Goodnow and Mr. Howe approached the matter
from the side of efficient city government rather than from
that of general educational considerations. While their report
is more reserved than Professor Moore's, their specific recommendations all looked to securing for the Board of Estimate
more complete and responsible supervision of all funds paid
for the schools out of the city treasury. So the case stands.
The conflict is a real one, not only in fact but in the principles involved. The reasons advanced for regarding education as on a different footing from street-cleaning or police
service are genuine and weighty. The dangers of injection
into the public educational system of a petty and sordid kind
of politics, in case the schools become in effect a city department, are not fanciful. Under an assured Tammany régime,
for instance, one might imagine what would happen if the
Board of Estimate could fix the number of school officials
and employees and their salaries. One can imagine under any
system what might happen if teachers, as great in number as
they are in New York City, had a motive to organize politically with place and salary in view. But on the other hand it
is difficult to see how a scientific budget control with efficiency of administration is to be secured if the municipal authorities cannot control the expenditure of the moneys which
they have to raise by taxation and bonded debt.

It is easy to construct a mental picture of a situation in
which the balance would fall heavily on the side of education
as a state function under its complete control. Education is
the concern of the whole of organized society in a way in

which other governmental services (unless that of public health) are not. It would be easy for the state to secure the services of a large body of educational experts—organize the information bearing on the best methods of administration and instruction, and put both experts and knowledge at the disposal of every community. It would be easier for the state than for a particular community to achieve a broad intellectual outlook, to free educational endeavor from the ruts and prejudices of local custom, to undertake well-planned experiments, and to secure a progressively developing educational tradition. The state could look ahead, and act less from local pressure and more from the bidding of constructive intelligence. However, such statesmanship has not in the past been the characteristic feature of our state educational officials. New York State has a more centralized machinery for affecting the public schools than most other states, but its management has been largely in the hands of routineers who have been more interested in imposing mechanical uniformity, and in that kind of administrative efficiency denoted by reports and examinations, than in educational leadership. Our state boards of education have much to learn from the methods of the national and state agricultural officials in the way of stimulating local action and guiding it by expert help. In some Western states the state universities have rendered signal service, but their influence has been confined to the high schools.

The fact is, I think, that we have no experience which will enable us to decide conclusively in behalf of either state or local control. If the experiment of complete municipal control could be tried under favorable auspices, the result might be an immense furthering of the interests of the schools in all our larger municipalities. The difficulty with the present system is that it is in practice, whatever be the theory, an ill-digested mixture of both methods, with the same dispersion of power and responsibility and the same empirical puttering-along that marks our other civic governmental services. In at least eight or ten of the largest cities of the United States the development of playgrounds, recreation centres, public baths, child hygiene work, social centres, together with the general extension of "social service" activities on the part of the municipality, give good grounds quite apart from fiscal reasons for making the experiment of whole-hearted municipal control. The peculiar industrial conditions of large cities also demand freedom of educational action.

But the experiment, to have a fair chance, must be whole-hearted. The municipal authority must be plenary. However it may be with financial needs, educational requirements are not in the least met merely by conferring power upon the city authorities to regulate expenditures. The appropriate city body must also have freedom from all mandatory provisions regarding the nature and powers of the educational administrators and even from statutory provisions, so far as possible, regarding the course of study. The chief objection — and it is a very serious one — to the action referred to in the opening paragraph is that it does not go far enough. It may aid in getting fiscal autonomy for the city, but it does not do the least thing for securing its educational autonomy. On the contrary, it increases the existing facilities for concealing responsibility and paralyzing initiative. If it becomes a law without further changes of the charter it will enable the Board of Education and the Board of Estimate endlessly to lay the blame for educational stagnation upon each other. It is an invitation to friction for which the children in the schools and the city itself will ultimately have to pay the penalties. It was reported in the press that Mr. McAneny, the author of the resolution adopted, objected to the more radical proposition to which reference has been made, that it involved changes so sweeping that they ought to be taken up only in connection with a general revision of the city charter. So far as the schools are concerned, the same objection applies to Mr. McAneny's own resolution. If complete fiscal control is to pass from the Board of Education as a separate corporation, by all means let us also provide for the freedom of the educational system and for bringing it into the closest possible touch with the other administrative agencies of the city.

I doubt if this can be accomplished without the abolition of the Board of Education in its existing form. All authorities are in favor of a great reduction in its size. Their imagination does not seem to have been adequate to conceiving it reduced to zero. But city boards of education are an anomaly at present. They are a monumental symbol of the haphazard way in which the enterprise of education is carried on, and of a fatal dispersion of initiative and direction. They are historic relics of a theory of state control which does not exist in fact. They are the middleman of our educational organization, and like the middleman in other fields they divide instead of bringing together. They are supposed to check and enlighten the professional wisdom of educational officers by bringing to bear the advice of other specialists and the general fund of municipal common sense. In small towns they render this service. In our large cities they have as much representative capacity as any other colossal accident. The Goodnow-Howe report expressly lays down as one reason why the Board of Estimate should have control over the school budget the fact that it would then control the elimination and extension of school activities—in other words, everything that is vital and not a matter of established custom. In all important aspects the recommendation gave to the Board of Estimate the main functions of the Board of Education and yet retained the latter in corporeal existence.

The principle, as I have been trying to say, is the correct one, provided the Board of Estimate is to take complete control of school finance. But in the form in which it was presented it was not thought out. It properly involves the elimination of the Board of Education, and the establishment of a paid expert educational department, one member of which shall be a member of the Board of Estimate, and which shall be responsible for submitting educational policies to the Board of Estimate, with the facts and reasons upon which they rest, so far as they involve the expenditure of funds. The late Mayor Gaynor's proposal of a small paid board of education was a halfway step in this direction. But it contemplated the retention of the Board of Superintendents, thus continuing in intensified form the existing division of intellectual responsibility and the existing causes of friction. The Board of Superintendents should be the heads of the Educational Department of the city, and put it in direct and reciprocal touch with all departments through the body supremely concerned with municipal policy and planning. Will it prove easier to patch than to construct?

German Philosophy and Politics

Preface

The will of John Calvin McNair established a Foundation at the University of North Carolina upon which public lectures are to be given from time to time to the members of the University. This book contains three lectures which were given in February of this year upon this Foundation. It is a pleasure to acknowledge the many courtesies enjoyed during my brief stay at Chapel Hill, the seat of the University.

J. D.

Columbia University,
   New York City, April, 1915.

1. GERMAN PHILOSOPHY: THE TWO WORLDS

The nature of the influence of general ideas upon practical affairs is a troubled question. Mind dislikes to find itself a pilgrim in an alien world. A discovery that the belief in the influence of thought upon action is an illusion would leave men profoundly saddened with themselves and with the world. Were it not that the doctrine forbids any discovery influencing affairs—since the discovery would be an idea—we should say that the discovery of the wholly *ex post facto* and idle character of ideas would profoundly influence subsequent affairs. The strange thing is that when men had least control over nature and their own affairs, they were most sure of the efficacy of thought. The doctrine that nature does nothing in vain, that it is directed by purpose, was not engrafted by scholasticism upon science; it formulates an instinctive tendency. And if the doctrine be fallacious, its pathos has a noble quality. It testifies to the longing of human thought for a world of its own texture. Yet just in the degree in which men, by means of inventions and political arrangements, have found ways of making their thoughts effective, they have come to question whether any thinking is efficacious. Our notions in physical science tend to reduce mind to a bare spectator of a machine-like nature grinding its unrelenting way. The vogue of evolutionary ideas has led many to regard intelligence as a deposit from history, not as a force in its making. We look backward rather than forward; and when we look forward we seem to see but a further unrolling of a panorama long ago rolled up on a cosmic reel. Even Bergson, who, to a casual reader, appears to reveal vast unexplored vistas of genuinely novel possibilities, turns out, upon careful study, to regard *intellect* (everything which in the past has gone by the name of observation and reflection) as but an evolutionary deposit whose importance is confined to the conservation of a life already achieved, and bids us trust to instinct, or something akin to instinct, for the future: —as if there were hope and consolation in bidding us trust to that which, in any case, we cannot intelligently direct or control.

I do not see that the school of history which finds Bergson mystic and romantic, which prides itself upon its hardheaded and scientific character, comes out at a different place. I refer to the doctrine of the economic interpretation of history in its extreme form—which, so its adherents tell us, is its only logical form. It is easy to follow them when they tell us that past historians have ignored the great part played by economic forces, and that descriptions and explanations have been correspondingly superficial. When one reflects that the great problems of the present day are those attending economic reorganization, one might even take the doctrine as a half-hearted confession that historians are really engaged in construing the past in terms of the problems and interests of an impending future, instead of reporting a past in order to discover some mathematical curve which future events are bound to describe. But no; our strictly scientific economic interpreters will have it that economic forces present an inevitable evolution, of which state and church, art and literature, science and philosophy are by-products. It is useless to suggest that while modern industry has given an immense stimulus to scientific inquiry, yet nevertheless the industrial revolution of the eighteenth century comes after the scientific revolution of the seventeenth. The dogma forbids any connection.

But when we note that Marx gave it away that his materialistic interpretation of history was but the Hegelian idealistic dialectic turned upside down, we may grow wary. Is it, after all, history we are dealing with or another philosophy of history? And when we discover that the great importance of the doctrine is urged upon us, when we find that we are told that the general recognition of its truth helps us out of our present troubles and indicates a path for future effort, we positively take heart. These writers do not seem to mean just what they say. Like the rest of us, they are human, and infected with a belief that ideas, even highly abstract theories, are of efficacy in the conduct of human affairs influencing the history which is yet to be.

I have, however, no intention of entering upon this controversy, much less of trying to settle it. These remarks are but preliminary to a consideration of some of the practical affiliations of portions of the modern history of philosophical thought with practical social affairs. And if I set forth my own position in the controversy in question, the statement is frankly a personal one, intended to make known the prepossessions with which I approach the discussion of the political bearings of one phase of modern philosophy. I do not believe, then, that *pure* ideas, or pure thought, ever exercised any influence upon human action. I believe that very much of what has been presented as philosophic reflection is in effect simply an idealization, for the sake of emotional satisfaction, of the brutely given state of affairs, and is not a genuine discovery of the practical influence of ideas. In other words, I believe it to be esthetic in type even when sadly lacking in esthetic form. And I believe it is easy to exaggerate the practical influence of even the more vital and genuine ideas of which I am about to speak.

But I also believe that there are no such things as *pure* ideas or *pure* reason. Every living thought represents a gesture made toward the world, an attitude taken to some practical situation in which we are implicated. Most of these gestures are ephemeral; they reveal the state of him who makes them rather than effect a significant alteration of conditions. But at some times they are congenial to a situation in which men in masses are acting and suffering. They supply a model for the attitudes of others; they condense into a dramatic type of action. They then form what we call the "great" systems of thought. Not all ideas perish with the momentary response. They are voiced and others hear; they are written and others read. Education, formal and informal, embodies them not so much in other men's minds as in their permanent dispositions of action. They are in the blood, and afford sustenance to conduct; they are in the muscles and men strike or retire. Even emotional and esthetic systems may breed a disposition toward the world and take overt effect. The reactions thus engendered are, indeed, superficial as compared with those in which more primitive instincts are embodied. The business of eating and drinking, buying and selling, marrying and being given in marriage, making war and peace, gets somehow carried on along with any and every system of ideas which the world has known. But how, and when and where and for what men do even these things is tremendously affected by the abstract ideas which get into circulation.

I take it that I may seem to be engaged in an emphatic urging of the obvious. However it may be with a few specialized schools of men, almost everybody takes it as a matter of course that ideas influence action and help determine the subsequent course of events. Yet there is a purpose in this insistence. Most persons draw the line at a certain kind of general ideas. They are especially prone to regard the ideas which constitute philosophic theories as practically innocuous—as more or less amiable speculations significant at the most for moments of leisure, in moments of relief from preoccupation with affairs. Above all, men take the particular general ideas which happen to affect their own conduct of life as normal and inevitable. Pray what other ideas would any sensible man have? They forget the extent to which these ideas originated as parts of a remote and technical theoretical system, which by multitudes of non-reflective channels has infiltrated into their habits of imagination and behavior. An expert intellectual anatomist, my friends, might dissect you and find Platonic and Aristotelian tissues, organs from St. Augustine and St. Thomas Aquinas, Locke and Descartes, in the make-up of the ideas by which you are habitually swayed, and find, indeed, that they and other thinkers of whose names you have never heard constitute a larger part of your mental structure than does the Calvin or Kant, Darwin or Spencer, Hegel or Emerson, Bergson or Browning to whom you yield conscious allegiance.

Philosophers themselves are naturally chiefly responsible for the ordinary estimate of their own influence, or lack of influence. They have been taken mostly at their own word as to what they were doing, and what for the most part they have pretended to do is radically different from what they have actually done. They are quite negligible as seers and reporters of ultimate reality, or the essential natures of things. And it is in this aspect that they have mostly fancied seeing themselves. Their actual office has been quite other.

They have told about nature and life and society in terms of collective human desire and aspiration as these were determined by contemporary difficulties and struggles.

I have spoken thus far as if the influence of general ideas upon action were likely to be beneficial. It goes against the grain to attribute evil to the workings of intelligence. But we might as well face the dilemma. What is called pure thought, thought freed from the empirical contingencies of life, would, even if it existed, be irrelevant to the guidance of action. For the latter always operates amid the circumstance of contingencies. And thinking which is colored by time and place must always be of a mixed quality. In part, it will detect and hold fast to more permanent tendencies and arrangements; in part, it will take the limitations of its own period as necessary and universal—even as intrinsically desirable.

The traits which give thinking effectiveness for the good give it also potency for harm. A physical catastrophe, an earthquake or conflagration, acts only where it happens. While its effects endure, it passes away. But it is of the nature of ideas to be abstract: that is to say, severed from the circumstances of their origin, and through embodiment in language capable of operating in remote climes and alien situations. Time heals physical ravages, but it may only accentuate the evils of an intellectual catastrophe—for by no lesser name can we call a systematic intellectual error. To one who is professionally preoccupied with philosophy there is much in its history which is profoundly depressing. He sees ideas which were not only natural but useful in their native time and place, figuring in foreign contexts so as to formulate defects as virtues and to give rational sanction to brute facts, and to oppose alleged eternal truths to progress. He sees movements which might have passed away with change of circumstance as casually as they arose, acquire persistence and dignity because thought has taken cognizance of them and given them intellectual names. The witness of history is that to think in general and abstract terms is dangerous; it elevates ideas beyond the situations in which they were born and charges them with we know not what menace for the future. And in the past the danger has been the greater because philosophers have so largely purported to be concerned not with contemporary problems of living, but with essential Truth and Reality viewed under the form of eternity.

In bringing these general considerations to a close, I face an embarrassment. I must choose some particular period of intellectual history for more concrete illustration of the mutual relationship of philosophy and practical social affairs—which latter, for the sake of brevity, I term Politics. One is tempted to choose Plato. For in spite of the mystic and transcendental coloring of his thought, it was he who defined philosophy as the science of the State, or the most complete and organized whole known to man; it is no accident that his chief work is termed the *Republic*. In modern times, we are struck by the fact that English philosophy from Bacon to John Stuart Mill has been cultivated by men of affairs rather than by professors, and with a direct outlook upon social interests. In France, the great period of philosophy, the period of *les philosophes*, was the time in which were forged the ideas which connect in particular with the French Revolution and in general with the conceptions which spread so rapidly through the civilized world—of the indefinite perfectibility of humanity, the rights of man, and the promotion of a society as wide as humanity, based upon allegiance to reason.

Somewhat arbitrarily I have, however, selected some aspects of classic German thought for my illustrative material. Partly, I suppose, because one is piqued by the apparent challenge which its highly technical, professorial and predominantly *a priori* character offers to the proposition that there is close connection between abstract thought and the tendencies of collective life. More to the point, probably, is the fact that the heroic age of German thought lies almost within the last century, while the creative period of continental thought lies largely in the eighteenth century, and that of British thought still earlier. It was Taine, the Frenchman, who said that all the leading ideas of the present day were produced in Germany between 1780 and 1830. Above all, the Germans, as we say, have philosophy in their blood. Such phrases generally mean something not about hereditary qualities, but about the social conditions under which ideas propagate and circulate.

Now Germany is the modern state which provides the greatest facilities for general ideas to take effect through social inculcation. Its system of education is adapted to that end. Higher schools and universities in Germany are really, not just nominally, under the control of the state and part of the state life. In spite of freedom of academic instruction when once a teacher is installed in office, the political authorities have always taken a hand, at critical junctures, in determining the selection of teachers in subjects that had a direct bearing upon political policies. Moreover, one of the chief functions of the universities is the preparation of future state officials. Legislative activity is distinctly subordinate to that of administration conducted by a trained civil service, or, if you please, bureaucracy. Membership in this bureaucracy is dependent upon university training. Philosophy, both directly and indirectly, plays an unusually large role in the training. The faculty of law does not chiefly aim at the preparation of practicing lawyers. Philosophies of jurisprudence are essential parts of the law teaching; and every one of the classic philosophers took a hand in writing a philosophy of Law and of the State. Moreover, in the theological faculties, which are also organic parts of state-controlled institutions, the theology and higher criticism of Protestant Germany have been developed, and developed also in close connection with philosophical systems—like those of Kant, Schleiermacher and Hegel. In short, the educational and administrative agencies of Germany provide ready-made channels through which philosophic ideas may flow on their way to practical affairs.

Political public opinion hardly exists in Germany in the sense in which it obtains in France, Great Britain or this country. So far as it exists, the universities may be said to be its chief organs. They, rather than the newspapers, crystallize it and give it articulate expression. Instead of expressing surprise at the characteristic utterances of university men with reference to the great war, we should then rather turn to the past history in which the ideas now uttered were generated.

In an account of German intellectual history sufficiently extensive we should have to go back at least to Luther. Fortunately, for our purposes, what he actually did and taught is not so important as the more recent tradition concerning his peculiarly Germanic status and office. All peoples are proud of all their great men. Germany is proud of Luther as its greatest national hero. But while most nations are proud of their great men, Germany is proud of itself rather for producing Luther. It finds him as a Germanic product quite natural—nay, inevitable. A belief in the universal character of his genius thus naturally is converted into a belief of the essentially universal quality of the people who produced him.

Heine was not disposed by birth or temperament to over-estimate the significance of Luther. But here is what he said:

Luther is not only the greatest but the most *German* man in our history. . . . He possessed qualities that we seldom see associated—nay, that we usually find in the most hostile antagonism. He was at once a dreamy mystic and a practical man of action. . . . He was both a cold scholastic word-sifter and an inspired God-drunk prophet. . . . He was full of the awful reverence of God, full of self-sacrificing devotion to the Holy Spirit, he could lose himself entirely in pure spirituality. Yet he was fully acquainted with the glories of this earth; he knew how estimable they are; it was his lips that uttered the famous maxim—

"Who loves not woman, wine and song,
Remains a fool his whole life long."

He was a complete man, I might say an absolute man, in whom there was no discord between matter and spirit. To call him a spiritualist would be as erroneous as to call him a sensualist. . . . Eternal praise to the man whom we have to thank for the deliverance of our most precious possessions.

And again speaking of Luther's work:

Thus was established in Germany spiritual freedom, or as it is called, freedom of thought. Thought became a right and the decisions of reason legitimate.

The specific correctness of the above is of slight importance as compared with the universality of the tradition which made these ideas peculiarly Germanic, and Luther, therefore, a genuine national hero and type.

It is, however, with Kant that I commence. In Protestant Germany his name is almost always associated with that of Luther. That he brought to consciousness the true meaning of the Lutheran reformation is a commonplace of the German historian. One can hardly convey a sense of the unique position he occupies in the German thought of the last two generations. It is not that every philosopher is a Kantian, or that the professed Kantians stick literally to his text. Far from it. But Kant must always be reckoned with. No position unlike his should be taken up till Kant has been reverently disposed of, and the new position evaluated in his terms. To scoff at him is fair sacrilege. In a genuine sense, he marks the end of the older age. He *is* the transition to distinctively modern thought.

One shrinks at the attempt to compress even his leading ideas into an hour. Fortunately for me, few who read my attempt will have sufficient acquaintance with the tomes of Kantian interpretation and exposition to appreciate the full enormity of my offense. For I cannot avoid the effort to seize from out his highly technical writings a single idea and to label that his germinal idea. For only in this way can we get a clue to those general ideas with which Germany characteristically prefers to connect the aspirations and convictions that animate its deeds.

Adventuring without further preface into this field, I find that Kant's decisive contribution is the idea of a dual legislation of reason by which are marked off two distinct realms—that of science and that of morals. Each of these two realms has its own final and authoritative constitution: On one hand, there is the world of sense, the world of phenomena in space and time in which science is at home; on the other hand, is the supersensible, the noumenal world, the world of moral duty and moral freedom.

Every cultivated man is familiar with the conflict of science and religion, brute fact and ideal purpose, what is and what ought to be, necessity and freedom. In the domain of science causal dependence is sovereign; while freedom is lord of moral action. It is the proud boast of those who are Kantian in spirit that Kant discovered laws deep in the very nature of things and of human experience whose recognition puts an end forever to all possibility of conflict.

In principle, the discovery is as simple as its application

is far-reaching. Both science and moral obligation exist. Analysis shows that each is based upon laws supplied by one and the same reason (of which, as he is fond of saying, reason is the legislator); but laws of such a nature that their respective jurisdictions can never compete. The material for the legislation of reason in the natural world is sense. In this sensible world of space and time, causal necessity reigns: such is the decree of reason itself. Every attempt to find freedom, to locate ideals, to draw support for man's moral aspirations in nature, is predoomed to failure. The effort of reason to do these things is contrary to the very nature of reason itself: it is self-contradictory, suicidal.

When one considers the extent in which religion has been bound up with belief in miracles, or departures from the order of nature; when one notes how support for morals has been sought in natural law; how morals have been tied up with man's natural tendencies to seek happiness and with consequences in the way of reward of virtue and punishment of vice; how history has been explained as a play of moral forces—in short, the extent to which both the grounds and the sanctions for morality have been sought within the time and space world, one realizes the scope of the revolution wrought by Kant, provided his philosophy be true. Add to this the fact that men in the past have not taken seriously the idea that every existence in space, every event in time, is connected by bonds of causal necessity with other existences and events, and consequently have had no motive for the systematic pursuit of science. How is the late appearance of science in human history to be accounted for? How are we to understand the comparatively slight influence which science still has upon the conduct of life? Men, when they have not consciously looked upon nature as a scene of caprice, have failed to bring home to themselves that nature is a scene of the legislative activity of reason in the material of sense. This fact the Kantian philosophy brings home to man once for all; it brings it home not as a pious wish, nor as a precarious hope confirmed empirically here and there by victories won by a Galileo or a Newton, but as an indubitable fact necessary to the existence of any cognitive experience at all. The reign of law in nature is the work of the same reason which proceeds empirically and haltingly to the discovery of law here and there. Thus the acceptance of the Kantian philosophy not only frees man at a single stroke from superstition, sentimentalism and moral and theological romanticism, but gives at the same stroke authorization and stimulation to the detailed efforts of man to wrest from nature her secrets of causal law. What sparse groups of men of natural science had been doing for the three preceding centuries, Kant proclaimed to be the manifestation of the essential constitution of man as a knowing being. For those who accept the Kantian philosophy, it is accordingly the *magna charta* of scientific work: the adequate formulation of the constitution which directs and justifies their scientific inquiries. It is a truism to say that among the Germans as nowhere else has developed a positive reverence for science. In what other land does one find in the organic law mention of Science, and read in its constitution an express provision that "Science and its teaching are free"?

But this expresses only half of Kant's work. Reason is itself supersensible. Giving law to the material of sense and so constituting nature, it is in itself above sense and nature, as a sovereign is above his subjects. The supersensible world is thus a more congenial field for its legislative activity than the physical world of space and time. But is any such field open to human experience? Has not Kant himself closed and locked the gates in his assertion that the entire operation of man's knowing powers is confined to the realm of sense in which causal necessity dominates? Yes, as far as knowledge is concerned. No, as far as moral obligation is concerned. The fact of duty, the existence of a categorical command to act thus and so, no matter what the pressure of physical surroundings or the incitation of animal inclinations, is as much a fact as the existence of knowledge of the physical world. Such a command cannot proceed from nature. What is cannot introduce man to what ought to be, and thus impose its own opposite upon him. Nature only enmeshes men in its relentless machine-like movement. The very existence of a command in man to act for the sake of what ought to be—no matter what actually is—is thus of itself final proof of the operation of supersensible reason within human experience:

not, indeed, within theoretical or cognitive experience, but within moral experience.

The moral law, the law of obligation, thus proceeds from a source in man above reason. It is token of his membership as a moral being in a kingdom of absolute ends above nature. But it is also directed to something in man which is equally above nature: it appeals to and demands freedom. Reason is incapable of anything so irrational, so self-contradictory, as imposing a law of action to which no faculty of action corresponds. The freedom of the moral will is the answer to the unqualified demand of duty. It is not open to man to accept or reject this truth as he may see fit. It is a principle of reason which is involved in every exercise of reason. In denying it in name, man none the less acknowledges it in fact. Only men already sophisticated by vice who are seeking an excuse for their viciousness ever try to deny, even in words, the response which freedom makes to the voice of duty. Since, however, freedom is an absolute stranger to the natural and sensible world, man's possession of moral freedom is the final sign and seal of his membership in a supersensible world. The existence of an ideal or spiritual realm with its own laws is thus certified to by the fact of man's own citizenship within it. But, once more, this citizenship and this certification are solely moral. Scientific or intellectual warrant for it is impossible or self-contradictory, for science works by the law of causal necessity with respect to what is, ignorant of any law of freedom referring to what should be.

With the doors to the supersensible world now open, it is but a short step to religion. Of the negative traits of true religion we may be sure in advance. It will not be based upon intellectual grounds. Proofs of the existence of God, of the creation of nature, of the existence of an immaterial soul from the standpoint of knowledge are all of them impossible. They transgress the limits of knowledge, since that is confined to the sensible world of time and space. Neither will true religion be based upon historic facts such as those of Jewish history or the life of Jesus or the authority of a historic institution like a church. For all historic facts as such fall within the realm of time which is sensibly conditioned.

From the points of view of natural theology and historic religions Kant was greeted by his contemporaries as the "all-shattering." Quite otherwise is it, however, as to moral proofs of religious ideas and ideals. In Kant's own words: "I have found it necessary to deny knowledge of God, freedom and immortality in order to find a place for faith"—faith being a moral act.

Then he proceeds to reinterpret in terms of the sensuous natural principle and the ideal rational principle the main doctrines of Lutheran Protestantism. The doctrines of incarnation, original sin, atonement, justification by faith and sanctification, while baseless literally and historically, are symbols of the dual nature of man, as phenomenal and noumenal. And while Kant scourges ecclesiastical religions so far as they have relied upon ceremonies and external authority, upon external rewards and punishments, yet he ascribes transitional value to them in that they have symbolized ultimate moral truths. Although dogmas are but the external vesture of inner truths, yet it may be good for us "to continue to pay reverence to the outward vesture since that has served to bring to general acceptance a doctrine which really rests upon an authority within the soul of man, and which, therefore, needs no miracle to commend it."

It is a precarious undertaking to single out some one thing in German philosophy as of typical importance in understanding German national life. Yet I am committed to the venture. My conviction is that we have its root idea in the doctrine of Kant concerning the two realms, one outer, physical and necessary, the other inner, ideal and free. To this we must add that, in spite of their separateness and independence, the primacy always lies with the inner. As compared with this, the philosophy of a Nietzsche, to which so many resort at the present time for explanation of what seems to them otherwise inexplicable, is but a superficial and transitory wave of opinion. Surely the chief mark of distinctively German civilization is its combination of self-conscious idealism with unsurpassed technical efficiency and organization in the varied fields of action. If this is not a realization in fact of what is found in Kant, I am totally at loss for a name by which to characterize it. I do not mean that conscious adherence to the philosophy of Kant has been the cause of the marvelous advances made in Germany in the natural sciences and in the systematic application of the fruits of intelligence to industry, trade, commerce, military affairs, education, civic administration and industrial organization. Such a claim would be absurd. But I do mean, primarily, that Kant detected and formulated the direction in which the German genius was moving, so that his philosophy is of immense prophetic significance; and, secondarily, that his formulation has furnished a banner and a conscious creed which in solid and definite fashion has intensified and deepened the work actually undertaken.

In bringing to an imaginative synthesis what might have remained an immense diversity of enterprises, Kantianism has helped formulate a sense of a national mission and destiny. Over and above this, his formulation and its influence aids us to understand why the German consciousness has never been swamped by its technical efficiency and devotion, but has remained self-consciously, not to say self-righteously, idealistic. Such a work as Germany has undertaken might well seem calculated to generate attachment to a positivistic or even materialistic philosophy and to a utilitarian ethics. But no; the teaching of Kant had put mechanism forever in its subordinate place at the very time it inculcated devotion to mechanism in its place. Above and beyond as an end, for the sake of which all technical achievements, all promotion of health, wealth and happiness, exist, lies the realm of inner freedom, of the ideal and the supersensible. The more the Germans accomplish in the way of material conquest, the more they are conscious of fulfilling an ideal mission; every external conquest affords the greater warrant for dwelling in an inner region where mechanism does not intrude. Thus it turns out that while the Germans have been, to employ a catchword of recent thought, the most technically pragmatic of all peoples in their actual conduct of affairs, there is no people so hostile to the spirit of a pragmatic philosophy.

The combination of devotion to mechanism and organization in outward affairs and of loyalty to freedom and consciousness in the inner realm has its obvious attractions.

Realized in the common temper of a people it might well seem invincible. Ended is the paralysis of action arising from the split between science and useful achievements on one side and spiritual and ideal aspirations on the other. Each feeds and reinforces the other. Freedom of soul and subordination of action dwell in harmony. Obedience, definite subjection and control, detailed organization is the lesson enforced by the rule of causal necessity in the outer world of space and time in which action takes place. Unlimited freedom, the heightening of consciousness for its own sake, sheer reveling in noble ideals, the law of the inner world. What more can mortal man ask?

It would not be difficult, I imagine, to fill the three hours devoted to these lectures with quotations from representative German authors to the effect that supreme regard for the inner meaning of things, reverence for inner truth in disregard of external consequences of advantage or disadvantage, is the distinguishing mark of the German spirit as against, say, the externality of the Latin spirit or the utilitarianism of Anglo-Saxondom. I content myself with one quotation, a quotation which also indicates the same inclination to treat historic facts as symbolic of great truths which is found in Kant's treatment of church dogmas. Speaking of the Germanic languages, an historian of German civilization says:

> While all other Indo-European languages allow a wide liberty in placing the accent and make external considerations, such as the quantity of the syllables and euphony, of deciding influence, the Germanic tribes show a remarkable and intentional transition to an internal principle of accentuation. . . . Of all related peoples the Germanic alone puts the accent on the root syllable of the word, that is, on the part that gives it its meaning. There is hardly an ethnological fact extant which gives so much food for thought as this. What leads these people to give up a habit which must have been so old that it had become instinctive, and to evolve out of their own minds a principle which indicates a power of discrimination far in advance of anything we are used to attribute to the lower stages of civilization? Circumstances of which we are not now aware must have compelled them to distinguish the inner essence of things from their external form, and must have taught them to appreciate the former as of higher, indeed as of sole, importance. It is this accentuation of the real substance of things, the ever-powerful

desire to discover this real substance, and the ever-present impulse to give expression to this inner reality which has become the controlling trait of the Germanic soul. Hence the conviction gained by countless unfruitful efforts, that reason alone will never get at the true foundation of things; hence the thoroughness of German science; hence a great many of the qualities that explain Germanic successes and failures; hence, perhaps, a certain stubbornness and obstinacy, the unwillingness to give up a conviction once formed; hence the tendency to mysticism; hence that continuous struggle which marks the history of German art,—the struggle to give to the contents powerful and adequate expression, and to satisfy at the same time the requirements of esthetic elegance and beauty, a struggle in which the victory is ever on the side of truth, though it be homely, over beauty of form whenever it appears deceitful; hence the part played by music as the only expression of those imponderable vibrations of the soul for which language seems to have no words; hence the faith of the German in his mission among the nations as a bringer of truth, as a recognizer of the real value of things as against the hollow shell of beautiful form, as the doer of right deeds for their own sake and not for any reward beyond the natural outcome of the deed itself.

The division established between the outer realm, in which of course acts fall, and the inner realm of consciousness explains what is otherwise so paradoxical to a foreigner in German writings: The constant assertion that Germany brought to the world the conscious recognition of the principle of freedom coupled with the assertion of the relative incompetency of the German folk *en masse* for political self-direction. To one saturated by the English tradition which identifies freedom with power to act upon one's ideas, to make one's purposes effective in regulation of public affairs, the combination seems self-contradictory. To the German it is natural. Readers who have been led by newspaper quotations to regard Bernhardi as preaching simply a gospel of superior force will find in his writings a continual assertion that *the* German spirit is the spirit of freedom, of complete intellectual self-determination; that the Germans have "always been the standard bearers of free thought." We find him supporting his teachings not by appeal to Nietzsche, but by the Kantian distinction between the "empirical and rational ego."

It is Bernhardi who says:

Two great movements were born from the German intellectual life, on which, henceforth, *all the intellectual and moral progress of mankind must rest*: —The Reformation and the critical philosophy. The Reformation that broke the intellectual yoke imposed by the Church, which checked all free progress; and the Critique of Pure Reason which put a stop to the caprice of philosophic speculation by defining for the human mind the limitations of its capacities for knowledge, and at the same time pointed out the way in which knowledge is really possible. On this substructure was developed the intellectual life of our time, whose deepest significance consists in the attempt to reconcile the result of free inquiry with the religious needs of the heart, and thus to lay a foundation for the harmonious organization of mankind. . . . The German nation not only laid the foundations of this great struggle for a harmonious development of humanity but took the lead in it. We are thus incurring an obligation for the future from which we cannot shrink. We must be prepared to be the leader in this campaign which is being fought for the highest stake that has been offered to human efforts. . . . To no nation except the German has it been given to enjoy in its inner self "that which is given to mankind as a whole." . . . It is this quality which especially fits us for leadership in the intellectual domain and *imposes upon us the obligation to maintain that position.*[1]

More significant than the words themselves are their occasion and the occupation of the one who utters them. Outside of Germany, cavalry generals who employ philosophy to bring home practical lessons are, I think, rare. Outside of Germany, it would be hard to find an audience where an appeal for military preparedness would be reinforced by allusions to the *Critique of Pure Reason*.

Yet only by taking such statements seriously can one understand the temper in which opinion in Germany meets a national crisis. When the philosopher Eucken (who received a Nobel prize for contributing to the idealistic literature of the world) justifies the part taken by Germany in a world war because the Germans alone do not represent a particularistic and nationalistic spirit, but embody the "universalism" of humanity itself, he utters a conviction bred in German thought by the ruling interpretation of German philosophic idealism. By the side of this *motif* the glorification of

1. Bernhardi, *Germany and the Next War*, pp. 73–74. Italics not in the original text.

war as a biologic necessity, forced by increase of population, is a secondary detail, giving a totally false impression when isolated from its context. The main thing is that Germany, more than any other nation, in a sense alone of all nations, embodies the essential principle of humanity: freedom of spirit, combined with thorough and detailed work in the outer sphere where reigns causal law, where obedience, discipline and subordination are the necessities of successful organization. It is perhaps worth while to recall that Kant lived, taught and died in Königsberg; and that Königsberg was the chief city of east Prussia, an island still cut off in his early years from western Prussia, a titular capital for the Prussian kings where they went for their coronations. His life-work in philosophy coincides essentially with the political work of Frederick the Great, the king who combined a régime of freedom of thought and complete religious toleration with the most extraordinary display known in history of administrative and military efficiency. Fortunately for our present purposes, Kant, in one of his minor essays, has touched upon this combination and stated its philosophy in terms of his own thought.

The essay in question is that entitled "What is the Enlightenment?" His reply in substance is that it is the coming of age on the part of humanity: the transition from a state of minority or infancy wherein man does not dare to think freely to that period of majority or maturity in which mankind dares to use its own power of understanding. The growth of this power of free use of reason is the sole hope of progress in human affairs. External revolutions which are not the natural expression of an inner or intellectual revolution are of little significance. Genuine growth is found in the slow growth of science and philosophy and in the gradual diffusion throughout the mass of the discoveries and conclusions of those who are superior in intelligence. True freedom is inner freedom, freedom of thought together with the liberty consequent upon it of teaching and publication. To check this rational freedom "is a sin against the very nature of man, the primary law of which consists in just the advance in rational enlightenment."

In contrast with this realm of inner freedom stands that

of civil and political action, the principle of which is obedience or subordination to constituted authority. Kant illustrates the nature of the two by the position of a military subordinate who is given an order to execute which his reason tells him is unwise. His sole duty in the realm of practice is to obey—to do his duty. But as a member not of the State but of the kingdom of science, he has the right of free inquiry and publication. Later he might write upon the campaign in which this event took place and point out, upon intellectual grounds, the mistake involved in the order. No wonder that Kant proclaims that the age of the enlightenment is the age of Frederick the Great. Yet we should do injustice to Kant if we inferred that he expected this dualism of spheres of action, with its twofold moral law of freedom and obedience, to endure forever. By the exercise of freedom of thought, and by its publication and the education which should make its results permeate the whole state, the habits of a nation will finally become elevated to rationality, and the spread of reason will make it possible for the government to treat men, not as cogs in a machine, but in accord with the dignity of rational creatures.

Before leaving this theme, I must point out one aspect of the work of reason thus far passed over. Nature, the sensible world of space and time, is, as a knowable object, constituted by the legislative work of reason, although constituted out of a non-rational sensible stuff. This determining work of reason forms not merely the Idealism of the Kantian philosophy but determines its emphasis upon the *a priori*. The functions of reason through which nature is rendered a knowable object cannot be derived from experience, for they are necessary to the existence of experience. The details of this *a priori* apparatus lie far outside our present concern. Suffice it to say that as compared with some of his successors, Kant was an economical soul and got along with only two *a priori* forms and twelve *a priori* categories. The mental habitudes generated by attachment to *a priori* categories cannot however be entirely neglected in even such a cursory discussion as the present.

If one were to follow the suggestion involved in the lately quoted passage as to the significant symbolism of the place of the accent in German speech, one might discourse upon the deep meaning of the Capitalization of Nouns in the written form of the German language, together with the richness of the language in abstract nouns. One might fancy that the dignity of the common noun substantive, expressing as it does the universal or generic, has bred an intellectual deference. One may fancy a whole nation of readers reverently bowing their heads at each successively capitalized word. In such fashion one might arrive at a picture, not without its truth, of what it means to be devoted to *a priori* rational principles.

A number of times during the course of the world war I have heard someone remark that he would not so much mind what the Germans did if it were not for the reasons assigned in its justification. But to rationalize such a tangled skein as human experience is a difficult task. If one is in possession of antecedent rational concepts which are legislative for experience, the task is much simplified. It only remains to subsume each empirical event under its proper category. If the outsider does not see the applicability of the concept to the event, it may be argued that his blindness shows his ineptness for truly universal thinking. He is probably a crass empiric who thinks in terms of material consequences instead of upon the basis of antecedent informing principles of reason.

Thus it has come about that no moral, social or political question is adequately discussed in Germany until the matter in hand has been properly deduced from an exhaustive determination of its fundamental *Begriff* or *Wesen*. Or if the material is too obviously empirical to allow of such deduction, it must at least be placed under its appropriate rational form. What a convenience, what a resource, nay, what a weapon is the Kantian distinction of *a priori* rational form and *a posteriori* empirical matter. Let the latter be as brutely diversified, as chaotic as you please. There always exists a form of unity under which it may be brought. If the empirical facts are recalcitrant, so much the worse for them. It only shows how empirical they are. To put them under a rational form is but to subdue their irrational opposition to reason, or to invade their lukewarm neutrality. Any violence done them is more than indemnified by the favor of bringing them under the sway of *a priori* reason, the incarnation of the Absolute on earth.

Yet there are certain disadvantages attached to *a priori* categories. They have a certain rigidity, appalling to those who have not learned to identify stiffness with force. Empirical matters are subject to revision. The strongest belief that claims the support of experience is subject to modification when experience testifies against it. But an *a priori* conception is not open to adverse evidence. There is no court having jurisdiction. If, then, an unfortunate mortal should happen to be imposed upon so that he was led to regard a prejudice or predilection as an *a priori* truth, contrary experience would have a tendency to make him the more obstinate in his belief. History proves what a dangerous thing it has been for men, when they try to impose their will upon other men, to think of themselves as special instruments and organs of Deity. The danger is equally great when an *a priori* Reason is substituted for a Divine Providence. Empirically grounded truths do not have a wide scope; they do not inspire such violent loyalty to themselves as ideas supposed to proceed directly from reason itself. But they are discussable; they have a humane and social quality, while truths of pure reason have a paradoxical way, in the end, of escaping from the arbitrament of reasoning. They evade the logic of experience, only to become, in the phrase of a recent writer, the spoil of a "logic of fanaticism." Weapons forged in the smithy of the Absolute become brutal and cruel when confronted by merely human resistance.

The stiffly constrained character of an *a priori* Reason manifests itself in another way. A category of pure reason is suspiciously like a pigeon-hole. An American writer, speaking before the present war, remarked with witty exaggeration that "Germany is a monstrous set of pigeon-holes, and every mother's son of a German is pigeoned in his respective hole—tagged, labeled and ticketed. Germany is a huge human check-room, and the government carries the checks in its pocket." John Locke's deepest objection to the older form of the *a priori* philosophy, the doctrine of innate ideas, was the readiness with which such ideas become strongholds be-

hind which authority shelters itself from questioning. And
John Morley pointed out long ago the undoubted historic
fact that the whole modern liberal social and political movement has allied itself with philosophic empiricism. It is hard
here, as everywhere, to disentangle cause and effect. But one
can at least say with considerable assurance that a hierarchi-
cally ordered and subordered State will feel an affinity for a
philosophy of fixed categories, while a flexible democratic
society will, in its crude empiricism, exhibit loose ends.

There is a story to the effect that the good townspeople
of Königsberg were accustomed to set their watches by the
time at which Kant passed upon his walks—so uniform was
he. Yielding to the Teutonic temptation to find an inner
meaning in the outer event, one may wonder whether German thought has not since Kant's time set its intellectual
and spiritual clocks by the Kantian standard: the separation
of the inner and the outer, with its lesson of freedom and
idealism in one realm, and of mechanism, efficiency and organization in the other. A German professor of philosophy
has said that while the Latins live in the present moment, the
Germans live in the infinite and ineffable. His accusation
(though I am not sure he meant it as such) is not completely
justified. But it does seem to be true that the Germans, more
readily than other peoples, can withdraw themselves from
the exigencies and contingencies of life into a region of *Innerlichkeit* which at least *seems* boundless; and which can
rarely be successfully uttered save through music, and a
frail and tender poetry, sometimes domestic, sometimes
lyric, but always full of mysterious charm. But technical
ideas, ideas about means and instruments, can readily be
externalized because the outer world is in truth their abiding
home.

2. GERMAN MORAL AND POLITICAL PHILOSOPHY

It is difficult to select sentences from Kant which are intelligible to those not trained in his vocabulary, unless the selection is accompanied by an almost word-by-word commentary. His writings have proved an admirable *terrain* for the display of German *Gründlichkeit*. But I venture upon the quotation of one sentence which may serve the purpose of at once recalling the main lesson of the previous lecture and furnishing a transition to the theme of the present hour.

Even if an immeasurable gulf is fixed between the sensible realm of the concept of nature and the supersensible realm of the concept of freedom, so that it is not possible to go from the first to the second (at least by means of the theoretical use of reason) any more than if they were two separate worlds of which the first could have no influence upon the second,—yet the second is *meant* to have an influence upon the first. The concept of freedom is meant to actualize in the world of sense the purpose proposed by its laws. . . .

That is, the relation between the world of space and time where physical causality reigns and the moral world of freedom and duty is not a symmetrical one. The former cannot intrude into the latter. But it is the very nature of moral legislation that it is meant to influence the world of sense; its object is to realize the purposes of free rational action within the sense world. This fact fixes the chief features of Kant's philosophy of Morals and of the State.

It is a claim of the admirers of Kant that he first brought to recognition the true and infinite nature of the principle of Personality. On one side, the individual is *homo phenomenon*—a part of the scheme of nature, governed by its laws as much as any stone or plant. But in virtue of his citizenship in the kingdom of supersensible Laws and Ends, he is elevated to true universality. He is no longer a mere occurrence. He is a Person—one in whom the purpose of

Humanity is incarnate. In English and American writings the terms subjective and subjectivism usually carry with them a disparaging color. Quite otherwise is it in German literature. This sets the age of subjectivism, whose commencement, roughly speaking, coincides with the influence of Kantian thought, in sharp opposition to the age of individualism, as well as to a prior period of subordination to external authority. Individualism means isolation; it means external relations of human beings with one another and with the world; it looks at things quantitatively, in terms of wholes and parts. Subjectivism means recognition of the principle of free personality: the self as creative, occupied not with an external world which limits it from without, but, through its own self-consciousness, finding a world within itself; and having found the universal within itself, setting to work to recreate itself in what had been the external world, and by its own creative expansion in industry, art and politics to transform what had been mere limiting material into a work of its own. Free as was Kant from the sentimental, the mystic and the romantic phases of this Subjectivism, we shall do well to bear it in mind in thinking of his ethical theory. Personality means that man as a rational being does not receive the end which forms the law of his action from without, whether from Nature, the State or from God, but from his own self. Morality is autonomous; man, humanity, is an end in itself. Obedience to the self-imposed law will transform the sensible world (within which fall all social ties so far as they spring from natural instinct or desire) into a form appropriate to universal reason. Thus we may paraphrase the sentence quoted from Kant.

The gospel of duty has an invigorating ring. It is easy to present it as the most noble and sublime of all moral doctrines. What is more worthy of humanity, what better marks the separation of man from brute, than the will to subordinate selfish desire and individual inclination to the commands of stern and lofty duty? And if the idea of command (which inevitably goes with the notion of duty) carries a sinister suggestion of legal authority, pains and penalties and of subservience to an external authority who issues the commands, Kant seems to have provided a final corrective in insisting that duty is self-imposed. Moral commands are imposed by the higher, supranatural self upon the lower empirical self, by the rational self upon the self of passions and inclinations. German philosophy is attached to antitheses and their reconciliation in a higher synthesis. The Kantian principle of Duty is a striking case of the reconciliation of the seemingly conflicting ideas of freedom and authority.

Unfortunately, however, the balance cannot be maintained in practice. Kant's faithful logic compels him to insist that the concept of duty is empty and formal. It tells men that to do their duty is their supreme law of action, but is silent as to what men's duties specifically are. Kant, moreover, insists, as he is in logic bound to do, that the motive which measures duty is wholly inner; it is purely a matter of inner consciousness. To admit that consequences can be taken into account in deciding what duty is in a particular case would be to make concessions to the empirical and sensible world which are fatal to the scheme. The combination of these two features of pure internality and pure formalism leads, in a world where men's *acts* take place wholly in the external and empirical region, to serious consequences.

The dangerous character of these consequences may perhaps be best gathered indirectly by means of a quotation.

> While the French people in savage revolt against spiritual and secular despotism had broken their chains and proclaimed their *rights,* another quite different revolution was working in Prussia—the revolution of *duty.* The assertion of the rights of the individual leads ultimately to individual irresponsibility and to a repudiation of the State. Immanuel Kant, the founder of the critical philosophy, taught, in opposition to this view, the gospel of moral duty, and Scharnhorst grasped the idea of universal military service. By calling upon each individual to sacrifice property and life for the good of the community, he gave the clearest expression to the idea of the State, and created a sound basis on which the claims to individual rights might rest.[2]

The sudden jump, by means of only a comma, from the gospel of moral duty to universal military service is much more logical than the shock which it gives to an American reader would indicate. I do not mean, of course, that Kant's

2. Bernhardi, *Germany and the Next War,* pp. 63–64.

teaching was the cause of Prussia's adoption of universal military service and of the thoroughgoing subordination of individual happiness and liberty of action to that capitalized entity, the State. But I do mean that when the practical political situation called for universal military service in order to support and expand the existing state, the gospel of a Duty devoid of content naturally lent itself to the consecration and idealization of such specific duties as the existing national order might prescribe. The sense of duty must get its subject-matter somewhere, and unless subjectivism was to revert to anarchic or romantic individualism (which is hardly in the spirit of obedience to authoritative law) its appropriate subject-matter lies in the commands of a superior. Concretely what the State commands is the congenial outer filling of a purely inner sense of duty. That the despotism of Frederick the Great and of the Hohenzollerns who remained true to his policy was at least that hitherto unknown thing, an enlightened despotism, made the identification easier. Individuals have at all times, in epochs of stress, offered their supreme sacrifice to their country's good. In Germany this sacrifice in times of peace as well as of war has been systematically reinforced by an inner mystic sense of a Duty elevating men to the plane of the universal and eternal.

In short, the sublime gospel of duty has its defects. Outside of the theological and the Kantian moral traditions, men have generally agreed that duties are relative to ends. Not the obligation, but some purpose, some good, which the fulfillment of duty realizes, is the principle of morals. The business of reason is to see that the end, the good, for which one acts is a reasonable one—that is to say, as wide and as equitable in its working out as the situation permits. Morals which are based upon consideration of good and evil consequences not only allow, but imperiously demand the exercise of a discriminating intelligence. A gospel of duty separated from empirical purposes and results tends to gag intelligence. It substitutes for the work of reason displayed in a wide and distributed survey of consequences in order to determine where duty lies an inner consciousness, empty of content, which clothes with the form of rationality the demands of existing social authorities. A consciousness which is not based upon and checked by consideration of actual results upon human welfare is none the less socially irresponsible because labeled Reason.

Professor Eucken represents a type of idealistic philosophy which is hardly acceptable to strict Kantians. Yet only where the fundamental Kantian ideas were current would such ethical ideas as the following flourish:

> When justice is considered as a mere means of securing man's welfare, and is treated accordingly—whether it be the welfare of individuals or of society as a whole makes no essential difference—it loses all its characteristic features. No longer can it compel us to see life from its own standpoint; no longer can it change the existing condition of things; no longer can it sway our hearts with the force of a primitive passion, and oppose to all consideration of consequences an irresistible spiritual compulsion. It degenerates rather into the complaisant servant of utility; it adapts itself to her demands, and in so doing suffers inward annihilation. It can maintain itself only when it comes as a unique revelation of the Spiritual Life within our human world, as a lofty Presence transcending all considerations of expediency.[3]

Such writing is capable of arousing emotional reverberations in the breasts of many persons. But they are emotions which, if given headway, smother intelligence, and undermine its responsibility for promoting the actual goods of life. If justice loses all its characteristic features when regarded as a means (the word "mere" inserted before "means" speaks volumes) of the welfare of society as a whole, then there is no objective and responsible criterion for justice at all. A justice which, irrespective of the determination of social well-being, proclaims itself as an irresistible spiritual impulsion possessed of the force of a primitive passion, is nothing but a primitive passion clothed with a spiritual title so that it is protected from having to render an account of itself. During an ordinary course of things, it passes for but an emotional indulgence; in a time of stress and strain, it exhibits itself as surrender of intelligence to passion.

The passage (from Bernhardi) quoted earlier puts the

3. Eucken, *The Meaning and Value of Life*, translated by Gibson, p. 104.

German principle of duty in opposition to the French principle of rights—a favorite contrast in German thought. Men like Jeremy Bentham also found the Revolutionary Rights of Man doctrinaire and conducing to tyranny rather than to freedom. These Rights were *a priori*, like Duty, being derived from the supposed nature or essence of man, instead of being adopted as empirical expedients to further progress and happiness. But the conception of duty is one-sided, expressing command on one side and obedience on the other, while rights are at least reciprocal. Rights are social and sociable in accord with the spirit of French philosophy. Put in a less abstract form than the revolutionary theory stated them, they are things to be discussed and measured. They admit of more or less, of compromise and adjustment. So also does the characteristic moral contribution of English thought—intelligent self-interest. This is hardly an ultimate idea. But at least it evokes a picture of merchants bargaining, while the categorical imperative calls up the drill sergeant. Trafficking in ethics, in which each gives up something which he wants to get something which he wants more, is not the noblest kind of morals, but at least it is socially responsible as far as it goes. "Give so that it may be given to you in return" has at least some tendency to bring men together; it promotes agreement. It requires deliberation and discussion. This is just what the authoritative voice of a superior will not tolerate; it is the one unforgiveable sin.

The morals of bargaining, exchange, the mutual satisfaction of wants may be outlived in some remote future, but up to the present they play an important part in life. To me there is something uncanny in the scorn which German ethics, in behalf of an unsullied moral idealism, pours upon a theory which takes cognizance of practical motives. In a highly esthetic people one might understand the display of contempt. But when an aggressive and commercial nation carries on commerce and war simply from the motive of obedience to duty, there is awakened an unpleasant suspicion of a suppressed "psychic complex." When Nietzsche says, "Man does not desire happiness; only the Englishman does that," we laugh at the fair hit. But persons who profess no regard for happiness as a test of action have an unfortunate way of living up to their principle by making others *un*happy. I should entertain some suspicion of the complete sincerity of those who profess disregard for their own happiness, but I should be quite certain of their sincerity when it comes to a question of *my* happiness.

Within the Kantian philosophy of morals there is an idea which conducts necessarily to a philosophy of society and the State. Leibniz was the great German source of the philosophy of the enlightenment. Harmony was the dominant thought of this philosophy; the harmony of nature with itself and with intelligence; the harmony of nature with the moral ends of humanity. Although Kant was a true son of the enlightenment, his doctrine of the radically dual nature of the legislation of Reason put an end to its complacent optimism. According to Kant, morality is in no way a work of nature. It is the achievement of the self-conscious reason of man through conquest of nature. The ideal of a final harmony remains, but it is an ideal to be won through a battle with the natural forces of man. His breach with the enlightenment is nowhere as marked as in his denial that man is by nature good. On the contrary, man is by nature evil—that is his philosophical rendering of the doctrine of original sin. Not that the passions, appetites and senses are of themselves evil, but they tend to usurp the sovereignty of duty as the *motivating* force of human action. Hence morality is a ceaseless battle to transform all the natural desires of man into willing servants of the law and purpose of reason.

Even the kindly and sociable instincts of man, in which so many have sought the basis of both morality and organized society, fall under Kant's condemnation. As natural desires, they aspire to an illegitimate control in man's motives. They are parts of human self-love: the unlawful tendency to make happiness the controlling purpose of action. The natural relations of man to man are those of an unsocial sociableness. On the one hand, men are forced together by natural ties. Only in social relations can individuals develop their capacities. But no sooner do they come together than disintegrating tendencies set in. Union with his fellows gives a stimulus to vanity, avarice and gaining power over others—traits which cannot show themselves in individuals when they are isolated. This mutual antagonism is, however, more of a force in evolving man from savagery to civilization than are the kindly and sociable instincts.

Without these unlovely qualities which set man over against man in strife, individuals would have lived on in perfect harmony, contentment and mutual love, with all their distinctive abilities latent and undeveloped.

In short, they would have remained in Rousseau's paradise of a state of nature, and

perhaps Rousseau was right when he preferred the savage state to the state of civilization provided we leave out of account the last stage to which our species is yet destined to rise.

But since the condition of civilization is but an intermediary between the natural state and the truly or rational moral condition to which man is to rise, Rousseau was wrong.

Thanks then be to nature for the unsociableness, the spiteful competition of vanity, the insatiate desires for power and gain.

These quotations, selected from Kant's little essay on an "Idea for a Universal History," are precious for understanding two of the most characteristic traits of subsequent German thought, the distinctions made between Society and the State and between Civilization and Culture. Much of the trouble which has been experienced in respect to the recent use of *Kultur* might have been allayed by a knowledge that *Kultur* has little in common with the English word "culture" save a likeness in sound. *Kultur* is sharply antithetical to civilization in its meaning. Civilization is a natural and largely unconscious or involuntary growth. It is, so to speak, a by-product of the needs engendered when people live close together. It is external, in short. Culture, on the other hand, is deliberate and conscious. It is a fruit not of men's natural motives, but of natural motives which have been transformed by the inner spirit. Kant made the distinction when he said that Rousseau was not so far wrong in preferring savagery to civilization, since civilization meant simply social decencies and elegancies and outward proprieties, while morality, that is, the rule of the end of Reason, is necessary to culture. And the real significance of the term "culture" becomes more obvious when he adds that it involves the slow toil of education of the Inner Life, and that the attainment of culture on the part of an individual depends upon long effort by the community to which he belongs. It is not primarily an individual trait or possession, but a conquest of the community won through devotion to "duty."

In recent German literature, Culture has been given even a more sharply technical distinction from Civilization and one which emphasizes even more its collective and nationalistic character. Civilization as external and uncontrolled by self-conscious purpose includes such things as language in its more spontaneous colloquial expression, trade, conventional manners or etiquette, and the police activities of government. *Kultur* comprises language used for purposes of higher literature; commerce pursued not as means of enriching individuals but as a condition of the development of national life; art, philosophy (especially in that untranslatable thing, the "Weltanschauung"); science, religion, and the activities of the state in the nurture and expansion of the other forms of national genius, that is, its activities in education and the army. The legislation of Bismarck with reference to certain Roman Catholic orders is nicknamed *Kultur-kampf*, for it was conceived as embodying a struggle between two radically different philosophies of life, the Roman, or Italian, and the true Germanic, not simply as a measure of political expediency. Thus it is that a trading and military post like Kiao-Chou is officially spoken of as a "monument of Teutonic *Kultur*." The war now raging is conceived of as an outer manifestation of a great spiritual struggle, in which what is really at stake is the supreme value of the Germanic attitude in philosophy, science and social questions generally, the "specifically German habits of feeling and thinking."

Very similar motives are at work in the distinction between society and the State, which is almost a commonplace of German thought. In English and American writings the State is almost always used to denote society in its more organized aspects, or it may be identified with government as a special agency operating for the collective interests of men in association. But in German literature society is a technical term and means something empirical and, so to speak, external; while the State, if not avowedly something mystic and transcendental, is at least a moral entity, the creation of self-conscious reason operating in behalf of the spiritual and ideal interests of its members. Its function is cultural, educative. Even when it intervenes in material interests, as it does in regulating lawsuits, poor laws, protective tariffs, etc., etc., its action has ultimately an ethical significance: its purpose is the furthering of an ideal community. The same thing is to be said of wars when they are really national wars, and not merely dynastic or accidental.

Society is an expression of man's egoistic nature; his natural seeking for personal advantage and profit. Its typical manifestation is in competitive economic struggle and in the struggle for honor and recognized social status. These have their proper place; but with respect even to them it is the duty of the State to intervene so that the struggle may contribute to ideal ends which alone are universal. Hence the significance of the force or power of the State. Unlike other forms of force, it has a sort of sacred import, for it represents force consecrated to the assertion and expansion of final goods which are spiritual, moral, rational. These absolute ends can be maintained only in struggle against man's individualistic ends. Conquest through conflict is the law of morals everywhere.

In Kant we find only the beginnings of this political philosophy. He is still held back by the individualism of the eighteenth century. Everything legal and political is conceived by him as external and hence outside the strictly moral realm of inner motivation. Yet he is not content to leave the State and its law as a wholly unmoral matter. The *natural* motives of man are, according to Kant (evidently following Hobbes), love of power, love of gain, love of glory. These motives are egoistic; they issue in strife—in the war of all against all. While such a state of affairs does not and cannot invade the inner realm of duty, the realm of the moral motive, it evidently presents a régime in which the conquest of the world of sense by the law of reason cannot be effected.

Man in his rational or universal capacity must, therefore, will an outward order of harmony in which it is at least possible for acts dictated by rational freedom to get a footing. Such an outer order is the State. Its province is not to promote moral freedom directly—only the moral will can do that. But its business is to hinder the hindrances to freedom: to establish a social condition of outward order in which truly moral acts may gradually evolve a kingdom of humanity. Thus while the State does not have a directly moral scope of action (since the coercion of motive is a moral absurdity), it does have a moral basis and an ultimate moral function.

It is the law of reason, "holy and inviolable," which impels man to the institution of the State, not natural sociability, much less considerations of expediency. And so necessary is the State to humanity's realization of its moral purpose that there can be no right of revolution. The overthrow and execution of the sovereign (Kant evidently had the French Revolution and Louis XVI in mind) is "an immortal and inexpiable sin like the sin against the Holy Ghost spoken of by theologians, which can never be forgiven in this world or in the next."

Kant was enough of a child of the eighteenth century to be cosmopolitan, not nationalistic, in his feeling. Since humanity as a whole, in its universality, alone truly corresponds to the universality of reason, he upheld the ideal of an ultimate republican federation of states; he was one of the first to proclaim the possibility of enduring peace among nations on the basis of such a federated union of mankind.

The threatened domination of Europe by Napoleon following on the wars waged by republican France put an end, however, to cosmopolitanism. Since Germany was the greatest sufferer from these wars, and since it was obvious that the lack of national unity, the division of Germany into a multitude of petty states, was the great source of her weakness; since it was equally obvious that Prussia, the one strong and centralized power among the German states, was the only thing which saved them all from national extinction, subsequent political philosophy in Germany rescued the idea of the State from the somewhat ambiguous moral position in which Kant had left it. Since a state which is an absolute moral necessity and whose actions are nevertheless lacking in inherent moral quality is an anomaly, the doctrine almost calls for a theory which shall make the State the supreme moral entity.

Fichte marks the beginning of the transformation; and, in his writings, it is easy to detect a marked difference of attitude toward the nationalistic state before and after 1806, when in the battle of Jena Germany went down to inglorious defeat. From the time of Fichte, the German philosophy of the State blends with its philosophy of history, so that my reservation of the latter topic for the next section is somewhat arbitrary, and I shall not try rigidly to maintain the division of themes.

I have already mentioned the fact that Kant relaxes the separation of the moral realm of freedom from the sensuous realm of nature sufficiently to assert that the former is *meant* to influence the latter and finally to subjugate it. By means of the little crack thus introduced into nature, Fichte rewrites the Kantian philosophy. The world of sense must be regarded from the very start as material which the free, rational, moral Ego has created in order to have material for its own adequate realization of will. Fichte had a longing for an absolute unity which did not afflict Kant, to whom, save for the concession just referred to, a complete separation of the two operations of legislative reason sufficed. Fichte was also an ardently *active* soul, whose very temperament assured him of the subordination of theoretical knowledge to moral action.

It would be as difficult to give, in short space, an adequate sketch of Fichte's philosophy as of Kant's. To him, however, reason was the expression of the will, not (as with Kant) the will an application of reason to action. *"Im Anfang war die That"* is good Fichteanism. While Kant continued the usual significance of the term Reason (with only such modifications as the rationalism of his century had made current), Fichte began the transformation which consummated in later German idealism. If the world of nature and of human relations is an expression of reason, then reason must be the sort of thing, and have the sort of attributes by means of which the world may be construed, no matter how far away this conception of reason takes us from the usual meaning of the term. To Fichte the formula which best described such aspects of the world and of life as he was interested in was effort at self-realization through struggle with difficulties and overcoming opposition. Hence his formula for reason was a Will which, having "posited" itself, then "posited" its antithesis in order, through further action subjugating this opposite, to conquer its own freedom.

The doctrine of the primacy of the Deed, and of the Duty to achieve freedom through moral self-assertion against obstacles (which, after all, are there only to further this self-assertion) was one which could, with more or less plausibility, be derived from Kant. More to our present point, it was a doctrine which could be preached with noble moral fervor in connection with the difficulties and needs of a divided and conquered Germany. Fichte saw himself as the continuator of the work of Luther and Kant. His final "science of knowledge" brought the German people alone of the peoples of the world into the possession of the idea and ideal of absolute freedom. Hence the peculiar destiny of the German scholar and the German State. It was the duty and mission of German science and philosophy to contribute to the cause of the spiritual emancipation of humanity. Kant had already taught that the acts of men were to become gradually permeated by a spirit of rationality till there should be an equation of inner freedom of mind and outer freedom of action. Fichte's doctrine demanded an acceleration of the process. Men who have attained to a consciousness of the absolute freedom and self-activity must necessarily desire to see around them similar free beings. The scholar who is truly a scholar not merely knows, but he knows the nature of knowledge—its place and function as a manifestation of the Absolute. Hence he is, in a peculiar sense, the direct manifestation of God in the world—the true priest. And his priestly function consists in bringing other men to recognize moral freedom in its creative operation. Such is the dignity of education as conducted by those who have attained true philosophic insight.

Fichte made a specific application of this idea to his own

country and time. The humiliating condition of contemporary Germany was due to the prevalence of egoism, selfishness and particularism: to the fact that men had lowered themselves to the plane of sensuous life. The fall was the worse because the Germans, more than any other people, were by nature and history conscious of the ideal and spiritual principle, the principle of freedom, lying at the very basis of all things. The key to the political regeneration of Germany was to be found in a moral and spiritual regeneration effected by means of education. The key, amid political division, to political unity was to be sought in devotion to moral unity. In this spirit Fichte preached his *Addresses to the German Nation*. In this spirit he collaborated in the foundation of the University of Berlin, and zealously promoted all the educational reforms introduced by Stein and Humboldt into Prussian life.

The conception of the State as an essential moral Being charged with an indispensable moral function lay close to these ideas. Education is *the* means of the advancement of humanity toward realization of its divine perfection. Education is the work of the State. The syllogism completes itself. But in order that the State may carry on its educational or moral mission it must not only possess organization and commensurate power, but it must also control the conditions which secure the possibility offered to the individuals composing it. To adopt Aristotle's phrase, men must live before they can live nobly. The primary condition of a secure life is that everyone be able to live by his own labor. Without this, moral self-determination is a mockery. The business of the State, outside of its educational mission, is concerned with property, and this business means insuring property to everyone as well as protecting him in what he already possesses. Moreover, property is not mere physical possession. It has a profound moral significance, for it means the subjugation of physical things to will. It is a necessary part of the realization of moral personality: the conquest of the non-ego by the ego. Since property does not mean mere appropriation, but is a right recognized and validated by society itself, property has a social basis and aim. It is an expression not of individual egotism but of the universal will. Hence it is essential to the very idea of property and of the State that all the members of society have an equal opportunity for property. Hence it is the duty of the State to secure to its every member the right to work and the reward of his work.

The outcome, as expressed in his essay on "The Closed Industrial State," is State Socialism, based on moral and idealistic grounds, not on economic considerations. In order that men may have a real opportunity to develop their moral personalities, their right to labor and to adequate living, in return for their labor, must be assured. This cannot happen in a competitive society. Industry must be completely regulated by the State if these indispensable rights to labor and resulting comfort and security of life as means to moral volition are to be achieved. But a state engaged in unrestricted foreign trade will leave its workingmen at the mercy of foreign conditions. It must therefore regulate or even eliminate foreign commerce so far as is necessary to secure its own citizens. The ultimate goal is a universal state as wide as humanity, and a state in which each individual will act freely, without state-secured rights and state-imposed obligations. But before this cosmopolitan and philosophically anarchic condition can be reached, we must pass through a period of the nationalistic closed state. Thus at the end a wide gulf separates Fichte from Kant. The moral individualism of the latter has become an ethical socialism. Only in and by means of a circle of egos or personalities does a human being attain the moral reason and freedom which Kant bestowed upon him as his birthright. Only through the educational activities of the State and its complete regulation of the industrial activities of its members does the potential moral freedom of individuals become an established reality.

If I have devoted so much space to Fichte it is not because of his direct influence upon affairs or even upon thought. He did not found a school. His system was at once too personal and too formal. Nevertheless, he expressed ideas which, removed from their special context in his system, were taken up into the thought of cultivated Germany. Heine, speaking of the vogue of systems of thought, says with profound truth that "nations have an instinctive presentiment of what they require to fulfill their mission."

And Fichte's thought infiltrated through many crevices.

Rodbertus and Lassalle, the socialists, were, for example, profoundly affected by him. When the latter was prosecuted in a criminal suit for his *The Working Man's Programme*, his reply was that his programme was a distinctively philosophic utterance, and hence protected by the constitutional provision for freedom of science and its teaching. And this is his philosophy of the State:

> The State is the unity and coöperation of individuals in a moral whole. . . . The ultimate and intrinsic end of the State is, therefore, to further the positive unfolding, the progressive development of human life. Its function is to work out the true end of man; that is to say, the full degree of culture of which human nature is capable.

And he quotes with approval the words:

> The concept of the State must be broadened so as to make the State the contrivance whereby all human virtue is to be realized to the full.

And if he differs from Fichte, it is but in the assertion that since the laboring class is the one to whom the need most directly appeals, it is workingmen who must take the lead in the development of the true functions of the State.

Pantheism is a philosophic nickname which should be sparingly employed; so also should the term Monism. To call Fichte's system an ethical pantheism and monism is not to say much that is enlightening. But with free interpretation, the designation may be highly significant in reference to the spiritual temper of the Germany of the first part of the nineteenth century. For it gives a key to the presentiment of what Germany needed to fulfill its mission.

It is a commonplace of German historians that its unity and expansion to a great state powerful externally, prosperous internally, was wrought, unlike that of any other people, from within outward. In Lange's words, "our national development started from the most ideal and approximated more and more to the real." Hegel and Heine agree that in Germany the French Revolution and the Napoleonic career were paralleled by a philosophic revolution and an intellectual empire. You recall the bitter word that, when Napoleon was finally conquered and Europe partitioned, to Germany was assigned the kingdom of the clouds. But this aerial and tenuous kingdom became a mighty power, working with and in the statesmen of Prussia and the scholars of Germany to found a kingdom on the solid earth. Spiritual and ideal Germany made common cause with realistic and practical Prussia. As says Von Sybel, the historian of *The Founding of the German Empire*:

> Germany had been ruined through its own disintegration and had dragged Prussia with it into the abyss. It was well known that the wild fancies of the Conqueror hovered about the utter annihilation of Prussia; if this should take place, then east as well as west of the Elbe, not only political independence, but every trace of a German spirit, the German language and customs, German art and learning—everything would be wiped out by the foreigners. But this fatal danger was perceived just at the time when everybody had been looking up to Kant and Schiller, had been admiring Faust, the world-embracing masterpiece of Goethe's, and had recognized that Alexander von Humboldt's cosmological studies and Niebuhr's "Roman History" had created a new era in European science and learning. In such intellectual attainments the Germans felt that they were far superior to the vanquisher of the world and his great nation; and so the political interests of Prussia and the salvation of the German nationality exactly coincided. Schleiermacher's patriotic sermons, Fichte's stirring addresses to the German people, Humboldt's glorious founding of the Berlin University, served to augment the resisting power of Prussia, while Scharnhorst's recruits and militia were devoted to the defense of German honor and German customs. Every one felt that German nationality was lost if Prussia did not come to its rescue, and that, too, there was no safety possible for Prussia unless all Germany was free.
>
> What a remarkable providence it was that brought together, as in the Middle Ages, on this ancient colonial ground, a throng of the most energetic men from all districts of Germany. For neither Stein nor his follower, Hardenberg, nor the generals, Scharnhorst, Blücher and Gneisenau, nor the authors, Niebuhr, Fichte and K. F. Eichhorn, nor many others who might be mentioned, were born in Prussia; yet because their thoughts centred in Germany, they had become loyal Prussians. The name Germany had been blotted from the political map of Europe, but never had so many hearts thrilled at the thought of being German.
>
> Thus on the most eastern frontier of German life, in the midst of troubles which seemed hopeless, the idea of German unity, which had lain dormant for centuries, now sprang up in a new birth. At first this idea was held exclusively by the great men of the times and remained the invaluable possession of the

cultivated classes; but once started it spread far and wide among the younger generation. . . . But it was easier to defeat the mighty Napoleon than to bend the German sentiments of dualism and individualism to the spirit of national unity.

What I have called the ethical pantheism and monistic idealism of Fichte (a type of philosophy reigning almost unchallenged in Germany till almost the middle of the century) was an effective weapon in fighting and winning this more difficult battle. In his volume on *The Romantic School in Germany,* Brandes quotes from the diary of Hoffman a passage written in 1809.

Seized by a strange fancy at the ball on the 6th, I imagine myself looking at my own Ego through a kaleidoscope. All the forms moving around me are Egos and annoy me by what they do and leave undone.

It is a temptation to find in this passage a symbol both of German philosophy and of the temper of Germany at the time. Its outer defeats, its weakness in the world of action, had developed an exasperated introspection. This outer weakness, coinciding, as Von Sybel points out, with the bloom of Germany in art, science, history, philology and philosophy, made the Ego of Germany the noblest contemporary object of contemplation, yet one surrounded with other national Egos who offended by what they did and what they did not do. Patriotism, national feeling, national consciousness are common enough facts. But nowhere save in Germany, in the earlier nineteenth century, have these sentiments and impulses been transformed by deliberate nurture into a mystic cult. This was the time when the idea of the *Volks-seele,* the *Volks-geist,* was born; and the idea lost no time in becoming a fact. Not merely poetry was affected by it, but philology, history and jurisprudence. The so-called historic school is its offspring. The science of social psychology derives from it at one remove. The soul, however, needed a body, and (quite in accord with German idealism) it formed a body for itself— the German State as a unified Empire.

While the idealistic period came first, it is important to bear in mind the kind of idealism it was. At this point the pantheistic allusion becomes significant. The idealism in question was not an idealism of another world but of *this* world, and especially of the State. The embodiment of the divine and absolute will and ideal is the existing world of nature and of men. Especially is the human ego the authorized and creative agent of absolute purpose. The significance of German philosophy was precisely to make men aware of their nature and destiny as the direct and active representatives of absolute and creative purpose.

If I again quote Heine, it is because, with his contempt for technical philosophy, he had an intimate sense of its human meaning. Of German pantheistic idealism, he wrote in 1833 while it was still in its prime:

> God is identical with the world. . . . But he manifests himself most gloriously in man, who feels and thinks at the same time, who is capable of distinguishing his own individuality from objective nature, whose intellect already bears within itself the ideas that present themselves to him in the phenomenal world. In man Deity reaches self-consciousness, and this self-consciousness God again reveals through man. But this revelation does not take place in and through individual man, but in and through collective humanity . . . which comprehends and represents in idea and in reality the whole God-universe. . . . It is an error to suppose that this religion leads men to indifference. On the contrary, the consciousness of his divinity will inspire man with enthusiasm for its manifestation, and from this moment the really noble achievements of true heroism glorify the earth.

In one respect, Heine was a false prophet. He thought that this philosophy would in the end accrue to the profit of the radical, the republican and revolutionary party in Germany. The history of German liberalism is a complicated matter. Suffice it in general to say that the honey the libertarians hived was appropriated in the end by the party of authority. In Heine's assurance that these ideas would in due time issue in action he was profoundly right. His essay closes with burning words, from which I extract the following:

> It seems to me that a methodical people, such as we, must begin with the reformation, must then occupy ourselves with systems of philosophy, and only after their completion pass to the political revolution. . . . Then will appear Kantians, as little tolerant of piety in the world of deeds as in the world of ideas, who will mercilessly upturn with sword and axe the soil of our European life to extirpate the last remnants of the past. Then will come upon the scene armed Fichteans, whose fanati-

cism of will is to be restrained neither by fear nor self-interest, for they live in the spirit. . . . Most of all to be feared would be the philosophers of nature,[4] were they actively to mingle. . . . For if the hand of the Kantian strikes with strong unerring blow; if the Fichtean courageously defies every danger, since for him danger has in reality no existence;—the Philosopher of Nature will be terrible in that he has allied himself with the primitive powers of nature, in that he can conjure up the demoniac forces of old German pantheism; and having done so, aroused in him that ancient Germanic eagerness which combats for the joy of the combat itself. . . . Smile not at my counsel as at the counsel of a dreamer. . . . The thought precedes the deed as the lightning the thunder. . . . The hour will come. As on the steps of an amphitheater, the nations will group themselves around Germany to witness the terrible combat.

In my preoccupation with Heine, I seem to have wandered somewhat from our immediate topic: the connection of the idealistic philosophy with the development and organization of the national state of Germany. But the necessity of the organized State to care for the moral interests of mankind was an inherent part of Fichte's thought. At first, *what* state was a matter of indifference. In fact his sympathies were largely French and republican. Before Jena, he writes:

What is the nation for a truly civilized Christian European? In a general way, Europe itself. More particularly at any time the State which is at the head of civilization. . . . With this cosmopolitan sense, we can be tranquil before the vicissitudes and catastrophes of history.

In 1807 he writes:

The distinction between Prussia and the rest of Germany is external, arbitrary and fortuitous. The distinction between Germany and the rest of Europe is founded in nature.

The seeming gulf between the two ideas is easily bridged. The *Addresses on the Fundamental Features of the Present Age* had taught that the end of humanity on earth is the establishment of a kingdom in which all relations of

4. He refers to the followers of Schelling, who as matter of fact had little vogue. But his words may not unjustly be transferred to the naturalistic schools, which have since affected German thought.

humanity are determined with freedom or according to Reason—according to Reason as conceived by the Fichtean formula. In his *Addresses to the German Nation,* in 1807–08, the unique mission of Germany in the establishment of this kingdom is urged as a motive for securing national unity and the overthrow of the conqueror. The Germans are the sole people who recognize the principles of spiritual freedom, of freedom won by action in accord with reason. Faithfulness to this mission will "elevate the German name to that of the most glorious among all the peoples, making this Nation the regenerator and restorer of the world." He personifies their ancestors speaking to them, and saying: "We in our time saved Germany from the Roman World Empire." But "yours is the greater fortune. You may establish once for all the Kingdom of the Spirit and of Reason, bringing to naught corporeal might as the ruling thing in the world." And this antithesis of the Germanic and the Roman principles has become a commonplace in the German imagination. Moreover, for Germany to win is no selfish gain. It is an advantage to all nations. "The great promise of a kingdom of right reason and truth on earth must not become a vain and empty phantom; the present iron age is but a transition to a better estate." Hence the concluding words: "There is no middle road: If you sink, so sinks humanity entire with you, without hope of future restoration."

The premises of the historic syllogism are plain. First, the German Luther who saved for mankind the principle of spiritual freedom against Latin externalism; then Kant and Fichte, who wrought out the principle into a final philosophy of science, morals and the State; as conclusion, the German nation organized in order to win the world to recognition of the principle, and thereby to establish the rule of freedom and science in humanity as a whole. The Germans are patient; they have a long memory. Ideas produced when Germany was divided and broken were retained and cherished after it became a unified State of supreme military power, and one yielding to no other people in industrial and commercial prosperity. In the grosser sense of the words, Germany has not held that might makes right. But it has been instructed by a long line of philosophers that it is the business of ideal right to gather might to itself in order that it may cease to be merely ideal. The State represents exactly this incarnation of ideal law and right in effective might. The military arm is part of this moral embodiment. Let sentimentalists sing the praises of an ideal to which no actual force corresponds. Prussian faith in the reality and enforcement among men of the ideal is of a more solid character. As past history is the record of the gradual realization in the Germanic State of the divine idea, future history must uphold and expand what has been accomplished. Diplomacy is the veiled display of law clothed with force in behalf of this realization, and war is its overt manifestation. That war demands self-sacrifice is but the more convincing proof of its profound morality. It is the final seal of devotion to the extension of the kingdom of the Absolute on earth.

For the philosophy stands or falls with the conception of an Absolute. Whether a philosophy of absolutes is theoretically sound or unsound is none of my present concern. But that philosophical absolutism may be practically as dangerous as matter of fact political absolutism history testifies. The situation puts in relief what finally is at issue between a theory which is pinned to a belief in an Absolute beyond history and behind experience, and one which is frankly experimental. For any philosophy which is not consistently experimental will always traffic in absolutes no matter in how disguised a form. In German political philosophy, the traffic is without mask.

3. THE GERMANIC PHILOSOPHY OF HISTORY

The unity of the German people longed for and dreamed of after 1807 became an established fact through the war of 1870 with France. It is easy to assign symbolic significance to this fact. Ever since the time of the French Revolution—if not before—German thought has taken shape in conflict with ideas that were characteristically French and in sharp and conscious antithesis to them. Rousseau's deification of Nature was the occasion for the development of the conception of Culture. His condemnation of science and art as socially corrupting and socially divisive worked across the Rhine to produce the notion that science and art are the forces which moralize and unify humanity. The cosmopolitanism of the French Enlightenment was transformed by German thinkers into a self-conscious assertion of nationalism. The abstract Rights of Man of the French Revolution were set in antithesis to the principle of the rights of the citizen secured to him solely by the power of the politically organized nation. The deliberate breach of the revolutionary philosophy with the past, the attempt (foreshadowed in the philosophy of Descartes) to make a *tabula rasa* of the fortuitous assemblage of traditions and institutions which history offers, in order to substitute a social structure built upon Reason, was envisaged as the *fons et origo* of all evil. That history is itself incarnate reason; that history is infinitely more rational than the formal abstracting and generalizing reason of individuals; that individual mind becomes rational only through the absorption and assimilation of the universal reason embodied in historic institutions and historic development, became the articles of faith of the German intellectual creed. It is hardly an exaggeration to say that for almost a century the characteristic philosophy of Germany has been a philosophy of history even when not such in apparent form.

Yet the meaning of this appeal to history is lost unless we bear in mind that the Enlightenment after all transmitted to Germany, from medieval thought, its foundation principle. The appeal was not from reason to experience, but from analytic thought (henceforth condemned to be merely "Understanding"—"*Verstand*") to an absolute and universal Reason (*Vernunft*) partially revealed in nature and more adequately manifested in human history as an organic process. Recourse to history was required because not of any empirical lessons it has to teach, nor yet because history bequeaths to us stubborn institutions which must be reckoned with, but because history is the dynamic and evolving realization of immanent reason. The contrast of the German attitude with that of Edmund Burke is instructive. The latter had the same profound hostility to cutting loose from the past. But his objection was not that the past is an embodiment of transcendent reason, but that its institutions are an "inheritance" bequeathed to us from the "collected wisdom" of our forefathers. The continuity of political life centres not about an inner evolving Idea, but about "our hearths, our sepulchres and our altars." He has the same suspicion of abstract rights of man. But his appeal is to experience and to practical consequences. Since "circumstances give in reality to every principle its distinguishing color and discriminating effect," there is no soundness in any principle when "it stands stripped of every relation in all the nakedness and solitude of metaphysical abstraction."

According to the German view, the English protested because of interference with empirically established rights and privileges; the Germans, because they perceived in the Revolution a radical error as to the nature and work of reason. In point of fact, the Germans never made that break with tradition, political or religious, of which the French Revolution is an emphatic symbol. I have already referred to Kant's disposition to regard church dogmas (of which, as dogmas, he disapproved) as vehicles of eternal spiritual truths—husks to preserve an inner grain. All of the great German idealists gave further expression to this disposition. To Hegel, for example, the substance of the doctrines of Protestant Christianity is identical with the truths of absolute philosophy, except that in religion they are expressed in a form not adequate to their meaning, the form, namely, of imaginative thought in which most men live. The disposition to philosophize Christianity is too widely shown in Germany to be dismissed as a cowardly desire at accommodation with things established. It shows rather an intellectual piety among a people where freedom of thought and conscience had been achieved without a violent political upheaval. Hegel finds that the characteristic weakness of Romance thought was an inner split, an inability to reconcile the spiritual and absolute essence of reality with which religion deals with the detailed work of intelligence in science and politics. The Germans, on the contrary, "were predestined to be the bearers of the Christian principle and to carry out the Idea as the absolutely Rational end." They accomplished this, not by a flight away from the secular world, but by realizing that the Christian principle is in itself that of the unity of the subjective and the objective, the spiritual and the worldly. The "Spirit finds the goal of its struggle, its harmony, in that very sphere which it made the object of its resistance,—it finds that secular pursuits are a spiritual occupation";—a discovery, surely, which unites simplicity with comprehensiveness and one which does not lead to criticism of the secular pursuits carried on. Whatever is to be said of this as philosophy, it expresses, in a way, the quality of German life and thought. More than other countries, Germany has had the fortune to preserve as food for its imaginative life and as emotional sanction the great ideas of the past. It has carried over their reinforcement into the pursuit of science and into politics—into the very things which in other countries, notably in the Latin countries, have been used as weapons of attack upon tradition.

Political development tells a somewhat similar tale. The painful transition from feudalism to the modern era was, for the most part, accomplished recently in Germany, and accomplished under the guidance of established political authorities instead of by revolt against them. Under their supervision, and mainly at their initiative, Germany has passed in less than a century to the régime of modern capitalistic competitive enterprise, moderated by the State, out

of the dominion of those local and guild restrictions which
so long held economic activity in corporate bonds. The governing powers themselves secured to members of the State
what seems, at least to Germans, to be a satisfying degree
of political freedom. Along with this absence of internal
disturbance and revolution, we must put the fact that every
step in the development of Germany as a unified political
power has been effected by war with some of the neighbors
by which it is hemmed in. There stands the unfolding
sequence: 1815 (not to go back to Frederick the Great),
1864, 1866, 1870. And the significant thing about these wars
is not that external territory was annexed as their consequence, but the rebound of external struggle upon the achieving of internal unity. No wonder the German imagination
has been impressed with the idea of an organic evolution
from within, which takes the form of a unity achieved
through conflict and the conquest of an opposing principle.

Such scattering comments as these prove nothing. But
they suggest why German thought has been peculiarly sensitive to the idea of historic continuity; why it has been prone
to seek for an original implicit essence which has progressively unfolded itself in a single development. It would take
much more than an hour to give even a superficial account
of the growth of the historical sciences and historic methods
of Germany during the first half of the eighteenth century.
It would involve an account of the creation of philology, and
the philological methods which go by the name of higher
criticism; of their extension to archeology; of the historic
schools of jurisprudence and political economy, as well as
of the ways in which such men as Niebuhr, Mommsen and
Ranke remade the methods of studying the past. I can only
say here that Germany developed such an effective historical
technique that even mediocre men achieved respectable
results; and, much more significantly, that when Taine made
the remark (quoted earlier) that we owe to the Germany of
the half century before 1830 all our distinctively modern
ideas, his remarks apply above all to the disciplines concerned with the historical development of mankind.

The bases of this philosophy are already before us. Even
in Kant we find the idea of a single continuous development

of humanity, as a progress from a reign of natural instinct to a final freedom won through adherence to the law of reason. Fichte sketched the stages already traversed on this road and located the point at which mankind now stands. In his later writings, the significance of history as the realization of the absolute purpose is increasingly emphasized. History is the continuous life of a divine Ego by which it realizes in fact what it is in idea or destiny. Its phases are successive stages in the founding of the Kingdom of God on earth. It and it only is the revelation of the Absolute. Along with this growing deification of history is the increased significance attached to nationalism in general and the German nation in particular. The State is the concrete individual interposed between generic humanity and particular beings. In his words, the national folk is the channel of divine life as it pours into particular finite human beings. He says:

> While cosmopolitanism is the dominant will that the purpose of the existence of humanity be actually realized in humanity, patriotism is the will that this end be first realized in the particular nation to which we ourselves belong, and that this achievement *thence* spread over the entire race.

Since the State is an organ of divinity, patriotism is religion. As the Germans are the only truly religious people, they alone are truly capable of patriotism. Other peoples are products of external causes; they have no self-formed Self, but only an acquired self due to general convention. In Germany there is a self which is self-wrought and self-owned. The very fact that Germany for centuries has had no external unity proves that its selfhood is metaphysical, not a gift of circumstance. This conception of the German mission has been combined with a kind of anthropological metaphysics which has become the rage in Germany. The Germans alone of all existing European nations are a pure race. They alone have preserved unalloyed the original divine deposit. Language is the expression of the national soul, and only the Germans have kept their native speech in its purity. In like vein, Hegel attributes the inner disharmony characteristic of Romance peoples to the fact that they are of mixed Germanic and Latin blood. A purely artificial cult of race has so flourished in Germany that many social movements—like anti-Semitism—and some of Germany's political ambitions cannot be understood apart from the mystic identification of Race, Culture and the State. In the light of actual science, this is so mythological that the remark of an American periodical that race means a number of people reading the same newspapers is sober scientific fact compared with it.[5]

At the beginning of history Fichte placed an "*Urvolk.*" His account of it seems an attempt to rationalize at one stroke the legends of the Golden Age, the Biblical account of man before the Fall and Rousseau's primitive "state of nature." The *Urvolk* lived in a paradise of innocence, a paradise without knowledge, labor or art. The philosophy which demands such a Folk is comparatively simple. Except as a manifestation of Absolute Reason, humanity could not exist at all. Yet in the first stage of the manifestation, Reason could not have been appropriated by the self-conscious effort of man. It existed without consciousness of itself, for it was given, not, like all true self-consciousness, won by morally creative struggle. Rational in substance, in form it was but feeling or instinct. In a sense, all subsequent history is but a return to this primitive condition. But "humanity must make the journey on its own feet; by its own strength it must bring itself back to that state in which it was once without its own coöperating labor. . . . If humanity does not re-create its own true being, it has no real life." While philosophy compels us to assume a Normal People who, by "the mere fact of their existence, without science and art, found

5. Chamberlain, for example, holds that Jesus must have been of Teutonic birth—a perfect logical conclusion from the received philosophy of the State and religion. Quite aware that there is much Slav blood in northern Germany and Romance blood in southern Germany, he explains that while with other peoples crossing produces a mongrel race, the potency of the German blood is such that cross-breeding strengthens it. While at one time he explains the historic strength of the Jew on the ground that he has kept his race pure, another place he allows his indignation at the Jews to lead him to include them among the most mongrel of all peoples. To one thing he remains consistent: By the very essence of race, the Semites represent a metaphysical principle inherently hostile to the grand Germanic principle. It perhaps seems absurd to dignify the vagaries of this garrulous writer, but according to all report the volumes in which such expressions occur, *The Foundations of the Nineteenth Century,* have had august approval and much vogue.

themselves in a state of perfectly developed reason," there is no ground for not admitting the existence at the same time of "timid and rude earth-born savages." Thus the original state of humanity would have been one of the greatest possible inequality, being divided between the Normal Folk existing as a manifestation of Reason and the wild and savage races of barbarism.

In his later period of inflamed patriotism this innocuous speculation grew a sting. He had determined that the present age—the Europe of the Enlightenment and the French Revolution—is the age of liberation from the external authority in which Reason had presented itself in the second age. Hence it is inherently negative: "an age of absolute indifference toward the Truth, an age of entire and unrestrained licentiousness." But the further evolution of the Divine Idea demands a Folk which has retained the primitive principle of Reason, which may redeem, therefore, the corrupt and rebellious modes of humanity elsewhere existing. Since the Germans are this saving remnant, they are the *Urvolk*, the Normal Nation, of the modern period. From this point on, idealization of past Germanic history and appeal to the nation to realize its unique calling by victory over Napoleon blend.

The Fichtean scaffolding tumbled, but these ideas persisted. I doubt if it is possible to exaggerate the extent to which German history has been systematically idealized for the last hundred years. Technically speaking, the Romantic movement may have passed away and an age of scientific history dawned. Actually the detailed facts have been depicted by use of the palette of Romanticism. Space permits but one illustration which would be but a literary curiosity were it not fairly typical. Tacitus called his account of the northern barbarians *Germania*—an unfortunate title in view of later developments. The characteristics assigned by him to the German tribes are such as any anthropologist could duplicate from any warlike barbaric tribe. Yet over and over again these traits (which Tacitus idealized as Cooper, say, idealized the North American Indian traits) are made the basis of the philosophic history of the German people. The Germans, for example, had that psychological experience now known as mana, manitou, tabu, etc. They identified their gods, in Tacitus' phrase, with "that mystery which they perceive by experiencing sacred fear." This turns out to be the germinal deposit of spiritual-mindedness which later showed itself in Luther and in the peculiar genius of the Germans for religious experience.

The following words are from no less an authority than Pfleiderer:

> Cannot we recognize in this point that truly German charac-teristic of *Innerlichkeit* which scorns to fix for sensuous percep-tion the divine something which makes itself felt in the depths of the sensitive soul, which scorns to drag down the sublime mys-tery of the unknowable to the vulgar distinctness of earthly things? The fact that the Germans attached but little importance to religious ceremonies accords with this view.

To others, this sense of mystery is a prophetic anticipa-tion of the Kantian thing-in-itself.

A similar treatment has been accorded to the personal and voluntary bond by which individuals attached them-selves to a chieftain. Thus early was marked out the fidelity or loyalty, *Treue*, which is uniquely Germanic—although some warlike tribes among our Indians carried the system still further. I can allow myself but one more example of the way in which the philosophic sophistication of history has worked. No historian can be unconscious of the extent to which European culture has been genuinely European—the extent to which it derives itself from a common heritage of the ancient world and the extent to which intermixtures and borrowings of culture have gone on ever since. As to Ger-many, however, these obvious facts have to be accommo-dated to the doctrine of an original racial deposit steadily evolving from within.

The method is simple. As respects Germany, these cul-tural borrowings and crosses represent the intrinsic univer-sality of its genius. Through this universality, the German spirit finds itself at home everywhere. Consequently, it con-sciously appropriates and assimilates what other peoples have produced by a kind of blind unconscious instinct. Thus it was German thought which revealed the truth of Hellenic culture, and rescued essential Christianity from its Roman-

ized petrifaction. The principle of Reason which French enlightenment laid hold of only in its negative and destructive
aspect, the German spirit grasped in its positive and constructive form. Shakespeare happened to be born in England,
but only the Germans have apprehended him in his spiritual
universality so that he is now more their own than he is
England's—and so on. But with respect to other peoples, similar borrowings reveal only their lack of inner and essential
selfhood. While Luther is universal because he is German,
Shakespeare is universal because he is not English.

I have intimated that Fichte's actual influence was limited. But his basic ideas of the State and of history were absorbed in the philosophy of Hegel, and Hegel for a considerable period absolutely dominated German thinking. To set
forth the ground principles of his "absolute idealism" would
be only to repeat what has already been said. Its chief difference, aside from Hegel's encyclopedic knowledge, his
greater concrete historic interest and his more conservative
temperament, is his bottomless scorn for an Idea, an Absolute, which merely ought to be and which is only going to be
realized after a period of time. "The Actual *is* the Rational
and the Rational *is* the Actual"—and the actual means the
actuating force and movement of things. It is customary to
call him an Idealist. In one sense of much abused terms, he
is the greatest realist known to philosophy. He might be
called a Brutalist. In the inquiry Bourdon carried on in Germany a few years ago (published under the title of *The German Enigma*), he records a conversation with a German
who deplores the tendency of the Germans to forsake the
solid bone of things in behalf of a romantic shadow. As
against this he appeals to the realistic sense of Hegel, who,

in opposition to the idealism which had lifted Germany on wings,
arrayed and marshaled the maxims of an unflinching realism.
He had formulae for the justification of facts whatever they
might be. "That which *is*," he would say, "is reason realised."
And what did he teach? That the hour has sounded for the third
act in the drama of humanity, and that the German opportunity
is not far off. . . . I could show you throughout the nineteenth
century the torrent of political and social ideas which had their
source here.

I have said that the essential points of the Fichtean philosophy of history were taken up into the Hegelian system. This assimilation involved, however, a rectification of an inconsistency between the earlier and the later moral theories of Fichte. In his earlier ethical writings, emphasis fell upon conscious moral personality—upon the deliberate identification by the individual will of its career and destiny with the purpose of the Absolute. In his later patriotic philosophy, he asserts that the organized nation is the channel by which a finite ego acquires moral personality, since the nation alone transmits to individuals the generic principle of God working in humanity. At the same time he appeals to the resolute will and consciously chosen self-sacrifice of individuals to overthrow the enemy and re-establish the Prussian state. When Hegel writes that victory has been obtained, the war of Independence has been successfully waged. The necessity of emphasizing individual self-assertion had given way to the need of subordinating the individual to the established state in order to check the disintegrating tendencies of liberalism.

Haym has said that Hegel's *Philosophy of Right* had for its task the exhibition as the perfect work of Absolute Reason up to date of the "practical and political condition existing in Prussia in 1821." This was meant as a hostile attack. But Hegel himself should have been the last to object. With his scorn for an Ideal so impotent that its realization must depend upon the effort of private selves, an Absolute so inconsequential that it must wait upon the accidents of future time for manifestation, he sticks in politics more than elsewhere to the conviction that the actual *is* the rational. "The task of philosophy is to comprehend that which is, for that which is, is Reason." Alleged philosophies which try to tell what the State should be or even what a state ought in the future to come to be, are idle fantasies. Such attempts come too late. Human wisdom is like "the bird of Minerva which takes its flight only at the close of day."[6] It comes, after the issue, to acknowledge what has happened. "The State is the

6. Marx said of the historic schools of politics, law and economics that to them, as Jehovah to Moses on Mt. Sinai, the divine showed but its posterior side.

rational in itself and for itself. Its substantial unity is an absolute end in itself. To it belongs supreme right in respect to individuals whose first duty is—just to be members of the State." . . . The State "is the absolute reality and the individual himself has objective existence, truth and morality only in his capacity as a member of the State." It is a commonplace of idealistic theism that nature is a manifestation of God. But Hegel says that nature is only an externalized, unconscious and so incomplete expression. The State has more, not less, objective reality than physical nature, for it is a realization of Absolute spirit in the realm of consciousness. The doctrine presents an extreme form of the idea, not of the divine right of kings, but of the divine right of States.

The march of God in history is the cause of the existence of states; their foundation is the power of reason realizing itself as will. Every state, whatever it be, participates in the divine essence. The State is not the work of human art; only Reason could produce it.

The State is God on earth.

His depreciation of the individual as an individual appears in every theme of his *Philosophy of Right* and *Philosophy of History*. At first sight, his theory of great world heroes seems inconsistent with his disregard of individuals. While the morality of most men consists simply in assimilating into their own habits the customs already found in the institutions about them, great men initiate new historic epochs. They derive

their purposes and their calling not from the calm regular course of things sanctioned by the existing order, but from a concealed fount, from that inner spirit hidden beneath the surface, which, striking the outer world as a shell, bursts it to pieces.

The heroes are thus the exception which proves the rule. They are world characters; while they seem to be seeking personal interests they are really acting as organs of a universal will, of God in his further march. In his identification with the Absolute, the world-hero can have but one aim to which

he is devoted regardless of all else. Such men may even treat other great and sacred interests inconsiderately. . . . But so

mighty a form must trample down many an innocent flower—
crush to pieces many an object in its path.

We are not surprised to see that Alexander, Caesar and Napoleon are the characters he prefers to cite. One can only
regret that he died before his contemplative piety could behold Bismarck.

A large part of the intellectual machinery by which
Hegel overcame the remnants of individualism found in
prior philosophy came from the idea of organic development
which had been active in German thought since the time of
Herder. In his chief work (*Outlines of a Philosophy of the
History of Man*), written in the closing decades of the eighteenth century, Herder holds that history is a progressive
education of humanity. This idea, had from Lessing, is combined with the idea of Leibniz that change is evolution, by
means of an internal force, of powers originally implicit in
existence, and with the idea of Spinoza of an all-comprehen-
sive substance. This idea of organic growth was then applied
to language, literature and institutions. It soon obtained reinforcement from the rising science of biology. Long before
the days of Darwin or Spencer, the idea of evolution had
been a commonplace of German thought with respect to
everything concerning the history of humanity. The notion
was set in sharp antithesis to the conception of "making" or
manufacturing institutions and constitutions, which was
treated as one of the fallacies of the French philosophy of
the Enlightenment. A combination of this notion of universal
organic growth with the technique of prior idealism may
fairly be said to have determined Hegel's whole philosophy.
While Leibniz and Herder had emphasized the notion of harmony as an essential factor of the working of organic forces,
Hegel took from Fichte the notion of a unity or synthesis
arrived at by "positing," and overcoming an opposite. Struggle for existence (or realization) was thus an "organic" part
of German thinking long before the teaching of Darwin,
who, in fact, is usually treated by German writers as giving
a rather superficial empirical expression to an idea which
they had already grasped in its universal speculative form.
It is characteristic of the extent in which Hegel thought in
terms of struggle and overcoming that after stating why it

was as yet impossible to include the Americas in his philosophy of history, and after saying that in the future the burden
of world history will reveal itself there, he surmises that it
may take the form of a "contest" between North and South
America. No philosopher has ever thought so consistently
and so wholly in terms of strife and overcoming as Hegel.
When he says the "world history is the world judgment" he
means judgment in the sense of assize, and judgment as
victory of one and defeat of another—victory being the final
proof that the world spirit has now passed from one nation
to take up its residence in another. To be defeated in a way
which causes the nation to take a secondary position among
nations is a sign that divine judgment has been passed upon
it. When a recent German writer argues that for Germany to
surrender any territory which it has conquered during the
present war would be sacrilegious, since it would be to refuse
to acknowledge the workings of God in human history, he
speaks quite in the Hegelian vein.

Although the phenomenon of nationalism was very recent when Hegel wrote, indeed practically contemporary
with his own day, he writes in nationalistic terms the entire
history of humanity. The State is the Individual of history;
it is to history what a given man is to biography. History
gives us the progressive realization or evolution of the Absolute, moving from one National Individual to another. It is
law, the universal, which makes the State a State, for law is
reason, not as mere subjective reflection, but in its manifestation as supreme over and in particulars. On this account,
Hegel's statement that the fundamental principle of history
is the progressive realization of freedom does not mean what
an uninstructed English reader would naturally take it to
mean. Freedom is always understood in terms of Reason. Its
expression in history means that Thought has progressively
become conscious of itself; that is, has made itself its own
object. Freedom is the *consciousness* of freedom. Liberty of
action has little to do with it. Obviously it is only in the German idealistic system—particularly in the system of Hegel
himself—that this has fully taken place. Meantime, when citizens of a state (especially of the state in which this philosophic insight has been achieved) take the laws of their state

as their own ends and motives of action, they attain the best possible substitute for a reason which is its own object. They appropriate as their own personal reason the objective and absolute Reason embodied perforce in law and custom.

After this detour, we are led back to the fact that the Germans possess the greatest freedom yet attained by humanity, for the Prussian political organization most fully exemplifies Law, or the Universal, organizing under and within itself all particular arrangements of social and personal life. Some other peoples—particularly the Latin—have thought they could *make* constitutions, or at least that the form of their constitution was a matter of choice. But this is merely setting up the private conceit of individuals against the work of Absolute Reason, and thus marks the disintegration of a state rather than its existence. Other peoples have tried to found the government on the consent of the governed, unwitting of the fact that it is the government, the *specific* realization of Reason, which makes a state out of what is otherwise an anarchic mass of individuals. Other peoples have made a parliament or representative body the essential thing in government; in philosophic reality this is only a consultative body, having as its main function communication between classes (which are indispensable to an "organic" state) and the real government. The chief function of parliament is to give the opinion of the social classes an opportunity to feel it is being considered and to enable the real government to take advantage of whatever wisdom may chance to be expressed. Hegel seems quite prophetic when he says: "By virtue of this participation subjective liberty and conceit, with their general opinion, can show themselves palpably efficacious and enjoy the satisfaction of feeling themselves to count for something." Finally, the State becomes wholly and completely an organized Individual only in its external relations, its relations to other states. As his philosophy of history ignores the past in seizing upon the national state as the unit and focus of history, so it ignores all future possibility of a genuinely international federation to which isolated nationalism shall be subordinated. Bernhardi writes wholly in the Hegelian sense when he says that to expand the idea of the State into the idea of humanity is a

Utopian error, for it would exclude the essential principle of life, struggle.

Philosophical justification of war follows inevitably from a philosophy of history composed in nationalistic terms. History is the movement, the march of God on earth through time. Only one nation at a time can be the latest and hence the fullest realization of God. The movement of God in history is thus particularly manifest in those changes by which unique place passes from one nation to another. War is the signally visible occurrence of such a flight of the divine spirit in its onward movement. The idea that friendly intercourse among all the peoples of the earth is a legitimate aim of human effort is in basic contradiction of such a philosophy. War is explicit realization of "dialectic," of the negation by which a higher synthesis of reason is assured. It effectively displays the "irony of the divine Idea." It is to national life what the winds are to the sea, "preserving mankind from the corruption engendered by immobility." War is the most effective preacher of the vanity of all merely finite interests; it puts an end to that selfish egoism of the individual by which he would claim his life and his property as his own or as his family's. International law is not properly law; it expresses simply certain usages which are accepted so long as they do not come into conflict with the purpose of a state—a purpose which always gives the supreme law of national life. Particularly against the absolute right of the "present bearer of the world spirit, the spirits of the other nations are absolutely without right. The latter, just like the nations whose epochs have passed, count no longer in universal history." Since they are already passed over from the standpoint of the divine idea, war can do no more than exhibit the fact that their day has come and gone. World history is the world's judgment seat.

For a period Hegelian thought was almost supreme in Germany. Then its rule passed away almost as rapidly as it had been achieved. After various shiftings, the trend of philosophic thought was definitely "Back to Kant." Kant's greater sobriety, the sharp distinction he drew between the realm of phenomena and science and the ideal noumenal world, commended him after the unbridled pretensions of

Hegelian absolutism. For more than a generation Hegel was spoken of with almost universal contempt. Nevertheless his ideas, loosed from the technical apparatus with which he surrounded them, persisted. Upon the historical disciplines his influence was peculiarly deep and abiding. He fixed the ideas of Fichte and fastened them together with the pin of evolution. Since his day, histories of philosophy, or religion, or institutions have all been treated as developments through necessary stages of an inner implicit idea or purpose according to an indwelling law. And the idea of a peculiar mission and destiny of German history has lost nothing in the operation. Expressions which a bewildered world has sought since the beginning of the war to explain through the influence of a Darwinian struggle for existence and survival of the fittest, or through the influence of a Nietzschean philosophy of power, have their roots in the classic idealistic philosophy culminating in Hegel.

Kant still remains the philosopher of Germany. The division of life between the world of sense and of mechanism and the world of the supersensible and purpose, the world of necessity and the world of freedom, is more congenial than a complete monism. The attempts of his successors to bridge the gap and set up a wholly unified philosophy failed, historically speaking. But, nevertheless, they contributed an indispensable ingredient to the contemporary German spirit; they helped people the Kantian void of the supersensible with the substantial figures of the State and its Historical Evolution and Mission. Kant bequeathed to the world an intellect devoted to the congenial task of discovering causal law in external nature, and an inner intuition which, in spite of its sublimity, had nothing to look at except the bare form of an empty law of duty. Kant was kept busy in proving the existence of this supernal but empty region. Consequently he was not troubled by being obliged to engage in the unremunerative task of spending his time gazing into a blank void. His successors were not so fortunate. The existence of this ideal realm in which reason, purpose and freedom are one was axiomatic to them; they could no longer busy themselves with proving its existence. Some of them, called the Romanticists, filled it with visions, more or less poetic, which frankly drew their substance from an imagination inflamed by emotional aspiration in revolt at the limitations of outward action. Others, called the idealistic philosophers, filled in the void, dark because of excess of light, with less ghostly forms of Law and the unfolding in History of Absolute Value and Purpose. The two worlds of Kant were too far away from each other. The later idealistic world constructions crumbled; but their débris supplied material with which to fill in the middle regions between the Kantian worlds of sense and of reason. This, I repeat, is their lasting contribution to present German culture. Where Kantianism has not received a filling in from the philosophy of history and the State, it has remained in Germany, as elsewhere, a critique of the methodology of science; its importance has been professional rather than human.

In the first lecture we set out with the suggestion of an inquiry into the influence of general ideas upon practical affairs, upon those larger practical affairs called politics. We appear to have concluded with a conviction that (in the instance before us at least) politics has rather been the controlling factor in the formation of philosophic ideas and in deciding their vogue. Yet we are well within limits when we say that ideas which were evoked in correspondence with concrete social conditions served to articulate and consolidate the latter. Even if we went so far as to say that reigning philosophies simply reflect as in a mirror contemporary social struggles, we should have to add that seeing one's self in a mirror is a definite practical aid in carrying on one's undertaking to its completion.

When what a people sees in its intellectual looking glass is its own organization and its own historic evolution as an organic instrument of the accomplishment of an Absolute Will and Law, the articulating and consolidating efficacy of the reflection is immensely intensified. Outside of Germany, the career of the German idealistic philosophy has been mainly professional and literary. It has exercised considerable influence upon the teaching of philosophy in France, England and this country. Beyond professorial circles, its influence has been considerable in theological directions. Without doubt, it has modulated for many persons the transition from a supernatural to a spiritual religion; it has enabled them to give up historical and miraculous elements as indifferent accretions and to retain the moral substance and emotional values of Christianity. But the Germans are quite right in feeling that only in Germany is this form of idealistic thinking both indigenous and widely applied.

A crisis like the present forces upon thoughtful persons a consideration of the value for the general aims of civilization of a philosophy of the *a priori*, the Absolute, and of their immanent evolution through the medium of an experience which as just experience is only a superficial and negligible vehicle of transcendent Laws and Ends. It forces a consideration of what type of general ideas is available for the articulation and guidance of our own life in case we find ourselves looking upon the present world scene as an *a priori* and an absolutistic philosophy gone into bankruptcy.

In Europe, speaking generally, "Americanism" is a synonym for crude empiricism and a materialistic utilitarianism. It is no part of my present task to try to show how largely this accusation is due to misunderstanding. It is simpler to inquire how far the charge points to the problem which American life, and therefore philosophy in America, must meet. It is difficult to see how any *a priori* philosophy, or any systematic absolutism, is to get a footing among us, at least beyond narrow and professorial circles. Psychologists talk about learning by the method of trial and error or success. Our social organization commits us to this philosophy of life. Our working principle is to try: to find out by trying, and to measure the worth of the ideas and theories tried by the success with which they meet the test of application in practice. Concrete consequences rather than *a priori* rules supply our guiding principles. Hegel found it "superficial and absurd to regard as objects of choice" social constitutions; to him "they were necessary structures in the path of development." To us they are the cumulative result of a multitude of daily and ever-renewed choices.

That such an experimental philosophy of life means a dangerous experiment goes without saying. It permits, sooner or later it may require, every alleged sacrosanct principle to submit to ordeal by fire—to trial by service rendered.

From the standpoint of *a priorism*, it is hopelessly anarchic; it is doomed, *a priori*, to failure. From its own standpoint, it is itself a theory to be tested by experience. Now experiments are of all kinds, varying from those generated by blind impulse and appetite to those guided by intelligently formed ideas. They are as diverse as the attempt of a savage to get rain by sprinkling water and scattering thistledown, and that control of electricity in the laboratory from which issue wireless telegraphy and rapid traction. Is it not likely that in this distinction we have the key to the failure or success of the experimental method generalized into a philosophy of life, that is to say, of social matters—the only application which procures complete generalization?

An experimental philosophy differs from empirical philosophy as empiricism has been previously formulated. Historical empiricisms have been stated in terms of precedents; their generalizations have been summaries of what has previously happened. The truth and falsity of these generalizations depended then upon the accuracy with which they catalogued, under appropriate heads, a multiplicity of past occurrences. They were perforce lacking in directive power except so far as the future might be a routine repetition of the past. In an experimental philosophy of life, the question of the past, of precedents, of origins, is quite subordinate to prevision, to guidance and control amid future possibilities. Consequences rather than antecedents measure the worth of theories. Any scheme or project may have a fair hearing provided it promise amelioration in the future; and no theory or standard is so sacred that it may be accepted simply on the basis of past performance.

But this difference between a radically experimental philosophy and an empiristic philosophy only emphasizes the demand for careful and comprehensive reflection with respect to the ideas which are to be tested in practice. If an *a priori* philosophy has worked at all in Germany it is because it has been based on an *a priori* social constitution—that is to say, on a state whose organization is such as to determine in advance the main activities of classes of individuals, and to utilize their particular activities by linking them up with one another in definite ways. It is a commonplace to say that

Germany is a monument to what can be done by means of conscious method and organization. An experimental philosophy of life in order to succeed must not set less store upon methodic and organized intelligence, but more. We must learn from Germany what methodic and organized work means. But instead of confining intelligence to the technical means of realizing ends which are predetermined by the State (or by something called the historic Evolution of the Idea), intelligence must, with us, devote itself as well to construction of the ends to be acted upon.

The method of trial and error or success is likely, if not directed by a trained and informed imagination, to score an undue proportion of failures. There is no possibility of disguising the fact that an experimental philosophy of life means a hit-and-miss philosophy in the end. But it means missing rather than hitting, if the aiming is done in a happy-go-lucky way instead of by bringing to bear all the resources of inquiry upon locating the target, constructing propulsive machinery and figuring out the curve of trajectory. That this work is, after all, but hypothetical and tentative till it issue from thought into action does not mean that it might as well be random guesswork; it means that we can do still better next time if we are sufficiently attentive to the causes of success and failure this time.

America is too new to afford a foundation for an *a priori* philosophy; we have not the requisite background of law, institutions and achieved social organization. America is too new to render congenial to our imagination an evolutionary philosophy of the German type. For our history is too obviously future. Our country is too big and too unformed, however, to enable us to trust to an empirical philosophy of muddling along, patching up here and there some old piece of machinery which has broken down by reason of its antiquity. We must have system, constructive method, springing from a widely inventive imagination, a method checked up at each turn by results achieved. We have said long enough that America means opportunity; we must now begin to ask: Opportunity for what, and how shall the opportunity be achieved? I can but think that the present European situation forces home upon us the need for constructive planning. I can but think that while it gives no reason for supposing that creative power attaches *ex officio* to general ideas, it does encourage us to believe that a philosophy which should articulate and consolidate the ideas to which our social practice commits us would clarify and guide our future endeavor.

Time permits of but one illustration. The present situation presents the spectacle of the breakdown of the whole philosophy of Nationalism, political, racial and cultural. It is by the accident of position rather than any virtue of our own that we are not sharers in the present demonstration of failure. We have borrowed the older philosophy of isolated national sovereignty and have lived upon it in a more or less half-hearted way. In our internal constitution we are actually interracial and international. It remains to see whether we have the courage to face this fact and the wisdom to think out the plan of action which it indicates. Arbitration treaties, international judicial councils, schemes of international disarmament, peace funds and peace movements, are all well in their way. But the situation calls for more radical thinking than that which terminates in such proposals. We have to recognize that furtherance of the depth and width of human intercourse is the measure of civilization; and we have to apply this fact without as well as within our national life. We must make the accident of our internal composition into an idea, an idea upon which we may conduct our foreign as well as our domestic policy. An international judicial tribunal will break in the end upon the principle of national sovereignty.

We have no right to cast stones at any warring nation till we have asked ourselves whether we are willing to forego this principle and to submit affairs which limited imagination and sense have led us to consider strictly national to an international legislature. In and of itself, the idea of peace is a negative idea; it is a police idea. There *are* things more important than keeping one's body whole and one's property intact. Disturbing the peace is bad, not because peace is disturbed, but because the fruitful processes of cooperation in the great experiment of living together are disturbed. It is futile to work for the negative end of peace unless we are committed to the positive ideal which it cloaks: Promoting the efficacy of human intercourse irrespective of class, racial, geographical and national limits. Any philosophy which should penetrate and particulate our present social practice would find at work the forces which unify human intercourse. An intelligent and courageous philosophy of practice would devise means by which the operation of these forces would be extended and assured in the future. An American philosophy of history must perforce be a philosophy for its future, a future in which freedom and fullness of human companionship is the aim, and intelligent cooperative experimentation the method.

Schools of To-Morrow

A test with books open. (Fairhope, Alabama.) *Frontispiece.*

Preface

There has been no attempt in this book to develop a complete theory of education nor yet review any "systems" or discuss the views of prominent educators. This is not a textbook of education, nor yet an exposition of a new method of school teaching, aimed to show the weary teacher or the discontented parent how education should be carried on. We have tried to show what actually happens when schools start out to put into practice, each in its own way, some of the theories that have been pointed to as the soundest and best ever since Plato, to be then laid politely away as precious portions of our "intellectual heritage." Certain views are well known to every teacher who has studied pedagogy, and portions of them form an accepted part of every theory of education. Yet when they are applied in a classroom the public in general and other teachers in particular cry out against that classroom as a place of fads and caprices; a place lacking in any far-reaching aim or guiding principle. We have hoped to suggest to the reader the practical meaning of some of the more widely recognized and accepted views of educational reformers by showing what happens when a teacher applies these views.

The schools we have used for purposes of illustration are all of them directed by sincere teachers trying earnestly to give their children the best they have by working out concretely what they consider the fundamental principles of education. More and more schools are growing up all over the country that are trying to work out definite educational ideas. It is the function of this book to point out how the applications arise from their theories and the direction that education in this country seems to be taking at the present time. We hope that through the description of classroom work we may help to make some theories living realities to the reader. On the other hand, we have dwelt on theoretical aspects in order to point out some of the needs of modern education and the way in which they are being met.

The schools that are used for illustration were chosen more or less at random; because we already knew of them or because they were conveniently located. They do not begin to represent all that is being done to-day to vitalize the school life of children. Schools with like traits may be found in every part of the country. Space has forced us to omit a very important movement—the reorganization of the rural school and the utilization of agriculture in education. But this movement shows the tendencies that mark the schools we have described; tendencies towards greater freedom and an identification of the child's school life with his environment and outlook; and, even more important, the recognition of the role education must play in a democracy. These tendencies seem truly symptoms of the times, and with a single exception proved to be the most marked characteristics of all the schools visited.

Without the very material help and interest of the teachers and principals of the schools visited this book would not have been possible. We thank them most sincerely for the unfailing courtesy they have shown in placing their time and the material of their classrooms at our disposal. Our thanks are especially due to Mrs. Johnson of Fairhope and to Miss Georgia Alexander of Indianapolis for information and suggestions. The visiting of the schools with one exception was done by Miss Dewey, who is also responsible for the descriptive chapters of the book.

J. D.

List of Illustrations

"We know nothing of childhood, and with our mistaken notions of it the further we go in education the more we go astray. The wisest writers devote themselves to what a man ought to know without asking what a child is capable of learning." These sentences are typical of the *Émile* of Rousseau. He insists that existing education is bad because parents and teachers are always thinking of the accomplishments of adults, and that all reform depends upon centering attention upon the powers and weaknesses of children. Rousseau said, as well as did, many foolish things. But his insistence that education be based upon the native capacities of those to be taught and upon the need of studying children in order to discover what these native powers are, sounded the key-note of all modern efforts for educational progress. It meant that education is not something to be forced upon children and youth from without, but is the growth of capacities with which human beings are endowed at birth. From this conception flow the various considerations which educational reformers since his day have most emphasized.

It calls attention, in the first place, to a fact which professional educators are always forgetting: What is learned in school is at the best only a small part of education, a relatively superficial part; and yet what is learned in school makes artificial distinctions in society and marks persons off from one another. Consequently we exaggerate school learning compared with what is gained in the ordinary course of living. We are, however, to correct this exaggeration, not by despising school learning, but by looking into that extensive and more efficient training given by the ordinary course of events for light upon the best ways of teaching within school walls. The first years of learning proceed rapidly and securely before children go to school, because that learning is so closely related with the motives that are furnished by their own powers and the needs that are dictated by their own conditions. Rousseau was almost the first to see that learning is a matter of necessity; it is a part of the process of self-preservation and of growth. If we want, then, to find out how education takes place most successfully, let us go to the experiences of children where learning is a necessity, and not to the practices of the schools where it is largely an adornment, a superfluity and even an unwelcome imposition.

But schools are always proceeding in a direction opposed to this principle. They take the accumulated learning of adults, material that is quite unrelated to the exigencies of growth, and try to force it upon children, instead of finding out what these children need as they go along.

A man must indeed know many things which seem useless to a child. Must the child learn, can he learn, all that the man must know? Try to teach a child what is of use to him as a child, and you will find that it takes all his time. Why urge him to the studies of an age he may never reach, to the neglect of those studies which meet his present needs? But, you ask, will it not be too late to learn what he ought to know when the time comes to use it? I cannot tell. But this I know; it is impossible to teach it sooner, for our real teachers are experience and emotion, and adult man will never learn what befits *him* except under his own conditions. A child knows he must become a man; all the ideas he may have as to man's estate are so many opportunities for his instruction, but he should remain in complete ignorance of those ideas that are beyond his grasp. My whole book is one continued argument in support of this fundamental principle of education.

Probably the greatest and commonest mistake that we all make is to forget that learning is a necessary incident of dealing with real situations. We even go so far as to assume that the mind is naturally averse to learning—which is like assuming that the digestive organs are averse to food and have either to be coaxed or bullied into having anything to do with it. Existing methods of instruction give plenty of evidence in support of a belief that minds are opposed to learning—to their own exercise. We fail to see that such aversion is in reality a condemnation of our methods; a sign that we are presenting material for which the mind in its existing state of growth has no need, or else presenting it in such ways as to cover up the real need. Let us go further. We say only an adult can really learn the things needed by the adult. Surely the adult is much more likely to learn the things befitting him when his hunger for learning has been kept alive continuously than after a premature diet of adult nutriment has deadened desire to know. We are of little faith and slow to believe. We are continually uneasy about the things we adults know, and are afraid the child will never learn them unless they are drilled into him by instruction before he has any intellectual or practical use for them. If we could really believe that attending to the needs of present growth would keep the child and teacher alike busy, and would also provide the best possible guarantee of the learning needed in the future, transformation of educational ideals might soon be accomplished, and other desirable changes would largely take care of themselves.

It is no wonder, then, that Rousseau preaches the necessity of being willing to lose time.

The greatest, the most important, the most useful rule of education is: Do not save time, but lose it. If the infant sprang at one bound from its mother's breast to the age of reason, the present education would be quite suitable; but its natural growth calls for quite a different training.

And he says, again,

The whole of our present method is cruel, for it consists in sacrificing the present to the remote and uncertain future. I hear from afar the shouts of the false wisdom that is ever dragging us on, counting the present as nothing, and breathlessly pursuing a future that flies as we pursue; a false wisdom that takes us away from the only place we ever have and never takes us anywhere else.

In short, if education is the proper growth of tendencies and powers, attention to the process of growing *in the particular form in which it goes on from day to day* is the only way of making secure the accomplishments of adult life. Maturity is the result of the slow growth of powers. Ripening takes time; it cannot be hurried without harm. The very meaning of childhood is that it is the time of growth, of developing. To despise the powers and needs of childhood, in

behalf of the attainments of adult life, is therefore suicidal.
Hence

Hold childhood in reverence, and do not be in any hurry to judge
it for good or ill. Give nature time to work before you take upon
yourself her business, lest you interfere with her dealings. You
assert that you know the value of time and are afraid to waste
it. You fail to perceive that it is a greater waste of time to use it
ill than to do nothing, and that a child ill taught is further from
excellence than a child who has learnt nothing at all. You are
afraid to see him spending his early years doing nothing. What!
Is it nothing to be happy, nothing to jump and run all day? He
will never be so busy again all his life long. . . . What would
you think of a man who refused to sleep lest he should waste
part of his life?

Reverence for childhood is identical with reverence for the
needs and opportunities of growth. Our tragic error is that
we are so anxious for the results of growth that we neglect
the process of growing.

Nature would have children be children before they are men. If
we try to invert this order we shall produce a forced fruit, immature and flavourless, fruit that rots before it can ripen. . . .
Childhood has its own ways of thinking, seeing, and feeling.

Physical growth is not identical with mental growth but
the two coincide in time, and normally the latter is impossible without the former. If we have reverence for childhood,
our first specific rule is to make sure of a healthy bodily development. Even apart from its intrinsic value as a source
of efficient action and of happiness, the proper development
of the mind directly depends upon the proper use of the
muscles and the senses. The organs of action and of reception are indispensable for getting into relation with the materials of knowledge. The child's first business is self-preservation. This does not mean barely keeping himself alive, but
preservation of himself as a growing, developing being.
Consequently, the activities of a child are not so aimless as
they seem to adults, but are the means by which he becomes
acquainted with his world and by which he also learns the
use and limits of his own powers. The constant restless activities of children seem senseless to grown-up people, simply because grown-up people have got used to the world

around them and hence do not feel the need of continual experimentation. But when they are irritated by the ceaseless movements of a child and try to reduce him to a state of quiescence, they both interfere with the child's happiness and health, and cut him off from his chief means of real knowledge. Many investigators have seen how a sound bodily state is a *negative* condition of normal mental development; but Rousseau anticipated our present psychology as to the extent in which the action of the organs of sense and movement is a positive cause of the unfolding of intelligence.

If you follow rules that are the opposite of the established practice and instead of taking your pupil far afield, wandering to distant places, far-off lands, remote centuries, the ends of the world and to heavens themselves, you keep him to himself, to his own concerns, he will be able to perceive, to remember, and to reason in nature's order of development. As the sentient infant grows into an active being, his discernment keeps pace with his increase in strength. Not till strength is developed beyond the needs of self-preservation is the faculty of speculation manifested, for this is the faculty of employing superfluous strength for other than necessary purposes. Hence, if you would cultivate your pupil's intelligence, *cultivate the strength it is meant to control.* Give his body constant exercise, make it strong and healthy in order to make him good and wise; let him work, let him do things; let him run and shout; let him be on the go. . . . It is a lamentable mistake to imagine that bodily activity hinders the working of the mind, as if the two kinds of activity ought not to advance hand in hand, and as if the one were not *intended to act as guide to the other.*

In the following passage Rousseau is more specific as to the way in which the physical activities which conduce to health and the growth of mind reenforce each other.

Physical exercise teaches us to use our strength, to perceive the relation between our own and neighboring bodies, to use natural tools which are within our reach and adapted to our senses. . . . At eighteen we are taught in our schools the use of the lever; every village boy of twelve knows how to use a lever better than the cleverest mechanician in the academy. The lessons the scholars give one another on the playground are worth a hundredfold more than what they learn in the classroom. Watch a cat when she first comes into a room. She goes from place to place; she sniffs about and examines everything. She is not still for a moment. It is the same with a child when he begins to walk and

(1) Nature would have children be children before they are men.

(2) Teach the child what is of use to him as a child. (Teachers College, N. Y. City.)

enters, as it were, the room of the world about him. Both use sight, and the child uses his hands as the cat her nose.

As man's first natural impulse is to measure himself upon his environment, to find in every object he sees the qualities that may concern himself, so his first study is a kind of experimental physics for his own preservation. He is turned away from this, and sent to speculative studies before he has found his own place in the world. While his delicate and flexible limbs and keen senses can adjust themselves to the bodies upon which they are intended to act is the time to exercise senses and limbs in their proper business—the time to learn the relation between themselves and things. Our first teachers in natural philosophy are our feet, hands, and eyes. To substitute books for them does not teach us to reason; it teaches us to use the reason of others rather than our own; it teaches us to believe much and to know little.

Before you can get an art, you must first get your tools; and if you are to make good use of your tools, they must be fashioned sufficiently strong to stand use. To learn to think, we must accordingly exercise our limbs, our senses, and our bodily organs, for these are the tools of intellect. To get the best use of these tools, the body that supplies us with these tools must be kept strong and healthy. Not only is it a mistake that true reason is developed apart from the body, but it is a good bodily constitution that makes the workings of the mind easy and correct.

The passage shows how far Rousseau was from considering bodily development as a complete end in itself. It also indicates how far ahead he was of the psychology of his own day in his conception of the relation of the senses to knowledge. The current idea (and one that prevails too much even in our own time) was that the senses were a sort of gateway and avenue through which impressions traveled and then built up knowledge pictures of the world. Rousseau saw that they are a part of the apparatus of action by which we adjust ourselves to our environment, and that instead of being passive receptacles they are directly connected with motor activities—with the use of hands and legs. In this respect he was more advanced than some of his successors who emphasized the importance of sense contact with objects, for the latter thought of the senses simply as purveyors of information about objects instead of instruments of the necessary adjustments of human beings to the world around them.

Consequently, while he makes much of the senses and suggests many games for cultivating them, he never makes the mere training of the senses an object on its own account. "It is not enough," he says,

to use the senses in order to train them; we must learn to judge by their means—we cannot really see, hear, or touch except as we have learned. A merely mechanical use of the senses may strengthen the body without improving the judgment. It is all very well to swim, run, jump, whip a top, throw stones. But we have eyes and ears as well as arms and legs, and these organs are necessary for learning the use of the rest. Do not, then, merely exercise strength, but exercise the senses as the powers by which strength is guided. Make the best use of every one of them, and check the results of one by another. Measure, count, weigh, compare. Do not use force till you have estimated the resistance; let estimation of the effect always precede application of the means. Get the child interested in avoiding superfluous and insufficient efforts. If you train him to calculate the consequences of what he does and then to correct the errors of his prevision by experience, the more he does, the wiser he will become.

One more contrast between teaching which guides natural growth and teaching which imposes adult accomplishments should be noticed. The latter method puts a premium upon accumulating information in the form of symbols. Quantity rather than quality of knowledge is emphasized; results that may be exhibited when asked for rather than personal attitude and method are demanded. Development emphasizes the need of intimate and extensive personal acquaintance with a small number of typical situations with a view to mastering the way of dealing with the problems of experience, not the piling up of information. As Rousseau points out, the facility with which children lend themselves to our false methods is a constant source of deception to us. We know—or fancy we know—what statements mean, and so when the child uses the proper form of words, we attribute the same understanding to him. "The apparent ease with which children learn is their ruin. We fail to see that this very ease proves that they are not learning. Their shining, polished brain merely reflects, as in a mirror, the things we show them." Rousseau describes in a phrase the defect of teaching *about* things instead of bringing to pass an acquaintance with the relations of the things themselves. "You think you are teaching him what the world is like; he is only learning the map." Extend the illustration from geography to the whole wide realm of knowledge, and you have the gist of much of our teaching from the elementary school through the college.

Rousseau has the opposite method in mind when he says, "Among the many short cuts to science we badly need one to teach us the art of learning with difficulty." Of course his idea is not to make things difficult for the sake of having them difficult, but to avoid the simulation of learning found in repeating the formulae of learning, and to substitute for it the slow and sure process of personal discovery. Text-books and lectures give the results of other men's discoveries, and thus seem to provide a short-cut to knowledge; but the outcome is just a meaningless reflecting back of symbols with no understanding of the facts themselves. The further result is mental confusion; the pupil loses his original mental sure-footedness; his sense of reality is undermined. "The first meaningless phrase, the first thing taken for granted on the authority of another without the pupil's seeing its meaning for himself, is the beginning of the ruin of judgment." And again: "What would you have him think about, when you do all the thinking for him?" (And we must not forget that the organized material of our texts and set lessons represents the thinking of others.) "You then complete the task of discrediting reason in his mind by making him use such reason as he has upon the things which seem of the least use to him."

If it was true in Rousseau's day that information, knowledge, as an end in itself, is an "unfathomable and shoreless ocean," it is much more certain that the increase of science since his day has made absurd the identification of education with the mere accumulation of knowledge. The frequent criticism of existing education on the ground that it gives a smattering and superficial impression of a large and miscellaneous number of subjects, is just. But the desired remedy will not be found in a return to mechanical and meagre teaching of the three R's, but rather in a surrender of our feverish desire to lay out the whole field of knowledge into various studies, in order to "cover the ground." We must substitute for this futile and harmful aim the better ideal of

To learn to think, we must exercise our limbs. (Francis Parker School, Chicago.)

dealing thoroughly with a small number of typical experiences in such a way as to master the tools of learning, and present situations that make pupils hungry to acquire additional knowledge. By the conventional method of teaching, the pupil learns maps instead of the world—the symbol instead of the fact. What the pupil really needs is not exact information about topography, but how to find out for himself. "See what a difference there is between the knowledge of your pupils and the ignorance of mine. They learn maps; he makes them." *To find out how to make knowledge when it is needed* is the true end of the acquisition of information in school, not the information itself.

2. AN EXPERIMENT IN EDUCATION AS NATURAL DEVELOPMENT

Rousseau's teaching that education is a process of natural growth has influenced most theorizing upon education since his time. It has influenced the practical details of school work to a less degree. Occasionally, however, experimenters have based their plans upon his principles. Among these experiments is one conducted by Mrs. Johnson at Fairhope, Alabama. To this spot during the past few years students and experts have made pilgrimages, and the influence of Mrs. Johnson's model has led to the starting of similar schools in different parts of the United States. Mrs. Johnson carries on a summer course for training teachers by giving a working object lesson in her ideas at Greenwich, Connecticut, where a school for children has been conducted as a model.

Her main underlying principle is Rousseau's central idea; namely: The child is best prepared for life as an adult by experiencing in childhood what has meaning to him as a child; and, further, the child has a right to enjoy his childhood. Because he is a growing animal who must develop so as to live successfully in the grown-up world, nothing should be done to interfere with growth, and everything should be done to further the full and free development of his body and his mind. These two developments go on together; they are inseparable processes and must both be constantly borne in mind as of equal importance.

Mrs. Johnson criticizes the conventional school of today. She says it is arranged to make things easy for the teacher who wishes quick and tangible results; that it disregards the full development of the pupils. It is arranged on the fatal plan of a hothouse, forcing to a sterile show, rather than fostering all-around growth. It does not foster an individuality capable of an enduring resistance and of creative activities. It disregards the *present* needs of the child; the fact that he is living a full life each year and hour, not waiting to live in some period defined by his elders, when school is a thing of the past. The distaste of children for school is a natural and necessary result of such mistakes as these. Nature has not adapted the young animal to the narrow desk, the crowded curriculum, the silent absorption of complicated facts. His very life and growth depend upon motion, yet the school forces him into a cramped position for hours at a time, so that the teacher may be sure he is listening or studying books. Short periods of exercise are allowed as a bribe to keep him quiet the rest of the time, but these relaxations do not compensate for the efforts which he must make. The child is eager to move both mentally and physically. Just as the physical growth must progress together with the mental, so it is in the separate acts of a child. His bodily movements and his mental awakening are mutually dependent upon each other.

It is not enough to state this principle without carrying its proof into practice, says Mrs. Johnson. The child with the well-nourished, active body is the child who is most anxious to do and to know things. The need of activity must be met in the exercise of the school, hour by hour; the child must be allowed to move about both in work and in play, to imitate and to discover for himself. The world of objects around him is an unexplored hemisphere to the child even at the age of six years, a world constantly enlarging to his small vision as his activities carry him further and further in his investigations, a world by no means so commonplace to him as to the adult. Therefore, let the child, while his muscles are soft and his mind susceptible, look for himself at the world of things both natural and artificial, which is for him the source of knowledge.

Instead of providing this chance for growth and discovery, the ordinary school impresses the little one into a narrow area, into a melancholy silence, into a forced attitude of mind and body, till his curiosity is dulled into surprise at the strange things happening to him. Very soon his body is tired of his task and he begins to find ways of evading his teacher, to look about him for an escape from his little prison. This means that he becomes restless and impatient, in the language of the school, that he loses interest in the small tasks set for him and consequently in that new world so alluring a little while ago. The disease of indifference has attacked his sensitive soul, before he is fairly started on the road to knowledge.

The reason for having a school where children work together is that the child must learn to work with others. Granting this, Mrs. Johnson has tried to find a plan giving the utmost liberty of individual development. Because the young child is unfitted by reason of his soft muscles and his immature senses to the hard task of settling down to fine work on the details of things, he should not begin school life by learning to read and write, nor by learning to handle small playthings or tools. He must continue the natural course he began at home of running from one interesting object to another, of inquiring into the meaning of these objects, and above all of tracing the relation between the different objects. All this must be done in a large way so that he gets the names and bearings of the obvious facts as they appear in their order. Thus the obscure and difficult facts come to light one after another without being forced upon the child's attention by the teacher. One discovery leads to another, and the interest of pursuit leads the child of his own accord into investigations that often amount to severe intellectual discipline.

Following this path of natural growth, the child is led into reading, writing, arithmetic, geography, etc., by his own desire to know. We must wait for the desire of the child, for the consciousness of need, says Mrs. Johnson; then we must promptly supply the means to satisfy the child's desire. Therefore, the age of learning to read is put off until the child is well grounded in his experience and knowledge of the larger relations of things. Mrs. Johnson goes so far as to prevent children from learning to read at too early an age. At eight or nine years, she thinks they are keen to explore books just as they have previously explored things. By this time they recognize the need and use of the information contained in books; they have found out they can get this information in no other way. Hence, the actual learning to read is hardly a problem; children teach themselves. Under the stimulus of interest in arriving at the knowledge of some particular subject, they overcome the mechanical difficulty of reading with ease and rapidity. Reading is not to them an isolated exercise; it is a means of acquiring a much-desired object. Like climbing the pantry shelves, its difficulties and dangers are lost sight of in the absorbing desire to satisfy the mental appetite.

Each of the subjects of the curriculum should be given to the child to meet a demand on his part for a greater knowledge of relations than he can get from studying objects. Arithmetic and abstract notions represented by figures are meaningless to the child of six, but numbers as a part of the things he is playing with or using every day are so full of meaning that he soon finds he cannot get along without a knowledge of them.

Mrs. Johnson is trying an experiment under conditions which hold in public schools, and she believes that her methods are feasible for any public-school system. She charges practically no tuition, and any child is welcome. She calls her methods of education "organic" because they follow the natural growth of the pupil. The school aims to provide for the child the occupations and activities necessary at each stage of development for his unfolding at that stage. Therefore, she insists that general development instead of the amount of information acquired, shall control the classification of the pupils. Division into groups is made where it is found that the children naturally divide themselves. These groups are called "Life Classes" instead of grades. The first life class ends between the eighth and ninth years; the second between the eleventh and twelfth, and since an even more marked change of interests and tastes occurs at the period of adolescence, there are distinct high-school classes. The work within the group is then arranged to give the pupils the experiences which are needed at that age for the development of their bodies, minds, and spirits.

Doing forced tasks, assignment of lessons to study, and ordinary examinations have no share in the Fairhope curriculum. Hence, the children do not acquire that dislike of learning and mistrust of what a teacher or text-book says, which are unfortunately so common among scholars in the ordinary school. They exercise their instincts to learn naturally, without that self-consciousness which comes from having been forced to keep their minds on examinations and promotions.

Bright and intelligent children often acquire a distaste for the schoolroom and what comes out of it, which they not only never wholly outgrow but which is a real handicap to them as they grow up, often preventing them from taking their college work seriously, and making them suspicious of all ideas not actually deduced from their own experience outside the classroom. Perhaps they grow so docile they acquiesce in all authoritative statements whatsoever, and lose their sense of reality. We tell our children that books are the storehouses of the world, and that they contain the heritage of the past without which we would be savages; then we teach them so that they hate books of information and discount what a teacher tells them. Incompetency is general not because people are not instructed enough as children, but because they cannot and do not make any use of what they learn. The extent to which this is due to an early mistrust of school and the learning associated with it cannot be overstated.

The students at Fairhope will never have this handicap to contend with. They are uniformly happy in school, and enthusiastically proclaim their "love" for it. Not only is the work interesting to the group as a whole, but no individual child is forced to a task that does not appeal; each pupil may do as he pleases as long as he does not interfere with any one else. The children are not freed, however, from all discipline. They must keep at work while they are in school, and learn not to bother their neighbors, as well as to help them when necessary. Caprice or laziness does not excuse a child from following a healthy or useful régime.

Mrs. Johnson feels that children in their early years are neither moral nor immoral, but simply unmoral; their sense of right and wrong has not yet begun to develop. Therefore, they should be allowed as much freedom as possible; prohibitions and commands, the result of which either upon themselves or their companions they cannot understand, are bound to be meaningless; their tendency is to make the child secretive and deceitful. Give a child plenty of healthy activity. When he must be disciplined, do not appeal to a sense which he has not got, but show him by a little pain if necessary what his naughty act meant to his playmate. If he is to share in fun and good things with his family and friends, he must behave so that they will want his company. This is a motive which a young child can understand, for he knows when his friends are agreeable or disagreeable to him. There is less in such a scheme of discipline that impels the child to shirk or conceal, to lie or to become too conscious of his acts, than in a discipline based on moral grounds, which seems to the child to be a mere excuse for forcing him to do something simply because some grown person wants it done.

Lack of self-consciousness is a positive gain on the side of happiness. Mrs. Johnson's scheme of discipline contributes toward that love of school and work which all teaching aims to establish. When work is interesting, it is not necessary to hamper children in their performance of it by meaningless restrictions and petty prohibitions. When children work willingly they come to associate learning with the doing of what is congenial. This is undoubtedly of positive moral value. It helps develop a confident, cheerful attitude toward work; an ability to face a task without dislike or repulsion, which is of more real value in character building than doing hard, distasteful tasks, or forcing attention and obedience.

The division into age groups or "life classes" takes away that emphasis upon the pupils' failures and shortcomings which is bound to be more or less evident where pupils are graded according to their proficiency in books. The child who is slow mentally is not made to feel that he is disgraced. Attention is not called to him and he is not prodded, scolded, or "flunked." Unaware of his own weaknesses, he retains the moral support of confidence in himself; and his handwork and physical accomplishments frequently give him prestige among his fellows. Mrs. Johnson believes that the recitations and examination of the ordinary schoolroom are merely devices to make the work easier for the teacher; while the consciousness of what he does or does not "know," resulting from marks and grades, is harmful to the child just as an emphasis of his failures is harmful.

Especially marked is the contrast of the classroom exercises at Fairhope with recitations where, sitting still with their books closed, the children are subject to a fire of questions from the teacher to find out how much they remember of a lesson they are supposed to have "studied" alone. To quote again from Rousseau:

He (the teacher) makes a point of showing that no time has been wasted; he provides his pupils with goods that can be readily displayed in the shop windows, accomplishments which can be shown off at will. . . . If the child is to be examined, he is set to display his wares; he spreads them out; satisfies those who behold them, packs up his bundle, and goes his way. Too many questions are tedious and revolting to most of us and especially to children. After a few minutes their attention flags; they cease to listen to your everlasting questions and they answer at random.

At Fairhope the children do the work, and the teacher is there to help them to know, not to have them give back what they have memorized. Tests are often conducted with books open, since they are not to show the teacher what the child can remember, but rather to discover his progress in ability to use books. Lessons are not assigned, but the books are open in the hands of the pupils and with the teacher they discuss the text, getting out of it all the joy and information possible. This stimulates a real love of books, so that these children who have never been assigned a lesson to study, voluntarily study the text after the class work. They are not tempted to cheat, for they are not put in the position of having to show off.

The result of this system of discipline and study over and above satisfactory progress in the "three R's," is freedom from self-consciousness on the mental and moral side; the ability of a child to put all his native initiative and enthusiasm into his work; the power to indulge his natural desire to learn; thus preserving joy in life and a confidence in himself which liberates all his energies for his work. He likes school and forgets that he is "learning"; for learning comes unconsciously as a by-product of experiences which he recognizes as worth while on their own account.

The following activities have been worked out at Fair-

(1) An hour a day spent in the "Gym."

(2) The Gully is a favorite text-book. (Fairhope, Ala.)

hope as a substitute for the usual curriculum: physical exercise, nature study, music, handwork, field geography, story telling, sense culture, fundamental conceptions of number, dramatizations, and games. In the second class map drawing and descriptive geography are added, for reading is acquired, and the number work is modified by the knowledge of figures. Each lesson is planned as a concrete experience with a definite end in view, appealing to the child as desirable. As would be expected from the emphasis put upon following the development of the child, physical exercise plays an important part in the day's work. It comes every day, during the regular school hours and usually in the first part of the morning while the children are fresh and energetic. For an hour the school is outdoors in a field the children call "the gym." Bars, horses, etc., are scattered about, and there is some one there to help them try new things and see that the work is well balanced, but formal gymnastics in the accepted meaning of the term do not exist. Mrs. Johnson believes that the distaste of children is sufficient reason for doing away with them, and that, since the growing child is constantly seeking of his own accord opportunities to stretch and exercise his muscles, all the school needs to do is to supply the opportunity, seeing to it that this is not indulged to the point of harming the child. The children fall naturally into groups; those who want to swing on the bars and rings, those who want to climb, to jump, or run, or throw, etc. Running usually takes the form of races; a tree is used as a target in the stone throwing contests. The children themselves have invented games to use on the apparatus, and the hour in the "gym" is one of the busiest in the day. It leaves the children eager and stimulated for their mental work, since it has meant no overworking of one set of muscles, no dull repetition of meaningless movements at some one else's command. Besides this regular time for exercise, the children may study outdoors, and many of the classes are conducted in the open air. Indoors there are games, handwork, and dramatizations, all of which contribute to the physical well-being of the children. There are no cramping desks, the pupil may sit where or how he pleases, or even move from place to place if he does not disturb his fellows. The classes go on in a room in which two groups, each of fifteen or more children, are working, and the necessary quiet and order exist.

Nature study and field geography are conducted almost entirely out of doors. The children go into the fields and woods and look at the trees and flowers, ask questions about them, examine the differences in bark, leaves, and flowers, tell each other what they think, and use their books to answer questions that the trees and plants have suggested to them. They learn the meaning of the words pistils, stamens, and petals with flowers they have gathered, or watch a bee carrying pollen from plant to plant. Individual pupils are encouraged to tell the class what they may have learned at home, to bring flowers from their gardens, or to tell of things they have seen. The class visit a neighboring truck farm, recognize as many vegetables as they can, and learn the names and characteristics of the new ones. When they are back in the schoolroom those that can write make a list of all the vegetables they can remember, thus combining with their nature lesson a lesson in writing. There is a garden in the school grounds where the pupils learn to plow, rake, and plant, watch their seeds come up and grow and flower. In a little plot of ground that is their own, they observe all the phases in the cycle of plant life, and besides get the benefits of the moral training that comes from carrying through a piece of work that lasts several months and demands constant thought and care. This sort of work plays a large part in the curriculum of the younger children, for it seems to belong particularly to their world; to the world of definite concrete objects which they see about them every day, which they can handle and play with, and which consequently arouse their curiosity.

The field geography is conducted in much the same way. Even the very young children acquire a good idea of the different sorts of rock formations, of the action of the wind and rain, of river currents, by direct observation; if textbooks are used they come afterwards, to explain or amplify something the pupils have seen. The soil about the school is clay and after a rain the smallest stream furnishes excellent examples of the ways of rivers, erosions, watersheds, floods, or changing currents, while an explanation of tides or the

Gulf Stream is made vital by a little trip to the Bay. A gully near the school building not only furnishes a splendid place for play but serves as a text-book in mountain ranges, valleys, and soil and rock formation. All this serves as an excellent foundation and illustration for the descriptive geography which comes later. The more advanced geography is principally commercial geography; and with the scientific background that the pupils have already obtained, the real significance of the relations between climates and crops, industries, exports and imports, and social conditions is much more likely to be understood.

The value of handwork is strongly emphasized at Fairhope, consistently with the emphasis put on physical growth. The little child must go on learning to coordinate with more and more skill his muscular movements if his body is to be developed to the highest standards of health and efficiency, and nothing contributes to this better than the controlled and rather delicate motions necessary for making things with the hands. The fact that he is making things gives just the stimulus the child needs to enable him to keep on at the task, to repeat over and over the same efforts of mind, hand, and eye, to give him real control of himself in the process. The benefits of handwork on the utilitarian side are just as great. The child learns how to use the ordinary tools of life, the scissors, knife, needle, plane, and saw, and gets an appreciation of the artists' tools, paint and clays, which lasts the rest of his life. If he is a child with initiative and inventiveness he finds a natural and pleasant outlet for his energies. If he is dreamy or unpractical, he learns a respect for manual work, and gains something toward becoming a well-rounded human being. Boys and girls alike do cooking and carpentry work, for the object of the work is not to train them for any trade or profession, but to train them to be capable, happy members of society. Painting or clay modeling play quite as large a role, even with the little ones, as carpentry or sewing, providing they serve a purpose or are sufficiently connected with other work to hold the pupil's interest. A sense of the beautiful is not consciously present in small children and must be developed through their handling of every-day objects if it is to become a real force in their lives. Therefore "art" is taught as part of the handwork, the story telling, the dramatization, or the nature study. The youngest children in clay modeling, painting, weaving paper mats, making paper or wooden toys, etc., are asked as much as possible to suggest things they want to make. With the acquisition of skill, they go on making more and more difficult objects; pupils of nine or ten make raffia baskets, boats, and dolls' furniture.

The story telling and dramatization are very closely connected and (up to the age of about ten) take the place of the usual bookwork. Stories of literary value, suited in subject-matter to the age of the pupils, are told or read to them, and they in turn are asked to tell stories they have heard outside of school. After the ninth or tenth year, when the children have learned to read, they read stories from books, either to themselves or aloud, and then the whole class discuss them. The Greek myths, the *Iliad*, and the *Odyssey* are favorites at this age, and very frequently without directions from the teacher, a class will act out a whole story, such as the Fall of Troy, or any tale that has appealed especially to their dramatic imagination. The school believes that this is the true way for young people to approach literature, if they are to learn to love and appreciate it, not simply to study the text for strange words and figures of speech. The pupils are not allowed to use books until the eighth or ninth year, and by this time they have realized so keenly their need, they beg for help in learning. The long, tiresome drill necessary for six-year-old children is eliminated. Each child is anxious to read some particular book, so there is little or no need to trap his attention, or to insist on an endless repetition. Mrs. Johnson believes also that it is better for the natural physical and mental development of the child, if learning to write and figure is put off as late as possible. Then pupils approach it with a consciousness of their real need for it, of the help it will be to them in their daily life. Their background of knowledge of things and skill acquired through handwork renders the actual processes of learning comparatively simple. Mrs. Johnson is convinced that a child who does not learn to read and write in her school until he is ten years old, is as well read at fourteen, and writes and spells as well as a child of fourteen in a school where the usual curriculum is followed.

The fundamental conception of number is taught orally.

The smallest children begin by counting one another or the things about them. Then perhaps at the blackboard they will divide a line in half, then into three parts, then quarters. By means of objects or lines on the blackboard they next begin to add, to subtract, to take three-fourths, even to divide. The oral drill in this kind of work is constant, and the children become thoroughly familiar with the fundamental processes of arithmetic, before they can write a number or know the meaning of the addition or multiplication sign. Then when the time comes, at about the age of nine, to learn to write numbers, the drill is repeated by using the conventional signs instead of lines or objects. The school has found that this method does away with the usual struggles, especially in learning fractions and their handling. Long division and the other complicated processes are taught after the pupils can write well and easily, and no emphasis is put on formal analysis until repeated drill has made the children fairly familiar with, and proficient in, the process. Games and contests of all sorts invented by the individual teacher are used to make this drill interesting to the pupils.

Sense culture means the specific training of the child's body and muscles to respond accurately to the desire to perform definite muscular or other sense acts; or more technically it means motor-sensory coordination. Besides the general training coming from handwork and physical exercise, special games are arranged to exercise the different senses. The youngest class does relatively most of this sense gymnastic. The whole class sits motionless and in absolute silence; some child tiptoes from his seat to another part of the room, and then with his eyes shut every other child tries to tell where he is; or one child says something and the others try to guess who it was, by the voice. To train the sense of touch, a blindfolded child is given some ordinary objects, and by touching them tries to recognize them. One of the favorite games of the whole school was invented to train muscular accuracy. Children of different ages, divided into groups, throw stones at a large tree in the yard. This game has all the zest of competition, while teaching the eye and hand to work together, and exercising the whole body. The unusual physical control of the Fairhope pupils is seen best in the carpenter shop, where even the youngest children work and handle full-sized tools, hammers, saws, and planes and do not hurt themselves. There is a foot power jig-saw in the shop and it is an instructive sight to see a child of seven, too small to work the pedal, holding his piece of wood, turning and shaping it in the saw without hurting himself.

The Fairhope pupils compare favorably with pupils in the ordinary public schools. When for any reason they make a change, they have always been able to work with other children of their age without extra effort; they are apt to be stronger physically and are much more capable with their hands, while they have a real love of books and study that makes them equally strong on the purely cultural side of their work. The organic curriculum has been worked out in detail and in use longest for the younger children, but Mrs. Johnson is convinced the principle of her work will apply equally well to high-school pupils and is beginning an experiment with high-school children. Under her direction the school has proved a decided success. Time and larger opportunities will undoubtedly correct the weak spots and discrepancies that are bound to appear while any school is in the experimental stage. The school has provided conditions for wholesome, natural growth in small enough groups for the teacher (as a leader rather than an instructor) to become acquainted with the weaknesses of each child individually and then to adapt the work to the individual needs. It has demonstrated that it is possible for children to lead the same natural lives in school that they lead in good homes outside of school hours; to progress bodily, mentally, and morally in school without factitious pressure, rewards, examinations, grades, or promotions, while they acquire sufficient control of the conventional tools of learning and of study of books—reading, writing, and figuring—to be able to use them independently.

The Elementary School of the University of Missouri, at Columbia, under the direction of Prof. J. L. Meriam, has much in common with Mrs. Johnson's school at Fairhope. In its fundamental idea, that education shall follow the natural development of the child, it is identical, but its actual organization and operation are sufficiently different to make a description of it suggestive. In common with most educational reformers, Professor Meriam believes the schools of the past have been too much concerned with teaching children adult facts. In attempting to systematize and standardize, the curriculum has ignored the needs of the individual child. He believes that the work and play of the school should be children's work and play; that the children should enjoy school. The life there should be like, only better than, the life of the children outside the school; better because they are helped to know how to play and work correctly and to do it with other children.

Do children remember how they learned to talk? No, but their parents remember for them. Yet most of us, both children and adults, remember how we struggled in learning to read and write at school. We learned to talk simply by talking when we were in need or had something to say. We learned to say, "Please, Mamma, give me a drink," when we wanted a drink. We did not practice on such words at nine o'clock each morning. The pupils in the University Elementary School learn to read, to write, to draw, and to do other things, just when they need to do so. The pupils do in this school about what they would do at home, but they learn to do it better. They work and play. At home they are very active most of the time doing many things; and so they are in this school.

What would these children naturally be doing if there were no school? On the answer to this question Professor Meriam has based his curriculum, which contains but one subject that appears on the ordinary program; namely, handwork. They would, he says, be playing outdoors, exercising their bodies by running, jumping, or throwing; they would be talking together in groups, discussing what they had seen or heard; they would be making things to use in their play: boats, bean bags, dolls, hammocks, or dresses; if they live in the country they would be watching animals or plants, making a garden or trying to fish. Every one recognizes that the child develops quite as much through such activities as through what he learns in school, and that what he learns out of school is much more apt to become a part of his working knowledge, because it is entirely pleasurable and he recognizes the immediate use of it. Again, these occupations are all closely connected with the business of living; and we send our children to school to learn this. What, then, could be more natural than making the school's curriculum of such material? This is what Professor Meriam does. The day is divided into four periods, which are devoted to the following elements: play, stories, observation, and handwork. For the younger children the work is drawn almost entirely from the community in which they live; they spend their time finding out more about the things they are already familiar with. As they grow older their interest naturally reaches out to remoter things and to the processes and reasons back of things; and they begin to study history, geography, and science.

The time of the first three grades is divided in this way: From 9 to 10:30, observation; 10:30 to 11, physical exercises; from 11 to 12, play; 1:30 to 3, stories; and 3 to 4, handwork.

The observation period is devoted to the study of one topic, and this topic may take only a single morning or it may take several weeks. While there is a general plan for the year's work, if the children bring up anything which seems of importance to them and which fits in, the program is laid aside and the teacher helps the pupils in their study of their own problem. This might be true of any of the studies of the day; the program is flexible, the school aims to meet the individual needs of the child and the group. The observation periods of the first three grades are devoted to a study of flowers, trees, and fruits; birds and animals, of the weather and the changing seasons, of holidays, of the

Games often require muscular skill, reading, writing, and arithmetic.

town grocery store, or the neighborhood dwellings, and the clothing that the children see for sale in the stores. The pupils learn to read and write and figure only as they feel the need of it to enlarge their work. The nature work is taught as much as possible out of doors; the children take walks with the teacher and talk about the trees, plants, and animals they meet on their way; they gather tadpoles and fish for the school aquarium and pick out a tree to watch and keep a record of for the whole year. Their study of the weather also lasts through the whole year; they watch the changing seasons, what things look like in the fall and what happens as winter begins, what the plants and animals do in winter, etc. In this way they watch the whole cycle of the year, and learn unconsciously the relation between their own climate and the vegetation and animal life about them.

The study of their own food, shelter, and clothing is concentrated into a consecutive period, and as interest and time dictate it is added to by a study of some phases of local life that are not concerned with the actual necessities of life. They learn about their neighbors' recreations and pleasures by studying the jewelry store and the circus, or the community interests of their parents by studying the local fire department and post-office.

The method of study is the same for all work. First, with help from the teacher the children tell all they know about the subject they are beginning to study; if it is food, each child has an opportunity to say anything he can think of about it; what his own family eats, where the food comes from, how it is taken care of, what he has noticed in the grocery stores, etc. Then the whole class with the teacher make a visit to the grocery store, spend perhaps all the morning there, each child trying to see how much he can find out for himself. Before they start the teacher has called their attention to the fact that the things are sold by the quart, etc., for the subject of weights and measures seems to be of absorbing interest to the children when approached from this side. Some first grade children have proved to be remarkably keen detectives in noticing the grocer's innumerable devices for making quantities look greater than they are. The pupils are also encouraged to note and compare prices, and to bring food budgets from home whenever their parents are willing. When they return to their classroom they again discuss what they have seen, and those who can write make a list with prices of all the articles which they can remember, or write an account of their visit, which is dictated by the teacher from the oral accounts the children themselves have given of it.

The pupils who cannot read will draw a picture of the grocery store or perhaps have a reading lesson in the catalogue the grocer has given them. Later they will study the way the grocer delivers his goods to his patrons, and in a very general way where the things come from. They will bring grocers' bills from home, compare them, add them up, and discuss the question of economical and nutritious food. Perhaps they will do the same thing with the milk and bakery business, before moving on to the question of the houses in the neighborhood. This and the clothing and recreation of the town will be studied in the same way. Later the class will visit the fire department and the post-office and find out what each is for and how they are conducted. This and the study of local amusements usually come in the third grade. The opportunity for the constant use of reading, writing, and arithmetic, and for drill in the correct use of spoken English, is obvious. Professor Meriam is insistent upon the fact that this study of the community in which the child lives is made for the educational value of the work itself to the pupil, never as a mere cloak for the teaching of "the three R's," which must be done only as it contributes directly to the work the children are doing.

The period devoted to games by the first three grades is of the same educational value. The children are exercising their bodies, learning to control them and to make skillful motions aimed at some immediate result. Much variety and liberty is allowed in this work, and the teacher is only an observer. Most of the games the children play are competitive, for they have found that the element of skill and chance is what the pupils need to make them work hard at the games. Bean bags and nine pins are favorites; any game, in fact, where they can keep score; the teacher acts as scorekeeper for the little children, and when the game is over they copy the score in a folder to refer to and see how they progress. The better they play, the more they enjoy the game; so they watch the best player, studying how he moves and stands, and make drawings. The teacher also writes on the board some of the things the pupils say as they play, and at the end of the game they find a reading lesson which they have made themselves and which gives an account of their game; in copying this into their folders they have a writing lesson. The children are allowed to talk and laugh as much as they please while they are playing, and this is an English lesson. Great variety is introduced into the games so as to encourage the pupils to talk freely, and added stimulus is given by using interesting things to play with, bright colored balls, dolls, and gaily painted "roly-polys." The new words and phrases the children use are written down in the daily account of the game, and in this way their vocabulary is enlarged in a natural way.

The hour devoted to stories is no more a reading and writing lesson than all the rest of the day's work. Children immensely enjoy good stories, therefore they ought to be given plenty of opportunity to become acquainted with them. During this period, the teacher and the children tell stories to each other; not stories they have studied from their primers, but stories that they already know, that they have listened to, or read because they enjoyed them. Every child likes to be listened to, and they soon discover they must tell their story well or they will get no audience. Some stories they tell by acting them out, others by drawing. Soon they want to learn a new group of stories, and then, quite naturally, they go to the school library, pick out a story book and read. It has been found that the first grade pupils read from twelve to thirty books during the year; the second grade pupils from twenty-five to fifty. In this way they learn to read, to read good books—for there is nothing else in the library—and to read them well, for they always have the desire to find a story to tell to their class, or one that they can act. Appreciation of good literature begins very early in this way, or rather, it is never lost. Very small children always enjoy most the best stories—Mother Goose, Hans Andersen, or Kipling's *Just So Stories*. The dislike of books gained in school turns children from literature to trash. But if children are allowed and encouraged to hear, and read, and act out these stories in school just as they would at home —that is, for the sake of the fun there is in it—they will keep their good taste and enjoyment of good books. Songs, says Professor Meriam, are another sort of story, and little children sing for the fun of it, for the story of the song; so the singing at this school is part of the story work, and the children work and learn to sing better, in order to increase their enjoyment.

Children are always clamoring to "make something." Professor Meriam takes this fact as sufficient grounds for making handwork a regular part of the curriculum and having it occupy an hour a day, a period which usually seems so short to the pupils that they take their work home. The youngest children, boys and girls alike, go into the carpenter shop and learn to handle tools and to make things: furniture for their dolls, a boat, or some present to take home. Weaving and sewing interest both boys and girls alike and give scope to the young child for beauty and utility, so they do a lot of it. The youngest begin usually with dolls' hammocks; then they learn to do coarse cross-stitching and crocheting. An entire class, especially among the youngest children, usually make the same thing at the same time, but they may suggest what they want to make, and the older children are allowed a great deal of liberty. The work naturally increases in variety and complexity as the pupils grow older, and as they acquire skill in the handling of tools. Some of the fifth and sixth grade boys have made excellent pieces of furniture which are in constant use in the school. The handwork furnishes another opportunity for drawing and color work, in the making of drawings for patterns.

With the fourth grade there is a marked shift in the work, due to the widening interests that are coming to the child. The day is divided then into three periods, which are devoted to industries, stories, and handwork. Organized games no longer appeal to the pupils; they want their play outdoors, or in the freedom of a big gymnasium, where they can play rougher, noisier games, and they are big enough to keep their own scores in their heads. The "industries" period takes the place of the "observation" of the younger children, and continues the same sort of work. The child has learned the meaning of the immediate objects he sees about him, their relation to himself and his friends, and he is ready to go on and enlarge this knowledge so as to take in the things he cannot see, processes and reasons, and relations that embrace the whole community, or more communities, and finally the whole world.

In the same way that the younger children study their immediate environment, the fourth grade studies the industries that go on in their own neighborhood: the shoe factory, the flour mill, the work in the wheat and corn fields. They go on excursions to the factory and farm, and their work in the classroom is based on what they see on their trips. Their writing and composition are the stories of their trips, which they write; their reading, the books that tell about farming or shoemaking; their arithmetic the practical problems they find the farmer or foreman doing; all done so that it will contribute to the pupils' understanding of the industry he is studying. Geography too comes from these trips. It answers the questions: Why do they grow wheat? Where will it grow best in the neighborhood and why? etc. This school happens to be situated in a small town where the industries are chiefly agricultural, but obviously such a plan could easily be adapted to any community by substituting the industries that are found in the immediate neighborhood.

In the fifth and sixth years the study of industries is continued, but the scope is extended to include the principal industries of the world. Here, of course, pupils must learn to substitute more and more the printed page for their former excursions. This includes drill in reading, writing, and mathematics, related to earlier studies, and also more and more geography. The use of the library becomes of great importance, for the pupils are not given one text-book from which they study and recite. Work in geography begins with this question: What becomes of the things made in this town, which we do not use up? The next step is: Where else are these same things made, and are they made in the same way? What else is made in that place and how is it done?

Then, where and how are the things made that we get from elsewhere? No one text-book could suffice for this work, and if it did it would contradict the idea of the school that the children should learn by investigation. They must find for themselves from among the books in the library the ones that tell about the particular industry they are studying. Every child does not read the same book, and as far as possible each pupil makes some contribution to the discussion. Just as in the lower grades, the older pupils all make folders where they keep their descriptions of the industries and illustrations of machines and processes.

In the seventh and highest grade in the school, the study of industries is continued as history; that is, the history of the industries connected with clothing, feeding, and housing is taken up. The pupils study the history of shelter from the first beginnings with a cave or a brush thicket, through the tents of the wandering tribes and the Greek and Roman house, to the steel skyscraper of to-day. They study the history of agriculture and learn to understand the development of the steam reaper and thresher from the wooden stick of the savage. The study of the industries in these four higher grades includes a study of the institutions of government. The fourth grade studies the local post-office, in the fifth and sixth they study the mail system of the United States, and then how letters are carried to all parts of the world. The seventh grade studies the history of some of these institutions. Part of their time during the past year was devoted to finding out how the different peoples of the world have fought their battles and organized their armies, first by means of reading and then by discussing what they had read. Each pupil kept a record of this work, writing a short paper on the army of each country he studied and illustrating it as he cared to.

The story period of the four highest grades continues the work begun in the lower grades. Music and art become more and more concentrated into it. The children continue reading and discussing what they have read. Each pupil keeps a record of the books he reads with a short account of the story and reasons why he liked it, and these records are kept on a shelf in the library where any other pupil can consult them for help in his choice of books. Even in high school, Professor Meriam does not believe in teaching composition for its own sake, nor literature by the usual method of analysis. All the work of the school is a constant drill in English, and by helping the pupils to use and write good English during every school hour, more is accomplished than by concentrating the work into one hour of formal drill.

The teaching of French and German is also considered part of story work. It is a study the pupils take for the pleasure they get from talking and reading another language; for the sake of the literature they will be able to read. For this reason it finds its place in the curriculum among the things that are purely cultural: for recreation and pleasure. The studies that come under the title of "stories" are the only ones where homework is given. The children come to school to do their work, and it is not fair to ask them to do this same work at home as well. They should look forward to school as a pleasure, if they are to get the utmost benefit out of it, but if the doing of set tasks becomes associated with school work, the pupil's interest in his work in school is bound to diminish. If, however, some of the school work is regarded as appropriate to leisure and recreation, it is natural that the children should keep on with it out of school hours, in their homes.

The school has been working with this program for eight years, and has about 120 pupils. The school building has few rooms and these are connected with large folding doors. At least two and usually three grades work in the same room, and the pupils are allowed freedom to move about and talk to each other as long as they do not disturb their classmates. One teacher takes charge of an entire room, about thirty-five children, divided into several groups, each doing a different thing. Individual teachers in some of the neighboring country public schools have also followed the program through one grade and have found that the pupils were all ready for promotion at the end of the year and that they did their work in the next grade with as much ease as if they had followed the usual formal drill. Records are being kept of the graduates of the elementary school. Most of them go into the high school of the university, where there is

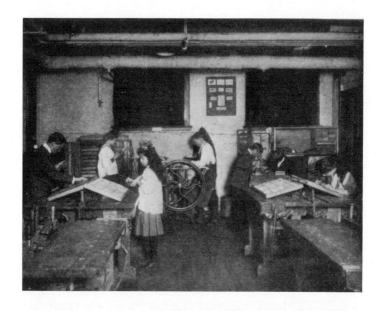

(1) Printing teaches English. (Francis Parker School, Chicago.)

(2) The basis of the year's work. (Indianapolis.)

every opportunity to watch them closely. They find no unusual difficulty in keeping up with the regular college preparatory work, and their marks and the age at which they enter college indicate that their elementary training has given them some advantages over the public-school pupils in ability to do the hard formal studying.

Professor Meriam is also director of the high school, but has not as yet changed the regular college preparatory curriculum, except in the English. He expects to do so, however, and believes an equally radical reorganization of the work will have beneficial results. In the high school, English is not taught at all as a separate study, but work on it is continued along the same lines followed in the elementary school. A study of a certain number of graduates from the university schools and an equal number from the town high school, has indicated that the pupils who have received none of the usual training in English during their high-school course do better work in their English courses in college than those who have followed the regular routine.

Of course, judging an educational experiment by the pupil's ability to "keep up" with the system the experiment is trying to improve, is of very little value. The purpose of the experiment is not to devise a method by which the teacher can teach more to the child in the same length of time, or even prepare him more pleasantly for his college course. It is rather to give the child an education which will make him a better, happier, more efficient human being, by showing him what his capabilities are and how he can exercise them, both materially and socially, in the world he finds about him. If, while a school is still learning how best to do this for its pupils, it can at the same time give them all they would have gained in a more conventional school, we can be sure there has been no loss. Any manual skill or bodily strength that their schooling has given them, or any enjoyment of the tasks of their daily life and the best that art and literature has to offer, are further definite gains that can be immediately seen and measured. All contribute to the larger aim, but the lives of all the pupils will furnish the only real test of the success or failure of any educational experiment that aims to help the whole of society by helping the whole individual.

4. THE REORGANIZATION OF THE CURRICULUM

Rousseau, while he was writing his *Émile*, was allowing his own children to grow up entirely neglected by their parents, abandoned in a foundling asylum. It is not strange then that his readers and students should centre their interest in his theories, in his general contribution to education rather than in his account of the impractical methods he used to create that exemplary prig—Émile. If Rousseau himself had ever tried to educate any real children he would have found it necessary to crystallize his ideas into some more or less fixed program. In his anxiety to reach the ideal described in his theories, the emphasis of his interest would have unconsciously shifted to the methods by which he could achieve his ideal in the individual child. The child should spend his time on things that are suited to his age. The teacher immediately asks what these things are? The child should have an opportunity to develop naturally, mentally, spiritually, and physically. How is the teacher to offer this opportunity and what does it consist in? Only in the very simplest environment where one teacher is working out her own theories is it possible to get along without a rather definite embodiment of the ideal in specific materials and methods. Therefore in reviewing some of the modern attempts at educational reform, we quite naturally find that emphasis has been put upon the curriculum.

Pestalozzi and Froebel were the two educators most zealous in reducing inspiration got from Rousseau into the details of schoolroom work. They took the vague idea of natural development and translated it into formulae which teachers could use from day to day. Both were theorists, Froebel by temperament, Pestalozzi by necessity; but both made vigorous efforts to carry their theories into practice. They not only popularized the newer ideas about education, but influenced school practice more than any other modern educators. Pestalozzi substantially created the working methods of elementary education; while, as everybody knows, Froebel created a new kind of school, the kindergarten, for children too young to attend regular primary classes.

This combination of theoretical and practical influence makes it important to discriminate between the points where they carried the idea of education as growth forward, and the points where, in their anxiety to supply a school program to be followed by everybody, they fell back upon mechanical and external methods. Personally, Pestalozzi was as heroic in life as Rousseau was the reverse. Devotion to others took with him the place occupied by a sentimental egotism in Rousseau. For this very reason, perhaps, he had a firm grasp on a truth which Rousseau never perceived. He realized that natural development for a man means a social development, since the individual's vital connections are with others even more than with nature. In his own words: "Nature educated man for social relations, and by means of social relations. Things are important in the education of man in proportion to the intimacies of social relations into which man enters." For this reason family life is the centre of education, and, in a way, furnishes the model for every educational institution. In family life physical objects, tables, chairs, the trees in the orchard, the stones of the fence, have a social meaning. They are things which people use together and which influence their common actions.

Education in a medium where things have social uses is necessary for intellectual as well as for moral growth. The more closely and more directly the child learns by entering into social situations, the more genuine and effective is the knowledge he gains. Since power for dealing with remoter things comes from power gained in managing things close to us,

the direct sense of reality is formed only in narrow social circles, like those of family life. True human wisdom has for its bedrock an intimate knowledge of the immediate environment and trained capacity for dealing with it. The quality of mind thus engendered is simple and clear-sighted, formed by having to do with uncompromising realities and hence adapted to future situations. It is firm, sensitive and sure of itself.

The opposite education is scattering and confused; it is superficial, hovering lightly over every form of knowledge, without putting any of it to use: a medley, wavering and uncertain.

The moral is plain: Knowledge that is worthy of being called knowledge, training of the intellect that is sure to amount to anything, is obtained only by participating intimately and actively in activities of social life.

This is Pestalozzi's great positive contribution. It represents an insight gained in his own personal experience; for as an abstract thinker he was weak. It not only goes beyond Rousseau, but it puts what is true in Rousseau upon a sound basis. It is not, however, an idea that lends itself readily to formal statement or to methods which can be handed from one to another. Its significance is illustrated in his own early undertaking when he took twenty vagabond children into his own household and proceeded to teach them by means of farm pursuits in summer and cotton spinning and weaving in the winter, connecting, as far as possible, book instruction with these active occupations. It was illustrated again, later in his life, when he was given charge of a Swiss village, where the adults had been practically wiped out for resistance to an army of Napoleon. When a visitor once remarked: "Why, this is not a school; this is a household," Pestalozzi felt he had received his greatest compliment.

The other side of Pestalozzi is found in his more official school teaching career. Here also he attacked the purely verbal teaching of current elementary education and struggled to substitute a natural development. But instead of relying upon contact with objects used in active social pursuits (like those of the home), he fell back upon bare contact with the objects themselves. The result was a shift in Pestalozzi's fundamental idea. Presentation of objects by the teacher seemed to take the place of growth by means of personal activities. He was dimly conscious of the inconsistency, and tried to overcome it by saying that there are certain fixed laws of development which can be abstracted from the various experiences of particular human beings. Education cannot follow the development going on in individual children at a particular time; that would lead to confusion and chaos, anarchy and caprice. It must follow general laws derived from the individual cases.

At this point, the emphasis is taken from participation in social uses of things and goes over to dependence upon objects. In searching for general laws which can be abstracted from particular experiences, he found three constant things: geometrical form, number, and language—the latter referring, of course, not to isolated verbal expressions but to the statement of the qualities of things. In this phase of his activity as teacher, Pestalozzi was particularly zealous in building up schemes of object-lesson teaching in which children should learn the spatial and numerical relations of things and acquire a vocabulary for expressing all their qualities. The notion that object-lessons, by means of presentation of things to the senses, is the staple of elementary education thus came from Pestalozzi. Since it was concerned with external things and their presentation to the senses, this scheme of education lent itself to definite formulation of methods which could be passed on, almost mechanically, from one person to another.

In developing such methods, Pestalozzi hit upon the idea that the "order of nature" consists in going from the simple to the complex. It became his endeavor to find out in every subject the A B C (as he called it) of observation in that topic—the simplest elements that can be put before the senses. When these were mastered, the pupils were to pass on to various complications of these elements. Thus, in learning to read, children were to begin with combinations like A B, E B, I B, O B; then take up the reverse combinations B A, B E, B I, B O, etc., until having mastered all the elements, they could go on to complex syllables and finally to words and sentences. Number, music, drawing were all taught by starting with simple elements which could be put before the senses, and then proceeding to build up more complex forms in a graded order.

So great was the vogue of this procedure that the very word "method" was understood by many to signify this sort of analysis and combination of external impressions. To this day, it constitutes, with many people, a large part of what is understood by "pedagogy." Pestalozzi himself called it the psychologizing of teaching, and, more accurately, its mechanizing. He gives a good statement of his idea in the following words:

In the world of nature, imperfection in the bud means imperfect maturity. What is imperfect in its germ is crippled in its growth. In the development of its component parts, this is as true of the growth of the intellect as of an apple. We must, therefore, take care, in order to avoid confusion and superficiality in education, to make *first impressions of objects as correct and as complete as possible.* We must begin with the infant in the cradle, and take the training of the race out of the hands of blind sportive nature, and bring it under the power which the experience of the centuries has taught us to abstract from nature's own processes.

These sentences might be given a meaning to which no one could object. All of the educational reformers have rightly insisted upon the importance of the first years in which fundamental attitudes controlling later growth are fixed. There can be no doubt that if we could regulate the earlier relations of children to the world about them so that *all* ideas gained are certain, solid, definite, and right as far as they go, we might give children unconscious, intellectual standards which would operate later on with an efficacy quite foreign to our present experience. But the certainty and definiteness of geometrical forms, and of isolated qualities of objects are artificial. Correctness and completeness are gained at the expense of isolation from the every-day human experience of the child. It is possible for a child to learn the various properties of squares, rectangles, etc., and to acquire their names. But unless the squares and rectangles enter into his purposeful activities he is merely accumulating scholastic information. Undoubtedly it is better that the child should learn the names in association with the objects than to learn mere strings of words. But one is almost as far from real development as the other. Both are very far from the "firm, sensitive, and sure knowledge" which comes from using things for ends which appeal to the child. The things that the child uses in his household occupations, in gardening, in caring for animals, in his plays and games, have real simplicity and completeness of meaning for him. The simplicity of straight lines, angles, and quantities put before him just to be learned is mechanical and abstract.

For a long time the practical influence of Pestalozzi was confined to expelling from the schools reliance upon memorizing words that had no connection with things; to bringing object-lessons into the schools, and to breaking up every topic into its elements, or A B C, and then going on by graded steps. The failure of these methods to supply motives and to give real power made many teachers realize that things which the child has a use for are really simpler and more complete to him, even if he doesn't understand *everything* about them, than isolated elements. In the newer type of schools, there is a marked return (though of course quite independently of any reference to Pestalozzi) to his earlier and more vital idea of learning by taking a share in occupations and pursuits which are like those of daily life and which are engaged in by the friends about him.

Different schools have worked the matter out in different ways. In the Montessori schools there is still a good deal of effort to control the growth of mind by the material presented. In others, as in the Fairhope experiment, the material is incidental and informal, and the curriculum follows the direct needs of the pupils.

Most schools fall, of course, between these two currents. The child must develop, and naturally, but society has become so complicated, its demands upon the child are so important and continuous, that a great deal must be presented to him. Nature is a very extensive as well as compact thing in modern life, including not only the intricate material environment of the child, but social relations as well. If the child is to master these he must cover a great deal of ground. How is this to be done in the best way? Methods and materials must be used which are in themselves vital enough to represent to the child the whole of this compact nature which constitutes his world. The child and the curriculum are two operative forces, both of them developing and reacting on each other. In visiting schools the things that are interesting and helpful to the average school teacher are the methods, and the curriculum, the way the pupils spend their time; that is, the way the adjustment between the child and his environment is brought about.

"Learning by doing" is a slogan that might almost be offered as a general description of the way in which many teachers are trying to effect this adjustment. The hardest lesson a child has to learn is a practical one, and if he fails to learn it no amount of book knowledge will make up for it:

it is this very problem of adjustment with his neighbors and his job. A practical method naturally suggests itself as the easiest and best way of solving this problem. On the face of it, the various studies—arithmetic, geography, language, botany, etc.—are in themselves experiences. They are the accumulation of the past of humanity, the result of its efforts and successes, for generation after generation. The ordinary school studies present this not as a mere accumulation, not as a miscellaneous heap of separate bits of experience, but in some organized way. Hence, the daily experiences of the child, his life from day to day, and the subject-matter of the schoolroom, are parts of the same thing; they are the first and last steps in the life of a people. To oppose one to the other is to oppose the infancy and maturity of the same growing life; it is to set the moving tendency and the final result of the same power over against each other; it is to hold that the nature and the destiny of the child war with each other.

The studies represent the highest development possible in the child's simple every-day experiences. The task of the school is to take these crude experiences and organize them into science, geography, arithmetic, or whatever the lesson of the hour is. Since what the child already knows is part of some one subject that the teacher is trying to teach him, the method that will take advantage of this experience as a foundation stone on which to build the child's conscious knowledge of the subject appears as the normal and progressive way of teaching. And if we can enlarge the child's experience by methods which resemble as nearly as possible the ways that the child has acquired his beginning experiences, it is obvious that we have made a great gain in the effectiveness of our teaching. It is a commonplace that until a child goes to school he learns nothing that has not some direct bearing on his life. How he acquires this knowledge, is the question that will furnish the clue for natural school method. And the answer is, not by reading books or listening to explanations of the nature of fire or food, but by burning himself and feeding himself; that is, by doing things. Therefore, says the modern teacher, he ought to do things in school.

Education which ignores this vital impulse furnished by the child is apt to be "academic," "abstract," in the bad sense of these words. If text-books are used as the sole material, the work is much harder for the teacher, for besides teaching everything herself she must constantly repress and cut off the impulses of the child towards action. Teaching becomes an external presentation lacking meaning and purpose as far as the child is concerned. Facts which are not led up to out of something which has previously occupied a significant place for its own sake in the child's life, are apt to be barren and dead. They are hieroglyphs which the pupil is required to study and learn while he is in school. It is only after the child has learned the same fact out of school, in the activities of real life, that it begins to mean anything to him. The number of isolated facts to which this can happen, which appear, say, in a geography text-book, are necessarily very small.

For the specialist in any one subject the material is all classified and arranged, but before it can be put in a child's text-book it must be simplified and greatly reduced in bulk. The thought provoking character is obscured and the organizing function disappears. The child's reasoning powers, the faculty of abstraction and generalization, are not adequately developed. This does not mean that the text-book must disappear, but that its function is changed. It becomes a guide for the pupil by which he may economize time and mistakes. The teacher and the book are no longer the only instructors; the hands, the eyes, the ears, in fact the whole body, become sources of information, while teacher and text-book become respectively the starter and the tester. No book or map is a substitute for personal experience; they cannot take the place of the actual journey. The mathematical formula for a falling body does not take the place of throwing stones or shaking apples from a tree.

Learning by doing does not, of course, mean the substitution of manual occupations or handwork for text-book studying. At the same time, allowing the pupils to do handwork whenever there is opportunity for it, is a great aid in holding the child's attention and interest.

Public School 45 of the Indianapolis school system is try-

Songs and games help arithmetic. (Public School 45, Indianapolis.)

ing a number of experiments where the children may be said to be learning by doing. The work done is that required by the state curriculum, but the teachers are constantly finding new ways to prevent the work becoming a mere drill in text-book facts, or preparation for examinations. In the fifth grade, class activities were centered around a bungalow that the children were making. The boys in the class made the bungalow in their manual training hours. But before they started it every pupil had drawn a plan to scale of the house, and worked out, in their arithmetic period, the amount and cost of the lumber they would need, both for their own play bungalow and for a full sized one; they had done a large number of problems taken from the measurements for the house, such as finding the floor and wall areas and air space of each room, etc. The children very soon invented a family for their house and decided they would have them live on a farm. The arithmetic work was then based on the whole farm. First this was laid out for planting, plans were drawn to scale, and from information the children themselves gathered they made their own problems, basing them on their play farm: such as the size of the corn field, how many bushels of seeds would be needed to plant it; how big a crop they could expect, and how much profit. The children showed great interest and ingenuity in inventing problems containing the particular arithmetical process they were learning and which still would fit their farm. They built fences, cement sidewalks, a brick wall, did the marketing for the family, sold the butter, milk and eggs, and took out fire insurance. When they were papering the house the number of area problems connected with buying, cutting, and fitting the paper, were enough to give them all the necessary drill in measurement of areas.

English work centered in much the same way around the building of the bungalow and the life of its inhabitants. The spelling lessons came from the words they were using in connection with the building, etc. The plans for the completed bungalow, a description of the house and the furnishings, or the life of the family that dwelt in it, furnished inexhaustible material for compositions and writing lessons. Criticism of these compositions as they were read aloud to the class by their authors became work in rhetoric; even the grammar work became more interesting because the sentences were about the farm.

Art lessons were also drawn from the work the children were actually doing in building and furnishing the house. The pupils were very anxious that their house should be beautiful, so the color scheme for both the inside and outside furnished a number of problems in coloring and arrangement. Later they found large opportunities for design, in making wallpaper for the house, choosing and then decorating curtains and upholstery. Each pupil made his own design, and then the whole class decided which one they wanted to use. The pupils also designed and made clay tiles for the bathroom floor and wall, and planned and laid out a flower garden. The girls designed and made clothes for the doll inmates of the house. The whole class enjoyed their drawing lessons immensely because they drew each other posing as different members of the family in their different occupations on the farm. The work of this grade in expression consisted principally in dramatizations of the life on the farm which the children worked out for themselves. Not only were the children "learning by doing" in the sense that nearly all the school work centered around activities which had intrinsic meaning and value to the pupils, but most of the initiative for the work came from the children themselves. They made their own number problems; suggested the next step in the work on the house; criticised each other's compositions, and worked out their own dramatizations.

In almost all the grades in the school the pupils were conducting the recitations themselves whenever there was an opportunity. One pupil took charge of the class, calling on the others to recite; the teacher becoming a mere observer unless her interference was necessary to correct an error or keep the lesson to the point. When the class is not actually in charge of a pupil, every method is used to have the children do all the work, not to keep all the responsibility and initiative in the hands of the teacher. The pupils are encouraged to ask each other questions, to make their objections and corrections aloud, and to think out for themselves each problem as it comes up. This is not done by giving a class a set lesson in a text-book as an introduction to a new problem, but by suggesting the problem to the class and by means of questions and discussion, helped out whenever possible by actual experiments by the pupils, trying to bring out the solution of the problem, or at the least to give the pupil an understanding of what the problem is about before he sees it in print.

The method can be applied to all the classroom work, but one illustration taken from a geography lesson is especially suggestive. One grade was studying the Panama Canal, and had great difficulty in understanding the purpose or working of the canal, and especially the locks; in other words, they were not intellectually interested in what the teacher told them. She changed her method entirely and starting from the beginning, asked the class to pretend that Japan and the United States were at war, and that they were the Government at Washington and had to run the army. They at once became interested, and discovered that a canal across Panama was a necessity if the United States' ships were to arrive in the Pacific in time to defend the coast and the Hawaiian Islands. The mountain range seemed an impossible barrier, until the locks were explained to them again, when they seized the principle. Many of them, indeed, became so interested that they made models of locks at home to bring to school. They used the map freely and accurately in their interest in saving the country from invasion, but until one pupil asked why the United States did not actually build a canal across the Isthmus, they did not notice that their exciting game had anything to do with the puzzling facts that they had previously been trying to memorize from their text-book.

The teachers in the school make use of any illustrations from the practical life about them that fit in well with the work the grade is doing. Thus the third grade set up a parcel post system in their classroom, basing all their English and arithmetic work on it for some time, and learning to use a map and scales and weights as well. A retail shoe store gave the first grade plenty of work and fun, and games and dances with little songs have proved a great help in their number work. Most of the furniture in the school office was made by the big boys in their shop work, and several of the rooms are decorated with stencil designs the pupils made in their art lessons. The number work of the whole school is taught from the concrete side. The little children have boxes of tooth-picks and paper counters, which they use for adding and subtracting; the older pupils may tear paper or draw squares when they are learning a new process. The class is given something to do which illustrates the process to be taught; then the children themselves analyze what they have done and, as the last step, they do examples with pure numbers.

Many of the public schools of Chicago are also trying in every way possible to vitalize their work; to introduce into the curriculum material which the children themselves can handle and from which they may get their own lessons. This work is fitted into the regular curriculum; it is not dependent on any peculiarities of an individual teacher, but may be introduced throughout the entire system, just as text-books are now uniform through a large number of schools. The work has been applied principally in history and civics for the younger grades, but it is easy to imagine how the same sort of thing could be used in geography or some of the other subjects. The history in the younger grades is taught largely by means of sand tables. The children are perhaps studying the primitive methods of building houses, and on their sand table they build a brush house, a cave dwelling, a tree house, or an eskimo snow hut. The children themselves do all the work. The teacher steps in with advice and help only when necessary to prevent real errors, but the pupils are given the problem of the manufacture of the house they are study-ing, and are expected to solve it for themselves. Sand tables are used in the same way by a third grade in their study of the early history of Chicago. They mold the sand into a rough relief map of the neighborhood and then with twigs build the forts and log cabins of the first frontier settlement, with an Indian encampment just outside the stockade. They put real water in their lake and river, and float canoes in it. Other grades do the same thing with the history of trans-portation among the first settlers in this country, and with the logging and lumber industry. The older grades are studying the government of their city, and make sand tables to illustrate the different departments of city government. One room has a life-saving station, with different types of boats, and life lines that work. Others have the telephone, mail carrier, and parcel posts systems, and a system of street cleaning of which the children are particularly proud, because they have copied conditions which they actually found in some of the alleys near the school buildings. Beside the alleys which were dirty, like those in the neighborhood, they have constructed a model alley with sanitary garbage appliances made on the best plan based on what the teacher has told them about systems in other cities.

In another building all the pupils above the fourth grade have organized into civic clubs. They divided the school district into smaller districts and one club took charge of each district, making surveys and maps of their own territory, counting lamp posts, alleys, and garbage cans, and the number of policemen, or going intensively into the one thing which interested them most. Then each club decided what they wanted to do for their own district and set out to accomplish it, whether it was the cleaning up of a bad alley or the better lighting of a street. They used all the methods that an adult citizens' club would employ, writing letters to the city departments, calling at the City Hall, and besides actually went into the alleys and cleaned them up. The interest and enthusiasm of the pupils in this work was remarkable and they are now undertaking a campaign to get a playground for the school, by means of advertising and holding neighborhood meetings. The English work in these grades is based on the work of the clubs; the pupils keep track of the work they do, make maps and write letters.

Most of the hand and industrial work, which is not taught for strictly vocational purposes illustrates the principles which "learning by doing" stand for. Examples of this are to be found in nearly all schools to-day which aim to be progressive. Many school systems all over the country have tried having a printing press operated by pupils with great success. The presses were installed not to teach the pupils the different processes in the trade, but so that the children might themselves print some of the pamphlets, posters, or other papers that any school is constantly needing. Besides the interest that the pupils have shown in setting up the type, operating the presses, and getting out the printed matter, the work has proved itself especially valuable in the teaching of English. Type setting is an excellent method of drilling in spelling, punctuation, paragraphing, and grammar, for the fact that the copy is going to be printed furnishes a motive for eliminating mistakes which exercises written by a pupil for his teacher never provide. Proofreading is another exercise of the same sort. In such schools the press publishes practically all the printed matter that is needed during the year, including spelling lists, programs, and school papers.

Schools are trying all sorts of experiments to make the work in English concrete. The text-book method of teaching —learning rules and definitions and then doing exercises in their application—has proved unsuccessful. Every teacher is familiar with the story of the boy who wrote, "I have gone," on a piece of paper fifty times, in order to impress the correct form on his mind, and then on the bottom of the page left a note for the teacher beginning, "I have went home." A purpose in English work seems absolutely necessary, for the child sees no gain in efficiency in the things he is most interested in due to progress in isolated grammar or spelling. When the progress is brought about as a by-product of the scholars' other work the case is quite otherwise. Give him a reason for writing, for spelling, punctuating, and paragraphing, for using his verbs correctly, and improvement becomes a natural demand of experience. Mr. Wirt in the Gary, Ind., schools has found this so true that the regular English required by the state curriculum has been supplemented by "application periods in English." In these hours the class in carpentry or cooking discusses the English used in doing their work in those subjects, and corrects from the language point of view any written work done as part of their other activity. A pupil in one of these classes, who had been corrected for a mistake in grammar, was overheard saying, "Well, why didn't they tell us that in English?" to which her neighbor answered, "They did, but we didn't know what they were talking about."

In some schools as in the Francis Parker School, Chicago, and in the Cottage School at Riverside, Ill., English is not taught as a separate subject to the younger grades, but the pupils have compositions to write for their history lessons, keep records of their excursions, and of other work where they do not use text-books. The emphasis is put on helping the child to express his ideas; but such work affords ample opportunity for the drill in the required mechanics of writing. Grammar no longer appears as a separate subject in the Chicago public-school curriculum; the teacher gives a lesson in grammar every time any one in the classroom talks and with every written exercise.

However, grammar can be given a purpose and made interesting even to eleven-year-old children, if the pupils are helped to make their own grammar and rules by doing their own analyzing as the first step instead of the last. This is being done with great success in the Phoebe Thorn Experimental School of Bryn Mawr College. Grammar had no place on the curriculum, but the pupils asked so many questions that their teacher decided to let them discover their own grammatical rules, starting from the questions they had asked. A few minutes were taken from the English hour two or three times a week for their lessons. At the end of three months the class could analyze any simple sentence, could tell a transitive from an intransitive verb instantly, and were thoroughly familiar with the rules governing the verb to be. The grammar lesson was one of the favorite lessons; the teacher and pupils together had invented a number of games to help their drill. For example, one child had a slip of paper pinned to her back describing a sentence in grammatical terms; the class made sentences that fitted the sentence, and the first pupil had to guess what her paper said. No text-book was used in the work, and the teacher started with the sentence, called it a town, and by discussion helped the pupils to divide it up into districts—singular, plural, etc. Starting from this, they developed other grammatical rules. The general tendency in the progressive schools to-day, nevertheless, seems to be toward the elimination of the separate study of grammar, and toward making it and the remainder of the English work (with the exception of literature) a part of other subjects which the class is studying.

The motto of the boys' school at Interlaken, Ind., "To

The pupils build the schoolhouses. (Interlaken School, Ind.)

teach boys to live," is another way of saying, "learning by doing." Here this is accomplished, not so much by special devices to render the curriculum more vital and concrete, and by the abolition of text-books with the old-fashioned reservoir and pump relation of pupil and teacher, as by giving the boys an environment which is full of interesting things that need to be done.

The school buildings have been built by the pupils, including four or five big log structures, the plans being drawn, the foundations dug and laid, and the carpentry and painting on the building done by boy labor. The electric light and heating plant is run by the boys, and all the wiring and bulbs were put in and are kept in repair by them. There is a six hundred acre farm, with a dairy, a piggery and hennery, and crops to be sowed and gathered. Nearly all this work is also done by pupils; the big boys driving the reapers and binders and the little boys going along to see how it is done. The inside of the houses are taken care of in the same way by the students. Each boy looks after his own room, and the work in the corridors and schoolrooms is attended to by changing shifts. There is a lake for swimming and canoeing, and plenty of time for the conventional athletics. Most of the boys are preparing for college, but this outdoor and manual work does not mean that they have to take any longer for their preparation than the boy in the city high school.

The school has also bought the local newspaper from the neighboring village and edits and prints a four-page weekly paper of local and school news. The boys gather the news, do much of the writing and all of the editing and printing, and are the business managers, getting advertisements and tending to the subscription list. The instructors in the English department give the boys any needed assistance. They do all these things, not because they want to know certain processes that will help them earn a living after they are through school, but because to use tools, to move from one kind of work to another, to meet different kinds of problems, to exercise outdoors, and to learn to supply one's daily needs are educating influences, which develop skill, initiative, independence, and bodily strength—in a word, character and knowledge.

Work in nature study is undergoing reorganization in many schools in all parts of the country. The attempt is to vitalize the work, so that pupils shall actually get a feeling for plants and animals, together with some real scientific knowledge, not simply the rather sentimental descriptions and rhapsodizings of literature. It is also different from the information gathering type of nature study, which is no more real science than is the literary type. Here the pupils are taught a large number of isolated facts, starting from material that the teacher gathers in a more or less miscellaneous way; they learn all about one object after another, each one unrelated to the others or to any general plan of work. Even though a child has gone over a large number of facts about the outdoor world, he gains little or nothing which makes nature itself more real or more understandable.

If nature study is turned into a science, the real material of the subject must be at hand for the students; there must be a laboratory, with provision for experimentation and observation. In the country this is easy, for nature is just outside the school doors and windows. The work can be organized in the complete way that has already been described in the schools at Fairhope and Columbia.

The Cottage School at Riverside, Ill., and the Little School in the Woods at Greenwich, Conn., both put a great deal of stress on their nature study work. At the former, the children have a garden where they plant early and late vegetables, so that they can use them for their cooking class in the spring and fall; the pupils do all the work here, plant, weed, and gather the things. Even more important is the work they do with animals. They have, for example, a rare bird that is as much a personality in the school life as any of the children, and the children, having cared for him and watched his growth and habits, have become much more interested in wild birds. In the backyard is a goat, the best liked thing on the place, which the children have raised from a little kid; and they still do all the work of caring for him. They are encouraged in every way to watch and report on the school pets and also on the animals they find in the woods.

In the Little School in the Woods at Greenwich outdoor work is the basis of the whole school organization. Nature study plays a large part in this. Groups of pupils take long walks through the woods in all seasons and weathers, learning the trees in all their dresses, and the flowers which come with each season. They learn to know the birds and their habits; they study insects in the same way, and learn about the stars. In fact, so much of their time is spent out of doors, that the pupils acquire first hand a large fund of knowledge of the world of nature in all its phases. The basis of this work, the director of the school calls Woodcraft; he believes that experience in the things the woodman does—riding, hunting, camping, scouting, mountaineering, Indian-craft, boating, etc.—will make strong, healthy, and independent young people with well-developed characters and a true sense of the beauty of nature. The nature study then is a part of this other training. A teacher is always with the pupils, whether they are boating, walking, or gardening, to explain what they are doing and why, and to call their attention to the things about them. There is no doubt that the children in the school, even the very little ones, have a knowledge and appreciation of nature which are very rare even among country children.

Nature study in the big city, where the only plants are in parks and formal yards and where the only animals are the delivery horse and the alley cat, offers a very different problem. The teacher may well be puzzled as to the best way to teach her pupils to love nature when they never see it; or be doubtful as to the value of trying to develop powers of observation when the things which they are asked to observe not only do not play any part in the lives of the pupils but are in quite artificial surroundings. Yet while wild nature, the world of woods and fields and streams, is almost meaningless to the city bred child, there is plenty of material available to make nature a very real thing even for the child who has never seen a tree or cow. The modern teacher takes as a starting point anything that is familiar to the class; a caged canary, a bowl of gold fish, or the dusty trees on the playground, and starting from these she introduces the children to more and more of nature, until they can really get some idea of "the country" and the part it plays in the lives of every one. The vegetable garden is the obvious starting point for most city children; if they do not have tiny gardens in their own backyards, there is a neighbor who has, or they are interested to find out where the vegetables they eat come from and how they are grown.

Both in Indianapolis and Chicago, the public schools realize the value of this sort of work for the children. In Indianapolis, gardening is a regular department in the seventh and eighth grades and the high school. The city has bought a large tract of land far enough in town to be accessible, and any child who cannot have a garden at home may, by asking, have a garden plot together with lessons in the theory and practice of gardening. The plots are large enough for the pupils to gain considerable experience and to put into practice what they learn in the classroom. Both boys and girls have the gardens, and are given credit for work in them just as for other work. All through the school system every attempt is made to arouse an interest in gardening. From the first grade on, statistics are kept of the numbers of children with gardens at home, whether they are vegetable or flower gardens, and what is grown. Seeds are given to the children who wish to grow new things, and the child is supposed to account to his grade for the use he has made of his garden.

This work has become a matter of course in many rural districts; every one is familiar with the "corn clubs" among the school children of the South and West, and the splendid example they have set the farmers as to the possibilities of the soil. In many small towns seeds are given to the children who want gardens, and in the fall a competitive flower and vegetable show is held, where prizes are given, as a means of keeping track of the work and arousing community interest. It is true that most of these efforts have been grafted on to the schools by the local agricultural interests, in an effort to improve the crops and so increase the wealth of the neighborhood; but local school boards are beginning to take the work over, and it is no less real nature study work because of its utilitarian color. It may be made a means of making a real science of nature study; in no way does it hinder the teaching of the beauty and usefulness of nature, which was the object of the old-fashioned study. In fact, it is the strongest weapon the school can make use of for this purpose. Every one, and children especially, enjoy and respect most the things about which their fund of knowledge is largest. The true value of anything is most apparent to the person who knows something about it. Familiarity with growing things and with the science of getting food supplies for a people, cannot fail to be a big influence towards habits of industry and observation, for only the gardener who watches all the stages and conditions of his garden, seeking constantly for causes, will be successful. Added to this is the purely economic value of having our young people grow up with a real respect for the farmer and his work, a respect which should counteract that overwhelming flow of population toward congested cities.

The work in the Chicago public schools has not been organized as it is in Indianapolis, but in some districts of the city a great deal of emphasis is put on nature study work through gardens. Many of the schools have school gardens where all the children get an opportunity to do real gardening, these gardens being used as the basis for the nature study work, and the children getting instruction in scientific gardening besides. The work is given a civic turn; that is to say, the value of the gardens to the child and to the neighborhood is demonstrated: to the child as a means of making money or helping his family by supplying them with vegetables, to the community in showing how gardens are a means of cleaning up and beautifying the neighborhood. If the residents want their backyards and empty lots for gardens, they are not going to throw rubbish into them or let other people do so. Especially in the streets around one school has this work made a difference. Starting with the interest and effort of the children, the whole community has become tremendously interested in starting gardens, using every bit of available ground. The district is a poor one and, besides transforming the yards, the gardens have been a real economic help to the people. With the help of one school a group of adults in the district hired quite a

Real gardens for city nature study. (Public School 45, Indianapolis.)

large tract of land outside the city and started truck gardens. The experiment was a great success. Inexperienced city dwellers, by taking advantage of the opportunities for instruction which the school could offer, were able to plan and do the work and make the garden a success from the start. The advantage to the school was just as great, for a large group of foreign parents came into close touch with it, discovered that it was a real force in the neighborhood, and that they could cooperate with it. This element of the population usually stands quite aloof from the school its children go to, through timidity and ignorance, or simply through feeling that it is an institution above them.

The impetus to "civic nature study" in Chicago, aside from the district just described, has come largely from the Chicago Teachers' College, where the teacher of biology has devoted himself especially to working out this problem. In addition to the familiar gardening work, with especial attention to the organization of truck gardening, plants are grown in the classroom for purposes of developing appreciation of beauty, scientific illustration, and assistance in geography. But plants are selected with special reference to local conditions, and with the desire to furnish a stimulus to beautifying the pupils' own environment. For it is found that the scientific principles of botany can be taught by means of growing plants which are adapted to home use as well as by specimens selected on abstract scientific grounds. By making a special study of the parks, playgrounds, and yards of their surroundings, the children learn what can be done to beautify their city, and secure an added practical motive for acquiring information. They keep pets in the schoolroom, such as white mice, fish, birds, and rabbits. While these are utilized, of course, for illustrating principles of animal structure and physiology, they are also employed to teach humaneness to animals and a general sympathy for animal life. This is easy, for children are naturally even more interested in animals than in plants, and the animals become real individualities to the children whose needs are to be respected. As the effect of conditions upon the health and vigor of their pets is noted, there is a natural growth of interest in questions of personal hygiene.

It will be observed that while nature study is used to instill the elements of science, its chief uses are to cultivate a sympathetic understanding of the place of plants and animals in life and to develop emotional and aesthetic interest. In the larger cities the situation is very different from that of rural life and the country village. There are thousands of children who believe that cement and bricks are the natural covering of the ground, trees and grass being to them the unusual and artificial thing. Their thoughts do not go beyond the fact that milk and butter and eggs come from the store; cows and chickens are unknown to them— so much so that in a recent reunion of old settlers in a congested district of New York one of the greatest curiosities was a live cow imported from the country. Under such circumstances, it is difficult to make the scientific problems of nature study of vital interest. There are no situations of the children's experience into which the facts and principles enter as a matter of course. Even the weather is tempered and the course of the changing seasons has no special effect upon the lives of the pupils, save upon the need for greater warmth in winter. Nature study in the city is like one of the fine arts, such as painting or music; its value is aesthetic rather than directly practical. Nature is such a small factor in the activities of the children that it is hard to give it much "disciplinary" value, save as it is turned to civic ends. A vague feeling for this state of affairs probably accounts for much of the haphazard and half-hearted nature study teaching which goes on in city schools. There is a serious problem in finding material for city children which will do for observation what the facts of nature accomplish in the case of rural children.

A valuable experiment with this end in view is carried on in the little "Play School" taught by Miss Pratt in one of the most congested districts of New York City. Nature study is not taught at all to these little children. If they go to the park or have pets and plant flowers it is because these things make good play material, because they are beautiful and interesting; if the children ask questions and want to know more about them, so much the better. Instead of telling them about leaves and grass, cows and butterflies, and hunting out the rare opportunities for the children to observe them, use is made of the multitudes of things which the children see about them in the streets and in their homes. The new building going up across the street furnishes just as much for observation and questioning as does the park, and is a much more familiar sight to the children. They find out how the men get the bricks and mortar to the upper floors; they see the sand cart unloading; possibly one child knows that the driver has been to the river to get the sand from a boat. They notice the delivery man going through the streets, and find out where he got the bread to take to their mothers. They see the children on the playground and learn that besides the fun they have, the playing is good for their bodies. They walk to the river and see the ferries carrying people back and forth and the coal barges unloading. All these facts are more closely related to them than the things of country life; hence it is more important that they understand their meaning and their relation to their own lives, while acuteness of observation is just as well trained. Such work is also equally valuable as a foundation for the science and geography the pupils will study later on. Besides awakening their curiosity and faculties of observation, it shows them the elements of the social world, which the later studies are meant to explain.

The Elementary School at Columbia, Missouri, has arranged its curriculum according to the same principle. All the material from nature which the children use and study they find near the school or their homes, and their study of the seasons and the weather is made from day to day, as the Columbia weather and seasons change. Even more important is the work the children do in studying their own town, their food, clothing, and houses, so that the basis of the study is not instruction given by the teacher but what the children themselves have been able to find out on excursions and by keeping their eyes open. The material bears a relation to their own lives, and so is the more available for teaching children how to live. The reasons for teaching such things to the city bred child are the same as those for teaching the country child the elements of gardening and the possibilities of the local soil. By understanding his own environment child or adult learns the measure of the beauty and order about him, and respect for real achievement, while he is laying the foundations for his own control of the environment.

5. PLAY

All peoples at all times have depended upon plays and games for a large part of the education of children, especially of young children. Play is so spontaneous and inevitable that few educational writers have accorded to it in theory the place it held in practice, or have tried to find out whether the natural play activities of children afforded suggestions that could be adopted within school walls. Plato among the ancients and Froebel among the moderns are the two great exceptions. From both Rousseau and Pestalozzi, Froebel learned the principle of education as a natural development. Unlike both of these men, however, he loved intellectual system and had a penchant for a somewhat mystical metaphysics. Accordingly we find in both his theory and practice something of the same inconsistency noted in Pestalozzi.

It is easier to say natural development than to find ways for assuring it. There is much that is "natural" in children which is also naturally obnoxious to adults. There are many manifestations which do not seem to have any part in helping on growth. Impatient desire for a method which would cover the whole ground, and be final so as to be capable of use by any teacher, led Froebel, as it has led so many others, into working out alleged "laws" of development which were to be followed irrespective of the varying circumstances and experiences of different children. The orthodox kindergarten, which has often been more Froebellian than Froebel himself, followed these laws; but now we find attempts to return to the spirit of his teaching, with more or less radical changes in its letter.

While Froebel's own sympathy with children and his personal experience led him to emphasize the instinctive expressions of child-life, his philosophy led him to believe that natural development consisted in the *un*folding of an absolute and universal principle already *en*folded in the child. He believed also that there is an exact correspondence between the general properties of external objects and the unfolding qualities of mind, since both were manifestations of the same absolute reality. Two practical consequences followed which often got the upper hand of his interest in children on their own account. One was that, since the law of development could be laid down in general, it is not after all so important to study children in the concrete to find out what natural development consists in. If they vary from the requirements of the universal law so much the worse for them, not for the "law." Teachers were supposed to have the complete formula of development already in their hands. The other consequence was that the presentation and handling, according to prescribed formulae, of external material, became the method in detail of securing proper development. Since the general relations of these objects, especially the mathematical ones, were manifestations of the universal principle behind development, they formed the best means of bringing out the hidden existence of the same principle in the child. Even the spontaneous plays of children were thought to be educative not because of what they are, directly in themselves, but because they symbolize some law of universal being. Children should gather, for example, in a circle, not because a circular grouping is convenient for social and practical purposes, but because the circle is a symbol of infinity which will tend to evoke the infinite latent in the child's soul.

The efforts to return to Froebel's spirit referred to above have tried to keep the best in his contributions. His emphasis upon play, dramatization, songs and story telling, which involve the constructive use of material, his deep sense of the importance of social relations among the children— these things are permanent contributions which they retain. But they are trying with the help of the advances of psychological knowledge since Froebel's time and of the changes in social occupations which have taken place to utilize these factors directly, rather than indirectly, through translation into a metaphysics, which, even if true, is highly abstract. In another respect they are returning to Froebel himself, against an alteration in his ideas introduced by many of his disciples. These followers have set up a sharp contrast between play and useful activity or work, and this has rendered the practices of their kindergartens more symbolic and sentimental than they otherwise would have been. Froebel himself emphasized the desirability of children sharing in social occupations quite as much as did Pestalozzi —whose school he had visited. He says, for example,

The young, growing human being should be trained early for outer work, for creative and productive activities. Lessons through and by work, through and from life, are the most impressive and the most intelligible, the most continuous and progressive, in themselves and in their effect upon the learner. Every child, boy and youth, whatever his position and condition in life, should devote, say, at least one or two hours a day to some serious active occupation constructing some definite external piece of work. It would be a most wholesome arrangement in school to establish actual working hours similar to existing study hours, and it will surely come to this.

In the last sentence, Froebel showed himself a true prophet of what has been accomplished in some of the schools such as we are dealing with in this book.

Schools all over the country are at present making use of the child's instinct for play, by using organized games, toy making, or other construction based on play motives as part of the regular curriculum. This is in line with the vitalization of the curriculum that is going on in the higher grades by making use of the environment of the child outside the schoolroom. If the most telling lessons can be given children through bringing into the school their occupations in their free hours, it is only natural to use play as a large share of the work for the youngest pupils. Certainly the greatest part of the lives of very young children is spent in playing, either games which they learn from older children or those of their own invention. The latter usually take the form of imitations of the occupations of their elders. All little children think of playing house, doctor, or soldier, even if they are not given toys which suggest these games; indeed, half of the joy of playing comes from finding and making the necessary things. The educational value of this play is obvious. It teaches the children about the world they live in. The more they play the more elaborate becomes their paraphernalia, the whole game being a fairly accurate picture of the daily life of their parents in its setting, clothed in the language and bearing of the children. Through their games they learn about the work and play of the grown-up world. Besides noticing the elements which make up this world, they find out a good deal about the actions and processes that are necessary to keep it going.

While this is of real value in teaching the child how to live, it is evident as well that it supplies a strong influence against change. Imitative plays tend, by the training of habit and the turn they give to the child's attention and thoughts, to make his life a replica of the life of his parents. In playing house children are just as apt to copy the coarseness, blunders, and prejudices of their elders as the things which are best. In playing, they notice more carefully and thus fix in their memory and habits, more than if they simply lived it indifferently, the whole color of the life around them. Therefore, while imitative games are of great educational value in the way of teaching the child to notice his environment and some of the processes that are necessary for keeping it going, if the environment is not good the child learns bad habits and wrong ways of thinking and judging, ways which are all the harder to break because he has fixed them by living them out in his play.

Modern kindergartens are beginning to realize this more and more. They are using play, the sort of games they find the children playing outside of school hours, not only as a method of making work interesting to the children, but for the educational value of the activities it involves, and for giving the children the right sort of ideals and ideas about every-day life. Children who play house and similar games in school, and have toys to play with and the material to make the things they need in their play, will play house at home the way they played it in school. They will forget to imitate the loud and coarse things they see at home, their attention will be centered on problems which were designed by the school to teach better aims and methods.

The kindergarten of the Teachers College of Columbia University could hardly be recognized as a kindergarten

(1) Making a town, instead of doing gymnastic exercises. (Teachers College Playground, New York City.)

(2) Gymnasium dances in sewing-class costumes. (Howland School, Chicago.)

at all by a visitor who was thinking of the mechanism of instruction worked out by Froebel's disciples. The kindergarten is part of the training school of the university, and from the start has been considered as a real part of the school system, as the first step in an education, not as a more or less unnecessary "extra." With a view to laying a permanent basis for higher education, the authorities have been developing a curriculum that should make use of whatever was of real worth in existing systems of education and in the experiments tried by themselves. To find what is of real worth, experiments have been conducted, designed to answer the following questions:

Among the apparently aimless and valueless spontaneous activities of the child is it possible to discover some which may be used as the point of departure for ends of recognized worth? Are there some of these crude expressions which, if properly directed, may develop into beginnings of the fine and industrial arts? How far does the preservation of the individuality and freedom of the child demand self-initiated activities? Is it possible for the teacher to set problems or ends sufficiently childlike to fit in with the mode of growth, and to inspire their adoption with the same fine enthusiasm which accompanies the self-initiated ones?

The result showed that the best success came when the children's instinctive activities were linked up with social interests and experiences. The latter centre, with young children, in their home. Their personal relations are of the greatest importance to them. Children's intense interest in dolls is a sign of the significance attached to human relations. The doll thus furnished a convenient starting point. With this as a motive, the children have countless things they wish to do and make. Hand and construction work thus acquired a real purpose, with the added advantage of requiring the child to solve a problem. The doll needs clothes; the whole class is eager to make them, but the children do not know how to sew or even cut cloth. So they start with paper and scissors, and make patterns, altering and experimenting on the doll for themselves, receiving only suggestions or criticisms from the teacher. When they have made successful patterns, they choose and cut the cloth, and then learn to sew it. If the garments are not wholly successful, the class has had a great deal of fun making them, and has had the training that comes from working towards a definite end, besides acquiring as much control over scissors, paper, and needle, and manual dexterity as would accrue from the conventional paper cutting, pricking, and sewing exercises.

The doll needs a house. In a corner of the room there is a great chest of big blocks, so large that it takes the whole class to build the house, and then it is not done in one day. There are flat long blocks like boards for the walls and roof, and square blocks for the foundations and window frames. When the house is done, it is big enough for two or three children to go into to play with the doll. One readily sees that it has taken a great deal of hard thinking and experimenting to make a house that would really stand up and serve such uses. Then the house needs furniture; the children learn to handle tools in fashioning tables, chairs, and beds, from blocks of wood and thin boards. Getting the legs on a table is an especially interesting problem to the class, and over and over again they have discovered for themselves how it can be done. Dishes for the doll family furnish the motive for clay modeling and decoration. Dressing and undressing the dolls is an occupation the children never tire of, and it furnishes excellent practice in buttoning and unbuttoning and tying bows.

The changing seasons of the year and the procession of outdoor games they bring furnish other motives for production that meet a real need of the children. In the spring-time they want marbles and tops, in the fall, kites; the demand for wagons is not limited to any one season. Whenever possible the children are allowed to solve their own problems. If they want marbles they experiment until they find a good way to make them round, while if they are making something more difficult where the whole process is obviously beyond them, they are helped. This help, however, never takes the form of dictation as to how to perform each step in its order, for the object of the work is to train the child's initiative and self-reliance, to teach him to think straight by having him work on his own problems. The little carts which the older children make would be beyond them if they had to plan and shape the material for themselves; but when they are given the sawed boards and round pieces for wheels, they find out by trying how they can be put together, and thus make usable little wagons. Making bags for their marbles, and aprons to protect their clothes while they are painting the dolls' furniture or washing the dishes after lunch, offer additional opportunities for sewing.

From the needs of an individual doll the child's interest naturally develops to the needs of a family and then of a whole community. With paper dolls and boxes, the children make and furnish dolls' houses for themselves, until all together they produce an entire village. On their sand table the whole class may make a town with houses and streets, fences and rivers, trees and animals for the gardens. In fact, the play of the children furnishes more opportunity for making things than there is time for in the school year. This construction work not only fills the children with the interest and enthusiasm they always show for any good game, but teaches them the use of work. In supplying the needs of the dolls and their own games, they are supplying in miniature the needs of society, and are acquiring control over the tools that society actually uses in meeting these wants. Boys and girls alike take the same interest in all these occupations, whether they are sewing and playing with dolls, or marble making and carpentry. The idea that certain games and occupations are for boys and others for girls is a purely artificial one that has developed as a reflection of the conditions existing in adult life. It does not occur to a boy that dolls are not just as fascinating and legitimate a plaything for him as for his sister, until some one puts the idea into his head.

The program of this kindergarten is not devoted exclusively to play construction. It occupies the place of the paper folding, pricking and sewing and the object-lesson work of the older kindergartens, leaving plenty of time every day to try their playthings and to take care of their little gardens out of doors, as well as for group games, stories and songs.

An interesting application of the play motive is being tried at the Teachers College playground, by the same teachers who are conducting the kindergarten. There is an outdoor playground for the use of the younger grades after school hours. Instead of spending their time doing gymnastic exercises or playing group games the children are making a town. They use large packing cases for houses and stores, two or three children taking care of each one; and have worked out quite an elaborate town organization, with a telephone, mail and police service, a bank to coin money, and ingenious schemes for keeping the cash in circulation. Much of the time is spent in carpentry work, building and repairing the houses and making wagons, furniture for the houses, or stock for the two stores. The work affords almost as much physical exercise as the ordinary sort of playground. It keeps the children busy and happy in a much more effective way, for besides healthy play in the open air they are learning to take a useful and responsible share in a community.

A kindergarten conducted along the same lines exists in Pittsburgh as part of the city university. It is called "The School of Childhood," and emphasizes the healthy physical development of the children. The work is centered around the natural interests of children; and while they apparently do not do as much construction work as in the Teachers College kindergarten, there is more individual play. The writer has not visited the school, but it seems to embrace a number of novel elements that ought to be suggestive to any one interested in educational experiments.

The "Play School" conducted by Miss Pratt in New York City organizes all the work around the play activities of little children. Quoting Miss Pratt, her plan is:

To offer an opportunity to the child to pick up the thread of life in his own community, and to express what he gets in an individual way. The experiment concerns itself with getting subject-matter first hand, and it is assumed that the child has much information to begin with, that he is adding to it day by day, that it is possible to direct his attention so that he may get his information in a more related way; and with applying such information to individual schemes of play with related toys and blocks as well as expressing himself through such general means as drawing, dramatization, and spoken language.

The children are of kindergarten age and come from homes where the opportunities for real activity are limited. Each child has floor space of his own with a rug, and screens

to isolate him sufficiently so that his work is really individual. There is a small work shop in the room where
the pupils can make or alter things they need in their play.
The tools are full size, and miscellaneous scraps of wood are
used. In cupboards and shelves around the room are all sorts
of material: toys, big and little blocks, clay, pieces of cloth,
needle and thread, and a set of Montessori material. Each
child has scissors, paper, paints, and pencil of his own,
and is free to use all the material as he chooses. He selects
either isolated objects he wants to make, or lays out some
larger construction, such as a railroad track and stations,
or a doll's house, or a small town or farm, and then from the
material at hand works out his own execution of his idea.
One piece of work often lasts over several days, and involves
considerable incidental construction, such as tracks and
signals, clay dishes, furniture or new clothes for the doll.
The role of the teacher is to teach the pupil processes and
control of tools, not in a prearranged scale but as they are
needed in construction. The teacher has every opportunity
to see the individual's weaknesses and abilities and so to
check or stimulate at the proper time. Besides the motor
control which the pupils develop through their handling of
material, they are constantly increasing their ingenuity and
initiative.

The elements of number work are taught in connection
with the construction; and if a child shows a desire to make
letters or signs in connection with his other work, he is
helped and shown how. The toys used are particularly good.
There are flat wooden dolls about half an inch thick, men,
women, and children, whose joints bend so that they will
stay in any position; all sorts of farm animals and two or
three kinds of little wagons that fit the dolls; quantities of
big blocks that fasten together with wooden pegs, so that
the houses and bridges do not fall down. Everything is
strongly made on the simplest plan, so that material can be
used not only freely but also effectively. Each success is a
stimulus to new and more complicated effort. There is no
discouragement from slipshod stuff. The pupils take care
of the toys themselves, getting them out and putting them
away. They also care for the classroom and serve their mid-

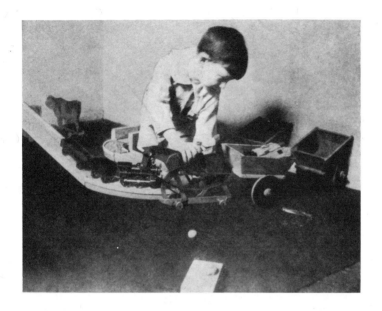

Constructing in miniature the things they see around them. (Play School, New York City.)

morning luncheon. This work, coupled with the fact that the constructions are almost always miniature copies of the things that the pupils see in their community, saves the work from any hint of artificiality. The children's constructions grow out of the observations already spoken of (p. 273), and give a motive for talking over what they have seen and making new, more extensive and more accurate observations.

The natural desire of children to play can, of course, be made the most of in the lowest grades, but there is one element of the play instinct which schools are utilizing in the higher grades—that is, the instinct for dramatization, for make-believe in action. All children love to pretend that they are some body or thing other than themselves; they love to make a situation real by going through the motions it suggests. Abstract ideas are hard to understand; the child is never quite sure whether he really understands or not. Allow him to act out the idea and it becomes real to him, or the lack of understanding is shown in what is done. Action is the test of comprehension. This is simply another way of saying that learning by doing is a better way to learn than by listening—the difference of dramatization from the work already described lies in the things the child is learning. He is no longer dealing with material where *things* are needed to carry an act to a successful result, but with *ideas* which need action to make them real. Schools are making use of dramatization in all sorts of different ways to make teaching more concrete. For older children dramatization is used principally in the strict sense of the word; that is, by having pupils act in plays, either as a means of making the English or history more real, or simply for the emotional and imaginative value of the work. With the little children it is used as an aid in the teaching of history, English, reading, or arithmetic, and is often combined with other forms of activity.

Many schools use dramatization as a help in teaching the first steps of any subject, especially in the lower grades. A first year class, for example, act the subject-matter of their regular reading lesson, each child having the part of one of the characters of the story, animal or person. This insures an idea of the situation as a whole, so that reading ceases to be simply an attempt to recognize and pronounce isolated words and phrases. Moreover, the interest of the situation carries children along, and enlists attention to difficulties of phraseology which might, if attacked as separate things, be discouraging. The dramatic factor is a great assistance in the expressive side of reading. Teachers are always having to urge children to read "naturally," "to read as they talk." But when a child has no motive for communication of what he sees in the text, knowing as he does that the teacher has the book and can tell it better than he can, even the naturalness tends to be forced and artificial. Every observer knows how often children who depart from humdrum droning, learn to exhibit only a superficial breathless sort of liveliness and a make-believe animation. Dramatization secures both attention to the thought of the text and a spontaneous endeavor, free from pretense and self-consciousness, to speak loudly enough to be heard and to enunciate distinctly. In the same way, children tell stories much more effectively when they are led to visualize for themselves the actions going on, than when they are simply repeating something as a part of the school routine. When children are drawing scenes involving action and posture, it is found that prior action is a great assistance. In the case of a pose of the body, the child who has done the posing is often found to draw better than those who have merely looked on. He has got the "feel" of the situation, which readily influences his hand and eye in the subsequent reproduction. In the early grades when pupils fail in a concrete problem in arithmetic, it is frequently found that resort to "acting out" the situation supplies all the assistance needed. The real difficulty was not with the numbers but in failure to grasp the meaning of the situation in which the numbers were to be used.

In the upper grades, literature and history, as already indicated, are often reenforced by dramatic activities. A sixth grade in Indianapolis engaged in dramatizing *Sleeping Beauty*, not merely composed the words and the stage directions, but also wrote songs and the music for them. Such concentration on a single purpose of studies usually pursued independently stimulates work in each. Literary expression is less monotonous, the phrasing of an idea more delicate and flexible, than when composition is an end in itself; and while of course the music is not likely to be remarkable, it almost always has a freshness and charm exceeding that which could be attained from the same pupils if they were merely writing music.

A shoe store in the second grade furnished the basis of the work for several days. The children set up a shop and chose pupils to take the part of the shoe clerk, the shoe-maker, and the family going to buy shoes. Then they acted out the story of a mother and children going to the store for shoes. Arithmetic and English lessons were based on the store, and the class wrote stories about it. This same class sang and acted out to a simple tune a little verse about the combinations that make ten. The same pupils were doing problems in mental arithmetic that were much beyond the work usually found in a second grade, adding almost instantly numbers like 74 and 57. They probably could not have gone so rapidly if they had not had so much of the dramatization work. It served to make their abstract problems seem real. In doing problems about Mrs. Baldwin's shoes they had come to think of numbers as having some meaning and purpose, so that when a problem in pure numbers was given they did not approach it with misgivings and uncertainty. One of the fifth grades had installed a parcel post office; they made money and stamps and brought bundles to school, then they played post office; two boys took the part of postmen, weighed the packages, looked up the rate of postage, and gave change for the customers. Tables of weights ceased to be verbal forms to be memorized; consultation of the map was a necessity; the multiplication table was a necessity; the system and order required in successful activity were impressed.

The Francis Parker School is one of many using the dramatic interest of the pupils as an aid in teaching history. The fourth grade studies Greek history, and the work includes the making of a Greek house, and writing poems about some Greek myth. The children make Greek costumes and wear them every day in the classroom. To quote Miss Hall, who teaches this grade:

They play sculptor and make clay statuettes of their favorite gods and mould figures to illustrate a story. They model Mycenae in sand-pans, ruin it, cover it, and become the excavators who bring its treasures to light again. They write prayers to Dionysius and stories such as they think Orpheus might have sung. They play Greek games and wear Greek costumes, and are continually acting out stories or incidents which please them. To-day as heroes of Troy, they have a battle at recess time with wooden swords and barrel covers. In class time, with prayers and dances and extempore song, they hold a Dionysiac festival. Again, half of them are Athenians and half of them Spartans in a war of words as to which city is more to be desired. Or they are freemen of Athens, replying spiritedly to the haughty Persian message.

Besides these daily dramatizations, they write and act for the whole school a little play which illustrates some incident of history that has particularly appealed to them. History taught in this way to little children acquires meaning and an emotional content; they appreciate the Greek spirit and the things which made a great people. The work so becomes a part of their lives that it is remembered as any personal experience is retained, not as texts are committed to memory to be recited upon.

The Francis Parker School takes advantage of the social value of dramatizations in its morning exercises. Studying alone out of a book is an isolated and unsocial performance; the pupil may be learning the words before him, but he is not learning to act with other people, to control and arrange his actions and thought so that other persons have an equal opportunity to express themselves in a shared experience. When the classes represent by action what they have learned from books, all the members have a part, so that they learn to cherish socially, as well as to develop, powers of expression and of dramatic and emotional imagery. When they act in front of the whole school they get the value of the work for themselves individually and help the growth of a spirit of unity and cooperation in the entire school. All the children, big and little, become interested in the sort of thing that is going on in the other grades, and learn to appreciate effort that is simple and sincere, whether it comes from the first grade or the seniors in high school. In their efforts to interest the whole school the actors learn to be simple and direct, and acquire a new respect for their work by seeing its value for others. Summaries of the work in different subjects are given in the morning exercises by any grade which thinks it has something to say that would interest the other children. The dramatic element is sometimes small, as in the descriptions of excursions, of curious processes in arithmetic or of some topic in geography; but the children always have to think clearly and speak well, or their audience will not understand them, and maps or diagrams and all sorts of illustrative material are introduced as much as possible. Other exercises, such as the Greek play written by the fourth grade, or a dramatization of one of Cicero's orations against Cataline, are purely dramatic in their interest.

The production of plays by graduating classes or for some specific purpose is of course a well-known method of interesting pupils or advertising a school. But recently schools have been giving plays and festivals for their educational value as well as for their interest to children and the public. The valuable training which comes from speaking to an audience, using the body effectively and working with other pupils for a common end, is present, whatever the nature of the play; and schools usually try to have their productions of some literary value. But until recently the resources of the daily work of the pupils for dramatic purposes have been overlooked. Being for purposes of public entertainment, plays were added on after school hours. But schools are beginning to utilize this natural desire of young people to "act something" for amplifying the curriculum. In many schools where dramatization of a rather elaborate character is employed for public performances, the subject-matter is now taken from English and history, while writing the play supplies another English lesson. The rehearsals take the place of lessons in expression and elocution, and involve self-control. The stage settings and costumes are made in the shop and art periods, the planning and management being done by the pupils, the teacher helping enough to prevent blunders and discouragement. At Riverside one of the classes had been reading Tolstoi's "Where Love Is There God Is Also" for their work in literature. They rewrote the story as a play and rehearsed it in their English lessons, the

Using the child's dramatic instinct to teach history. (Cottage School, Riverside, Ill.)

whole class acting as coach and critic. As their interest grew
they made costumes and arranged a stage setting and finally
gave the play to an audience of the school and its friends.
At another time the English class gave an outdoor performance of a sketch which they had written, based on the
Odyssey. The American history class at the Speyer School
give a play which they write about some incident in pioneer
history. During the rehearsal nearly all the children try
the parts, quite regardless of sex or other qualifications, and
the whole class chooses the final cast. The fifth grade was
studying Irving's *Sketch Book* in connection with its history
and literature work, and dramatized the story of Rip Van
Winkle, doing all its own coaching and costuming.

The Howland School, one of the public schools of
Chicago situated in a foreign district, gave a large festival
play during the past year. The principal wrote and arranged
a pageant illustrating the story of Columbus, and the whole
school took part in the acting. The story gave a simple
outline of the life of Columbus. A few tableaux were added
about some of the most striking events in pioneer history,
arranged to bring out the fact that this country is a democracy. The children made their own costumes for the most
part, and all the dances they had learned during the year in
gymnasium were introduced. Thus the whole exhibition
presented a very good picture of the outline of our history
and the spirit of the country, and at the same time offered
an interesting summary of the year's work. Its value as a
unifying influence in a foreign community was considerable,
for besides teaching the children something of the history
of their new country, it gave the parents, who made up the
audience, an opportunity to see what the school could do
for their children and the neighborhood. The patriotic value
of such exercises is greater than the daily flag salute or
patriotic poem, for the children understand what they are
supposed to be enthusiastic about, as they see before them
the things which naturally arouse patriotic emotions.

Exercises to commemorate holidays or seasons are more
interesting and valuable than the old-fashioned entertainment where individual pupils recited poems, and adults
made speeches, for they concentrate in a social expression

the work of the school. The community is more interested because parents know that their own children have had their share in the making of the production, and the children are more interested because they are working in groups on something which appeals to them and for which they are responsible. The graduating exercises at many schools are now of a kind to present in a dramatic review the regular work of the year. Each grade may take part, presenting a play which they have written for work in English, dancing some of the folk or fancy dances they have learned in gymnasium, etc. Many schools have a Thanksgiving exercise in which different grades give scenes from the first Thanksgiving at Plymouth, or present dramatic pictures of the harvest festivals of different nations. In similar fashion Christmas entertainments are often made up of songs, poems and readings by children from different grades, or by the whole grade, which have been arranged in the English and music classes. The possibilities for plays, festivals, and pageants arranged on this plan are endless; for it is always possible to find subject-matter which will give the children just as much training in reading, spelling, history, literature, or even some phases of geography, as would dry Gradgrind facts of a routine text-book type.

6. FREEDOM AND INDIVIDUALITY

The reader has undoubtedly been struck by the fact that in all of the work described, pupils must have been allowed a greater amount of freedom than is usually thought compatible with the necessary discipline of a schoolroom. To the great majority of teachers and parents the very word school is synonymous with "discipline," with quiet, with rows of children sitting still at desks and listening to the teacher, speaking only when they are spoken to. Therefore a school where these fundamental characteristics are lacking must of necessity be a poor school; one where pupils do not learn anything, where they do just as they please, quite regardless of what they please, even though it be harmful to the child himself or disagreeable to his classmates and the teacher.

There is a certain accumulation of facts that every child must acquire or else grow up to be illiterate. These facts relate principally to adult life; therefore it is not surprising that the pupil is not interested in them, while it is the duty of the school to see that he knows them nevertheless. How is this to be done? Obviously by seating the children in rows, far enough apart so that they cannot easily talk to each other, and hiring the most efficient person available to teach the facts; to tell them to the child, and have him repeat them often enough so that he can reasonably be expected to remember them, at least until after he is "promoted."

Again, children should be taught to obey; efficiency in doing as one is told is a useful accomplishment, just as the doing of distasteful and uninteresting tasks is a character builder. The pupil should be taught to "respect" his teacher and learning in general; and how can he be taught this lesson if he does not sit quietly and receptively in the face of both? But if he will not be receptive, he must at least be quiet, so that the teacher can teach him anyway. The very fact that the pupil so often is lawless, destructive, rude and noisy as soon as restraint is removed proves, according to the advocates of "discipline" by authority, that this is the only way of dealing with the child, since without such restraint the child would behave all day long as he does when it is removed for a few uncertain minutes.

If this statement of the disciplinarian's case sounds harsh and unadorned, think for a moment of the things that visitors to "queer schools" say after the visit is over; and consider whether they do not force the unprejudiced observer to the conclusion that their idea of schools and schooling is just such a harsh and unadorned affair. The discussion of freedom versus authoritative discipline in schools resolves itself after all into a question of the conception of education which is entertained. Are we to believe, with the strict disciplinarian, that education is the process of making a little savage into a little man, that there are many virtues as well as facts that have to be taught to all children so that they may as nearly as possible approach the adult standard? Or are we to believe, with Rousseau, that education is the process of making up the discrepancy between the child at his birth and the man as he will need to be, "that childhood has its own ways of seeing, thinking, and feeling," and that the method of training these ways to what a man will need is to let the child test them upon the world about him?

The phrase, "authoritative discipline," is used purposely, for discipline and freedom are not contradictory ideas. The following quotation from Rousseau shows very plainly what a heavy taskmaster even his freedom was, a freedom so often taken to mean mere lawlessness and license.

Give him [the pupil] no orders at all, absolutely none. Do not even let him think that you claim any authority over him. Let him know only that he is weak and you are strong, that his condition and yours puts him at your mercy; let this be perceived, learned and felt. Let him early find upon his proud neck the heavy yoke which nature has imposed upon us, the heavy yoke of necessity, under which every finite being must bow. Let him find the necessity in things, not in the caprices of man; let the curb be the force of conditions, not authority.

Surely no discipline could be more severe, more apt to develop character and reasonableness, nor less apt to develop disorder and laziness. In fact the real reason for the feeling against freedom in schools seems to come from a misunderstanding. The critic confuses physical liberty with moral and intellectual liberty. Because the pupils are moving about, or sitting on the floor, or have their chairs scattered about instead of in a straight line, because they are using their hands and tongues, the visitor thinks that their minds must be relaxed as well; that they must be simply fooling, with no more restraint for their minds and morals than appears for their bodies. Learning in school has been so long associated with a docile or passive mind that because that useful organ does not squirm or talk in its operations, observers have come to think that none of the child should do so, or it will interfere with learning.

Assuming that educational reformers are right in supposing that the function of education is to help the growing of a helpless young animal into a happy, moral, and efficient human being, a consistent plan of education must allow enough liberty to promote that growth. The child's body must have room to move and stretch itself, to exercise the muscles and to rest when tired. Every one agrees that swaddling clothes are a bad thing for the baby, cramping and interfering with bodily functions. The swaddling clothes of the straight-backed desk, head to the front and hands folded, are just as cramping and even more nerve racking to the school child. It is no wonder that pupils who have to sit in this way for several hours a day break out in bursts of immoderate noise and fooling as soon as restraining influences are removed. Since they do not have a normal outlet for their physical energy to spend itself, it is stored up, and when opportunity offers it breaks forth all the more impetuously because of the nervous irritation previously suffered in repressing the action of an imperfectly trained body. Give a child liberty to move and stretch when he needs it, with opportunities for real exercise all through the day and he will not become so nervously overwrought that he is irritable or aimlessly boisterous when left to himself. Trained in *doing* things, he will be able to keep at work and to think of other people when he is not under restraining supervision.

A truly scientific education can never develop so long as children are treated in the lump, merely as a class. Each child has a strong individuality, and any science must take stock of all the facts in its material. Every pupil must have a chance to show what he truly is, so that the teacher can find out what he needs to make him a complete human being. Only as a teacher becomes acquainted with each one of her pupils can she hope to understand childhood, and it is only as she understands it that she can hope to evolve any scheme of education which shall approach either the scientific or the artistic standard. As long as educators do not know their individual facts they can never know whether their hypotheses are of value. But how are they to know their material if they impose themselves upon it to such an extent that each portion is made to act just like every other portion? If the pupils are marched into line, information presented to them which they are then expected to give back in uniform fashion, nothing will ever be found out about any of them. But if every pupil has an opportunity to express himself, to show what are his particular qualities, the teacher will have material on which to base her plans of instruction.

Since a child lives in a social world, where even the simplest act or word is bound up with the words and acts of his neighbors, there is no danger that this liberty will sacrifice the interests of others to caprice. Liberty does not mean the removal of the checks which nature and man impose on the life of every individual in the community, so that one individual may indulge impulses which go against his own welfare as a member of society. But liberty for the child is the chance to test all impulses and tendencies on the world of things and people in which he finds himself, sufficiently to discover their character so that he may get rid of those which are harmful, and develop those which are useful to himself and others. Education which treats all children as if their impulses were those of the average of an adult society (whose weaknesses and failures are moreover constantly deplored) is sure to go on reproducing that same average society without even finding out whether and how it might be better. Education which finds out what children really are may be able to shape itself by this knowledge so that the best can be kept and the bad eliminated. Meantime much is lost by a mere external suppression of the bad which equally prevents the expression of the better.

If education demands liberty before it can shape itself according to facts, how is it to use this liberty for the benefit of the child? Give a child freedom to find out what he can and cannot do, both in the way of what is physically possible and what his neighbors will stand for, and he will not waste much time on impossibilities but will bend his energies to the possibilities. The physical energy and mental inquisitiveness of children can be turned into positive channels. The teacher will find the spontaneity, the liveliness, and initiative of the pupil aids in teaching, instead of being, as under the coercive system, nuisances to be repressed. The very things which are now interferences will become positive qualities that the teacher is cultivating. Besides preserving qualities which will be of use to the man and developing habits of independence and industry, allowing the child this freedom is necessary if pupils are really to learn by doing. Most doing will lead only to superficial muscle training if it is dictated to the child and prescribed for him step by step. But when the child's natural curiosity and love of action are put to work on useful problems, on finding out for himself how to adjust his environment to his needs, the teacher finds that the pupils are not only doing their lessons as well as ever, but are also learning how to control and put to productive use those energies which are simply disturbing in the average classroom. Unless the pupil has some real work on which to exercise his mind by means of his senses and muscles, the teacher will not be able to do away with the ordinary disciplinary methods. For in a classroom where the teacher is doing all the work and the children are listening and answering questions, it would be absurd to allow the children to place themselves where they please, to move about, or to talk. Where the teacher's role has changed to that of helper and observer, where the development of every child is the goal, such freedom becomes as much a necessity of the work as is quiet where the children are simply reciting.

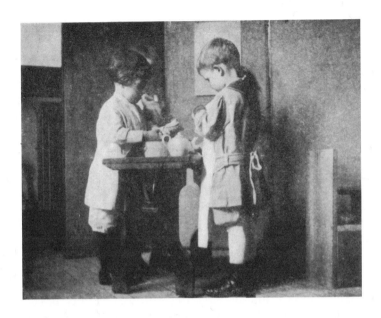

Learning to live through situations that are typical of social life. (Teachers College, N. Y. City.)

At present, the most talked of schools in which freedom and liberty are necessary for the children's work are the schools of Madame Maria Montessori in Italy and those of her pupils in this country. Madame Montessori believes, with many educators in this country, that liberty is necessary in the classroom if the teacher is to know the needs and capabilities of each pupil, if the child is to receive in school a well-rounded training making for the best development of his mind, character, and physique. In general, her reasons for insisting upon this liberty, which is the basis of her method, correspond with those outlined above, with one exception. She holds that liberty is necessary for the child if a scientific education is to be created, because without it data on which to base principles cannot be collected; also that it is necessary for the physical welfare of the pupils and for the best development of their characters in training them to be independent. The point of difference between the Italian educator and most reformers in this country lies in their respective views of the value of liberty in the use of material, and this point will be taken up later.

Madame Montessori believes that repressing children physically while they are in school and teaching them habits of mental passivity and docility is mistaking the function of the school and doing the children real harm. Scientific education not only needs freedom for the child in order to collect data, but liberty is its very basis; "liberty is activity," says Madame Montessori in her book called *The Montessori Method.* Activity is the basis of life; consequently training children to move and act is training them for life, which is the proper office of the schoolroom. The object of liberty is the best interests of the whole group; this becomes the end of the liberty allowed the children. Everything which does not contribute to it must be suppressed, while the greatest care is taken to foster every action with a useful scope. In order to give the pupils the largest possible scope for such useful activity, they are allowed a very large amount of freedom in the classroom. They may move about, talk to each other, place their tables and chairs where they please, and, what is of more significance, each pupil may choose what work he will do, and may work at one thing as long or as short a time as he wishes. She says, "A room in which all the children move about usefully, intelligently, and voluntarily, without committing any rough or rude act, would seem to me a classroom very well disciplined indeed." Discipline, in short, is ability to do things independently, not submission under restraint.

In order to bring about this active discipline, which allows free scope for any useful work, and at the same time does not stifle the spontaneous impulses of the child, the ordinary methods of discipline are done away with, and a technique is developed to emphasize the positive, not the negative, side of discipline. Montessori has described it in this way:

As to punishments, we have many times come in contact with children who disturbed the others, without paying any attention to our corrections. Such children were at once examined by the physician. When the case proved to be that of a normal child, we placed one of the little tables in a corner of the room, and in this way isolated the child, having him sit in a comfortable little arm-chair, so placed that he might see his companions at work, and giving him those games and toys to which he was most attracted. This isolation almost always succeeded in calming the child; from his position he could see the entire assembly of his companions, and the way in which they carried on their work was an object lesson much more efficacious than any words of the teacher could possibly have been. Little by little he would come to see the advantages of being one of the company working so busily before his eyes, and he would really wish to go back and do as the others did.

The corrections which the teachers first offer never take the form of scoldings; the child is quietly told that what he is doing is not polite or disturbs the other children. Then he is told how he ought to behave to be a pleasant companion, or his attention is diverted to a piece of work. Because children are working on something of their own choice, and when they want to, and because they may move and talk enough so that they do not get nervously tired, there is very little need for any "punishment." Except for an isolated case of real lawlessness, such as Montessori refers to in the quotation just cited, the visitor to one of her schools sees very little need of negative discipline. The teachers' corrections are practically all for small breaches of manners or for care-lessness.

Activity founded on liberty being the guiding principle of the Montessori schools, activity is expended by the child on two sorts of material. Montessori believes that the child needs practice in the actions of daily life; that, for example, he should be taught how to take care of and wait on himself. Part of the work is accordingly directed to this end. She also believes that the child possesses innate faculties which should be allowed to develop to their fullest; consequently part of the work is designed to give adequate expression to these faculties. These exercises for the culture of the inner potentialities of the child she considers the more important of the two. The child needs to know how to adjust himself to his environment in order to be independent and happy; but an imperfect development of the child's faculties is an imperfect development of life itself; so the real object of education consists in furnishing active help to the normal expansion of the life of the child. These two lines of develop-ment Madame Montessori considers to be so distinct one from the other that the exercises of practical life cannot perform the function of the exercises arranged to train the faculties and senses of the child.

The exercises of practical life are designed to teach the child to be independent, to supply his own wants, and to perform the actions of daily life with skill and grace. The pupils keep the schoolroom in order, dusting and arranging the furniture, and putting away each piece of material as soon as they are through with it. They wait on themselves while they are working, getting out the things they want, finding a convenient place to work, and then taking care of the apparatus when they have worked with it as long as they like. In schools where the children do not live in the building, a midday lunch is served for the pupils; and, except for the cooking, the children do all the work connected with the meal, setting tables, serving food, and then clearing away and washing the dishes. All the pupils share alike in this work, regardless of their age; children of three and four soon learn to handle the plates and glasses, and to pass the food. Wherever possible the schools have gardens, which

the children care for, and animal pets of a useful sort—
hens and chickens or pigeons. Even the youngest children
put on their own wraps, button and unbutton their aprons
and slippers, and when they cannot do it for themselves, they
help each other. The necessity of the pupils' learning to take
care of themselves as early as possible is so much insisted
upon that in order to help the youngest in learning this
lesson, Montessori has designed several appliances to give
them practice before they begin to wait upon themselves.
These are wooden frames, fitted with cloth which is opened
down the centre. Then the edges are joined either with
buttons, hooks and eyes, or ribbons, and practice consists
in opening and closing these edges by buttoning, hooking, or
tying as the case may be.

These appliances may be taken as a bridge between
the two sorts of exercises in use in the Montessori schools.
They mark a transition from the principles which are common to most educational reformers to those associated
particularly with the method worked out by Madame Montessori. Another quotation from her first book gives the clue
to an understanding of this method:

In a pedagogical method which is experimental the education of
the senses must undoubtedly assume the greatest importance.
. . . The method used by me is that of making a pedagogical experiment with a didactic object and awaiting the spontaneous
reaction of the child. . . . With little children, we must proceed
to the making of trials, and must select the didactic materials in
which they show themselves to be interested. . . . I believe,
however, that I have arrived at a selection of objects representing
the minimum necessary to a practical sense education.

Madame Montessori started her career as a teacher
among deficient children in the hospitals where Seguin had
worked. Naturally she experimented with the material used
with her subnormal pupils when she began working with
normal children. It is equally natural that many of the
objects which had proved useful with the former were also
usable with the average school child. Ordinary school methods succeed with deficient children when used more slowly
and with more patience; and in the same way Madame
Montessori found that many of the appliances which had

before been used only for deficients produced remarkably successful results with ordinary children, when used with more rapidity and liberty. Therefore her "didactic material" includes many things that are used generally to develop sensory consciousness among deficients. But instead of using the material in a fixed order and under the guidance of a teacher, the normal child is allowed complete liberty in its use; for the object is no longer to awaken powers that are nearly lacking, but to exercise powers that the child is using constantly in all his daily actions, so that he may have a more and more accurate and skillful control over them.

The exercises to develop the faculties of the child are especially so arranged as to train the power to discriminate and to compare. His sensory organs are nearly all exercised with apparatus designed, like the button frames, to allow the child to do one thing for one purpose. The pupil does not have to use these objects in any fixed order or work for any length of time on one thing. Except for the very youngest children, who do only the very simplest exercises, pupils are at liberty to work at any one they wish and for as long as they wish. Montessori believes that the child will turn naturally to the exercise he is ready for. The materials to develop the sense of touch are among the simplest. There are small boards with strips of sandpaper running from the roughest to the smoothest, and pieces of different kinds of cloth; these the child rubs his hands over while his eyes are blindfolded, distinguishing the differences. The appliances designed to teach the child to distinguish differences of form and size use the sense of touch as a strong aid to sight. There are blocks of wood with holes of different diameters and depths, and cylinders to fit each hole. The child takes all the cylinders out, rubs his fingers around their edge and then around the rim of the holes and puts them back in the proper hole. The ability to judge of size is also exercised by giving the child a set of graduated wooden blocks with which he builds a tower, and another set which he may use to make a stair. The power to distinguish form is developed by wooden insets of all shapes which fit into holes in a thin board. The child takes out the insets, feels of them and then replaces them. Later the teacher tells him the geometrical name of each form while he is touching it, and then has him distinguish them by name.

There are sets of cardboard forms to correspond to the wooden ones, and metal plaques where the form appears as a hole in the centre of the plaque. These are used in games which consist in matching the same form in the different materials, and for drawing the form in outline on paper to be filled in with colored pencils.

The method of teaching reading and writing uses the sense of touch to reenforce the lesson the pupil gets through the eye and ear. Sandpaper alphabets with each letter pasted on a square of cardboard are given a child. He rubs his finger over these as if he were writing and makes the sound of the letter as he rubs. Movable letters are used only after the child is familiar with the letters by touch, and with them he makes words. Writing usually precedes reading when children learn in this way; when they take pencil or chalk, they are able to trace the letters with very little difficulty because the muscles as well as the eye are familiar with the forms.

The sense of hearing is exercised by means of two sets of bells, one fixed to give the scale, the other movable, so that the child can make his own scale by comparing with the fixed scale. The children play a number of games where they are as quiet as possible, acting out simple, whispered directions from the teacher. There is as well a series of rattles filled with sand, gravel, and grains, and the game is to guess which rattle is being shaken. The sense of color is developed in the same way by means of specially arranged apparatus. This consists of small tablets wound with colored silks in all colors and shades, which are used in many different ways, according to the age and skill of the pupil. The youngest learn to distinguish two or three colors and to tell dark from light shades. The older pupils who are familiar with the colors acquire enough skill in their manipulation to be able to glance at one tablet and then go to the other side of the room and bring either an exact match or the next shade lighter or darker, according to what the teacher has asked for.

Muscular development is provided for by giving the

children plenty of time during the school day to run and play, and by means of apparatus for free gymnastics, while the finer coordinating muscles are being constantly exercised while the child is manipulating the appliances for sense training. The faculty of speech is trained by having the children practice the pronunciation of words and syllables. The fundamental conceptions of number are taught much as are reading and writing. Besides the sandpaper numbers and the plain cardboard ones, there is a series of wooden bars varying in length from one to ten decimeters, which the children use in connection with numbers in learning the combinations up to ten.

The foregoing description of the didactic material is very brief and general and omits many of the uses of the appliances as well as reference to some of the less used material, but it serves to illustrate the nature and purpose of the work done by the children. Pupils acquire a marked skill in the handling of the material which appeals especially to them, and children of four and five learn to write with very little effort. In fact, Madame Montessori believes that the average child is ready for many of the ideas which he usually does not get until his sixth year at an earlier age, when they can be acquired more easily; and that a system such as hers which allows the child to perform one set of acts at the time when he is ready for it saves him a great deal of time later on, besides giving a more perfect result than could then be achieved.

Each piece of material is designed to train singly one specific sense through the performance of one set of fixed acts. Consequently if liberty is confounded with doing as one pleases, this method must appear very strict. Liberty is found in the use the children make of the material. The amount of freedom the pupils are allowed in the classroom has already been described, and the role of the teacher is made to correspond with this liberty. She is trained not to interfere with any spontaneous activity of the child and never to force his attention where it is not given naturally. When a child has turned of his own accord to a certain apparatus the teacher may show him the proper use of it; or in rare cases she may try to direct the child's attention to a different type of work if he seems inclined to concentrate to excess on one thing, but if she fails she never insists. In fact nothing is done by the teacher to call the child's attention to his weaknesses and failures, or to arouse any negative associations in his mind. Madame Montessori says,

If he [the child] makes a mistake, the teacher must not correct him, but must suspend her lesson to take it up again another day. Indeed, why correct him? If the child has not succeeded in associating the name with the object, the only way in which to succeed would be to repeat both the action of the sense stimuli and the name; in other words, to repeat the lesson. But when the child has failed, we should know that he was not at that instant ready for the physic associations which we wished to provoke in him, and we must therefore choose another moment. If we should say, in correcting the child, "No, you have made a mistake," all these words, which, being in the form of a reproof, would strike him more forcibly than others, would remain in the mind of the child, retarding the learning of the names. On the contrary, the silence which follows the error leaves the field of consciousness clear, and the next lesson may successfully follow the first.

The simplicity and passivity of the teachers' role are increased by the nature of the didactic material. Once the child has been taught the nomenclature connected with the apparatus, the teacher ceases to teach. She becomes merely an observer as far as that pupil is concerned until he is ready to move on to another appliance. This is possible because of what Montessori calls the "self-corrective" nature of her material. That is, each thing is arranged so that the child can do but one complete thing with it, so that if he makes a mistake the apparatus does not work. Thus a child working with any one thing does not have to be told when he makes a mistake how to correct it. He is confronted with an obvious problem, which is solved by his own handling of the material. The child is educating himself in that he sees his own mistakes and corrects them, and the finished result is perfect; partial success or failure is not possible.

Take the simplest piece of material, the block of wood in which solid cylinders are set. There are ten of these cylinders, each varying, say, in length about a quarter of an inch from the one next it. The child takes all these cylinders from their proper holes and mixes them up; then he puts them back in their right places again. If he puts a cylinder in a hole too deep for it, it disappears; if the hole is too shallow it sticks up too far, while if every cylinder is put in its proper hole, the child has a solid block of wood again. All the geometrical insets are self-corrective in exactly the same way. Even the youngest child would know whether he had succeeded with the button and lacing frames. The tower blocks will not pile up into a tower unless the child piles them one on top of the other in decreasing sizes, nor will the stair blocks make a stair unless they are laid side by side according to the same principle. In using the color tablets the child needs rather more preparation; but when he has learned to distinguish the eight different shades of one of the eight colors, he is ready to arrange them so that they blend from dark to light, and if he makes a mistake the tablet placed in wrong sequence will appear to him as an inharmonious blot. Once the pupil gets the idea with one color he is able to work it out for himself for the other seven. Since the pupils are never allowed merely to play with an apparatus, it becomes associated in his mind with performing the right set of actions, so a misstep appears to him as something to be undone, something calling for another trial. The educational purpose Montessori aims to serve in making her material self-corrective, is that of leading the child to concentrate upon the differences in the parts of the appliances he is working with; that is, in trying for the fixed end he has to compare and discriminate between two colors, two sounds, two dimensions, etc. It is in making these comparisons that the intellectual value of training the senses lies. The particular faculty or sense that the child is exercising in using any one apparatus is sharpened by concentration upon the *relations* between the things. Sense-development of an intellectual character comes from the growth of this power of the sense organ to compare and discriminate, not from teaching the child to recognize dimensions, sounds, colors, etc., nor yet from simply going through certain motions without making a mistake. Montessori claims that intellectual result differentiates her work from the appliances of the kindergarten.

As we said above, the difference between the Montessori

method and the views of American reformers lies not in a difference of opinion as to the value of liberty, but rather in a different conception of the best use to be made of it. Physically the pupils of a Montessori class are freer than they are in the classes of most American educators with whose views this book has been dealing; intellectually they are not so free. They can come and go, work and be idle, talk and move about quite voluntarily; getting information about things and acquiring skill in movement are the ends secured. Each pupil works independently on material that is self-corrective. But there is no freedom allowed the child to create. He is free to choose which apparatus he will use, but never to choose his own ends, never to bend a material to his own plans. For the material is limited to a fixed number of things which must be handled in a certain way. Most American educators think that the training of the pupil to habits of right thinking and judgment is best accomplished by means of material which presents to him real problems, and they think that the measure of reality is found in connection with the experiences of life out of school. The big thing that children have to learn is twofold; for their adjustment to the world in which they find themselves involves relations to people and to things. Adjustment means not simply the ability to control their bodies, but an intellectual adjustment as well, an ability to see the relations between things, to look behind their surface and perceive their meaning not alone to the individual, but to the community as well. "The best way of making sure that children learn this double adjustment is," says the American school-teacher, "to give them work which represents truly the conditions they have to deal with out of school."

Outside the classroom the child is constantly having to bend material things to his own needs, and to satisfy the demands that are made upon him because he lives with other people. If he is to accomplish this successfully for himself and others it is important that he learn to see things as they are; that he be able to use his senses accurately to understand the meaning that things and people have to and for him as a member of society. Hence the need of freedom to meet and solve these problems in school,

Solving problems in school as they would have to be met out of school. (Francis Parker School, Chicago.)

much as one has to do out of school. Madame Montessori, on the other hand, believes that the technique of living can best be learned by the child through situations that are not typical of social life, but which have been arranged in order to exercise some special sense so as to develop the faculties of discrimination and comparison.

The difference of opinion resolves itself into the acceptance of different views of the nature of the human intelligence. Montessori, in common with the older psychologists, believes that people have ready-made faculties which can be trained and developed for general purposes, regardless of whether the acts by which they are exercised have any meaning other than the training they afford. The child is born with undeveloped faculties which can be made to blossom by suitable appliances, and then devoted at will to other uses. Most educators in this country agree with the newer psychological theories that skill cannot be achieved independently of the tools used and the object fashioned in the accomplishment of a special end. Exercises which distinguish for the child the abstract qualities like length and color, regardless of the things of which they are qualities, may give the child great skill in performing the special exercise, but will not necessarily result in making him more successful in dealing with these qualities as they appear as factors in the situations of life. Much less will they train powers of comparing and discriminating at large so that they may be transferred to any use. A child is not born with faculties to be unfolded, but with special impulses of action to be developed through their use in preserving and perfecting life in the social and physical conditions under which it goes on.

If, accordingly, the child in an American progressive school does not usually have as much freedom of moving about and of choice of his time for doing work, the explanation does not consist in a less degree of belief in the value of liberty. The emphasis falls on the larger freedom of using and testing senses and judgment in situations typical of life. Because these situations are social, they require that children work more together in common pursuits; because they are social they permit and often require the teacher's aid, just as one gains assistance from others in the ordinary affairs of life. Help from others is not to be feared as an encroachment upon liberty, but that kind of help which restricts the use of the children's own intelligence in forming ends and using ingenuity, initiative and inventiveness in the selection and adaption of materials. The limitation of material to performing exercises calculated to train an isolated sense—a situation that never presents itself in life—seems to the American teacher a greater limitation of freedom than that which arises from the need of cooperation with others in the performance of common activities. It is desirable not merely that the child should learn not to interfere with others as they execute their own ends, but also that he should learn to work with them in an intelligent way. Hence the scope of the material should not be limited to training the discriminations and comparisons of a single sense (however valuable this may be with very young children who are incapable of cooperative activity and whose main business is to master the use of their organs),[1] but should be varied enough to offer typical problems calling for the kind of comparison and discrimination used in ordinary life-situations. And when pupils are making real things for real uses, or finding out about the activities and materials of out-of-school life, several children need to work at the same thing and keep at one thing with some consecutiveness.

But if the educators of this country differ with Montessori as to the existence of innate faculties which can be trained for general application by special exercises designed only for training and not for the accomplishment of results in which training is incidental, they welcome her efforts to secure that degree of freedom in the schoolroom which will enable teachers to become acquainted with the real powers and interests of the child and thus secure the data for a scientific method in education. They appreciate the force of her point that artificial conditions of restraint prevent teachers from getting true knowledge of the material with which

---

1. It is significant that many who have experimented with the apparatus hold that its value is greatest with quite young children —three and four years old.

they are dealing, so that instruction is limited to repetition of traditional processes. They perceive that her insistence upon touch associated with muscular movement as a factor in learning to write and read, is a real contribution to the technique of elementary instruction. She has become a most important factor in the popularizing of the gospel of liberty as indispensable to any true education.

With a wider understanding of the meaning of intellectual and moral freedom, and the accompanying breakdown of the negative and coercive ideas of discipline, the chief obstacle to the use of the teacher's own powers of observation and experimentation will disappear. The scientific interest which requires personal observation, reflection, and experimental activity, will be added to the teacher's sympathetic interest in the welfare of children. Education that associates learning with doing will replace the passive education of imparting the learning of others. However well the latter is adapted to feudal societies, in which most individuals are expected to submit constantly and docilely to the authority of superiors, an education which proceeds on this basis is inconsistent with a democratic society where initiative and independence are the rule and where every citizen is supposed to take part in the conduct of affairs of common interest. It is significant of the wide-reaching development of the democratic spirit that the voice most influentially identified at the present time with the ideal of liberty in education should sound forth from Italy.

7. THE RELATION OF THE SCHOOL TO THE COMMUNITY

Work is essentially social in its character, for the occupations which people carry on are for human needs and ends. They are concerned with maintaining the relations with things and with others which make up the world we live in. Even the acts that are concerned with keeping alive are arranged to fit into a social scheme which has modified all man's instinctive acts and thoughts. Everything about this scheme is dependent upon the ability of people to work together successfully. If they can do this a well-balanced, happy and prosperous society results. Without these occupations, which are essentially social life—that is human life—civilization cannot go on. The result is a sort of social education by necessity, since every one must learn to adapt himself to other individuals and to whole communities. When it is left to circumstances this education, although necessary, is haphazard and only partial. We send children to school supposedly to learn in a systematic way the occupations which constitute living, but to a very large extent the schools overlook, in the methods and subject-matter of their teaching, the social basis of living. Instead of centering the work in the concrete, the human side of things, they put the emphasis on the abstract, hence the work is made academic —unsocial. Work then is no longer connected with a group of people all engaged in occupations, but is isolated, selfish and individualistic. It is based on a conception of society which no longer fits the facts, an every-man-for-himself society which ceased to exist a hundred years ago. The ordinary school curriculum ignores the scientific democratic society of to-day and its needs and ideals, and goes on fitting children for an individualistic struggle for existence, softened by a little intellectual "culture" for the individual's enjoyment.

Schools started in this country in pioneer days, when a comparatively small number of people were scattered over

an immense country that offered them unlimited and unexplored opportunities. The pioneer was dependent upon his
own ability in seizing these opportunities, in getting ahead,
in his use of nature's raw material. He lived much alone and
for himself; no one was really dependent upon his relations
with others; for there were few people, endless material,
and unorganized communities, without traditions or institutions. The welfare of the country was dependent upon the
spread of the doctrines of getting on, and every man for
himself. It was entirely natural that the new schools should
reflect this ideal and shape their work to drive home the
lesson. Our early settlers came from countries with traditions of culture and "learning"; and it was natural that
they should look to their schools to keep alive these trans-
planted ideals in the midst of their struggle with nature.
Culture did not mean to them a harmonious development of
all the child's faculties, but it meant rather the storing up
of historical facts and the acquiring of knowledge and the
literatures of the past. Learning, too, did not mean finding
out about the things around them or about what was going
on in other parts of the world; it meant reviewing the achievements of the past, learning to read the dead languages, the
deader the language the greater the reputation for "learning." The school curriculums were principally devoted, therefore, to turning the eyes of the pupils to the past, where
alone they could find things worth studying and where, too,
they might find the refinements of esthetic and intellectual
development. A knowledge of the "three R's" and a little
natural "smartness" was all the social equipment the child
needed, all the preparation that was necessary for him to
begin to get on in the world. Once he had that equipment
the schools could then turn their attention to giving him
culture.

However interesting or enlightening such culture might
be to the individual, obviously the first business of the public
school is to teach the child to live in the world in which he
finds himself, to understand his share in it, and to get a
good start in adjusting himself to it. Only as he can do these
things successfully will he have time or inclination to cultivate purely intellectual activities.

The public schools started with the awakening of the

spirit of liberty and democracy. More and more people realized that there was no possibility of an equal chance for
every one, if a very small minority of the population had
entire control of the material of science, which was so rapidly changing all social and industrial conditions. Naturally
enough when these popular schools were started, the community turned to the schools already in existence for their
curriculum and organization. The old schools, however, were
not conducted to give equal opportunity to all, but for just
the opposite purpose, to make more marked the line between
classes, to give the leisure and moneyed classes something
which every one could not get, to cater to their desire for
distinction and to give them occupation.

People lived generation after generation in the same
place, carrying on the same occupations under the same
conditions. Their world was so small that it did not seem to
offer much in the way of material for a school education;
and what it did offer was primarily concerned with earning
a living. But the schools were for people who did not earn
their own livings, for people who wished to be accomplished,
polished and interesting socially, so the material was abstract, purposely separated from the concrete and the useful.
Ideals of culture and education were and still are to a surprising extent based entirely upon the interests and demands
of an aristocratic and leisure class. Having such an ideal of
culture it was natural to the pioneers to copy the curriculum
of the schools made for this ideal, even when the purpose
of their schools was to give an equal industrial and social
chance to all. From the very beginning of the public schools
in this country the material of the curriculum reflected social conditions which were rapidly passing away: ideals of
education that a feudal society, dependent upon its aristocracy, had developed.

The tremendous change in society which the application of science to industry brought about, changes which
caused the French Revolution and the general revolution of
1848, effected a reconstruction of nearly all the institutions
of civilization, the death of a great many, and the birth of
many more. The need of popular education was one of the
results of the change, and with this need came the public

schools. As their form did not adapt itself to the new conditions, but simply copied the schools already existing, the process of reconstruction to fit the new society is still going on, and is only just beginning to become conscious. A democratic society, dependent upon applications of science for all its prosperity and welfare, cannot hope to use with any great success a system of education which grew up for the ruling body in an autocratic society using only human power for its industries and wealth. The ever-increasing dissatisfaction with the schools and the experiments in trade and industrial training which are being started, are protests against clinging to this outworn inheritance. They are the first steps in the process of building a new education which shall really give an equal chance to every one, because it will base itself on the world in which the children live.

There are three things about the old-fashioned school which must be changed if schools are to reflect modern society: first, the subject-matter, second, the way the teacher handles it, and third, the way the pupils handle it. The subject-matter will not be altered as to name. Reading, writing, arithmetic and geography will always be needed, but their substance will be greatly altered and added to. In the first place modern society realizes that the care and growth of the body are just as important as the development of the mind; more so, for the latter is dependent upon the former, so schools will become places for children to learn to live physically as well as mentally. Again we need to know how to read and write nowadays so that we may be able to do the simplest daily actions, take the right street-car, avoid dangerous places, and keep in touch with people and events we cannot see, and, in fact, do almost everything connected with our occupations. But the schools are still teaching reading and writing as if they were ends in themselves, simply luxuries to be acquired by pupils for their private edification. The same thing is true of geography; pupils learn boundaries, populations and rivers as if their object was to store up facts that everybody may not know. But in a society where railroads and steamboats, newspapers and telegraph, have made the whole world neighbors, and where no community is self-supporting, the desirability of really knowing about these neighbors is obvious. In other words our world has been so tremendously enlarged and complicated, our horizons so widened and our sympathies so stimulated, by the changes in our surroundings and habits brought about by machinery, that a school curriculum which does not show this same growth can be only very partially successful. The subject-matter of the schoolroom must be enlarged to take in the new elements and needs of society. This can be done without overburdening the pupils by effecting the second and third necessary changes.

The complication and multiplication due to machinery and the increase in the mere number of facts that are known about things through scientific discoveries, make the task of mastering even one subject almost impossible. When we consider all the facts connected with teaching the geography of our own country, the climatic and geological facts, the racial facts, the industrial and political facts, and the social and scientific facts, we begin to realize the hopelessness of teaching with lists of facts. Geography embraces nearly the entire range of human knowledge and endeavor. The same thing is true to a lesser extent of all the subjects in the curriculum. The great number of facts at our disposal in any one branch makes a mere classification of the principal ones seem like a makeshift. So teachers, instead of having their classes read and then recite facts from text-books, must change their methods. Facts present themselves to every one in countless numbers, and it is not their naming that is useful, but the ability to understand them and see their relation and application to each other. So the function of the teacher must change from that of a cicerone and dictator to that of a watcher and helper. As teachers come to watch their individual pupils with a view to allowing each one the fullest development of his thinking and reasoning powers, and to use the tables of reading, writing, and arithmetic as means of training the child's abilities to judge and act, the role of the child necessarily changes too. It becomes active instead of passive, the child becomes the questioner and experimenter.

It is the rare mind that can get relations or draw conclusions from simply hearing facts. Most people must see and handle things before they can tell how these things will behave and what their meaning is. The teacher then becomes the one who sees that the pupils get proper material, and that they use it in ways that are true; that is, in ways that represent relations and conditions that actually exist outside the classroom. This is simply another way of saying that in a society where every one is supposed to take care of himself, and is supposed to have liberty of person and action, up to the point of harming others, it is pretty important that every one should be able to conduct himself, that is, to act so that he can take care of himself successfully. For its own sake society cannot afford to train up its children in a way that blunts and dulls the quickness and accuracy of judgment of the baby before it begins school. If it does this it is increasing the number of incompetents who will be a drag on the whole of society. Dogmatic methods which prescribe and make for docility and passivity not only become ineffective in modern society but they actually hinder the development of the largest possibilities of society.

All the educational reformers following Rousseau have looked to education as the best means of regenerating society. They have been fighting against the feudal and pioneer notion that the reason for a good education was to enable your children and mine to get ahead of the rest of the community, to give individuals another weapon to use in making society contribute more to their purse and pleasure. They have believed that the real reason for developing the best possible education was to prevent just this, by developing methods which would give a harmonious development of all the powers. This can be done by socializing education, by making schools a real part of active life, not by allowing them to go their own way, shunting off all outside influences, and isolating themselves. Froebel, Pestalozzi, and their followers tried to effect just this linking up with society which would result in the development of a social spirit in every one. But they did not have the means for making their schools embryo communities. The demand for popular education was still so small that the community was not willing to recognize the schools as an integral part, and the idea that children were anything but miniature grown-ups, was

still so new that successful methods of handling groups of
children had not been developed. The role of the community
in making the schools vital is just as important as the role
of the school itself. For in a community where schools are
looked upon as isolated institutions, as a necessary convention, the school will remain largely so in spite of the most
skillful methods of teaching. But a community that demands
something visible from its schools, that recognizes the part
they play in the welfare of the whole just as it recognizes
its police and fire departments, that uses the energies and
interest of its youthful citizens, not simply controlling their
time until they are prepared to be turned out as citizens—
such a community will have social schools, and whatever its
resources, it will have schools that develop community spirit
and interests.

A great deal has been written lately about the public-
school system at Gary, Ind., with special reference to the
novel features of school administration that are being
worked out there, or else with emphasis on the opportunities
for industrial training. But the biggest idea there is the one
behind these new features. It is the social and community
idea. Mr. Wirt, the superintendent of schools, has had an
opportunity to make the schools of the steel town almost
from the very beginning of the town, and he has wanted to
do it right. He did not visit the most famous schools all over
the country or send for the best school architect; instead he
stayed right at home, and forgetting what had or had not
been done in other places, he tried to make the best possible
schools for Gary. The question he tried to answer was this:
What did the Gary children need to make them good citizens
and happy and prosperous human beings, and how could
the money available for educational purposes supply all
these needs? The industrial features of his schools will be
taken up later, but it may be well to point out in passing
that they were not instituted to turn out good workers for
the steel company, nor to save the factories the expense of
training their own workers, but for the educational value of
the work they involved. In the same way it would be a
mistake to consider the Gary schools simply as an attempt to
take the unpromising immigrant child and turn him into

The pupil stays in the same building from day nursery through high school. (Gary, Ind.)

a self-supporting immigrant, or as an attempt to meet the demand of an industrial class for a certain sort of training.

Mr. Wirt found himself the superintendent of schools in an American town, responsible for thousands of children coming from all sorts of surroundings. It was his problem to take care of them for a number of years in such a way that at the end of the time each child would be able to find his own job and do it successfully, whether this was feeding a machine or managing a business, whether it was taking care of a family or working in an office, or teaching school. His problem is not to give the special information each one may need for the details of his work, but to keep the natural interests and enthusiasms of childhood, to enable each pupil to gain control of his mind and body, and to insure his being able to do the rest for himself. To be successful as a human being and an American citizen, is the goal that the public schools of the country have set for their pupils: earning a living forms part of this ideal, and follows as a matter of course if the larger training is successful. There are many factors to be considered in deciding on the best ways of reaching this goal: such as the individual peculiarities of every child that goes to school; the people that will teach; the neighborhood in which the child lives; and the larger community which pays for the schools. Mr. Wirt's plan takes advantage to their full value of the contributions each one has to make to the whole scheme. Each factor is a contributory asset; without it the others could not perform their work; therefore it means a weak spot in the result if anything is overlooked.

A tremendous waste in the organization of the ordinary public school appears at the first glance to a critic who is seeking to spend the school taxes with the greatest possible benefit to the children and to the taxpayers. The entire school equipment of building, yard, and supplies stands empty for half of every school day, besides summer vacation and Saturdays. The buildings are expensive and for the greater part of the time are not in use at all. This is an extravagance in itself, but when we consider the way the average child who goes to public school in town or city spends the hours when he is not in school, and the very incomplete education he gets during the school hours, we begin to realize just how serious this extravagance is. Mr. Wirt decided to keep the schools open all day in Gary, so that the children would not be forced to spend the greater part of their time playing in the alleys and on crowded street corners, exposed to all the dangers to health and morals that such places offer for the loiterer. Still the buildings would be closed for many hours a day and for many weeks, and he decided that the people who built the buildings—the taxpayers—ought to have a chance to use them for public purposes during this time, so the Gary schools have evening school, Saturday classes, and summer sessions. This makes the upkeep of the buildings much more expensive than having them open for a few months only, therefore some way of running the plant more economically must be discovered.

Children cannot sit still all day at their desks as they do for five hours in most schools; therefore other things must be provided for them to do if they are to keep well and busy during eight hours of school. The Gary buildings obtain this necessary economy by using a building for twice as many pupils as the ordinary building is supposed to be able to take care of. There are two schools in every house, one from eight to three and the other from nine to four, and each takes its turn at the regular classrooms during alternate hours, the remaining half of the day being spent in the various occupations that make Gary unique. In this way enough money is saved to equip shops and pay extra teachers for the subjects that supplement the regular curriculum, and to pay for the extra sessions. Thus with taxes of ordinary size the people of Gary get schools that utilize the children's time, and give them greatly increased facilities for learning, besides offering the adults of the community opportunities for special courses in evening school. At present in Gary the number of adults using the school buildings is greater than the number of children, though of course the number of hours they attend school is much shorter. By having two duplicate schools in every building one half the usual cost per classroom is saved, and enough money to supply healthy activities for the children for eight hours a day and to keep the schools open evenings, holidays and Sundays for adults is obtained.

Each building is equipped with a gymnasium, swimming pool, and playground, and has physical directors that are in attendance for the entire eight hours. Physical training is as much a part of the regular school work as anything else, and besides the work that is part of every pupil's program there are two hours a day when the playground is open for the children to use as they please. Instead of going to the streets to play, the children stay in the school and use the play opportunities it offers. For the most part the physical training takes the form of supervised play and apparatus work. Experimentation has shown here as in so many other places that the pupils are not really interested in the formal group exercises, and that they go through with them under compulsion and so lose most of the benefit. So for the gymnastic drill, swimming pool, tennis courts, and apparatus are largely substituted. The directors see that the individual gets the special exercise that he needs so that the work does not lose its orderliness or effectiveness, and besides getting physical development suited to his needs, every child has a healthy and pleasant place to play or otherwise spend his time outdoors.

The Gary pupil is expected to gain physically during the school year just as he is expected to keep up with his grade in his other work. Each child is examined by a doctor, and the pupils who are not strong enough for the strain of the classroom work are not sent home to do nothing until they are stronger, but are kept in school and given a program suited to their strength, their classroom time is cut down to a minimum, and they spend most of the day on the playground or in the gymnasium, doing the sort of things the doctor says they need to get strong. The physical growth of the pupils is just as important as the mental, and by devoting the same care to it that is given to the child's progress through the grades, the schools go a long way towards making themselves a small community which gives every opportunity for a normal and natural life.

The schools are open eight hours a day, but the grade teachers teach for only six hours, while the physical directors are on duty for the whole time. Four hours of each school's time is given to the regular classroom work or laboratories, and one hour for the auditorium and one hour for "application" or play. Then there are the other two hours when the children may use the play facilities if they wish, and they all do use them. By rotating the classes the number of teachers does not have to be increased, and the pupils get the benefit of teachers especially trained for the subject they are teaching. By dividing each school into groups of pupils the classes are smaller than in most public schools. For the first two hours in the morning—from 8:15 to 10:15 —one school has the use of the classrooms, studios, shops and laboratories, one group in a recitation room for the first hour and in the shops for the second, the second group beginning with the shop work. The other school uses the playground for the first hour and attendance is not compulsory, for the second hour one group goes to the auditorium and the other remains on the playground for systematic gymnastics or has an "application" period. Then at 10:15 the first school goes to the auditorium and playgrounds for its work and the second school takes possession of the class and shop rooms for two hours. Grades one to five have two hours daily in regular classrooms for formal instruction in language, history, literature, and mathematics. Grades six to twelve have three hours daily for this formal instruction. The additional hour is taken from the play and application periods. Grades one to five have one hour of laboratory work in science or shop work in industrial training, thirty minutes for music or literature, and thirty minutes for physical training. Grades six to twelve have the entire two hours for shop work in industrial training, laboratory work in science, or music and drawing.

By this scheme of alternation of classes and schools twice the number of children that are usually cared for in one building are taken care of in smaller classes by teachers who are specialists in their subjects. For besides the industrial teachers, there are teachers for French, German, history, mathematics, literature, music, art, nature study, and the sciences. This additional efficiency is paid for by the saving on buildings effected by the two school systems. Each grade room is used by at least four different classes, so each child does not have a desk where he keeps his things and belongings, but has a locker for his books and changes his classroom at the end of the hour. No one teacher is responsible for one set of pupils, but for her own work, and in the same way the pupils are responsible for themselves. Obviously such a scheme as this requires a real spirit of cooperation among the pupils and teachers, and also good business management.

Mr. Wirt believes that lack of just this has been one of the reasons why the public schools have lost so many of the opportunities that Gary is using. Running a big institution successfully from the business end is a large order in itself, and Mr. Wirt feels that school principals and supervisors have been too greatly handicapped in being expected to do this business while carrying out an educational program. He believes that the school principal or superintendent should be a business manager, an administrative officer simply for the building or for the city. The educational policy of the schools, the program, and methods should be looked out for by experts who are free from the details of administration. These supervising educators should not be appointed for districts but for subjects, and should move their offices from time to time from one school to another, so that they may really keep in touch with all the work in their subject, and so that no one school will be overstrong in one subject. These supervisors should act as the educational principals of the schools where they have their offices for the time, and the whole body of supervisors arrange the curricula for all the schools. Gary has too few schools as yet to enable the completion of such a plan, but the present organization shows the same broad-mindedness and desire to get the cooperation and value of all the work of all the teachers through the system, from the newest assistant to the superintendent himself.

In discipline, in social life, and in the curriculum the Gary schools are doing everything possible, in cooperation with church and home, to use to the best educational purpose every resource of money, organization and neighborhood influence. The school is a small community in its discipline, and a democratic one. The work is so well arranged that the children want to go to school; there is no need to drag them with truant officers or overawe them by a show of stern authority. Once in the school building they feel at home and take the same interest and responsibility in the work that they take in their own homes. Each child knows what all the other children and classes are doing, for all the children are constantly meeting in the locker rooms or as they pass through the halls for their change of classroom at the end of every hour. The auditorium and the system of visiting classes, and the repairing and manufacturing of school equipment by the students, are strong factors in creating the spirit that prevails among the scholars. There is a student council in each school elected by the students to attend to the interests of the student body and to the order of the building. There are health campaigns carried on by the school doctors cooperating through the school printing press with the English classes and the auditorium periods. The children take such a keen interest in these, and work so hard that there is a larger per cent of contagious diseases among the children under school age than among those in school, in spite of the greater chances for contagion among the latter. Instead of simply enforcing the health laws, the school authorities tell the children what the laws are, why they were made and how they can help to keep down contagion and all sorts of sickness; in chemistry and cooking the pupils are taught enough about germs and physiology so that they understand what contagion and dirt mean. The result is that the children themselves take every precaution to prevent sickness, and when a classmate is sick they see to it that quarantine is enforced and that the school doctor is notified.

The schools have carried on a pure milk campaign in the same way; the pupils brought samples of milk from home and tested it, and then saw that their parents did something about it if impurities were found. An anti-fly campaign goes on all the time and meets with a real response from the children. In the matter of health the schools not only do their share as a part of the whole community, they do more than this, acting as assistants to the board of health and getting rid of the prejudice and fear of city doctors which is so common in our foreign communities, and which makes it so hard to keep down disease and take care of school children. Once the cooperation and understanding of the children is gained by the city doctors, it is not hard to have their adenoids or eyes attended to. The children know why these things need to be done even if their parents do not, and they see to it that the parents are kept from interfering and that they help.

Another difficult problem for the public schools in an industrial community with a foreign population is to keep the children in school after the legal age at which they may leave. The Gary schools go about this just as they attack the question of public health, not by making more rules or trying compulsion, but by getting the children themselves to help, by making the schools so obviously useful for each individual that he wants to stay. There are no "High Schools" in Gary! A pupil goes to school in one building from the day he enters kindergarten until he is ready for college or until he goes into business or the factory. There is no graduation with a celebration and a diploma at the end of the eighth grade. When a pupil begins the ninth grade his program deviates from the plan of previous years, but otherwise there is nothing done to make the child think he has gone as far as he needs, that from now on he will simply be getting frills and luxuries. The teachers do not change. The same history, language and literature teachers conduct all the grades; and in the shops the pupils get a chance to learn some one thing thoroughly. The pupils do not look forward to the last four years of school with dread of a hard and useless grind, they look at it as a continuation of their school life, getting harder from year to year as their own ability increases. And especially they regard this period as an opportunity to get training whose immediate value they can see. The arguments of the school to persuade the pupils to stay in school are practical, telling arguments, things the children can see. The school press prints from time to time bulletins explaining to the pupils and their parents the opportunities that the Gary schools offer in the way of general education and of special training. These bulletins give statistics and information about the opportunities in the different fields of work; they show the boys and girls in figures the relative positions and salaries of high-school graduates and those who leave school at fourteen—as they appear one, two, or ten years after leaving school. Business men come to the schools and tell the students what the chances for graduates and non-graduates are in their business and why they want better educated employees. Statistics of Gary pupils are kept and shown to the pupils. The usual break between the eighth grade and high school does not exist, and, therefore, parents do not think it necessary to take their children out of school. They find that the sacrifices they have made to keep the children in can be kept up for a few years more. If children are going to learn a trade better by staying in school than by leaving, and if children are keen to continue in school with definite plans for the future, even the most poverty-stricken parent is unwilling to thwart the advantage of his children. It is well known that in big cities where the proportion of pupils who leave school at fourteen is overwhelming, and where the usual reason given is that the parents need the financial help of the children, the real reason for defection is the indifference of the pupils themselves to school. The almost invariable answer given by the child to the question, "Why did you leave school?" is, "Because I did not like it." This fact taken with the poverty at home is enough to make them leave school at the first chance. Give the child work that he recognizes as interesting and valuable and a chance to play, and his hatred of school will speedily be forgotten.

The inflexibility of the ordinary public school tends to push the pupils out of school instead of keeping them in. The curriculum does not fit them, and there is no way of making it fit without upsetting the entire organization of the school. One failure sets a pupil back in all his work, and he soon gets the feeling that his own efforts are not important, because the school machinery works on at the same rate, regardless of any individual pupil or study. Indifference or dislike is almost surely the result of feeling that work is making no impression, that the machine for which he is working is not after all affected or dependent upon his work. In Gary organization has been made to fit each individual child, and is flexible enough so that even the most difficult pupil cannot upset its working. The child and the school get along together. We have explained in an earlier paragraph how the two-school system works so that an individual can spend more or less time on any one subject, or can drop it altogether. The child who is weak physically spends much of his time on the playground, while the child who is weak in arithmetic or geography can take these lessons with both schools or even with a grade below, and hundreds of children in the same building can make the same sort of change in their program without disturbing the orderly conduct of the school routine. A pupil who is stronger in one subject than in the rest of his work, can take that subject with a higher grade. The pupil who is losing interest in school and falling behind in most of his studies, or who is beginning to talk of leaving, is not punished for this lack of interest by being put still further back. His teachers find out in what he is good and give him plenty of time to work at it, and to get ahead in it so that his interest in his work is stimulated. If he later wakes up to an interest in the regular school program, so much the better. Every facility is given him to catch up with his grade in all the work. If this awakening does not come, the boy or girl has still been kept in school until he or she learned some one thing, probably the one most suited to the pupil's ability, instead of leaving or failing entirely by being held back in everything until even the one strong faculty died and the pupil was without either training or the moral stimulus of success.

The school program is reorganized every two months and the pupil may change his entire program at any one of these times, instead of having to struggle along for half a year with work that is too hard or too easy or not properly apportioned. For administrative convenience the schools still keep the grade classifications, but pupils are classified not according to the grade number, but as "rapid," "average," and "slow" workers. Rapid pupils finish the twelve years of school at about sixteen years of age, average workers at eighteen, and slow workers at twenty. This classification does not describe the quality of work done. The slow worker

Special teachers for special subjects from the very beginning. (Gary, Ind.)

may be a more thorough scholar than the rapid worker. The
classification is used not to distinguish between the abilities
of scholars, but to take advantage of the natural growth of
the child by letting his work keep abreast with it. The rapid
child moves as quickly as possible from grade to grade instead of being held back until his work has no stimulus for
him, and the slow worker is not pushed into work before
he is ready for it. Does this flexible system work successfully
or does it result in easy-going, slap-dash methods? We have
only to visit the schools and see the pupils hard at work,
each one responsible for his own movements through the
day, to be convinced that the children are happy and interested; while from the point of view of the teacher and
educator, the answer is even more positively favorable, when
we consult the school records. Fifty-seven per cent of all the
school children in Gary who are thirteen years old are in
the seventh grade or above it. This is a better showing than
most industrial communities can make, and means that the
majority of all the Gary school children go through school
at about the same rate as the average pupil who is preparing
for college. Even more remarkable than this are the figures
regarding the pupils who have gone on to higher schools or
colleges after leaving the Gary schools. One-third of all the
pupils that have left the Gary schools during the eight years
of their existence are now in the state university, in an
engineering school, or a business college. When we remember that the population of Gary is made up principally of
laborers in the steel mills, and is sixty per cent foreign born,
and compare with this the usual school history of the second generation in this country, we realize how successful
Mr. Wirt has been in making a system which meets the
needs of the pupils, a system that appeals to the community
as so good that they want to go on and get more education
than mere necessity requires.

The motive back of these changes from the routine
curriculum is always a social one. Mr. Wirt believes that if
the social end of the school is properly emphasized the
pedagogical will take care of itself. The public schools must
study the needs and qualities of its pupils, the needs of the
community and the opportunities that the community con-

tributes to the schools' welfare. We have seen how the physical life of the child and the health of the community are used in the school curriculum, so as to make the curriculum more interesting, and for the good of the community as well. This same close connection is kept up between the school work and other community interests and matters of daily life. Every advantage is taken of the social instincts of children in the teaching. Instead of isolating each grade and cutting off the younger children from the older, the two are thrown together as much as possible. The younger grades use the laboratories and shops which would be an unwarranted extravagance if the high-school pupils were not in the same buildings and using them also for technical training. They use them not only for beginning lessons in science or manual training, but they go into them when the older classes are working there to act as helpers or as an audience for the higher grades. Fourth and fifth grade pupils thus assist seventh, eighth, and ninth grade students in shops, studios, and laboratories.

The older children learn responsibility and cooperation from having to look out for the little people, and the latter learn an astonishing amount about the subject from waiting on, watching, and asking questions of the older pupils. Both grades find out what is going on in the school and get thereby a large feeling of fellowship, while the interest of the lower one grows and finds reasons for staying in school. The work of the older children is used, wherever it is feasible, in teaching the lower grades. Maps and charts made in drawing are used for less advanced pupils in nature study or geography; the printing shop makes the spelling lists and problem sheets for the whole school; the doctor in his health campaigns calls in the art and English workers to make posters and pamphlets. The halls of the schools are hung with notices of what is going on in the school, with especially good and interesting drawings or maps, with information about what is being made in the different shops, or about anything that the whole school ought to see or know.

Another strong element in making public opinion is the auditorium, where every pupil in the school spends one hour each day, sometimes for choral singing, sometimes to hear an older grade tell about an interesting experiment in physics, to find out from a cooking class about cheap and nutritious bills of fare, or to hear the doctor tell how the school can improve the health conditions in its home neighborhoods. The auditorium period is for the use of the general community as well. Ministers, politicians, any one in the city who is doing anything interesting, may come in and tell the children about it. The school invites all social agencies in the neighborhood to come in in this way.

The hour for "application" contributes to the same end. The children go to the nearest public library to read or to look up references for their class work, or simply for a lesson on the use of library books; or they may go to the neighboring Y. M. C. A. building to use the gymnasium or to listen to a lecture; or they may go to any church or club that offers religious instruction desired by the parents. The school is a social clearing house for the neighborhood. The application period is also used to supplement the regular classroom studies by means of practical work in the shops or on the playground. Thus an arithmetic class may get a lesson in applied mathematics by laying out the foundation for a house on the playground, or by spending an hour in the school store, a room fitted up like a grocery store, where the children get practice in mental and oral arithmetic and in English by playing "store." The application period may also be spent in doing work for the school building. Thus an older pupil, studying stenography and typewriting or bookkeeping, might go to the school office and do an hour of real work, helping one of the clerks. The boys in the fifth grade put in this time in tending the school storeroom. They take entire charge of the school supplies, check up all the material sent in by the board and distribute it through the building to the teachers and janitors. The records of the pupils in the different shops are kept by other pupils in their application time. One paid bookkeeper has general charge of an office, where the pupils come with printed slips filled out by the shop teacher, giving them credit for so much time at a certain rate of skill; the pupil clerks give the pupils credit on their record for this work and keep all the records. Pupils also run a post office for the building, and the writer saw a sixth grade boy delivering salary checks and collecting receipts for them through the building. Children who do this kind of work are not only learning arithmetic and bookkeeping, they are learning as well responsibility and reliability. They get an appreciation of what their school means, and are made wide-awake to its welfare; they learn that they are the real school, identical with its interests.

The school lunch room is conducted by the cooking department. When the Emerson School was first built it was equipped with the regulation cooking school desks, individual gas burners, tables and lockers. All this has since been turned into a serving table where student waiters serve the food they have cooked—real lunches to their fellow students, who pay a student cashier. The younger girls get their cooking lessons by going to the older girls' cooking lessons as helpers and watchers. The girls do all the menu planning and buying for the lunch room and keep the accounts. They have to pay expenses and serve menus that come up to the standard set by the chemistry department, where they have analyzed food and made tables of comparative values. The result is steaming hot food, nourishing and well cooked, sold very cheaply. The daily menu is posted with the price of each article and its food value, and the walls of the lunch room are hung with posters and charts showing the relative values of foodstuffs, sample menus for cheap and nourishing meals, and the extravagance of poor food. These have all been made by the cooking school students and are the result of actual experimentation.

Gary schools do not teach civics out of a text-book. Pupils learn civics by helping to take care of their own school building, by making the rules for their own conduct in the halls and on the playgrounds, by going into the public library, and by listening to the stories of what Gary is doing as told by the people who are doing it. They learn by a mock campaign, with parties, primaries, booths and ballots for the election of their own student council. Pupils who have made the furniture and the cement walks with their own hands, and who know how much it cost, are slow to destroy walks or furniture, nor are they going to be very easily fooled as to the value they get in service and improvements when they themselves become taxpayers. The health campaigns, the application work which takes them to the social agencies of the city, the auditorium periods when they learn more about their city, all give civics lessons that make their own appeal. The children can see the things with their own eyes; they are learning citizenship by being good citizens.

The value of this practical civics is doubly great because of the large number of children with foreign parents, who know nothing about the government or organization of the city in which they are living, and who, because they do not understand what they see about them, cannot know its possibilities and limitations. The parents learn nothing of the laws until they break them, of public health until they endanger it, nor of social resources until they want something. They are naturally suspicious of government and social authority in consequence, and it is very important that their children should have some real knowledge on which to base a sounder judgment. Besides giving them this, the schools try to teach American standards of living to the pupils and so to their parents. On entering school every pupil gives the school office, besides the usual name, age, and address, certain information about his family, its size, its resources, and the character of the home he lives in. This record is kept in the school and transferred if the child moves out of the school district. Every grade teacher takes a certain number of squares in the school district, and they make plans of this area. The children make a large scale map, with streets, walks, lamp posts and mail boxes, locating every house, barn, or shed and every empty lot. This is altered as changes are made. Every child brings measurements of the rooms in his home and draws a floor plan of his house. These plans are kept with the teacher's map of her district, so that she has a complete map of the neighborhood and home of every child living in it. By comparing these with any family record, it is a simple matter to tell if the family are living under proper moral and hygienic conditions.

The teacher has a district small enough to know it

thoroughly, and as far as possible she gets acquainted with all the children living in it. If bad conditions are due to ignorance or poverty, the teacher finds out what can be done to remedy them, and sees to it that the family learn how they can better themselves. If conditions are very bad, neighborhood public opinion is worked up through the other children on the block. From time to time an auditorium period is devoted to showing these maps and pointing out the good and bad features of blocks and neighborhoods. Children always carry the news home to their parents, and as rents and accommodations are freely discussed, these reports are often acted upon. The parents are encouraged to come to the school and ask for information, and on more than one occasion some newly arrived family has moved from an overcrowded rear shack to a comfortable flat with the same rent because through the children they found out that their bad quarters were unnecessary. Because the school does this work to help, and as part of its regular program, it is accepted by the children and their parents as a matter of course. Information about improvements, sanitation, the size and comfort of the houses, and the rents, is given to the parents. If a block is poor a good block near by where conditions are better and the rents the same, is shown them. Thus the schools not only teach the theory of good citizenship and social conditions, they give the children actual facts and conditions, so that they can see what is wrong and how it can be bettered.

Gary schools use the community as much as possible as a contributor to the educational facilities, and in so doing they give good return in immediate results, besides the larger return in alert and intelligent citizens. Conditions in Gary are not ideal. The schools have no larger sums to spend than any city of its size, the teachers might be found in any other town, and the pupils come for the most part from homes that offer their children no training, while the parents are trying to adjust themselves to entirely new surroundings. But these schools have done much by showing a good business management, by spending the taxpayers' money in an economical way so as to give the younger generation the largest possible facilities for spending their time profitably.

The results of the system as seen in the school buildings and playgrounds, the alert and happy students, and the statistics of their progress through school as well as their careers afterwards, are doubly inspiring just because they have been accomplished with the resources available in any public school.

8. THE SCHOOL AS A SOCIAL SETTLEMENT

Schools all over the country are finding that the most direct way of vitalizing their work is through closer relations with local interests and occupations. That period of American school history which was devoted to building up uniformity of subject-matter, method, and administration, was obliged to neglect everything characteristic of the local environment, for attention to that meant deviation from uniformity. Things remote in time and space, and things of an abstract nature, are most readily reduced to uniformity and doled out in doses to children in a mass. Unfortunately the consequences were too often that in aiming to hit all children by exactly the same educational ammunition, none of them were really deeply touched. Efforts to bring the work into vital connection with pupils' experiences necessarily began to vary school materials to meet the special needs and definite features of local life.

This closer contact with immediate neighborhood conditions not only enriches school work and strengthens motive force in the pupils, but it increases the service rendered to the community. No school can make use of the activities of the neighborhood for purposes of instruction without this use influencing, in turn, the people of the neighborhood. Pupils, for example, who learn civics by making local surveys and working for local improvements, are certain to influence the life of the locality, while lessons in civics learned from the purely general statements of a text-book are much less likely to have either applicability or application. In turn, the community perceives the local efficiency of the schools. It realizes that the service rendered to welfare is not remote, to appear when the pupils become adults, but a part of the regular, daily course of education. The statement that the schools exist for a democratic purpose, for the good of citizenship, becomes an obvious fact and not a formula. A community which perceives what a strong factor its school is in civic activities, is quick to give support and assistance in return, either by extending the use of its own facilities (as happens in Gary) or by the direct assistance of labor, money, or material when these are needed.

The supervising principal of public school No. 26 in Indianapolis is trying an experiment unlike any other known to us in an effort to make his plant a true school; that is, a place where the children of his neighborhood shall become healthy, happy, and competent both economically and socially, and where the connection of instruction with the life of the community shall be directly recognized both by children and parents. Mr. Valentine's school is located in the poor, crowded colored district of the city and has only colored pupils. It is not an attempt to solve the "race question" nor yet an experiment suited only to colored people. There is nothing in the school not entirely practical in any district where the children come from homes with limited resources and meagre surroundings. A visitor when leaving this school cannot fail to wish that such ventures might be started in all our great cities,—indeed in any community where people need to be aroused to a sense of their needs, including the fact that if they are to contribute to the best interests of the community, they must be taught how to earn a living, and how to use their resources for themselves and their neighbors both in leisure time and in working hours. Mr. Valentine's school is a school for colored children only in the sense that the work has been arranged in relation to the conditions in the neighborhood; these modify the needs of the particular children who are the pupils. Yet the success of the experiment would mean a real step forward in solving the "race question" and peculiar problems of any immigrant district as well. Mr. Valentine is not interested in illustrating any theories on these points, but in making up for gaps in the home life of the pupils; giving them opportunities to prepare for a better future; in supplying plenty of healthy occupation and recreation; and in seeing to it that their school work reacts at once to improve neighborhood conditions.

Mr. Valentine's school is really a social settlement for the neighborhood, but it has a decided advantage over the average settlement, for it comes in contact with all the children living within its district for a number of hours each day, while most settlements reach the children for only a few scattered hours each week. The school has a larger influence than most settlements because it is a public institution for which the people who use it are paying their share; they feel that their relation to it is a business one, not a matter of philanthropy. Because of this businesslike relation the school is able really to teach the doctrines of social welfare. In any settlement the work is always handicapped by the fact that the people who make use of it feel that they are receiving something for which they do not pay, that something is being done for them by people who are better off financially than they are. But giving a community facilities that it lacks for special classes and recreation through the public school of the district put the work on a different basis. The school is really the property of the people of the district; they feel that they are more or less responsible for what is done there. Any wider activities that a school may undertake are to a certain extent the work of the people themselves; they are simply making use of the school plant for their own needs.

The neighborhood around Mr. Valentine's school is one of the poorest in Indianapolis, and once had a bad reputation for lawlessness and disorder as well. The school had struggled along for years with little or no support from the community as a whole or from individual parents. The per cent of truancy was high, and a large number of cases were sent to the juvenile court each year. The children took no interest in their work as a whole, and cases of extreme disorder were not infrequent; one pupil tried to revenge himself on his teacher for a merited punishment with a butcher's knife, in another case it was necessary to arrest a boy's father as a lesson to the neighborhood. Besides this attitude of hostility and of unwilling attendance, the school had to contend with immoral surroundings which finally made it necessary to do something to isolate the school building from neighboring houses. Finally the school board bought the tract of land and wooden tenements around the school building. It was at first proposed to tear down the old buildings, but the authorities were persuaded to turn them over to the school for its use.

The school now found itself the possessor of a large playground and of three frame tenements in the worst possible condition, the board having stipulated that this added property should mean no further expense to the city after its purchase and the cleaning up of the grounds. It was decided to use the buildings for social and industrial purposes. One of them was fitted up by the pupils and neighbors interested as a manual training building. In this there is a carpenter shop, a sewing room, and a room for the class in shoemaking. Each grade devotes a regular number of hours a week to handwork, and has an opportunity to join other industrial classes after school. The immediate practical appeal of the work is never lost sight of, and the work is arranged to fit the needs of the individual pupil.

The carpenter shop is open all day, and there are classes for the girls as well as for the boys. Pupils are at liberty to go into the shop and work whenever they have any free time. The work is not confined to exercises to train the child in the use of tools, but each pupil makes something that he needs or wants, something that will be of real use to him. Processes and control of tools are taught the pupil by means of the piece of work he is doing. This is the keynote to all the industrial work done in the school. The more remote end of teaching the child processes which will be useful to him later is not lost sight of, but material is always used which has some immediate value to the child or to the school. The boys have learned carpentry work by making things that were needed in the school building—tables, cupboards, and bookcases— and by doing some of the repairing on the building. The girls have learned to sew by making clothes for themselves, for their brothers and sisters, and by making curtains and linen for the school. They have learned to cook by making soup for hot lunches for the school and the neighbors, and by cooking a whole meal for their own class. Besides the cooking and sewing department for the girls, there is a class in millinery and in crocheting. These two classes are conducted from the commercial point of view, to teach the girls to do something that will enable them to earn some money. In the millinery class the pupils start by making and trimming hats for themselves, so that they learn the different processes in the trade.

The girls in the class who show the most skill are then allowed to take orders from friends and neighbors and trim or make hats for them. Besides the cost of the material the buyer pays a very small sum for the work, and this goes into the school treasury. The millinery class has done quite a business in the neighborhood, and turned out some very successful hats. Crocheting is taught as a trade, and any girl who wishes to make some money has an opportunity to learn how to make lace, table doilies, and all sorts of crocheted articles, like hoods, etc., which will sell. As the girls are learning, they are working on something which they can use for themselves or in their homes.

The work for the boys is arranged in the same way. Besides the carpenter work and the repairing there is a boys' cooking class, a shoe-repairing department, and a tailoring shop. The cooking class is even more popular with the boys than with the girls. In the shoe-repairing shop, which holds classes after school hours, the boys learn to mend their own shoes. A professional cobbler is the teacher, and the mending must be neatly done. The boys begin work on their own old shoes and as they progress in skill, are allowed to bring shoes from home to be repaired, or to mend for the girls and for the younger boys in the school, who, however, pay a small sum for the work. The tailoring department is run on the same plan, to teach habits of personal neatness and of industry through giving the pupils work that results in neatness and gives some manual skill and control of tools. The class is taught by a tailor, and the boys learn to patch and mend their own clothes, as well as to sponge and press them. Attendance is entirely voluntary, and the class meets after the regular school work is over. Knowing how to keep themselves tidy has resulted in a very marked improvement in the appearance and habits of the boys in the class, and has had an influence not only on the whole school, but on the neighborhood as well. The boys no longer resent the attempts of the teachers to influence them towards cleanliness and neatness, for they have become conscious of the advantages of these habits.

The cooking and domestic science classes are taught in one of the tenements turned over to the school without hav-

ing been repaired, although the cooking equipment was supplied by the city. All the other work on the building—cleaning, painting, repairing, furnishing, and decorating—was
done and paid for by the pupils of the school with help from
the neighborhood clubs that use the building. There is a large
cooking room, a demonstration dining and sitting room, and
two bedrooms. The girls not only learn to cook real meals,
but they learn how to serve them, and then how to take care
of the demonstration house. The domestic science classes include lessons in buying, the comparative costs and values of
food, something of food chemistry and values, and large
quantity cooking. This work is done in connection with the
soup kitchen. A group of girls have charge of the kitchen
long enough to really learn about the work. They plan the
menu and do the buying, cooking and serving of the soup,
selling it for three cents a bowl to the pupils of the school and
to neighbors. They keep all the accounts and not only have
to make all their expenses, but are expected to make some
profit for the use of the school as well. They have made
enough profit in one year to furnish most of the demonstration house. Aside from teaching how to do housework thoroughly and easily, the purpose of the house is to furnish an
example of what can be done to make one of the regular
frame tenements of the district comfortable and attractive,
without more expense than most of the people now put into
their homes. The house is very simply furnished, with cheap
and strong things, in plain colors that are easily kept clean;
the painting and papering was done by the pupils. The sewing class has made all the curtains and linen for the house,
and made furniture by covering boxes, etc. Besides the class
work that goes on in the building, the rooms are also used as
a social centre for the girls of the school.

The third building left standing on the ground pur-
chased by the school authorities has been turned into a boys'
club house. There is a gymnasium, two club rooms, and a
shower bath room. This house was in exceedingly bad condition when it became part of the school property, and there
was no money and not much lumber available to repair it.
But the boys of the school wanted the club house, and were
not discouraged because it was not given to them all finished.

They started out, as they had done in the manual training and domestic science buildings, to do the work themselves. Under the direction of the manual training teacher, they pulled off old paper and broken plaster, tore up uneven floors and took out partitions. Then they laid floors, put in woodwork and painted it, rehung doors, mended windows, and made furniture and gymnastic apparatus. When there was a job they could not do, such as the plastering and plumbing, they went among their friends and asked for money or help in work. Plumbers and plasterers who lived near the school came in and gave their time and work to help the boys get their building in order, and other friends gave enough money to finish the work. Men in the neighborhood dug a long ditch through the school grounds for sewerage connections. Gradually they are adding to the gymnasium apparatus and to the simple bathing facilities, while cleaning and keeping up the painting continue to supply opportunities for useful work.

As already indicated, the reflex effect upon homes in the vicinity has been marked. The school board had intended to wreck the three tenement houses when they bought the land; but Mr. Valentine saw the opportunity to give the community something which they needed, and at the same time to arouse a spirit of coöperation and interest among both parents and pupils in place of the old spirit of distrust and antagonism, when he persuaded the board to turn the buildings over to the school. He told the pupils what could be done with them and asked for their help in doing it. He got a hearty response at once, and so went out into the district with the children and told their parents what he proposed to do and asked for help. He got the same generous response for the first building, the manual training shops, as for the boys' club. Besides the time and material which the skilled workers of the community have contributed, the community has given $350 in cash, no small sum for people as poor as they are. The value of the work being done in these buildings and of the training the boys have had in making them over, is proved by the fact that the community and the boys themselves wanted the work badly enough to pay for getting it in money and work. While it has undoubtedly been a struggle for the school and the district to contribute so much, the benefit to the school and to the community has been greater just because of these sacrifices and struggles. The work has made over the relations between the school and the pupils. The children like to go to school now, where before they had to be forced to go with threats of the truant officer, and their behavior is better when they get to school. The children's parents have changed their attitude in the same way. They not only see that the children go to school, but they want them to go because they appreciate that the school is giving them things they need to make them self-supporting; but they also see that they have their own share to do if the work is to be successful. The school has been the cause of the growth of community spirit in increased civic and social activities of the district. With improved attendance and discipline, the number of cases sent to the juvenile court has decreased one-half in proportion to the number of pupils in school. Meanwhile the educational value of the work done has undoubtedly been greater than that of work done in disconnected shops and kitchens.

The school is also carrying on definite work to arouse the pupils to a sense of responsibility for their community and neighbors. Giving the pupils as much liberty and responsibility as possible around the school buildings is an important factor. Each pupil in the higher grades is given some small child in one of the lower grades to look out for. On the playground they see to it that the charge has a fair chance to play, and that he behaves himself; they see that the little boy or girl comes to school clean and tidy, if necessary doing the washing or mending themselves. This work has proved especially successful in doing away with bullying and in arousing personal pride and a sense of responsibility in the older children; the younger ones are better looked after than before and have many opportunities to learn things from the older and more advanced pupils. The older pupils are also encouraged in every way to help in carrying on the outside activities of the school. They make calls and write notes to keep up the attendance at the night school; they see to the order of the principal's office and keep the boys' club house in order. All the teachers of the school are agreed upon a policy of frank discussion of the poverty of the district, and

(1) The boys like cooking more than the girls do.
(2) Mending their own shoes, to learn cobbling. (Public School 26, Indianapolis.)

of urging the pupils to earn money to help their parents by becoming as nearly self-supporting as possible. Each grade keeps track of what its members earn and how they earn it, and the grade with the largest sum to its credit feels that it has accomplished something worth while during the year.

There is a savings bank in the school to teach the children habits of thrift and economy; here a pupil may deposit any sum from a penny up. The pupil receives a bank book in which stamps are pasted for his deposits, the money being kept in a city savings bank. The school also has a branch library, and the pupils are taught how to use it. Part of the playground has been made into a school garden, and here every pupil in the higher grades has a garden plot, also instruction which enables him to grow successfully some of the commoner fruits and flowers. This work is made very practical; the children have the sort of garden that would be useful and ornamental if it were in their own back yard. The school carries on a neighborhood campaign for home gardens, and the pupils with school gardens do much of this work, telling the people who want gardens what to plant, and giving them practical help with their plot until it is well established. In all these ways the teachers are trying to make ambitious, responsible citizens out of the student body. Inside the school pupils are taught higher standards of living than prevail in their homes, and they are taught as well trades and processes which will at least give them a start towards prosperity, and then, too, they are aroused to a feeling of responsibility for the welfare of the whole community.

All these things are done as part of the regular work of the school, and to a large extent during regular school hours. But there are many other activities which, while not contributing so directly to the education of the children, are important for the general welfare of the whole community. There is a night school for the adults of the neighborhood who want to go on learning, the shops being used as well as the schoolrooms. A group of people especially interested in the school have formed a club to promote the interest of the night school, and to see that the men of the community understand the opportunities it offers for them to perfect themselves in a trade or in their knowledge and use of English. This club is made up of men who live near the school and who are sufficiently alive to the needs of the school and the community to work very hard to let all the district know what the school is already doing for its welfare and what it can do as the people come to demand more and more from it. Besides keeping up the attendance at the night school, the club has done much for the general welfare of the school, like helping raise money for remodeling the buildings and giving an expensive phonograph to the school. The success of the school as a social centre and the need for such a centre are realized when we remember that this club is made up of men who live in the district, whose children are using the school, and who are perhaps themselves going to the night school.

There is also a vacation school during the summer time for the children of the neighborhood, with some classroom work and a great deal of time spent on the playground and in the workshops. The school has an active alumni association which uses the school building for social purposes and keeps track of the pupils that leave. A parents' club has been started as an aid in gaining the cooperation of the pupils' parents in the work of the school and as a means of finding out the real needs of the neighborhood. The parents are brought in even closer contact with the school through the series of teas given by the grades for their parents during the year. Each grade serves tea once a year in the domestic science house for the mothers of its pupils. The children do the work for the teas as part of their domestic science work, and write the invitations in their English class. The teachers use these teas as an opportunity for visiting the children's homes and getting acquainted with their mothers. The teacher who knows the home conditions of each child is much better able to adjust the work to the child, being aware of his weak and strong points. To poverty-stricken, overworked mothers these social gatherings come as a real event.

The pupils of the school are given social as well as educational opportunities through their school life. The boys' club house is opened nearly every night to local boys' clubs, some of them being school organizations and some independent ones. There are rooms for the boys to hold meetings and to play games, and a well-equipped gymnasium. The teachers of the school take turns supervising these evening gatherings. The attendance is large for the size of the building. Giving the boys a place for wholesome activities has done much to break up the habits of street loafing and the gangs which were so common in the district. The girls of the school use the domestic science house for social purposes. Two chapters of the Camp Fire Girls hold regular meetings in the building and get help and advice from the teachers. Each domestic science class aims to teach the girls how to live a comfortable and self-respecting life, as well as how to do housework, and so becomes a social centre of its own. The girls learn to cook and serve good cheap meals, and then they sit down together and eat what they have cooked. They talk over their individual problems with the teacher and with each other, and give each other much practical help. The domestic science teacher helps the girls who have some skill find work to do after school hours so that they can help their families by helping themselves; she helps the pupils find steady work as they leave school and then keeps track of them, encouraging them to go on fitting themselves for better work.

The success of the settlement work the school has done points strongly to the fact that the schoolhouse is the natural and logical social centre in a neighborhood, the teachers coming into closer and more natural contact with both children and parents than is possible in the case of other district workers.

There are large economies combining the school and the settlement in districts where the social and economic standards of living are so low that the people are not especially successful citizens. Both the school and settlement facilities are enlarged by using the same group of buildings for both purposes. The settlement has the use of better and larger shops and classrooms than most settlements can command, and the school uses the social rooms and activities to become itself a community. The school comes in contact with almost all the families in a district so that community action is much easier to establish. But even more important than these economies are the far-reaching results which come from the fact that the school settlement is a democratic community, really reflecting the conditions of the community.

In using the school plant for any activities, whether simply for the usual eight classes or to supply the community with all sorts of opportunities, as the Gary schools are doing and as Mr. Valentine's school is doing, the people of the community feel that they are using for their own ends public facilities which have been paid for by their taxes. They want to see real, tangible results in the way of more prosperous and efficient families and better civic conditions, coming from the increased plant in the district school. Because the schools are public institutions in fact as well as in name, people know whether the schools are really meeting their needs and they are willing to work to see that they do. The school settlement reaps all the advantages of working for definite ends and of having the businesslike cooperation of the community as a body. In spite of the fact that the work of Mr. Valentine's school has been hampered by lack of funds, and that some of the special things done are suited to one particular local population, the changes which have taken place in the neighborhood in the relation between the school and the parents, and in the spirit of the pupils in their school attitude, show what a public school may mean to its neighborhood when it ceases to be an isolated academic institution.

The Gary schools and Mr. Valentine's school have effected an entire reorganization in order to meet the particular needs of the children of the community, physically, intellectually, and socially. Both schools are looking towards a larger social ideal; towards a community where the citizens will be prosperous and independent, where there will be no poverty-ridden population unable to produce good citizens. While changes in social conditions must take place before this can happen, these schools believe that such an education as they provide is one of the natural ways and perhaps the surest way of helping along the changes. Teaching people from the time they are children to think clearly and to take care of themselves is one of the best safeguards against exploitation.

A great many schools are doing some of the same sort of work, using the activities of the community as a means of enriching the curriculum, and using the school plant for a neighborhood centre. The civic clubs of the Chicago public schools, which have already been described, are aiming at the same thing: the better equipment of pupils for their life in the community with the hope of improving the community itself. The Cottage School at Riverside, Illinois, where pupils all come from well-to-do American families, has found a similar club valuable for the pupils and of real use to the town. The school organized by the pupils into a civic league has made itself responsible for the conditions of the streets in certain portions of the town, and is not only cleaning up but trying to get the rest of the town interested in the problem. Mock elections and "self-governments" based upon political organization are examples of attempts of education to meet the need for training in good citizenship. Using the school plant as a social centre is recognition of the need for social change and of the community's responsibility to help effect it.

The attempt to make this enlarged use of the school plant is not so much in order to train young people so that they can assume the burden of improvement for themselves as to give the neighborhood some immediate opportunities which it lacks for recreation, intercourse and improvement. The school plant is the natural and convenient place for such undertakings. Every community has the right to expect and demand that schools supported at public expense for public ends shall serve community uses as widely as possible. As attempts in socializing education have met with such success and such enthusiasm among the children that their value as educational tools is established, so giving the people of the community a real share in activities centered in school buildings and employing school equipment, is one of the surest ways of giving them a more intelligent public spirit and a greater interest in the right education of the youth of the land.

9. INDUSTRY AND EDUCATIONAL READJUSTMENT

The chief effort of all educational reforms is to bring about a readjustment of existing scholastic institutions and methods so that they shall respond to changes in general social and intellectual conditions. The school, like other human institutions, acquires inertia and tends to go on doing things that have once got started, irrespective of present demands. There are many topics and methods in existing education which date back to social conditions which are passing away. They are perpetuated because of tradition and custom. Especially is it true of our institutions of learning that their controlling ideals and ideas were fixed when industrial methods differed radically from those of the present. They grew up when the place of industry in life was much less important than it is now when practically all political and social affairs are bound up with economic questions. They were formed when there was no positive connection between science and the operations of production and distribution of goods; while at the present, manufacturing, railways, electric transportation, and all the agencies of daily life, represent just so much applied science. Economic changes have brought about a closer interdependence among men and strengthened the ideal of mutual service. These political, intellectual, and moral changes make questions connected with industrial education the most important problem of present-day public education in America.

The fact that the Greek word from which our word "school" is derived meant *leisure* suggests the nature of the change which has taken place. It is true at *all* times that education means relief from the pressure of having to make a living. The young have to be supported more or less by others while they are being instructed. They must be saved from the impact of the struggle for material existence. Opposition to child labor goes hand in hand with the effort to extend the

facilities of public schools to all the wards of the nation.
There must be free time for schooling, and pupils must not
come to their studies physically worn out. Moreover, the use
of imagination, thought and emotion in education demands
minds which are free from harassing questions of self-
support. There must be an atmosphere of leisure if there
is to be a truly liberal or free education.

Such things are as true now as when schools were
named after the idea of leisure. But there was once assumed a permanent division between a leisure class and a
laboring class. Education, beyond at least the mere rudiments, was intended only for the former. Its subject-matter
and its methods were designed for those who were sufficiently well off so that they did not have to work for a
living. The stigma attached to working with the hands was
especially strong. In aristocratic and feudal countries such
work was done by slaves or serfs, and the sense of social
inferiority attached to these classes naturally led to contempt for the pursuits in which they were engaged. Training for them was a servile sort of education, while *liberal*
education was an education for a free man, and a free man
was a member of the upper classes, one who did not have
to engage in labor for his own support or that of others. The
antagonism to industry which was generated extended itself
to all activities requiring use of the hands. A "gentleman"
would not use his hands or train them to skill, save for
sport or war. To employ the hands was to do useful work
for others, while to render personal service to others was
a badge of a dependent social and political status.

Strange as it may seem, the very notions of knowledge
and of mind were influenced by this aristocratic order of
society. The less the body in general, and the hands and the
senses in particular, were employed, the higher the grade of
intellectual activity. True thought resulting in true knowledge was to be carried on wholly within the mind without
the body taking any part at all. Hence studies which could
be carried on with a minimum of physical action were alone
the studies belonging to a liberal education. First in order
came such things as philosophy, theology, mathematics,
logic, etc., which were purely mental. Next in rank came

literature and language, with grammar, rhetoric, etc. The pursuit of even what we call the fine arts was relegated to a lower grade, because success in painting, sculpture, architecture, etc., required technical and manual training. Music alone was exempt from condemnation, partly because vocal music did not require the training of the hands, and partly because music was used for devotional purposes. Otherwise education should train men to appreciate art, not to produce it.

These ideas and ideals persisted in educational theory and practice long after the political and industrial conditions which generated them had begun to give way. Practically all the conceptions associated with culture and cultural education were created when the immense superiority of a leisure class over all working classes was a matter of course. Refinement, polish, esthetic taste, knowledge of classic literatures, acquaintance with foreign languages and with branches of sciences which could be studied by purely "mental" means, and which were not put to practical uses, were the marks of culture, just as they were the marks of leisure time and superior wealth. The learned professions—divinity, law, and, to a less extent, medicine—were admitted upon suffrance to the sphere of higher education, for the manual element in the service rendered to others was not so great as in industrial pursuits. But professional education was looked upon with disparagement in contrast with a liberal education just because its aim was rendering service to others. And for a long time medicine in particular occupied a mediocre and dubious position just because it required personal attention to the bodily needs of others.

Opposition to the introduction into higher education of the natural sciences was due not only to the conservative dread of change on the part of established institutions, but also to the fact that these sciences emphasized the use of the senses (which are physical organs), of physical apparatus, and of manual skill required in its manipulation. Even the representatives of mathematical science joined those of literary studies in assuming that the natural sciences must be less cultural than sciences like geometry, algebra, and calculus, which could be pursued in a more purely mental way. Even when the progress of social changes forced more and more useful studies into the curriculum, the idea of a graded rank in the cultural value of studies persisted. Occupations like banking and commerce involved less manual activity and less direct personal service to others than housekeeping, manufacturing, and farming, consequently the studies which prepared for them were at least more "genteel" than studies having to do with the latter. Even at the present time many people associate mental activity with physical acquiescence.

The first breach in this order of ideas occurred in elementary education. Along with the spread of democratic ideas which took place in the eighteenth century, there developed the idea that education was a need and right of the masses as well as a privilege of the upper classes. In reading Rousseau and Pestalozzi, an American student, who is used to the democratic idea of universal education, is not likely to notice that their conception of the educational development of all as a social necessity is even more revolutionary than the particular methods which they urged. But such was the case. Even so enlightened a liberal as John Locke wrote his educational essay with reference to the education of a gentleman, and assumed that the training of the laboring classes should be of a radically different kind. The idea that all the powers of all members of society are capable of development and that society owed it to itself and to its constituent members to see that the latter received this development, was the first great intellectual token of the democratic revolution which was occurring. It is noteworthy that Rousseau was Swiss by birth, that democratic political ideas were rife in France when he wrote, and that Pestalozzi was not only Swiss by birth but did his work in that republican country.

While the development of public elementary schools for the masses inevitably puts emphasis upon the usefulness of studies as a reason for education, the growth of the public curriculum and methods was profoundly affected by the surviving ideals of leisure class education. Elementary education, just because it was an education for the masses, was regarded as a kind of necessary political and economic concession rather than as a serious educative enterprise. A strict line was drawn between it, with its useful studies, and the higher education of the few conducted for genuinely cultural purposes. Reading, writing, arithmetic, the three R's, were to be taught because of their utility. They were needed to make individuals capable of self-support, of "getting on" better, and so capable of rendering better economic service under changed commercial conditions. It was assumed that the greater number of pupils would leave school as soon as they had mastered the practical use of these tools.

No better evidence could be found that primary education is still regarded with respect to the larger number of pupils, as a practical social necessity, not as an intrinsic educative measure, than the fact that the greater number of pupils leave school about the fifth grade—that is, when they have acquired rudimentary skill in reading, writing and figuring. The opposition of influential members of the community to the introduction of any studies, save perhaps geography and history, beyond the three R's, the tendency to regard other things as "frills and fads," is evidence of the way in which purely elementary schooling is regarded. A fuller and wider culture in literature, science and the arts may be allowed in the case of those better off, but the masses are not to be educatively developed so much as trained in the use of tools needed to make them effective workers. Elementary instruction to a larger extent than we usually admit, is a substitute, under the changed circumstances of production and distribution of goods, for the older apprenticeship system. The latter was never treated as educational in a fundamental sense; the former is only partially conducted as a thoroughly educational enterprise.

In part the older ideals of a predominantly literary and "intellectual" education invaded and captured the new elementary schools. For the smaller number of pupils who might go on to a higher and cultural education, the three R's were the tools of learning, the only really indispensable tools of acquiring knowledge. They are all of them concerned with language, that is, with *symbols* of facts and ideas, a fact which throws a flood of light upon the prevailing ideas of learning and knowledge. Knowledge consists of the ready-made material which others have found out, and mastery of language is the means of access to this fund. To learn is to appropriate something from this ready-made store, not to find out something for one's self. Educational reformers may go on attacking pouring-in methods of teaching and passive reception methods of learning; but as long as these ideas of the nature of knowledge are current, they make little headway. The separation of the activity of the mind from the activity of the senses in direct observation and from the activity of the hand in construction and manipulation, makes the material of studies academic and remote, and compels the passive acquisition of information imparted by text-book and teacher.

In the United States there was for a long time a natural division of labor between the book-learning of the schools and the more direct and vital learning of out-of-school life. It is impossible to exaggerate the amount of mental and moral training secured by our forefathers in the course of the ordinary pursuits of life. They were engaged in subduing a new country. Industry was at a premium, and instead of being of a routine nature, pioneer conditions required initiative, ingenuity, and pluck. For the most part men were working for themselves; or, if for others, with a prospect of soon becoming masters of their own affairs. While the citizens of old-world monarchies had no responsibility for the conduct of government, our forefathers were engaged in the experiment of conducting their own government. They had the incentive of a participation in the conduct of civic and public affairs which came directly home to them. Production had not yet been concentrated in factories in congested centres, but was distributed through villages. Markets were local rather than remote. Manufacturing was still literally *hand-making*, with the use of local water-power; it was not carried on by big machines to which the employed "hands" were mechanical adjuncts. The occupations of daily life engaged the imagination and enforced knowledge of natural materials and processes.

Children as they grew up either engaged in or were in intimate contact with spinning, weaving, bleaching, dyeing, and the making of clothes; with lumbering, and leather, saw-mills, and carpentry; with working of metals and making of candles. They not only saw the grain planted and reaped, but were familiar with the village grist-mill and the preparation of flour and of foodstuffs for cattle. These things were close to them, the processes were all open to inspection. They knew where things came from and how they were made or where they went to, and they knew these things by personal observation. They had the discipline that came from sharing in useful activities.

While there was too much taxing toil, there was also stimulus to imagination and training of independent judgment along with the personal knowledge of materials and processes. Under such conditions, the schools could hardly have done better than devote themselves to books, and to teaching a command of the use of books, especially since, in most communities, books, while a rarity and a luxury, were the sole means of access to the great world beyond the village surroundings.

But conditions changed and school materials and methods did not change to keep pace. Population shifted to urban centres. Production became a mass affair, carried on in big factories, instead of a household affair. Growth of steam and electric transportation brought about production for distant markets, even for a world market. Industry was no longer a local or neighborhood concern. Manufacturing was split up into a very great variety of separate processes through the economies incident upon extreme division of labor. Even the workingmen in a particular line of industry rarely have any chance to become acquainted with the entire course of production, while outsiders see practically nothing but either the raw material on one hand or the finished product on the other. Machines depend in their action upon complicated facts and principles of nature which are not recognized by the worker unless he has had special intellectual training. The machine worker, unlike the older hand worker, is following blindly the intelligence of others instead of his own knowledge of materials, tools, and processes. With the passing of pioneer conditions passed also the days when almost every individual looked forward to being at some time in control of a business of his own. Great masses of men have no other expectation than to be permanently hired for pay to work for others. Inequalities of wealth have multiplied, so that demand for the labor of children has become a pressing menace to the serious education of great numbers. On the other hand, children in wealthy families have lost the moral and practical discipline that once came from sharing in the round of home duties. For a large number there is little alternative, especially in larger cities, between irksome child labor and demoralizing child idleness. Inquiries conducted by competent authorities show that in the great centres of population opportunities for play are so inadequate that free time is not even spent in wholesome recreations by a majority of children.

These statements do not begin, of course, to cover the contrasts between present social conditions and those to which our earlier school facilities were adapted. They suggest, however, some of the obvious changes with which education must reckon if it is to maintain a vital connection with contemporary social life, so as to give the kind of instruction needed to make efficient and self-respecting members of the community. The sketch would be even more incomplete, however, if it failed to note that along with these changes there has been an immense cheapening of printed material and an immense increase in the facilities for its distribution. Libraries abound, books are many and cheap, magazines and newspapers are everywhere. Consequently the schools do not any longer bear the peculiar relation to books and book knowledge which they once did. While out of school conditions have lost many of the educative features they once possessed, they have gained immensely in the provision they make for reading matter and for stimulating interest in reading. It is no longer necessary or desirable that the schools should devote themselves so exclusively to this phase of instruction. But it is more necessary than it used to be that the schools shall develop such interest in the pupils as will induce them to read material that is intellectually worth while.

While merely learning the use of language symbols and of acquiring habits of reading is less important than it used to be, the question of the use to which the power and habits shall be put is much more important. To learn to use reading matter means that schools shall arouse in pupils problems and interests that lead students both in school and after they leave school to seek that subject-matter of history, science, biography, and literature which is inherently valuable, and not to waste themselves upon the trash which is so abundantly provided. It is absolutely impossible to secure this result when schools devote themselves to the formal sides of language instead of to developing deep and vital interest in subject-matter. Educational theorists and school authorities who attempt to remedy the deplorable reading habits with which many youth leave school by means of a greater amount of direct attention to language studies and literatures, are engaged in a futile task. Enlargement of intellectual horizon, and awakening to the multitude of interesting problems presented by contemporary conditions, are the surest guarantees for good use of time with books and magazines. When books are made an end in themselves, only a small and highly specialized class will devote themselves to really serviceable books. When there is a lively sense of the interest of social affairs, all who possess the sense will turn as naturally to the books which foster that interest as to the other things of which they feel a need.

These are some of the reasons for saying that the general problem of readjustment of education to meet present conditions is most acute at the angle of industry. The various details may be summed up in three general moral principles. First, never before was it as important as it is now that each individual should be capable of self-respecting, self-supporting, *intelligent* work—that each should make a living for himself and those dependent upon his efforts, and should make it with an intelligent recognition of what he is doing and an intelligent interest in doing his work well. Secondly, never before did the work of one individual affect the welfare of others on such a wide scale as at present. Modern conditions of production and exchange of commodities have made the whole world one to a degree never approximated before. A war to-day may close banks and paralyze trade in places thousands of miles away from the scene of action. This is only a coarse and sensational manifestation of an interdependence which is quietly and persistently operating in the activity of every farmer, manufacturer, laborer, and merchant, in every part of the civilized globe. Consequently there is a demand which never existed before that all the items of school instruction shall be seen and appreciated in their bearing upon the network of social activities which bind people together. When men lived in small groups which had little to do with each other, the harm done by an education which pursued exclusively intellectual and theoretic aims was comparatively slight. Knowledge might be isolated because men were isolated. But to-day the accumulation of information, just as information, apart from its social bearings, is worse than futile. Acquisition of modes of skill apart from realization of the social uses to which they may be put is fairly criminal. In the third place, industrial methods and processes depend to-day upon knowledge of facts and laws of natural and social science in a much greater degree than ever before. Our railways and steamboats, traction cars, telegraphs, and telephones, factories and farms, even our ordinary household appliances, depend for their existence upon intricate mathematical, physical, chemical, and biological insight. They depend for their best ultimate use upon an understanding of the facts and relationships of social life. Unless the mass of workers are to be blind cogs and pinions in the apparatus they employ, they must have some understanding of the physical and social facts behind and ahead of the material and appliances with which they are dealing.

Thus put, the problem may seem to be so vast and complicated as to be impossible of solution. But we must remember that we are dealing with a problem of readjustment, not of original creation. It will take a long time to complete the readjustment which will be brought about gradually. The main thing now is to get started, and to start in the right direction. Hence the great importance of the various experimental steps which have already been taken. And we must also remember that the essential thing to be brought about through the change is not amassing more information, but the formation of certain attitudes and interests, ways of looking at things and dealing with them.

If accomplishment of the educational readjustment meant that pupils must become aware of the whole scope of scientific and social material involved in the occupations of daily life, the problem would be absolutely impossible of solution. But in reality accomplishing the reform means *less* attention than under present conditions to mere bulk of knowledge.

What is wanted is that pupils shall form the habit of connecting the limited information they acquire with the activities of life, and gain ability to connect a limited sphere of human activity with the scientific principles upon which its successful conduct depends. The attitudes and interests thus formed will then take care of themselves. If we take arithmetic or geography themselves as subjects isolated from social activities and uses, then the aim of instruction must be to cover the whole ground. Any failure to do so will mark a defect in learning. But not so if what we, as educators, are concerned with is that pupils shall realize the connection of what they learn about number, or about the earth's surface, with vital social activities. The question ceases to be a matter simply of quantity and becomes one of motive and purpose. The problem is not the impossible one of acquainting the pupil with all the social uses to which knowledge of number is put, but of teaching him in such a way that each step which he takes in advance in his knowledge of number shall be connected with some situation of human need and activity, so that he shall see the bearing and application of what is learnt. Any child who enters upon the study of number already has experiences which involve number. Let his instruction in arithmetic link itself to these every-day social activities in which he already shares, and, as far as it goes, the problem of socializing instruction is solved.

The industrial phase of the situation comes in, of course, in the fact that these social experiences have their industrial aspect. This does not mean that his number work shall be crassly utilitarian, or that all the problems shall be in terms of money and pecuniary gain or loss. On the contrary, it means that the pecuniary side shall be relegated to its proportionate place, and emphasis put upon the place occupied by knowledge of weight, form, size, measure, numerical quantity, as well as money, in the carrying on of the activities of life. The purpose of the readjustment of education to existing social conditions is not to substitute the acquiring of money or of bread and butter for the acquiring of information as an educational aim. It is to supply men and women who as they go forth from school shall be intelligent in the pursuit of the activities in which they engage. That a part of that intelligence will, however, have to do with the place which bread and butter actually occupy in the lives of people to-day, is a necessity. Those who fail to recognize this fact are still imbued, consciously or unconsciously, with the intellectual prejudices of an aristocratic state. But the primary and fundamental problem is not to prepare individuals to work at particular callings, but to be vitally and sincerely interested in the calling upon which they must enter if they are not to be social parasites, and to be informed as to the social and scientific bearings of that calling. The aim is not to prepare bread-winners. But since men and women are normally engaged in bread-winning vocations, they need to be intelligent in the conduct of households, the care of children, the management of farms and shops, and in the political conduct of a democracy where industry is the prime factor.

The problem of educational readjustment thus has to steer between the extremes of an inherited bookish education and a narrow, so-called practical, education. It is comparatively easy to clamor for a retention of traditional materials and methods on the ground that they alone are liberal and cultural. It is comparatively easy to urge the addition of narrow vocational training for those who, so it is assumed, are to be the drawers of water and the hewers of wood in the existing economic régime, leaving intact the present bookish type of education for those fortunate enough not to have to engage in manual labor in the home, shop, or farm. But since the real question is one of reorganization of all education to meet the changed conditions of life—scientific, social, political—accompanying the revolution in industry, the experiments which have been made with this wider end in view are especially deserving of sympathetic recognition and intelligent examination.

The experiments of some of our cities in giving their children training which shall make them intelligent in all the activities of their life, including the important one of earning a living, furnish excellent examples of the best that is being done in industrial education. The cities chosen for description are Gary, Chicago, and Cincinnati. This book is not concerned with schools or courses which are designed simply to give the pupils control of one specialized field of knowledge; that is, which train people for the processes of one particular industry or profession. It is true that most of the experiments in industrial education tried so far in this country have taken the material offered by the largest skilled industries of the neighborhood for their basis, and as a result have trained pupils for one or more definite trades. But wherever the experiment has been prompted by a sincere interest in education and in the welfare of the community this has not been the object of the work. The interest of the teachers is not centered on the welfare of any one industry, but on the welfare of the young people of the community. If the material prosperity of a community is due almost entirely to one or two industries, obviously the welfare of the individuals of the community is very closely connected with those industries. Then the educational purpose of training the children to the most intelligent use of their own capabilities and of their environment, is most easily served by using these industries as the material for the strictly utilitarian part of this training. The problem of general public-school education is not to train workers for a trade, but to make use of the whole environment of the child in order to supply motive and meaning to the work.

In Gary this has been done more completely than in any other single place. Superintendent Wirt believes firmly in the value of muscular and sense training for children;

and instead of arranging artificial exercises for the purpose, he gives children the same sort of things to do that occupy their parents and call for muscular skill and fine coordination in the business of everyday life. Every child in Gary, boy and girl, has before his eyes in school finely equipped workshops, where he may, as soon as he is old enough, do his share of the actual work of running and keeping in order the school buildings. All of the schools except one small one where there are no high-school pupils, have a lunch room where the girls learn to cook, and a sewing room where they learn to make their own clothes; a printing shop, and carpenter, electrical, machine, pattern, forging, and molding shops, where boys, and girls if they wish, can learn how most of the things that they see about them every day are made. There are painting departments, and a metal working room, and also bookkeeping and stenography classes. The science laboratories help give the child some understanding of the principles and processes at work in the world in which he lives.

The money and space required to equip and run these shops are saved from an ordinary sized school budget by the "two school system" that has been described above, and by the fact that all the expense usually charged by a school to repairs and paid out to contractors, is spent on these shops and for the salaries of the skilled workmen who teach in them. The buildings are kept in better repair than where all the work is done during the summer vacation, because as soon as anything needs to be fixed the pupils who are working in the shop that does that kind of work get at the repairs under the direction of the teacher. These shops cannot be considered in any way an unnecessary luxury because they are used also by the high-school pupils who are specializing for one kind of work and by the night and summer school for their vocational classes. The school management says in regard to the success of this plan, "When you have provided a plant where the children may live a complete life eight hours a day in work, study, and play, it is the simplest thing imaginable to permit the children in the workshops, under the direction and with the help of well-trained men and women, to assume the responsibility for the equipment

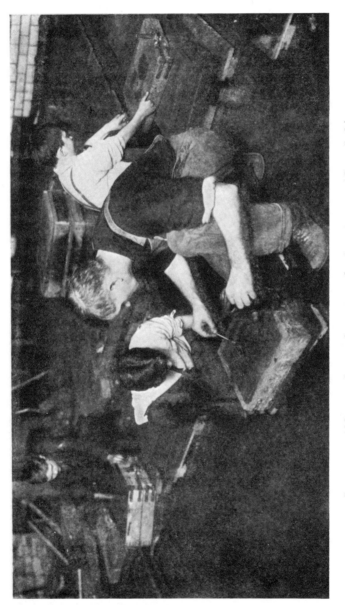

Learning molding, and manufacturing school equipment. (Gary, Ind.)

and maintenance of the school plant. An industrial and commercial school for every child is thus provided without extra cost to the taxpayers."

The first three grades spend one hour a day in manual training and drawing, which take the form of simple handwork and are not done in the shops, but in an especially equipped room with a trained teacher. The pupils draw, do painting and clay modeling, sewing and simple carpentry work. The five higher grades spend twice as much time on manual training and drawing. The little children go into the shops as helpers and watchers, much as they go into the science laboratories, and they pick up almost as much theory and understanding of processes as the older children possess. The art work and simpler forms of handwork are kept up for the definite training in control and technique that comes from carrying through a problem independently. Because the small child's love of creating is very great, they continue until the pupils are old enough to choose what shop they will go into as apprentices to the teacher. Since sixth grade children are old enough and strong enough to begin doing the actual work of repairing and maintaining the building, in this grade they cease to be watchers and helpers and become real workers. Distributing school supplies, keeping the school records and taking care of the grounds are done by the pupils under the direction of the school office or the botanical laboratory, and constitute a course in shop work just as much as does painting or repairing the electric lights. The school heat and power plant is also a laboratory for the pupils, in which they learn the principles of heating and lighting in a thoroughly practical way because they do much of the work connected with keeping the plant running.

The shop and science courses of the schools last only a third of the year, and there is a shorter probation course of five weeks. The pupils choose with the advice of their teachers what shop course they will take; if at the end of five weeks they do not like it they may change. They must change twice during the year. In this way the work cannot lose its educational character and become simply a method of making juvenile factory hands to do the school repairs.

Taking three shop courses in one school year results in giving the pupil merely a superficial knowledge of the theory and processes of any one kind of work. But this is as it should be, for the pupils are not taking the courses to become carpenters, or electricians, or dressmakers, but to find out how the work of the world is done. Moving as they do from one thing to another they learn as much of the theory of the industry as children of their age can understand, while an all-around muscular and sense training is insured. To confine the growing child too long to the same kind of muscular activity is harmful both mentally and physically; to keep on growing he must have work which exercises his whole body, which presents new problems, keeps teaching him new things, and thus develops his powers of reasoning and judgment. Any manual labor ceases to be educative the moment it becomes thoroughly familiar and automatic.

In Gary, the child of the newly arrived immigrant from the agricultural districts of eastern Europe has as much chance to prepare for a vocation, that is really to learn his own capabilities for the environment in which he finds himself, as the child of the educated American. From the time he enters the public-school system, whether day nursery, kindergarten, or first grade, he is among people who are interested in making him see things as they are, and in teaching him how to do things. In the nursery he has toys to play with which teach him to control his body; and he learns unconsciously, by being well taken care of, some of the principles of hygiene and right living. In the kindergarten the work to train his growing body to perform useful and accurate motions and coordination goes on. In the first three grades, emphasis is put on teaching him to read and write and obtain a good foundation for the theoretical knowledge which comes from books. His physical growth is taken care of on the playground, where he spends about two hours a day, doing things that develop his whole body in a natural way and playing games that give him opportunity to satisfy his desire to play. At the same time he is taking the first steps in a training which is more specifically vocational, in that it deals with the practical bread and butter side of life. He learns to handle the materials which lie at the foundations of civilization in much the same way that primitive people used them, because this way is suited to the degree of skill and understanding he has reached. On a little hand loom he weaves a piece of coarse cloth; with clay he makes dishes or other objects that are familiar to him; with reeds or raffia he makes baskets; and with pencil or paints he draws for the pleasure of making something beautiful; with needle and thread he makes himself a bag or apron. All these activities teach him the first steps in the manufacture of the things which are necessary to our life as we live it. The weaving and sewing show him how our clothing is made; the artistic turn that is given to all this work, through modeling and drawing, teach him that even the simplest things in life can be made beautiful, besides furnishing a necessary method of self-expression.

In the fourth grade the pupils stop the making of isolated things, the value of which lies entirely in the process of making, and where the thing's value lies solely in its interest to the child. They still have time, however, to train whatever artistic ability they may possess, and to develop through their music and art the esthetic side of their nature. But the rest of their handwork takes a further vocational turn. The time for manual occupation is now all spent on intensive and useful work in some one kind of work or industry. These pupils are now less interested in games, so they spend less time playing and more time making things. The girl goes into the dressmaking department and learns to sew from the point of view of the worker who has to produce her own things. She is still too young to carry through a long, hard piece of work, so she goes for the first two years as a watcher and helper, listening to the lessons in theory that the seventh, eighth, or ninth grade pupils are taking, and helping them with their work. A girl may choose dressmaking for her first course, but at the end of three months she must change to some other department, perhaps helping cook the lunch for the school and learning about wholesome foods and food chemistry for the next three months. Or if she is fond of drawing, she may devote nearly all her time for shop work to developing her talent for that.

In the same way the boy chooses what shop he will go

into for three months. In the carpenter shop he will be old enough really to make for himself some of the simpler things needed in the school building. If he choose the forging or casting shop he will have a chance to help at shoeing the horses for the use of the department of education, or to help an older boy make the mold for the iron stand to a school desk. In such ways he finds out something about the way iron is used for so many of our commonest things. In the fifth and sixth grades nearly all the boys try to get at least one course in storekeeping. Here they go into the school storerooms with the janitor; and with the school lists at hand unpack and check up the material which comes in both from the workshops and from outside. Then as these things are needed through the building they take the requisitions from the office, distribute the material, and make the proper entries on the books. They are taught practical bookkeeping and are responsible for the smooth running of the supply department while they are working there. As they learn the cost of all the material as well as the method of caring for it and distributing it, they get a good idea of the way a city spends its taxes and of the general business methods in use in stores. Both boys and girls may take a beginners' course in bookkeeping and office management. Here they go into what is called the school bank, and keep the records of the shop work of all the pupils in the school.

Before pupils can graduate from school they must have completed a certain number of hours of satisfactory work in the school shops. In order to fit the needs of every individual pupil, the amount of credit does not depend upon the mere attendance through a three months' course, but each pupil is given credit by the shop teacher for so many hours of work for the piece of work he has done. The rate of work is standardized, and thus a more equal training is insured for all, for the slow worker will get credit for only so much completed work regardless of the time it has taken him, and the fast worker will get credit for all he does even if he outstrips the average. A fixed number of "standard hours" of work entitle the pupil to "one credit," for which the pupil receives a credit certificate. When he has eight of these he has completed the work required by the vocational section

of the Gary schools for graduation. All the work connected
with keeping the records for these credit certificates is done
by pupils under the direction of an advanced pupil.

From the seventh grade the pupils are the responsible
workers in all the shops. A pupil who knows that he has to
leave school when he has finished the eighth grade can now
begin to specialize in the workrooms of some one department. If he wishes to become a printer he can work on the
school presses for an entire year, or he can put in all his
shop time in the bookkeeping department if he is attracted
by office work. The girls begin to take charge of the lunch
room, doing all the marketing and planning for the menus
and keeping the books. Sewing work takes in more and more
of the complications of the industry. The girls learn pattern drawing and designing, and may take a millinery course.
The work for the students in office work is now extended to
include stenography and typewriting and business methods.
The art work also broadens to take in designing and hand
metal work. There is no break between the work of the
grades and the high school in the vocational department,
except that as the pupil grows older he naturally tends to
specialize toward what is to be his life work. The vocational
department is on exactly the same level as the academic,
and the school takes the wholesome attitude that the boy
who intends to be a carpenter or painter needs to stay in
school just as many years as the boy who is going to college.
The result is the very high per cent of pupils who go on to
higher schools.

The ordinary view among children of laboring people in
large cities is that only those who are going to be teachers
need to continue at school after the age of fourteen; it does
not make any difference that one is leaving to go into a
factory or shop. But since the first day the Gary child began
going to school he has seen boys and girls in their last year
of high school still learning how to do the work that is
being done where, perhaps, he expects ultimately to go to
work. He knows that these pupils all have a tremendous
advantage over him in the shop, that they will earn more,
get a higher grade of work to do, and do it better. Through
the theory lessons in the school shop he has a general
idea of the scope and possibilities in his chosen trade, and

what is more to the purpose, he knows how much more he has to learn about the work. He is familiar with the statistics of workers in that trade, knows the wages for the different degrees of skill and how far additional training can take a man. With all this information about, and outlook upon, his vocation it is not strange that so few, comparatively, of the pupils leave school, or that so many of those who have to leave come back for evening or Sunday classes.

The pupil who stays in a Gary school through the four years of high school knows the purpose of the work he is doing, whether he is going to college or not. If he wants to go into office work, he shapes his course to that end, even before he gets his grammar grades diploma perhaps. But he is not taking any short-cut to mere earning capacity in the first steps of office work. He is doing all the work necessary to give him the widest possible outlook. His studies include, of course, lessons in typewriting and stenography, book-keeping and accounting, filing, etc.; but they include as well sufficient practice in English, grammar, and spelling so that he will be able to do his work well. They include work in history, geography and science, so that he will find his work interesting, and will have a background of general knowledge which will enrich his whole life. The student preparing for college does the work necessary for his entrance examinations, and a great deal of manual work besides, which most high-school pupils are not supposed to have time for. It is just as valuable for the man who works with his brain to know how to do some of the things that the factory worker is doing, as it is for the latter to know how the patterns for the machine he is making were drawn, and the principles that govern the power supply in the factory. In Gary the work is vocational in all of these senses. Before the pupil leaves school he has an opportunity to learn the specific processes for any one of a larger number of professions. But from the first day he went to school he has been doing work that teaches the motives and principles of the uses to which the material world is put by his social environment, so that whatever work he goes into will really be a vocation, a calling in life, and not a mere routine engaged in only for the sake of pay.

The value of the pupils' training is greatly increased by

the fact that all the work done is productive. All the shops are manufacturing plants for the Gary school; the business school finds a laboratory in the school office. In dressmaking or cooking the girls are making clothes which they need, or else cooking their own and other people's lunches. The science laboratories use the work of the shops for the illustration of their theories. The chemistry is the chemistry of food; botany and zoology include the care of the school grounds and animals. Drawing includes dress designing and house decoration, or pattern drawing for the hand metal shop. Arithmetic classes do the problems for their carpentry class, and English classes put emphasis on the things which the pupils say they need to know to work in the printing shop: usually paragraphing, spelling, and punctuation. The result of this cooperation is to make the book work better than if they put in all their time on books. The practical world is the real world to most people; but the world of ideas becomes intensely interesting when its connection with the world of action is clear. Because the work is real work constant opportunities are furnished to carry out the school policy of meeting the needs of the individual pupil. The classification according to fast, slow, and average workers, both in the vocational and academic departments, has already been described. It enables the pupil to do his work when he is ready for it, without being pushed ahead or held back by his fellow pupils; the slow worker may learn as much as the rapid worker, and the latter in turn does not develop shiftless habits because he has not enough to do. But if for any reason a pupil does not fit into any of the usual programs of classification, he is not forced to the conclusion that the school holds no place for him. The pupil who is physically unfit to sit at a desk and study goes to school, and spends all his time outdoors, with a teacher to help him get strong.

In the same way the two-school system enables the child who is weak in arithmetic to catch up without losing his standing in other subjects. He simply takes the arithmetic lessons with two grades. In the shops the poor pupil simply works longer on one thing, but as his progress is not bound up with that of the class it makes no difference. The pupil who thinks he hates school, or is too stupid to keep on going, is not dealt with by threats and punishments. His teachers take it for granted that there is something wrong with his program, and with his help fix it for him.

The child who hastens to leave school without any reason as soon as he may, is told that he may come back and spend all his time on the thing that he likes. This often results in winning back a pupil, for after he has worked for a few months in his favorite shop or the art room, he finds he needs more book knowledge to keep on there and so he asks to go back to his grade. The large number of foreign pupils is also more efficiently dealt with. The newcomer concentrates on English and reading and writing until he is able to go into the grade where his age would naturally place him, and the pupil who expects to go to school only a very short time before going to work can be put into the classes which will give him what he needs most, regardless of his age or grade. The work around the school buildings which cannot be done by the pupils under the direction of the shop or department heads, is not done by outside hired help, but is given to some school pupil who is interested in that sort of work and is ready to leave school. This pupil holds the position for a few months only, until he has no more to learn from his work or gets a better position outside. These pupil assistants are paid slightly less than they could earn if they went into an office, but the plan often serves to keep a pupil under school influences and learning when he would otherwise have to leave school in order to earn money, perhaps just before he finishes his technical training.

Gary has fortunately been able to begin with such an all-around system of education, putting it into operation in all her schools in a nearly complete form, because the town was made, as it were, at a stroke and has grown rapidly from a waste stretch of sand dunes to a prosperous town. But many other cities are realizing more and more strongly the necessity of linking their curriculum more closely to the lives of their pupils, by furnishing the children with a general training and outlook on life which will fit them for their place in the world as adults. Recently the

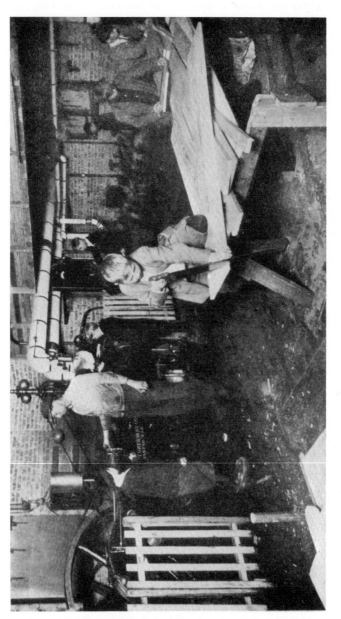

Real work in a real shop begins in the fifth grade. (Gary, Ind.)

Chicago public schools have been introducing vocational work in some of the school buildings, while technical high schools give courses that are vocational, besides work in trade-training. Of course such elaborate equipment as that in Gary is impractical in a building where the shops are not used by the high school as well as the grades. Twenty or more of the regular school buildings in the city have been fitted up with carpenter shops and cooking and sewing rooms as well as laboratories for work in science. Each one of these schools has a garden where the pupils learn how to do practical city gardening. From one-fourth to even a half of the children's time is spent on manual training instead of one-eighth as in the other schools of the city, and in other respects the regular curriculum is being followed. The teachers in the schools who were there before the change of program feel convinced that the pupils not only get through with as much book work as they did when practically all their time was given to it, but that they actually do their work better because of the motive furnished by the hand-work.

The courses given by the schools are not uniform, but most of the schools include courses in mechanical drawing, pattern making, metal work, woodwork, and printing for the boys, and for the girls, work in sewing, weaving, cooking, millinery, laundry, and general home-making. Both boys and girls have work in designing, pottery, bookbinding, and gardening. The program differs somewhat in different schools to meet the needs of the neighborhood or because of the resources of the building; but all the pupils of one school take the same work, so that when a pupil graduates from the eighth grade in one of these schools he has acquired a good beginner's knowledge of the principles and processes underlying two or three trades. This special work is supplemented by the regular work in music and art and this, with work in the elementary processes of sewing and weaving and pottery, constitutes the work for the younger grades. The object of this training is to enable the child to pick up the thread of life in his own community, by giving him an understanding of the elements of the occupations that supply man's daily needs; it is not to confine him to the industries of his neighborhood by teaching him some one skilled trade.

The laboratories for the study of the elements of science play a most important part in this work. In them the child learns to understand the foundations of modern industry, and so comes to his environment as a whole. Without this comprehensive vision no true vocational training can be successful, for it is only as he sees the place of different kinds of work and their relation to each other that the youth can truly choose what his own vocation is to be. Elementary courses in physics, chemistry, and botany are given pupils, and the bearing of the work on what they are doing in the shops is made clear. The botany is taught in connection with the gardening classes, chemistry for the girls is given in the form of the elements of food chemistry. One school gives a laboratory class in electricity, where the pupils make the industrial application of the laws they are studying, learning how to wire when they are learning about currents, and how to make a dynamo when they are working on magnets, etc. All the pupils take a course in the elements of science, so that they may get a true basis for their ideas about the way things work. There is no doubt that even in this rather tentative form the vocational schools have proved themselves a decided success, enabling pupils to do their book work better than before. Linking it with the things of everyday life gives it meaning and zest, and at the same time furnishes a mental and muscular control over the sort of thing they are going to need as adults while earning a living.

There are five technical high schools in Chicago, four for boys and one for girls. In all of these and in three other schools there are given what is known as "prevocational" courses. These are for pupils who have reached the legal age for leaving school, but who are so backward in their work that they ought not to be allowed to do so, while at the same time this backwardness makes them wish not to stay. These classes have proved again the great value of training for the practical things of everyday life to the city child. The boys and girls who are put into these classes are by no means deficient: they are simply children who for one reason or another have not been able to get along in the ordinary grade school as well as they ought; often the reason has been poor health, or because the child has had to move from one school to another, or simply because the usual curriculum made so little appeal that they were not able to hold themselves to the work. The prevocational classes include the sixth, seventh, and eighth grades, and give the greater part of the time to training the child through developing skill with his hands. Book work is not neglected, however, and the pupils are held up to the same standards that they would have to reach in an ordinary school, though they do not cover quite so much ground. The work can be made more varied than in the vocational grammar school because the equipment of the high school is available. Moreover, their ambition is so stimulated that very large numbers of them do additional work and transfer to the regular technical high school work, where in spite of their prior backwardness they do as well as the regular students. Ordinarily not a single one of them would ever have entered a high school.

The girls' technical high school does about what the vocational grammar schools are doing excepting that the work is more thorough, so that the graduate is more nearly prepared to take up work in some one industry. The cooking includes work in the school lunch room, and training in marketing, kitchen gardening and general housekeeping. The vocational classes proper take up large-quantity cooking, household administration, and restaurant management. In sewing the girls learn how to make their own clothes, but they learn as the work would have to be learned in a good dressmaking establishment; there is a course in machine operating for the girls who wish it. More advanced work teaches such principles of pattern making and designing as would be needed by a shop manager. But the most important difference is found in the emphasis that is put on the artistic side of women's traditional occupations. Drawing is taught while the girls are learning to design dresses, and color in the same way; how to make the home pleasing to the eye is made a vital problem in the housekeeping department, and the art department has decorated the model rooms. The pattern and coloring for any piece of work, whether it is a centerpiece to be embroidered, a dress, a piece of pottery, or weaving, has been carefully worked out in the art department by the worker herself before she begins upon it in the shop. The girls are not simply learning how to do the drudgery of housework more efficiently; they are learning how to lift it above drudgery by making it into a profession.

The vocational courses in the boys' technical high schools continue the pupils' study in the regular academic subjects, and give them work in excellently equipped shops. There is work in printing, carpentry, forging, metal work, mechanical drawing, and in the machine shop, well supplemented by the art department. The pupil does not specialize in one kind of work, but secures general training. The object of all the vocational courses in the grammar schools is to prepare the pupils for any branch of work that they may want to take up by giving them an outlook over all the branches of work carried on around them. The work is cultural in much the same way that it is cultural in Gary. The success of these courses in bringing boys back to school, in enabling others to catch up with their grade, and in keeping others in school, points strongly to the fact that for a great many pupils at least some work which will link their school course to the activities of everyday life is necessary.

The technical high schools give two-year courses for the pupils who cannot afford to stay in school for four years. They are designed to give a boy training for a definite vocation, and are at the same time broad enough to count for the first two years of high-school work if the boy should be able to go on later. At the Lane School two-year courses are given in patternmaking, machine shop work, carpentry, electricity, printing and mechanical drawing; all of these courses include work in English, shop arithmetic, drawing, and physiology. The four-year pupils take one of three courses, according to what they expect to do. The technical course prepares students for college, the architectural course prepares for work in an architect's office, and the general trade course prepares for immediate entry into industry. During the first two years of work the student devotes his time to the study of general subjects, and during the last two the major part of his time is put in on work that leads directly to the vocation that he has chosen. The two-year course has not cut down the total attendance at the school by offering a short-cut to pupils who would otherwise stay four years. On the contrary, it has drawn a different class of boys to school, those who had expected to go directly to work, but who were glad to make a sacrifice to stay on in school two years longer when an opportunity appeared to put those two years to definite account in training for the chosen occupation. All these technical high schools have shown conclusively that boys and girls like to go to school and like to learn, when they can see whither their lessons are leading. Giving the young work they want to do is a more effective method of keeping them in school than are truant officers or laws.

In the Lane School the work of the different departments is closely connected so that the pupil sees the relations of any one kind of work to everything he is doing. A problem being set to a group of students, such as the making of a gasoline engine or a vacuum cleaner, the different elements in its solution are worked out in the different classrooms. For the vacuum cleaner, for instance, the pupils must have reached a certain point in physics and electrical work before they are capable of trying to make the machine, since each pupil becomes in a sense the inventor, working out everything except the idea of the machine. When they are familiar with the principles which govern the cleaner they make rough sketches, which are discussed in the machine shop and altered until the sketch holds the promise of a practical result. In mechanical drawing, accurate drawings are made for the whole thing and for each part, from which patterns are made in the pattern shop. The pupils make their own molds and castings and when they have all the parts they construct the vacuum cleaner in the machine and electrical shops. The problem of the gasoline engine is worked out in a like way; and since all the work that is given the pupils has been chosen for its utility as well as its educational value, the pupil does everything connected with its production himself, from working out the theory in the laboratory or classroom to screwing the last bolt. The connection of theory and practice not only makes the former concrete and understandable, but it prevents the manual work from being routine and narrow. When a pupil has completed a problem of this sort he has increased knowledge and power. He has tested the facts he learned and knows what they stand for in terms of the use the world makes of them; and he has made a useful thing in a way which develops his own sense of independent intelligent power.

The attempts of the Cincinnati school board to give the school children of that city a better education, by giving them a better preparation for the future, have been made from a somewhat different point of view. Three-fourths of the school children of Cincinnati, as of so many other cities, leave school when they are fourteen years old; most of them do not go beyond the fifth grade. They do this because they feel they must go to work in order to give help at home. Of course a fifth-grade pupil of fourteen is fitted to do only the easiest and most mechanical work and so receives very low pay. Once at work in factory or shop on this routine kind of work, the chances for the worker to advance, or to become master of any trade, or branch of his trade, are slight. His schooling has given him only an elementary control of the three R's, and usually no knowledge of the theory or practice of the business he is engaged in. He soon finds himself in a position where he is not learning any more. It is only the very exceptional person who will go on educating himself and push ahead to a position of independence or responsibility under such conditions. The person who becomes economically swamped in the cheapest grades of work is not going to show much energy or intelligence in his life as citizen. The experiments of the Cincinnati schools in introducing manual and industrial training have been directed to remedying this evil by making the school work such that the pupil will desire to stay in school if this is in any way possible; and if it is not, by giving him opportunities to go on with his education while working.

The Ohio law requires children to stay in school until they are sixteen unless they must go to work, when they are given a certificate permitting them to work for the employer with whom they have found their first position. This permission must be renewed with each change of position. Consequently the pupil is kept in school until he has found work, and if for any reason he stops working, the school keeps in touch with him and can see that he goes back to school. The city also conducts continuation schools, where most of the pupils who leave between the ages of fourteen and sixteen have to return to school for a few hours a week, receiving theoretical instruction in the work they are doing. The cash girl has lessons in business English, arithmetic of the sort she has to use, and lessons in salesmanship, and receives a certain amount of general instruction about her special branch of trade. There are voluntary continuation classes for workers above sixteen years of age, by means of which any shop or store is able to use the facilities of the public schools to make their workers more efficient by giving them more knowledge of the theory of the trade.

These continuation classes are undoubtedly of the greatest value to the employee who cannot go back to school, but they do not give him that grasp of present problems and conditions which would enable him intelligently to choose the work for which he is best suited. They improve him in a particular calling, but the calling may have been selected by accident. Their function is to make up to the child somewhat for what he has lost by having to become a wage earner so young. The cooperative plan which is being thoroughly tried out in Cincinnati is less of a makeshift and more of a distinct contribution to education, and has so far proved so successful as to be of great suggestive value. More than any other vocational plan it takes advantage of the educational value of the industries that are most important in the community. The factory shops of the city become the school shops for the pupils. Many of the big factories of the city have shown themselves willing to cooperate with the city for the first year of the experiment. This has proved so successful that many more factories are anxious to get their beginning workers in this way. In a sense it is a return to the old-fashioned apprenticeship method that prevailed when manufacturing was done by hand; for the pupils get their manual skill and the necessary practice in processes and shop conditions by working for wages in the city factories.

When the plan is further along the factories and stores will not be the only community institutions that will furnish laboratories for the school children of the city. The city college will begin its plan of having the domestic science pupils get their practice by working as nurses, cooks, housekeepers, or bookkeepers in the city hospital, and the engineering and architectural students will get theirs by working in the machine shops and draught-room of the city. As far as possible the departments of the city government will be used for the pupils' workshops; where they cannot furnish opportunities for the kind of work the pupil needs, he will go into an office, store, or factory where conditions reach the standard set by the board of education. So far this plan has been tested only with the boys and girls who are taking the technical course in the city high schools. The pupils who have finished the first two years of work, which corresponds to the work of any good technical high school, begin working alternate weeks in shop and school. The pupil chooses a kind of work in which he wishes to specialize, and is then given a position in one of the factories or shops which are cooperating with the schools. He receives pay for his work as any beginner would, and does the regular work of the place, under the direction of, and responsible to, the shop superintendent. One week he works here under trade conditions, meeting the requirements of the place, the next week he returns to school, and his place in the factory is taken by another pupil who has chosen the same line of work. The week in school is devoted entirely to theoretical work. The pupil continues his work in English, history, mathematics, drawing, and science, and enriches his trade experience by a thorough study of the industry, all its processes and the science they involve, the use, history, and distribution of the goods, and the history of the industry. This alternation between factory and shop is kept up for the last two years of the course, and also during the pupil's college course, provided he goes on to a technical course in the city university.

From the standpoint of vocational guidance, this

method has certain distinct advantages over having the pupil remain in the classroom until he goes into a shop permanently. His practical work in the factory is in the nature of an experiment. If his first choice proves a failure, the pupil does not get the moral setback that comes from a failure to the self-supporting person. The school takes the attitude that the pupil did not make the right choice; by cooperating with him, the effort is made to have his second factory experience correspond more nearly to his abilities and interest. A careful record of the pupil's work in the factory is kept as well as of his classroom work, and these two records are studied, not as separate items, but as interacting and inseparable. If his class work is good and his factory record poor, it is evident that he is in the wrong factory; and the nature of the class work will often give a hint of the sort of work to which the pupil ought to change. If all the work is mediocre, a change to another kind of practical work will often result in a marked improvement in the theoretical work if the change has been the right one. The pupil has an opportunity to test his own interests and abilities, to find if his judgment of them is correct; if it is not, he has a scientific basis on which to form a more correct judgment.

The work is not approached from the trade point of view; that is, the schools do not aim to turn out workers who have finished a two years' apprenticeship in a trade and are to that extent qualified as skilled workmen for that particular thing. The aim is to give the pupil some knowledge of the actual conditions in trade and industry so that he will have standards from which to make a final intelligent choice. The school work forms a necessary part of the training for this choice, for it is just as much a guide to the interests and bent of the boy as would be his success in any one shop. And it lifts his judgments from the plane of mere likes and dislikes to that of knowledge based on theory as well as practice. For the exceptional pupil who really knows what he wants, and is eager to go ahead with it, this plan offers distinct advantages. The boy's desire to get to work is satisfied by his weeks in the shop, and in his classroom he is learning enough of the larger aspects and possibilities of

(1) Children are interested in the things they need to know
     about. (Gary, Ind.)
(2) Making their own clothes in sewing class. (Gary, Ind.)

the trade to make him realize the value of additional theoretical training for the satisfaction of his own practical purposes.

As a result of the first year of working on this plan a large number of factories, at first indifferent to the plan, have asked to receive apprentices in this way, and a number of pupils have decided to go to college who, when they were spending all their time in school, had no such intention. The technical course for girls includes only those occupations that are traditionally supposed to belong to women because they are connected with home-making. They may continue for the four years working in school, which is made practical by having the pupils trim hats to wear, make their own clothes, do some commercial cooking, with the buying, selling, and bookkeeping connected with it; or they may specialize during the last two years as the boys do, by working alternate weeks in shop and school. So far girls have gone only into millinery or sewing establishments, where they work just as do the boys under actual trade conditions. The aim of the work for the girl, just as it is for the boy, is to help her find her life work, to fit herself for it mentally and morally, and to give her an intelligent attitude toward her profession and her community, using the shop experience not as an end in itself but a means to these larger ends.

The schools that have been described were selected not because of any conviction that they represent all of the best work that is being done in this country, but simply because they illustrate the general trend of education at the present time, and because they seem fairly representative of different types of schools. Of necessity a great deal of material that would undoubtedly prove just as suggestive as what has been given, has been omitted. No attempt has been made to touch upon the important movement for the vitalization of rural education: a movement that is just as far reaching in its scope and wholesome in its aims as anything that is being done, since it purposes to overcome the disadvantages of isolation that have handicapped the country school-teacher, and to make use of the natural environment of the child to give him a vocational education, in the same way that the city schools use their artificial environment. And except as their work illustrates a larger educational principle, very little attention has been given to the work of individual teachers or schools in their attempt to teach the conventional curriculum in the most efficient way. While devices and ingenious methods for getting results from pupils often seem most suggestive and even inspiring to the teacher, they do not fit into the plan of this book when they have to do simply with the better use of the usual material of the traditional education.

We have been concerned with the more fundamental changes in education, with the awakening of the schools to a realization of the fact that their work ought to prepare children for the life they are to lead in the world. The pupils who will pass this life in intellectual pursuits, and who get the necessary training for the practical side of their lives from their home environment, are such a small factor numerically that the schools are not acting wisely to shape all the work for them. The schools we have been discussing are all working away from a curriculum adapted to a small and specialized class towards one which shall be truly representative of the needs and conditions of a democratic society.

While these schools are all alike in that they reflect the new spirit in education, they differ greatly in the methods that have been developed to bring about the desired results; their surroundings and the class of pupils dealt with are varied enough to suggest the influence that local conditions must exercise over methods even when the aim is identical. To the educator for whom the problems of democracy are at all real, the vital necessity appears to be that of making the connection between the child and his environment as complete and intelligent as possible, both for the welfare of the child and for the sake of the community. The way this is to be accomplished will, of course, vary according to the conditions of the community and to a certain extent according to the temperament and beliefs of the educator. But great as the differences are between the different schools, between such a plan as that worked out by Mr. Meriam in Columbia, Missouri, and the curriculum of the Chicago public schools, an analysis of the ideas back of the apparent extreme divergence of views, reveals certain resemblances that seem more fundamental than the differences. The resemblances are more fundamental because they illustrate the direction that educational reform is taking, and because many of them are the direct result of the changes that modern science and psychology have brought about in our way of looking at the world.

Curiously enough most of these points of similarity are found in the views advocated by Rousseau, though it is only very recently that they have begun to enjoy anything more than a theoretical respect. The first point of similarity is the importance that is accorded to the physical welfare of the pupils. The necessity of insuring the health of all young people as the foundation on which to build other qualities and abilities, and the hopelessness of trying to build where the body is weak, ill-nourished, or uncontrolled, is now so well recognized that it has become a commonplace and needs only a passing mention here. Health is as important from the social point of view as from the individual, so that attention to it is doubly necessary to a successful community.

While all schools realize the importance of healthy pupils, the possibilities of using the activities of the child that are employed in giving him a strong healthy body, for general educational purposes, are not so well understood. As yet it is the pioneer in education who realizes the extent to which young children learn through the use of their bodies, and the impossibility of insuring general intelligence through a system which does not use the body to teach the mind and the mind to teach the body. This is simply a re-statement of Rousseau's proposition that the education of the young child rests largely on whether he is allowed to "develop naturally" or not. It has already been pointed out to what an extent Mrs. Johnson depends on the physical growth of her pupils as a tool for developing their intellectual ability, as well as the important part that muscular skill plays in the educational system of Madame Montessori. This seems not only reasonable but necessary when we think of the mere amount of movement, handling, and feeling of things that a baby must indulge in to understand the most familiar objects in its environment, and remember that the child and the adult learn with the same mental machinery as the very small child. There is no difference in the way the organism works after it is able to talk and walk; the difference lies in the greater complexity of activities which is made possible by the preliminary exercises. Modern psychology has pointed out the fact that the native instincts of a human being are his tools for learning. Instincts all express themselves through the body; therefore education which stifles bodily activities, stifles instincts, and so prevents the natural method of learning. To the extent of making an educational application of this fact, all the schools described are using the physical activities of their pupils, and so the means of their physical development, as instruments for training powers of judgment and right thinking. That is to say the pupils are learning by doing. Aside from the psychological reasons for teaching by this method, it is the logical consequence of a realization of the importance of the physical welfare of the child, and necessarily brings changes in the material of the schoolroom.

What are the pupils to do in order to learn? Mere activity, if not directed toward some end, may result in developing muscular strength, but it can have very little effect on the mental development of the pupils. These schools have all answered the question in the same general way, though the definite problems on which they work differ. The children must have activities which have some educative content, that is, which reproduce the conditions of real life. This is true whether they are studying about things that happened hundreds of years ago or whether they are doing problems in arithmetic or learning to plane a board. The historical facts which are presented must be true, and whether the pupils are writing a play based on them or are building a viking boat, the details of the work as well as the main idea must conform to the known facts. When a pupil learns by doing he is reliving both mentally and physically some experience which has proved important to the human race; he goes through the same mental processes as those who originally did these things. Because he has done them he knows the value of the result, that is, the fact. A statement, even of facts, does not reveal the value of the fact, or the sense of its truth—of the fact that it is a fact. Where children are fed only on book knowledge, one "fact" is as good as another; they have no standards of judgment or belief. Take the child studying weights and measures; he reads in his text-book that eight quarts make a peck, but when he does examples he is apt, as every school-teacher knows, to substitute four for eight. Evidently the statement as he read it in the book did not stand for anything that goes on outside the book, so it is a matter of accident what figure lodges in his brain, or whether any does. But the grocer's boy who has measured out pecks with a quart measure *knows*. He has made pecks; he would laugh at anybody who suggested that four quarts made a peck. What is the difference in these two cases? The schoolboy has a result without the activity of which it is the result. To the grocer's boy the statement has value and truth, for it is the obvious result of an experience—it is a *fact*.

Thus we see that it is a mistake to suppose that practical activities have only or even mainly a utilitarian value in the schoolroom. They are necessary if the pupil is to understand the facts which the teacher wishes him to learn; if his knowledge is to be real, not verbal; if his education is to furnish standards of judgment and comparison. With the adult it is undoubtedly true that most of the activities of practical life have become simply means of satisfying more or less imperative wants. He has performed them so often that their meaning as types of human knowledge has disappeared. But with the school child this is not true. Take a child in the school kitchen; he is not merely preparing that day's midday meal because he must eat; he is learning a multitude of new things. In following the directions of the *recipe* he is learning accuracy, and the success or failure of the dish serves as an excellent measure of the pupil's success. In measuring quantities he is learning arithmetic and tables of measures; in mixing materials, he is finding out how substances act when they are manipulated; in baking or boiling he is discovering some of the elementary facts of physics and chemistry. Repetition of these acts by adults, after the muscular and intellectual mastery of the adjustments they call for has been established, gives the casual thinker the impression that pupils also are doing no more than wasting their time on insignificant things. The grocer's boy knows what a peck is because he has used it to measure things with, but since his stock of knowledge is not increased as he goes on measuring out peck after peck, the point is soon reached where intellectual discovery ends and mere performance of a task takes its place. This is the point where the school can see that the pupil's intellectual growth continues; while the activity of the mere worker who is doing the thing for its immediate practical use becomes mechanical. The school says the pupil has had enough of this particular experience; he knows how to do this thing when he needs to and he has understood the principles or facts which it illustrates; it is time he moved on to other experiences which will teach him other values and facts. When the pupil has learned how to follow a recipe, how to handle foodstuffs and use the stove he does not go on repeating the same elementary steps; he begins to extend his work to take in the larger aspects of cooking. The educative value of the cooking lessons continues because he is now studying questions of food values,

Training the hand, eye, and brain by doing useful work. (Gary, Ind.)

menus, the cost of food, and the chemistry of foodstuffs, and cooking. The kitchen becomes a laboratory for the study of a fundamental factor in human life.

The moral advantages of an active form of education reenforce its intellectual benefits. We have seen how this method of teaching necessitates greater freedom for the pupil, and that this freedom is a positive factor in the intellectual and moral development of the pupils. In the same way the substitution of practical activities for the usual isolated text-book study achieves positive moral results which are marked to any teacher who has used both methods. Where the accumulation of facts presented in books is the standard, memory must be relied upon as the principal tool for acquiring knowledge. The pupil must be stimulated to remember facts; it makes comparatively little difference whether he has to remember them in the exact words of the book, or in his own words, for in either case the problem is to see that he does store up information. The inevitable result is that the child is rewarded when his memory is successful, and punished by failure and low marks when it is not successful. The emphasis shifts from the importance of the work that is done to the pupil's degree of external success in doing it. Since no one's performance is perfect, the failures become the obvious and emphasized thing. The pupil has to fight constantly against the discouragement of never reaching the standard he is told he is expected to reach. His mistakes are constantly corrected and pointed out. Such successes as he achieves are not especially inspiring because he does no more than reproduce the lesson as it already exists in the book. The virtues that the good scholar will cultivate are the colorless, negative virtues of obedience, docility, and submission. By putting himself in an attitude of complete passivity he is more nearly able to give back just what he heard from the teacher or read in the book.

Rewards and high marks are at best artificial aims to strive for; they accustom children to expect to get something besides the value of the product for work they do. The extent to which schools are compelled to rely upon these motives shows how dependent they are upon motives which are foreign to truly moral activity. But in the schools where the children are getting their knowledge by doing things, it is presented to them through all their senses and carried over into acts; it needs no feat of memory to retain what they find out; the muscles, sight, hearing, touch, and their own reasoning processes all combine to make the result part of the working equipment of the child. Success gives a glow of positive achievement; artificial inducements to work are no longer necessary, and the child learns to work from love of the work itself, not for a reward or because he is afraid of a punishment. Activity calls for the positive virtues—energy, initiative, and originality—qualities that are worth more to the world than even the most perfect faithfulness in carrying out orders. The pupil sees the value of his work and so sees his own progress, which spurs him on to further results. In consequence his mistakes do not assume undue importance or discourage him. He can actively use them as helps in doing better next time. Since the children are no longer working for rewards, the temptation to cheat is reduced to the minimum. There is no motive for doing dishonest acts, since the result shows whether the child has done the work, the only end recognized. The moral value of working for the sake of what is being done is certainly higher than that of working for rewards; and while it is possible that a really bad character will not be reformed by being placed in a situation where there is nothing to be gained excepting through an independent and energetic habit of work, the weak character will be strengthened and the strong one will not form any of those small bad habits that seem so unimportant at first and that are so serious in their cumulative effect.

Another point that most of the present-day reformers have in common, in distinction from the traditional way of looking at school work, is the attempt to find work of interest to the pupils. This used to be looked at as a matter of very little importance; in fact a certain amount of work that did not interest was supposed to be a very good thing for the moral character of the pupil. This work was supposed to have even greater disciplinary qualities than the rest of the work. Forcing the child to carry through a task which did not appeal to him was supposed to develop perseverance and strength of character. There is no doubt that the ability to perform an irksome duty is a very useful accomplishment, but the usefulness does not lie in the irksomeness of the task. Things are not useful or necessary because they are unpleasant or tiresome, but in spite of these characteristics. The habit of giving work to pupils solely for the sake of its "disciplinary" value would seem to indicate a blindness to moral values rather than an excess of moral zeal, for after all the habit is little more than holding up a thing's defects as its virtues.

But if lack of interest is not to be admitted as a motive in selection of class work, it is fair enough to object that interest cannot serve as a criterion, either. If we take interest in its narrowest sense, as meaning something which amuses and appeals to the child because of its power of entertainment, the objection has truth. The critic of the new spirit in education is apt to assume that this narrow sense is what is meant when he hears that the pupils ought to be interested in what they are doing. Then logically enough he goes on to point out that such a system lacks moral fibre, that it caters to the whims of children, and is in reality an example of the general softening of the social fibre, of every one's desire for the easy way. But the work is not made easy for the pupils; nor yet is there any attempt to give the traditional curriculum a sugar coating. The change is of a more fundamental character and is based on sound psychological theory. The work given to the children has changed; the attempt is not to make all the child's tasks interesting to him, but to select work on the basis of the natural appeal it makes to the child. Interest ought to be the basis for selection because children are interested in the things they need to learn.

Every one is familiar with the way a baby will spend a long time making over and over again the same motions or feeling of some object, and of the intense interest children two and three years old take in building a tower of blocks, or filling a pail with sand. They do it not once but scores of times, and always with the same deep absorption, for it is real work to them. Their growing, unformed muscles have not yet learned to act automatically; every motion that is aimed at something must be repeated under the conscious direction of the child's mind until he can make it without being aware of effort towards an adjustment. Since the little child must adjust the things about him, his interests and his needs are identical; if they were not he could not live. As a child grows older his control over his immediate needs so rapidly becomes automatic, that we are apt to forget that he still learns as the baby does. The necessary thing is still, as it will be all his life, the power of adjustment. Good adjustment means a successful human being, so that instinctively we are more interested in learning these adjustments than in anything else. Now the child is interested in adjusting himself through physical activity to the things he comes up against, because he must master his physical environment to live. The things that are of interest to him are the things that he needs to work on. It is then the part of wisdom in selecting the work for any group of children, to take it from that group of things in the child's environment which is arousing their curiosity and interest at that time. Obviously as the child grows older and his control of his body and physical environment increases he will reach out to the more complicated and theoretical aspects of the life he sees about him.

But in just this same way the work in the classroom reaches out to include facts and events which do not belong in any obvious way to the child's immediate environment. Thus the range of the material is not in any way limited by making interest a standard for selection. Work that appeals to pupils as worth while, that holds out the promise of resulting in something to their own interests, involves just as much persistence and concentration as the work which is given by the sternest advocate of disciplinary drill. The latter requires the pupil to strive for ends which he cannot see, so that he has to be kept at the task by means of offering artificial ends, marks, and promotions, and by isolating him in an atmosphere where his mind and senses are not being constantly besieged by the call of life which appeals so strongly to him. But the pupil presented with a problem, the solution of which will give him an immediate sense of accomplishment and satisfied curiosity, will bend all his powers to the work; the end itself will furnish the stimulus necessary to carry him through the drudgery.

The conventional type of education which trains children to docility and obedience, to the careful performance of imposed tasks because they are imposed, regardless of where they lead, is suited to an autocratic society. These are the traits needed in a state where there is one head to plan and care for the lives and institutions of the people. But in a democracy they interfere with the successful conduct of society and government. Our famous, brief definition of a democracy, as "government of the people, for the people and by the people," gives perhaps the best clue to what is involved in a democratic society. Responsibility for the conduct of society and government rests on every member of society. Therefore, every one must receive a training that will enable him to meet this responsibility, giving him just ideas of the condition and needs of the people collectively, and developing those qualities which will insure his doing a fair share of the work of government. If we train our children to take orders, to do things simply because they are told to, and fail to give them confidence to act and think for themselves, we are putting an almost insurmountable obstacle in the way of overcoming the present defects of our system and of establishing the truth of democratic ideals. Our State is founded on freedom, but when we train the State of to-morrow, we allow it just as little freedom as possible. Children in school must be allowed freedom so that they will know what its use means when they become the controlling body, and they must be allowed to develop active qualities of initiative, independence, and resourcefulness, before the abuses and failures of democracy will disappear.

The spread of the realization of this connection between democracy and education is perhaps the most interesting and significant phase of present educational tendencies. It accounts for the growing interest in popular education, and constitutes a strong reenforcement to the arguments of science and psychology for the changes which have been outlined. There is no doubt that the text-book method of education is well suited to that small group of children who by environment are placed above the necessity of engaging in practical life and who are at the same time interested in abstract ideas. But even for this type of person the system leaves great gaps in his grasp of knowledge; it gives no place to the part that action plays in the development of intelligence, and it trains along the lines of the natural inclinations of the student and does not develop the practical qualities which are usually weak in the abstract person. For the great majority whose interests are not abstract, and who have to pass their lives in some practical occupation, usually in actually working with their hands, a method of education is necessary which bridges the gap between the purely intellectual and theoretical sides of life and their own occupations. With the spread of the ideas of democracy, and the accompanying awakening to social problems, people are beginning to realize that every one, regardless of the class to which he happens to belong, has a right to demand an education which shall meet his own needs, and that for its own sake the State must supply this demand.

Until recently school education has met the needs of only one class of people, those who are interested in knowledge for its own sake, teachers, scholars, and research workers. The idea that training is necessary for the man who works with his hands is still so new that the schools are only just beginning to admit that control of the material things of life is knowledge at all. Until very recently schools have neglected the class of people who are numerically the largest and upon whom the whole world depends for its supply of necessities. One reason for this is the fact that democracy is a comparatively new thing in itself; and until its advent, the right of the majority, the very people who work with their hands, to supply any of their larger spiritual needs was never admitted. Their function, almost their reason for existence, was to take care of the material wants of the ruling classes.

Two great changes have occurred in the last century and a half which have altered men's habits of living and of thinking. We have just seen how one of these, the growth of democratic ideals, demands a change in education. The other, the change that has come about through scientific discoveries, must also be reflected in the classroom. To piece

together all one's historical information into a rough picture
of society before the discovery of the steam engine and of
electricity, will hardly serve to delineate sufficiently the
changes in the very fundamentals of society that these and
similar discoveries have brought about. The one possibly
most significant from the point of view of education is the
incredible increase in the number of facts that must be part
of the mental furniture of any one who meets even the ordinary situations of life successfully. They are so many that
any attempt to teach them all from text-books in school hours
would be simply ridiculous. But the schools instead of facing
this frankly and then changing their curriculum so that
they could teach pupils how to learn from the world itself,
have gone on bravely teaching as many facts as possible.
The changes made have been in the way of inventing
schemes that would increase the consumption of facts. But
the change that is demanded by science is a more radical
one; and as far as it has been worked out at present it follows the general lines that have been suggested in this book.
This includes, as the curricula of these different schools
have shown, not alone teaching of the scientific laws that
have brought about the changes in society since their discovery, but the substitution of real work which itself teaches
the facts of life for the study and memorization of facts after
they have been classified in books.

If schools are to recognize the needs of all classes of
pupils, and give pupils a training that will insure their becoming successful and valuable citizens, they must give
work that will not only make the pupils strong physically
and morally and give them the right attitude towards the
state and their neighbors, but that will as well give them
enough control over their material environment to enable
them to be economically independent. Preparation for the
professions has always been taken care of; it is, as we have
seen, the future of the worker in industry which has been
neglected. The complications of modern industry due to
scientific discoveries make it necessary for the worker who
aspires to real success to have a good foundation of general
education on which to build his technical skill, and the
complications of human nature make it equally necessary

that the beginner shall find his way into work that is suited to his tastes and abilities. A discussion of general educational principles is concerned only with industrial or vocational education which supplies these two needs. The questions of specific trade and professional training fall wholly outside the scope of this book. However, certain facts connected with the movement to push industrial training in its narrower sense have a direct bearing on the larger question. For there is great danger just at present that, as the work spreads, the really educative type of work that is being done in Gary and Chicago may be overlooked in favor of trade training.

The attention of influential citizens is more easily focused on the need of skilled workers than on that of a general educational readjustment. The former is brought home to them by their own experience, perhaps by their self-interest. They are readily impressed with the extent to which Germany has made technical trade training a national asset in pushing the commercial rivalries of that empire. Nothing seems so direct and practical as to establish a system of continuation schools to improve workers between the ages of fourteen and eighteen who have left school at the earliest age, and to set up separate schools which shall prepare directly for various lines of shop work, leaving the existing schools practically unchanged to prepare pupils for higher schools and for the walks of life where there is less manual work.

Continuation schools are valuable and important, but only as palliatives and makeshifts; they deal with conditions which ought not to exist. Children should not leave school at fourteen, but should stay in school until they are sixteen or eighteen, and be helped to an intelligent use of their energies and to the proper choice of work. It is a commonplace among teachers and workers who come in contact with any number of pupils who leave school at fourteen to go to work, that the reason is not so much financial pressure as it is lack of conviction that school is doing them any good. Of course there are cases where the child enjoys school but is forced to leave at the first opportunity in order to earn money. But even in these rare instances it would usually be wiser to continue the family arrangements that were in vogue up to the child's fourteenth birthday, even if they include charity. The wages of the child of fourteen and fifteen are so low that they make a material difference only to the family who is already living on an inadequate scale.

The hopelessness of the situation is increased by the fact that these children increase their earning capacity much more slowly and reach as their maximum a much lower level than the child who is kept in school, so that in the long run the loss both to the child and his family more than offsets the precarious temporary gain. But the commonest reason advanced by pupils for leaving school is that they did not like it, and were anxious to get some real work to do. Not that they were prepared to go to work, or had finished any course of training, but simply that school seemed so futile and satisfied so few of their interests that they seized the first opportunity to make a change to something that seemed more real, something where there was a visible result.

What is needed then is a reorganization of the ordinary school work to meet the needs of this class of pupils, so that they will wish to stay in school for the value of what they are learning. The present system is bungling and short-sighted; continuation schools patch up some of its defects; they do not overcome them, nor do they enable the pupils to achieve a belated intellectual growth, where the malad-justment of the elementary school has served to check it. The ideal is not to use the schools as tools of existing in-dustrial systems, but to use industry for the reorganization of the schools.

There is danger that the concentrated interests of busi-ness men and their influential activity in public matters will segregate training for industry to the damage of both de-mocracy and education. Educators must insist upon the primacy of educational values, not in their own behalf, but because these represent the more fundamental interests of society, especially of a society organized on a democratic basis. The place of industry in education is not to hurry the preparation of the individual pupil for his individual trade. It should be used (as in the Gary, Indianapolis, and other schools) to give practical value to the theoretical knowledge that every pupil should have, and to give him an understanding of the conditions and institutions of his environment. When this is done the pupil will have the necessary knowledge and intelligence to make the right choice of work and to direct his own efforts towards getting the necessary technical skill. His choice will not be limited by the fact that he already knows how to do one thing and only one; it will be dictated only by his own ability and natural aptitude.

The trade and continuation schools take their pupils before they are old enough or have knowledge enough of their own power to be able to make a wise choice, and then they drill them in one narrow groove, both in their theoretical work and in their manual skill, so that the pupil finds himself marked for one occupation only. If it proves not to be the right one for him it is still the only one he is trained for. Such a system does not give an opportunity for the best development of the individual's abilities, and it tends to keep people fixed in classes.

The very industries that seem to benefit most by receiving skilled workers for the first steps of the trade will lose by it in the more difficult processes, for the workers will not have the background of general knowledge and wider experience that the graduate of a technical high school or vocational school should have acquired. But the introduction of the material of occupations into the schools for the sake of the control of the environment brought by their use will do much to give us the proportion of independent, intelligent citizens that are needed in a democracy.

It is fatal for a democracy to permit the formation of fixed classes. Differences of wealth, the existence of large masses of unskilled laborers, contempt for work with the hands, inability to secure the training which enables one to forge ahead in life, all operate to produce classes, and to widen the gulf between them. Statesmen and legislation can do something to combat these evil forces. Wise philanthropy can do something. But the only fundamental agency for good is the public-school system. Every American is proud of what has been accomplished in the past in fostering among very diverse elements of population a spirit of unity and of brotherhood so that the sense of common interests and aims has prevailed over the strong forces working to divide our people into classes. The increasing complexity of our life, with the great accumulation of wealth at one social extreme and the condition of almost dire necessity at the other makes the task of democracy constantly more difficult. The days are rapidly passing when the simple provision of a system in which all individuals mingle is enough to meet the need. The subject-matter and the methods of teaching must be positively and aggressively adapted to the end.

There must not be one system for the children of parents who have more leisure and another for the children of those who are wage-earners. The physical separation forced by such a scheme, while unfavorable to the development of a proper mutual sympathy, is the least of its evils. Worse is the fact that the over bookish education for some and the over "practical" education for others brings about a division of mental and moral habits, ideals and outlook.

The academic education turns out future citizens with no sympathy for work done with the hands, and with absolutely no training for understanding the most serious of present-day social and political difficulties. The trade training will turn out future workers who may have greater immediate skill than they would have had without their training, but who have no enlargement of mind, no insight into the scientific and social significance of the work they do, no education which assists them in finding their way on or in making their own adjustments. A division of the public-school system into one part which pursues traditional methods, with incidental improvements, and another which deals with those who are to go into manual labor means a plan of social predestination totally foreign to the spirit of a democracy.

The democracy which proclaims equality of opportunity as its ideal requires an education in which learning and social application, ideas and practice, work and recognition of the meaning of what is done, are united from the beginning and for all. Schools such as we have discussed in this book —and they are rapidly coming into being in large numbers all over the country—are showing how the ideal of equal opportunity for all is to be transmuted into reality.

Miscellany

PROFESSORIAL FREEDOM

*Teachers Whom Trustees Can Fire
Are Morally Public Employes*

Columbia University, Oct. 11, 1915
To the Editor of The New York Times:

It is doubtless fitting and natural that the *New York Times* should find university professors "chartered libertines of speech," given to "too much foolish babbling," whenever the results of the investigations of university scholars lead them to question any features of the existing economic order. The position of the *Times* in such matters is firmly established, and no one, I am sure, grudges economic interests such a competent organ.

Certain statements and implications of your editorial of Oct. 10, on academic freedom, entitled "The Philadelphia Martyr," seem, however, open to discussion. You apparently take the ground that a modern university is a personally conducted institution like a factory, and that if for any reason the utterances of any teacher, within or without the university walls, are objectionable to the Trustees, there is nothing more to be said. This view virtually makes the Trustees owners of a private undertaking. Perhaps I am mistaken in my understanding of the position of the *Times*. I hope I am. But your statements that it was the "right" of the Trustees not to renew the appointment of Dr. Nearing; that many teachers profess views "which set on edge the teeth of the sedate members of the corporation"; that "the Trustees are not obliged to give reasons for dismissal," give that impression.

[First published in *New York Times,* 22 October 1915. Reprinted in *School and Society* 2 (1915): 673, with the title "The Control of Universities."]

In any case, a discussion by the *Times* of whether modern universities should be conceived as privately owned and managed institutions, or as essentially public institutions, with responsibilities to the public, would be welcome.

Doubtless, college professors are attached to their jobs and salaries. Even if they are as unique in that regard as the *Times* would imply, I am quite sure that they will be satisfied with any adjustment of the difficulties connected with the control of universities which is based upon recognition that the modern university is in every respect, save its legal management, a public institution with public responsibilities. They are only too well aware that in many of our institutions of learning it is the legal right of a body of men (who are, educationally speaking, outsiders) to dismiss any teachers whose views set their teeth on edge, and give no reason. But they have been trained to think of the pursuit and expression of truth as a public function to be exercised in behalf of the interests of their moral employer—society as a whole. Consequently they regret, and are fast coming to resent, arbitrary exercises of a legal right based upon the conception of the relation of a factory employer to his employe. They ask for no special immunities or privileges for themselves. They will be content, for their own protection, with any system which protects the relation of the modern university to the public as a whole.

(Signed) JOHN DEWEY
President American Association of University Professors

THE SITUATION AT THE UNIVERSITY
OF UTAH

To the Editor of *The Nation*:

Sir: In view of the fact that seventeen members of the faculty of the University of Utah have resigned their positions on the ground that it seemed to them "impossible to retain their self-respect and remain in the University," the Council of the American Association of University Professors has authorized the appointment of a committee of inquiry to report upon the case. At the request of the president, the secretary of the Association recently spent four days in Salt Lake City investigating the situation in the University and collecting evidence to be laid before the committee. The special purposes and scope of the investigation are indicated in the following extract from the letter addressed by the secretary of the Association to the president of the University:

The situation that has developed at the University of Utah has aroused much concern throughout the country among persons interested in the work of the American universities, and especially among members of the university teaching profession. It has, however, been difficult for those at a distance to be sure that they had correctly gathered the essential facts of the case from the incomplete and more or less conflicting *ex-parte* statements which have appeared in newspapers and periodicals. It has therefore seemed advisable to the president of the American Association of University Professors to send a representative of that organization to secure as full and impartial a statement as may be of the relevant facts. . . .

It is perhaps advisable to explain the nature of the interest which the Association of University Professors takes in the matter. It is coming to be a well-recognized principle that the general body of university teachers is entitled to know, with regard to any institution, the conditions of the tenure of the professorial office therein, the methods of university government, and the policy

[Published simultaneously in *Nation* 100 (1915): 491–92, and as "Conditions at the University of Utah" in *Science*, n.s. 41 (1915): 685.]

and practice of the institution with respect to freedom of inquiry and of teaching. In the absence of information upon these points, it is impossible for members of the profession to judge whether or not the institution is one in which positions may properly be accepted or retained, by university teachers having a respect for the dignity of their calling, a sense of its social obligations, and a regard for the ideals of a university. It is, therefore, important to the profession that when criticisms or charges are made by responsible persons against any institution, with respect to its conduct or policy in the matters to which I have referred, the facts should be carefully ascertained in a judicial spirit by some committee wholly detached from any local or personal controversies, and in some degree representative of the profession at large. It is in this spirit and for these purposes that information is sought in the present instance.

The report of the committee of inquiry will be prepared and published at as early a date as is practicable. It is the purpose of the committee to present all the pertinent facts so fully in its report that university teachers may judge for themselves as to the administrative methods, and the conditions of professorial service, in the University. We make this statement in order that any one who is considering either the acceptance of a position in the University or the recommending of others for such a position may look forward to a full knowledge of the situation in the near future, and may postpone immediate action in case he deems such knowledge advisable before reaching a final decision.

(Signed)

John Dewey, President of the American Association of University Professors.

A. O. Lovejoy, Secretary of the American Association of University Professors.

Edwin R. A. Seligman, Chairman of the Committee of Inquiry.

April 30.

EDUCATION VS. TRADE-TRAINING:
REPLY TO DAVID SNEDDEN

Sir: I have written unclearly indeed when Dr. Snedden interprets me as giving, even in appearance, "aid and comfort to the opponents of a broader, richer and more effective program of education," or else Dr. Snedden has himself fallen a victim to the ambiguity of the word vocational. I would go farther than he is apparently willing to go in holding that education should be vocational, but in the name of a genuinely vocational education I object to the identification of vocation with such trades as can be learned before the age of, say, eighteen or twenty; and to the identification of education with acquisition of specialized skill in the management of machines at the expense of an industrial intelligence based on science and a knowledge of social problems and conditions. I object to regarding as vocational education any training which does not have as its supreme regard the development of such intelligent initiative, ingenuity and executive capacity as shall make workers, as far as may be, the masters of their own industrial fate. I have my doubts about theological predestination, but at all events that dogma assigned predestinating power to an omniscient being; and I am utterly opposed to giving the power of social predestination, by means of narrow trade-training, to any group of fallible men no matter how well-intentioned they may be. Dr. Snedden has been fortunate if he has not met those who are not so well-intentioned, and if he is so situated that he believes that "the interests" are a myth of muckrakers and that none of "the interests" have any designs upon the control of educational machinery.

Dr. Snedden's criticisms of my articles seem to me couched in such general terms as not to touch their specific contentions. I argued that a separation of trade education

[First published in *New Republic* 3 (1915): 42–43. For letter to which this was a reply, see this volume, pp. 460–65.]

and general education of youth has the inevitable tendency to make both kinds of training narrower, less significant and less effective than the schooling in which the material of traditional education is reorganized to utilize the industrial subject-matter—active, scientific and social—of the present-day environment. Dr. Snedden would come nearer to meeting my points if he would indicate how such a separation is going to make education "broader, richer and more effective." If he will undertake this task there will be something specific to discuss. In order that the discussion may be really definite, I suggest that he tell the readers of the *New Republic* what he thinks of the Gary system, and whether he thinks this system would have been possible in any of its significant features except by a mutual interpretation of the factors of general education and of industry. And as his article may be interpreted as an apology for the Cooley bill in Illinois, I should like to ask him whether he is familiar with the educational reorganization going on in Chicago, and whether he thinks that it would be helped or hindered if the Chicago schools came under a dual administration, with one agency looking after a traditional bookish education and another after a specific training for mechanical trades. I should like to know, too, how such educational cleavage is to be avoided unless each type of school extends its work to duplicate that of the other type.

Apart from light on such specific questions, I am regretfully forced to the conclusion that the difference between us is not so much narrowly educational as it is profoundly political and social. The kind of vocational education in which I am interested is not one which will "adapt" workers to the existing industrial régime; I am not sufficiently in love with the régime for that. It seems to me that the business of all who would not be educational time-servers is to resist every move in this direction, and to strive for a kind of vocational education which will first alter the existing industrial system, and ultimately transform it.

I can readily understand how a practical administrator becomes impatient with the slowness of social processes and becomes eager for a short-cut to desired results. He has a claim upon the sympathy of those who do not have to face the immediate problems. But as long as there are as many debatable questions as Dr. Snedden admits there are, and as long as conditions are as mobile as he indicates, it is surely well that those outside the immediate administrative field insist that particular moves having short-run issues in view be checked up by consideration of issues more fundamental although remoter.

(Signed) JOHN DEWEY

LETTER TO WILLIAM BAGLEY AND THE EDITORIAL STAFF OF *SCHOOL AND HOME EDUCATION*

20 September 1915

Dear Sirs: The accuracy of the representations of my educational philosophy and the pertinency of the strictures passed upon it in the September number of your journal are matters which may best be judged by students of my writings. In justice to others, however, there is a matter of fact about which I should like to speak. Dr. Bagley intimates that my writings have inspired those who conduct the schools which are described in the book *Schools of To-Morrow*, written by my daughter and myself. He even refers to "the disciples whose efforts to put it (my theory) into practice he so well describes." It was not modesty which made me refrain from claiming any responsibility for the efforts described, but regard for facts; and a perception that much of the significance of the various experiments lies in the fact that they have sprung up independently under diverse auspices. So far as Mrs. Johnson's Organic Education is not the result of her own public-school experience, it is inspired by the writings of Dr. Hanford Henderson. Dr. Meriam's scheme bears on its face signs of its independent authorship. At least two schools referred to derive quite obviously from the work of Col. Parker. Another to which considerable space is given, is certainly closely connected with the work of Dr. Reddie, Leete, etc. I should be proud to think that Supt. Wirt derived any help from the visits he made to the Laboratory School in Chicago years ago, but the highest flight of my flattered imagination does not enable me to conceive him as a disciple engaged in carrying out my theories. And so it goes.

May I also express my regret that Dr. Bagley should

[First published in *School and Home Education* 35 (1915): 35–36. For editorial to which this was a reply, see this volume, pp. 466–70.]

have derived the impression from anything which I have ever said that I would have no commerce with recorded knowledge—that I hold recorded knowledge in derision—that "The very notion that the child should be asked or required to assimilate the experience of others is repugnant to him." I am sorry, because I think that such a position as is ascribed to me would be literally nothing less than insanity. My chief preoccupation in behalf of opportunity for direct and active experience by pupils in the school is that they may thereby be better enabled "to assimilate the experiences of others"— so important and so difficult is that accomplishment.

Yours truly,

(Signed) JOHN DEWEY

REPLY TO CHARLES P. MEGAN'S "PAROCHIAL SCHOOL EDUCATION"

Sir: I regret repeating any false report; and upon the express statement of Mr. Megan, denying, on the basis of personal knowledge, the report to which I gave currency, I gladly withdraw it with this expression of regret.

I should have been glad to leave the matter with this withdrawal and utterance of regret. But Mr. Megan uses the following words: "'And why not?' asks Professor Dewey. That is to say, here is a measure which every good citizen ought to oppose, but the Catholics are for it; and their reason is easily understood." And there are other intimations that anti-Catholic feeling influenced my argument. There is neither by statement nor by implication any such element in my article. Any one turning to my original article will see that the context of the "Why not?" quoted by Mr. Megan is wholly different from the meaning which he gratuitously supplies. I held and still hold that the Roman Catholics have a better and stronger claim for a divided apportionment of school funds and school control than have industrial interests. But since I regret *any* such division in our public schools, the fact that the bill in question puts our Catholic fellow citizens in a still better position to urge a still further division is a good ground for opposition to the bill.

Mr. Megan's own position on this matter is not clear to me. As is undoubtedly known to Mr. Megan, it has been pretty constantly urged that parochial schools should receive a proportionate share of the public schools' funds. I do not understand whether he is disavowing for himself and friends any such desire; still less do I understand whether he is disavowing in behalf of the Roman Catholic Church

[First published in *New Republic* 3 (1915): 72. For Megan's letter, see this volume, pp. 471–72. Dewey's article, "Splitting Up the School System," to which Megan's letter refers, also appears in this volume on pp. 123–27.]

any disposition to press further this claim. If he has authority for making the latter disavowal, his letter is of immense importance. But one can hold that such a division of funds is educationally unwise without believing for a moment that Catholics are undesirable citizens or are actuated by anything other than sincere desire to have justice done as they see justice.

(Signed) JOHN DEWEY

REPLY TO WILLIAM ERNEST HOCKING'S "POLITICAL PHILOSOPHY IN GERMANY"

Sir: The correctness of my account of the historic development of the German temper of mind is of limited interest compared with the other question which Professor Hocking raises—a question which, as he truly says, concerns our own American political thinking. Shall our political philosophy be experimental, or shall it be *a priori* and absolutistic? My book on *German Philosophy and Politics* was certainly addressed to American, not German readers; it was animated by the hope that it might do something, however slight, to make Americans conscious of the discrepancy which exists between the tenor of our activity and our current theory and phraseology about that activity. To make a specific application, I do not feel easy when I find that, say, the divergence between President Wilson and Mr. Bryan as to the method of dealing with the present international situation rests upon a common assumption of "immutable principles," waiting ready-made to be fastened upon the situation; the divergence being that Mr. Wilson, as a lawyer, finds them already embodied in a legal code, and Mr. Bryan, as a sentimental moralist, finds them embodied in the great heart-throbs of an altruistic humanity. I can but think that we should be better off if we had recognized from the beginning that the question was to find out what we really wanted, and what the moving forces of the situation permitted, and how to go intelligently about getting the ends decided, after due deliberation, to be desirable.

But Professor Hocking disagrees. He finds that the matter with us is that we have been too pragmatic, too empirical and experimental, and that the conduct of Germany is an object lesson to us of what that sort of a philosophy leads to; a warning, presumably, to return to some absolute

[First published in *New Republic* 4 (1915): 236. For Hocking's letter, see this volume, pp. 473–77.]

and eternal code—just whose, however, he fails to tell us. And so it appears that the accuracy of my statement of Germany's mental diathesis is relevant to the issue between us. For Professor Hocking has not grasped my position. I have not said that the behavior of the rulers of Germany was dictated by an idealistic philosophy. I meant (and said) that it was a *Realpolitik*—highly pragmatic if you please. Of course it is; all action as action is pragmatic. But the prevalence of an idealistic philosophy full of talk of Duty, Will, and Ultimate Ideas and Ideals, and of the indwelling of the Absolute in German history for the redeeming of humanity, has disguised from the mass of the German people, upon whose support the policy of the leaders ultimately depends for success, the real nature of the enterprise in which they are engaged. Does Professor Hocking believe that the German people are supporting the war because *they* think it is a measure of "practical expediency"? If so, what and where is his evidence? For myself, while I should hesitate to accept the utterances of representative Germans in the present excitement as satisfactory evidence regarding objective facts, I think they are wholly acceptable evidence regarding their own state of mind. And that state of mind is one which naturally expresses itself by appeal to Kant, the categorical imperative, and the traditional idealism of Germany. Does Professor Hocking deny this? If not, what does he make of it?

What I make of it, I repeat, is not that the Germans are conscious hypocrites, but that in a world where men act pragmatically, it is dangerous to entertain a philosophy which is at odds with the facts of action, since such a philosophy will mask from men the real nature of their activities and encourage them to engage in one kind of action feeling that they have the sanction of ideas of a radically different kind. Yet I recognize that in a society organized as is Germany, class stratifications, and an efficiently organized hierarchy of subordinations, give appeal to *a priori* concepts a certain solid backing. "Immutable principles" are but sublimations of the emotions attending the actual organization of society. There is no such intellectual uncertainty and confusion in a German appeal to an absolute philosophy as there is, inevitably, in its American analogue—which to my ear always has a deplorable thinness and unreality.

Let it not be thought that to admit—or rather assert— that German action is pragmatic and experimental is to give away the case. What is at issue is the difference between an activity which is aware of its own character, which knows what it is about, which faces the consequences of its activities and accepts responsibility for them, and an activity which disguises its nature to the collective consciousness by appeal to eternal principles and the eulogistic predicates of pure idealism. Let me close by rewriting a sentence of Professor Hocking's:

Infected by a romantic idealism, the current popular philosophy of Germany justifies measures undertaken because of narrow expediency in the name of eternal principles; it justifies acts devoid of sympathy and humanity on the ground that they are in the interest of an ultimate evolution of humanity possible only through the leadership of a people which appreciates the truth of pure idealism and the meaning of pure duty; it justifies breaking of legal and therefore external and temporary obligations in behalf of an unconditional obligation to fulfill an historic mission as organ of the Absolute.

(Signed) JOHN DEWEY

THE ONE-WORLD OF HITLER'S
NATIONAL SOCIALISM

History has probably never beheld such a swift and complete reversal of conditions as that which took place in Germany after the close of the first World War. The transformation is so great in quality as well as in quantitative aspects that it raises the question whether the classic philosophy of Germany has any applicability to the Germany of the National Socialist epoch. A plausible case may be made out for the conclusion that the only factor of identity between the philosophy that brought Hitler to power and the philosophies reported upon in the chapters which follow is belief in the intrinsic superiority of the German people and its predestined right to determine the destiny of other nations. Doubts as to the relevance of the older outlook are not decreased when we recall that the man who effected the remarkable change in conditions is a man of slight education, in the school sense of education, who probably has never read a word of Kant, Fichte, or Hegel.

Facts which lie on the surface certainly forbid the attempt to trace *direct* influence of the established philosophical tradition of Germany upon Adolph Hitler's creed. Absence of direct channels of transmission does not, however, do away with the all but incredible one-to-one correspondence that has been proved by events to exist between the terms of the appeal of Hitler and the response aroused in the German people—a correspondence without which Hitler would have remained an obscure agitator with at most a nuisance value. Only a prepared soil and a highly favorable climate of opinion could have brought to fruition the seeds which Hitler sowed. It is reasonable to hold that absence of direct channels of influence but points the more

[First published as the Introduction to the second edition of *German Philosophy and Politics* (New York: G. P. Putnam's Sons, 1942), pp. 13–49.]

unerringly to a kind of preestablished harmony between the attitudes of belief in which Germans had been indoctrinated and the terms of the Hitlerian appeal: — terms whose adaptation to the state of German mentality must be judged by the triumph they speedily achieved.

It is not surprising that the demonstrated extraordinary success of an obscure man should have convinced Hitler that he was entrusted by God, or Destiny, or Nature (he uses different words at different times) with a mission from on high to awaken the slumbering German genius to consciousness of its own being and its intrinsic strength. Hitler believed or claimed to believe that he was divinely called to evoke what slumbered in German blood. We perhaps have reason for holding that what he attributes to blood and race is in fact a product of culture and cultivation, in the formation of which the classic philosophers were educational forces. Certain it is that the one thing upon which Hitler lays most emphasis is his success in bringing a small party, of which he was at the outset but the seventh member, to power in Germany, in order then to bring the Germany he ruled to a state in which it threatened — and promised — to rule the whole world. Over and over again he cites these facts as proof that he is the divinely appointed incarnation of the true German spirit and blood: — What else, he asks, could account for his and Germany's triumphant rise?

The factor which most effectually conceals the underlying strains of continuity connecting the creed of Hitler with the classic philosophic tradition of Germany is his own extraordinary flexibility in choice and use of means — combined, as he himself has said, with fanatical inflexibility of purpose. Hitler raised opportunism to the point of genius. The fact is familiar to us in the timing which marks his successive moves into surrounding lands. But it is shown equally in the measures taken between 1922 and 1933 by which he came to be undisputed master of his party and by which he made his party the undisputed master of Germany. The contemptuous underestimation of him which prevailed was an important factor in his success. It gave him time and room for the shrewd changes and shifts in manner of appeal by which he won over workingmen, with their millions of party-socialists, bankers and big industrialists, army leaders and old-time Junkers, to his aims and policies.

A less apparent but equally skillful aspect of his genius in opportunism is found in the way in which he borrowed and adapted to his own use all ideas he ran across provided they reinforced any angle or phase of his appeal. I do not think he can be called a disciple, in any literal sense, of Nietzsche, Houston Chamberlain, Treitschke, or Spengler any more than of Kant or Hegel. He showed his sense of timing in the ideas he used as weapons, and he never allowed considerations of logical consistency to keep him from appropriating any idea that would serve him as a weapon. Perhaps he had less use for Spengler than for any of the others mentioned. The idea of "decline of the west" was the offensive opposite of his own plan for its rise to new heights under his leadership. But he certainly derived inspiration from the following words of Spengler: "Money can be overthrown and its power abolished only by blood. Life is alpha and omega. Life and only life, the quality of blood, the triumph of will, counts in history."

"Opportunism" is altogether too weak a word to convey the meaning I want to bring out. If it is the essence of art to conceal its own traces, it is of the essence of the conditions which made Hitler's appeal successful that it aroused hopes and desires that accorded with the basic beliefs of every section of the German people, without display of ideas of an openly philosophical kind. His uncanny insight into the covert wishes and secret ambitions of every group with which he came in contact enabled him to put upon the German people all which the human traffic would bear— "bear" not only in the sense of standing at the time but even more in the sense of upholding and carrying forward.

It is not possible to say too much about the correspondence, the harmony, the coadaptation of the creed of Hitler and the dominant temper of the Germany to which he appealed; and its existence points to the necessity of considering the attitudes, the habitual beliefs, the acquired ideas of the German people, quite as much as the things Hitler himself has said and done. It is upon the side of infiltration of the teachings of the philosophic representatives of Germany into popular attitudes and habits that we find

underlying continuity between them and the powerful components of Hitler's appeal.

That post-war Germany was a defeated and humiliated
nation is a well-known fact. That this condition of affairs
provided the practical basis of Hitler's appeal is also a
familiar fact. Germany was down because it was weak; let
it become strong and it would rise. This simple consideration
is trumpeted forth by Hitler on every conceivable occasion
and in every conceivable guise. Germany had a mission in
the world to fulfill, and strength, power, was the absolute
prerequisite which would enable it to do its bounden duty.
Strength was virtue and virtue was power; weakness was,
fundamentally, the only vice. Quotations from Hitler's writings and speeches, and information about his deeds, have
made his gospel of force, carried to the pitch of fanatical
ruthlessness, brutal intimidation, and cruel persecution, a
matter of general knowledge. It is also well known that his
policy of suppression of every breath of criticism (initiated
by use of gangsters to break up public meetings of other
parties than his own) developed, when he came into power,
into rigid, forceful control of press, pulpit, public assembly,
radio, school, and every agency (including whenever possible
private conversation) by which opinions are expressed and
formed.
    There is no doubt about the place occupied in the
system of Hitler, in practical action as well as in doctrines
preached, of sheer unmitigated force. Hitler has never failed
to carry into prompt effect the dictum he uttered in a
speech of the year 1922: "The people needs pride and will-
power; defiance, hate, and hate and once again hate." To
imbue the German people with this attitude was, he asserted,
an important part of the "purifying" process the National
Socialist Party had to undertake in bringing the German
people from weakness to strength. He taught that "will is
the one constant factor, the condition of everything else,
even of success in war no matter how efficient arms might
be." And by will he understands sheer force in action. In a
later speech he used such words as these: "Always before
God and the world, the stronger has the right to carry

through what he wills. The whole world of nature is a mighty struggle between strength and weakness and an eternal victory of the strong over the weak."

Such passages as these can be multiplied indefinitely, and Hitler's conduct has never failed to accord with the beliefs he set forth in his speeches. There is no ground for doubt of the position of the doctrine of sheer force in the scheme of Hitler. It culminates in creation of a political state having absolute authority, since it has monopoly of all the organs of power, physical and cultural; a state whose leaders are moved "by fanatical devotion and ruthless decision" and in which the one virtue of subjects is implicit, loyal obedience. Popular representations of Hitler's creed, however, usually give a false idea of it, and consequently of the cause of the hold gained over the German people. The mistake consists in treating the gospel of force as if it were the whole of his doctrine. Even a nation like Germany in the state of defeat and depression, needs more than fanaticism, brutality, and hysteria (a word Hitler often associates with the fanaticism he commends) in order to transform itself.

Strange as it sounds, Hitler repeatedly stated that the cause of Germany's weakness, the weakness which produced its defeat, was "spiritual" (*geistige*) and that therefore its redemption must also first of all be spiritual. A rebirth of idealistic faith was the primary necessity. In his *Mein Kampf* Hitler along with glorification of force expressly states its subordination (military and economic alike) to ideas and ideals. Without this strand of continuity with the "idealistic" philosophers who were educators of the German people there is no reason to suppose the latter would have responded as it has in fact responded.

In a speech made soon after coming to power (in 1935), Hitler said there were still some even among the Germans themselves who failed to understand the reasons for the existence and for the victory of the National Socialist Party. They were the ones who did not know that the German people could be governed only by appeal "to its inner instincts, its conscience," so that the strength of idealism "alone accomplished the acts which have moved the world." The people came to him, he asserted, "because of the command of an inner voice; reason alone would have dissuaded them; overpowering idealistic faith alone gave the word of command."

We do not need to go to the unreasonable extreme of those who have passed over in silence the brutal side of Hitler's philosophy, that of the role accorded sheer force, and who, concentrating upon the "idealistic" aspects of his message, have seen in it the oncoming of the "wave of the future." But unless we are to indulge in serious miscalculation of the sources of his strength in Germany—a miscalculation which will affect injuriously our peace policies—we need to take account of the belief of the German people in the ideal qualities of his work, and give them, as far as they exist, full recognition.

One can hardly use the word *philosophy* in connection with Hitler's outgivings without putting quotation marks around it. Nevertheless, in connection with his emphasis upon the "spiritual" cause of both Germany's weakness and her recovery to strength, he himself does not hesitate to use the word *Weltanschauung*. Not only that, but he says that the absence of a unified *Weltanschauung* was the cause of Germany's defeat while its development is the prerequisite for her recovery. The word, like many German philosophical words, is vaguely ambiguous, and again, like many philosophical terms, owes considerable of its influence to its very vagueness. The usual English translation is "world-outlook," and this translation certainly carries part of its signification. But it may also be translated "world-intuition." It is characteristic of German philosophical procedure to hold that a look "without" must be based upon a prior look "within." Intuition is in philosophical discourse a method of looking "within" which reveals principles that are first and ultimate truths in spite of their hazy character.

In any case, Hitler has a truly Germanic devotion to a *Weltanschauung*. One of the most serious charges he brought against other political parties while he was striving to bring his own party to power was that at their gatherings no problems of *Weltanschauung* were ever brought up for discussion. A speech that he made to a group of industrialists shortly before coming to power, in 1932, is of first-rate importance in understanding the "idealistic" phase of Naziism. It is matter of common knowledge that Hitler was given to attributing the defeat of Germany in 1918 to a "stab in the back," he having regarded the German army as unconquerable till almost the end. This notion served him well for ordinary popular propaganda purposes. But it is far from expressing his actual explanation of the cause of Germany's defeat. In the address just mentioned (more reasoned and less purely emotional in tone than most of his speeches) he expressly said that it is a mistake to regard the Versailles Treaty as the source of the evils from which Germany was suffering. "I am bound to assert," he went on to say, "that if I am to hold the belief that the German people can exercise an influence in changing these evil conditions, there must have been responsibility within Germany itself for what happened." Logically enough, he held that if the cause for the evil state of the country was external, then the remedy must also come from outside. If cure and redemption could be effected from within, then there was also responsibility from within for Germany's weak and humiliated state.

"They are wrong," he said, "who seek the cause of Germany's distress in externals. Our position is certainly the result not merely of external events but also of our internal, I may almost say, aberration of spirit, our internal division, our own collapse." He then repudiated the idea that the purely "spiritual" side of the catastrophe Germany had undergone could be overlooked, and went on to repeat his protest against "those who claim that the Treaty of Versailles is the cause of our misfortunes." For that Treaty is only "*the consequence* of our own slow inner confusion and aberration of mind." Having supplemented this assertion with a corresponding one that only a change in the *Weltanschauung* of the German people will restore Germany to unity and strength, he went on to explain, on historic grounds, the cause of what he repeatedly calls "inner division," "inner conflict," "inner aberration," "spiritual collapse."[1]

His explanation of the lapse of Germany and the means of its recovery is as follows:

1. The cloudiness which adds emotional force to many German words is evident in the word *geistige*, here translated *spiritual*. It has the ordinary meaning of *mental*, psychological, and also bears the highly honorific significance many persons find in whatever is labeled "spiritual."

Germany once had a unified world-outlook. Accordingly it possessed the conditions required for large-scale organization, community of religion being the unifying principle. When the rise of Protestantism shattered this basis, the strength of the nation turned from external to internal conflicts, *since the very nature of man forces him by inner necessity to seek for a foundation in a common world-intuition* (or outlook). Otherwise man's nature is split into two, and falling into chaos is unable to turn its force outwards.

And just because Germany had failed to achieve a new spiritual unity, "its force turned inwards and was internally absorbed and exhausted." Its preoccupations with its own "internal tensions" rendered it "unresponsive to external events of world-wide significance."

I think we are justified in regarding this account as a confirmation of what I said over twenty-five years ago about the "two-world scheme" of German culture. As has been frequently pointed out, in the absence of anything comparable to the French Revolution, Germany's "revolution" took place in ideas isolated from habits and institutions in action. Hence Hitler's conclusion as to the sole method by which Germany can recover the unity which is a condition of both domestic and international power.

Unless Germany can master its internal division in world-outlooks (or world-intuitions), it can do nothing to arrest the decline of the German people. . . . We are not the victims of treaties, but the treaties are the consequence of our own mistakes, and if I wish to better the situation I must first change the values of the nation.

Hence the address closed with an appeal to the latent idealism of the nation, in which "material," that is, economic, interests are specifically set in opposition to higher "spiritual" interests. Dependence upon the former only leads to further dissipation of the inner spirit from which alone will proceed a unified world-outlook and hence strength. "The more you bring the people back, on the other hand, into the sphere of faith, of ideals, the more it will cease to regard material distress as the one thing which counts." For, he goes on to ask, did not the German people once wage wars for a hundred and fifty years "for religion, for an ideal, for a conviction, without a trace of an ounce of material interest?"

And his final word is that when the whole German people has the same faith in its national vocation that has moved the storm-troopers to make their sacrificial efforts (including use of violence on the streets and in the meetings of their party-opponents) the position of Germany in the world will be very different from what it has been. In short, it was Hitler's mission to overcome that division between the "inner" and the "outer," the ideal and the actual, between spiritual faith and the hard realities of action which had constituted "The Two Worlds of Germany," and for this reason I have felt justified in entitling this chapter "The One-World of Hitler's Germany."

A Berlin professor who left Germany because of opposition to its policies in the first World War, wrote in 1917 the following words under the caption *Philosophy as a Smoke-screen*:

Because of the strong religious bent in Germany, the Renaissance passed off there in religious disputes. The humanists properly so-called never had much influence there. . . . Men were so taken up with religious liberty they forgot there was such a thing as civil liberty. . . . Above all, Germany got into the habit of considering the world on which she depended as something far away, above the clouds, and anything "on this side" or "here below" as of small moment. . . . What the German genius needed was that in the free "world of thought" each person be a law unto himself, while in the actual world he was forced to bow the knee to his superiors.

Up to a certain point, there is here the same diagnosis of the source of Germany's troubles as that given by Hitler. Moreover, the writer went on:

The pleasing saying, "Well, if you won't be my brother, I'll bash your head in," has become a German proverb. And the German thinks this is the formula by which he can redeem the world. . . . A Frenchman will never understand this. He is too frivolous and materialistic.[2] He thinks a dead man is just a dead man, an asphyxiating bomb just an asphyxiating bomb. But the German knows that behind both there lurks something else—an idea. . . . Ideas lurking behind things are the excuse for everything, and behind the bombs every German seeks and finds what he wants

2. It is possible the author came from the Rhineland, whose culture has long been as much French as German.

to find. The Christian finds his God, the philosopher his Kant, the philanthropist his love of humanity, and the Philistine citizen finds universal order.

It will be recalled that Hegel attacked the Kantian separation of what is and what ought to be, of the actual and ideal. He declared that what is actual is the rational and what is rational becomes in virtue of its own activity the actual. But in his dialectic scheme, knowledge of their identity exists only in philosophy as the ultimate manifestation of Absolute Spirit. Any outward manifestation of the identity has to be left to the majestic onward procession of that spirit. Hitler's philosophy, or world-outlook, is that the identity of the ideal with hard fact may be effected here and now, by means of combining faith in the ideal to which destiny has called the German people with force which is thoroughly organized to control every aspect of life, economic, cultural, artistic, educational, as well as military and political.

I shall not multiply quotations of passages in which Hitler insists that his success in transformation of the German people from a weak, divided, and humiliated people to one which is strong, proud, and united springs from the fact that he was the one who understood their latent idealism and knew how to rouse it into action. His policies of "coordination," of totalitarianism, represent his "ideal" of social unification put into thoroughgoing practical operation. In Hitler's own words: "In place of a great number of parties, social ranks, and societies, a single community has arisen. You have sacrificed your parties, societies, associations. But you have obtained in return a great and strong Reich." Abolition of trades unions, of federated states, of *Staende*, ranks and "classes," and of diverse political parties, with the intention of doing away ultimately with differences of religious denominations and organizations; control of schools, press, radio, public and private gatherings: all these things are in the interest of the "ideal" of a community having "inner spiritual" unity and hence strong. They are but the special means by which Hitler did away with the conflict and laceration he attributed to acceptance of the two-world scheme.

A declaration he has issued since the war began says that the "ideal" of the nations against which Germany wars is "struggle for wealth, for capital, for family possessions, for personal egoism"—in short, for unmitigated "materialistic" supremacy of a separate "class" cloaked under a pretended regard for individual liberty. These other nations, he said, war on peaceful Germany because they hate its ideal of complete inner spiritual unity. Germany, on the other hand, is engaged in creating a world of complete mutuality, "a world of mutual work, mutual effort, mutual cares and mutual duties." In this process, "our tasks help bring our people closer and closer together and to create an ever more genuine community." And, as if moved by an inner urgent necessity for making his philosophy of the union of idealism and ruthless force complete, he added, "If there are those who are unwilling to cooperate, we shall give them a state funeral." The consistency of his policy is exhibited in the funerals he is giving the persons in occupied countries who decline to "cooperate."

There are those who are content to define the principle at stake in the struggle of democracy against authoritarianism as respect for personality in the abstract, that is, without regard to concrete social context, and, indeed, as if the bare principle of a personal self automatically produced its own proper social context. They will be surprised to discover that no one has been more ardent in profession of reverence for "personality" than Hitler himself. For example, he has said that

in periods of national decline two closely related factors appear. One of them is the substitution for the idea of the value of personality of a leveling idea of the supremacy of mere numbers— democracy. The other is negation of the value of a Folk; that is, the denial of differences in the inborn capacities and the achievements of different peoples.

Again, "it is absurd to recognize the authority of the principle of personality in economic life and deny it in the political domain. I am bound to put the authority of personality in the forefront." Again, "there are two diametrically opposed principles: the principle of democracy, which, when allowed to have practical effect, is a principle of destruction, and the

principle of personality, which is the principle of achievement."

I have no desire to interpret these professions as yielding even a verbal deference to the Kantian principle of
personality—as an "end in itself." The authority which Hitler
gives to personality is that of active or vital energy; the kind
of brutal force exhibited in his own career and in the sub-
leaders who rallied about him. But the passages should make
clear the emptiness of formal philosophical and theological
assertion of the supreme value of "personality," exactly as
other utterances make evident the barrenness, combined
with threat of social harm, of formal proclamations of idealism. To healthy common sense, an "ideal" has meaning
when it is taken as something to guide effort in production
of future concrete changes in the existing state of affairs.
In the two-world scheme of German philosophy, the ideal
was the future brought into the present in the form of a
remote but overarching heavenly sky—cloudy but still un-
utterably sublime. With Hitler the ideal became creation of
a completely unified "community" by means of force. Empty,
formal use of *ideals* and *personality* is not confined to German philosophy. It has found lodgment in the teaching of
philosophy in this country and Great Britain. Just as Hitler
could boast, with formal correctness, that he brought National Socialism to power under the form of constitutionality,
so idealism and personality separated from empirical analysis and experimental utilization of concrete social situations
are worse than vague mouthings. They stand for "realities,"
but these realities are the plans and desires of those who
wish to gain control, under the alleged cloak of high ends,
of the activities of other human beings. Hitler's success
within Germany and the threat to the peoples of the whole
world that success has produced is a tragic warning of the
danger that attends belief in abstract absolute "ideals."

I turn now to a summary statement of the main components of the philosophy of social unity constituting the
creed of National Socialism. Hitler outlined the creed in a
speech he made soon after coming to political power (in

1934), and briefly repeated its main points in 1941. The latter can be stated, accordingly, in a paraphrase of his own words. Rallying and unifying the idealism of Germany is the supreme need. This idealism was divided between two camps which opposed one another and which had therefore to be welded together into unity. The masses, the workers, were wedded to socialism. They perhaps did not have definite ideas of just what it signified but it presented to them a necessary and fixed goal. Over against this large group stood a smaller group devoted to the ideal of nationalism. The split was serious because the first and larger group represented the workers, the hand, the productive agency of the nation, while the nationalists represented its brain. The strength and the promise of triumph of Hitler came from the fact that he first, and alone, saw the underlying identity of the two ideals. "The purest form of socialism signifies the conscious elevation of the claims and interests of the life of the people over the interests and claims of the individual." On the other side, "the highest form of nationalism finds its expression only in the unconditional devotion of the individual to the people." In short, true socialism and true nationalism are manifestations of the same ultimate ideal, approached and viewed from its two ends. What one side saw as the superior claim of society, the other side saw as the subordination and devotion of the individual to society. In spite, however, of their intrinsic correspondence, "the task of immeasurable difficulty lying before the Party is translation of recognition of the identity from the world of ideals, of abstract thought, into the domain of hard actualities."

Looking back upon the work of the Party from the vantage point of 1941, he said that so much had been accomplished in overcoming the separation between socialism and nationalism and in effecting the necessary translation into hard fact of their inner kinship, that "today the evolution of the national state is looked upon as a matter of course. In 1918–19 it was looked upon as the figment of a diseased imagination." Then he went on to say: "The ideology of National Socialism represents the conquest of individualism—not in the sense of curtailing individual

faculties or paralyzing individual initiative but in the sense
of setting the interests of the community above the liberty
and initiative of the individual"—the interests of the community in question being of course those of the particular
"community" set up by Hitler himself.

There is one important matter in which Hitler's National Socialism represents a break with the orthodox German tradition of political philosophy. Contrary to what is
often said, Hitler did not indulge in deification of the State
or political organization. What he calls *society*, understood in
terms of the people or *volkische* nation, is supreme; the
state is reduced, in the theory of National Socialism, to an
organ, although an indispensable one, of promoting the
security and well-being of the community. At the outset, he
could hardly have had any other idea, since he was engaged
in a deliberate attempt to overthrow the existing state because it had failed utterly to perform its social function. But
as time went on he saw himself more and more as the
divinely commissioned representative of the people, of the
national community which the government or state he
created was bound to serve. It was also much simpler to
connect his theory of blood and race with a quasi-mystical
notion of the people than with the activities of the state,
which are often felt as a burden, as in having to pay taxes.

Hitler also made a change of an extraordinary character
in the theory of socialism. Previous creeds that called themselves socialistic attached primary importance to economic
factors, no matter what brand of socialism they presented.
Hitler comes out flatly for subordination of economic interests and affairs. Work, productive work put forth in behalf
of the community—the Hitlerian community, of course—is
the sole economic factor of importance. To it, all technical
economic questions and problems are completely subordinate; and in no affair has Hitler displayed his opportunism
on larger scale or with more immediate success than in his
manipulation of capitalists and laborers. Rauschning's statement that Hitler looked upon socialization of banks, factories, this and that industry, and of private property as
trifling matters, since the one thing of importance is the
socialization of human beings, is in line with the tenor of

Hitler's public speeches, although it is franker in tone than those he made in appealing to socialist workingmen.

Except when used in the service of national unity, economic activities are external and "materialistic." There is no reason for supposing that his attack upon Marxist Bolshevism on this score is not sincere. It was a factor in his success in converting millions of socialist voters to his cause. More important with respect to this latter matter, however, is his subordination of the economic, given the existing condition of Germany, to development of a powerful government and powerful army. In his own words, "There can be no economic life unless behind economic activity there stands the determined political will of the nation ready to strike and to strike hard." Not even agriculture could be revived without a prior revival of Germany as a political power. Foreign trade could be developed only by the same means. Even with respect to an "internal market, the problem of the Life-space (*Lebensraum*) of Germany must first be solved by making Germany into a political power factor."

As a means of reaching depressed laborers and the millions of unemployed, the appeal of the communist party to internationalism was indeed theoretical, pale, and remote compared to what Hitler told them—making his word good in his "guns before butter" war economy—he could do if they would assist in building up a powerful German political nationalist state. Present-day communists seem to have learned the lesson, possibly more from the example of Stalin in converting the U.S.S.R. from international socialism into a highly nationalistic state—which foolish liberals often take to be a move to the return of capitalistic economy. At all events, the communist party in the United States is quite willing to subordinate distinctively American interests to those of a foreign country which they hold up as a concrete example of a "socialist" state.

The distinctive feature of the ideal Folk-society is that its unity springs ultimately from blood or race. One may read everything Hitler has said and be none the wiser as to what he understands by race. According to good authority, Hitler once retorted impatiently to a critic that he knew the scientific facts about the composite racial structure of Germany as well as anyone. Certain it is that he employs "blood, race, and soil" in a mystical sense, if one defines "mystical" to mean the complete submergence of fact and idea in an overpowering emotion supposed to reveal higher truth than cold intelligence can compass. The following quotation gives a partial idea of the role of blood and race in his appeal.

First of all stands the inner value of a people which is transmitted through the generations, a value which suffers change when the Folk who is the custodian of the value changes its inner blood-conditioned composition. Traits of character are bound to recur as long as the nature of a people, its blood-conditioned state, does not alter. This value, not to be destroyed without a change in blood substance, *is the chief source of all hope for revival of our people.* Otherwise the mystic hope of millions for a new Germany would be incomprehensible.

Scientific facts about race were as nothing in comparison with a simple, easily grasped, symbol which could be used as a weapon in an emotional appeal to fanatical action. Hitler's contempt for intellectual measures and for science, except when used as an effective technical instrument in propaganda, are the obverse side of his belief in the power of emotion to reach the masses, and of his conviction that when "intellectuals" are emotionally stirred they fade into the mass. For it is characteristic of intense emotion to rule out discrimination; emotion is an all or none state. We fear and hate all over; the emotions are inherently totalitarian. When they are once kept excited they control belief and every semblance of intellectual operation. Indifference, apathy, Hitler called his chief foe; excitement, and always some new source of excitement, is the consistent quality in his inconsistent policies. Since emotion is total, it knows only black and white, not intermediate shades. Hence the ideal value of Germanic blood needed for effective presentation an extreme and wholly dark opposite.

There is, accordingly, good reason to believe the report that Hitler once said that if the Jews were destroyed, it would be necessary to invent them. Just as he always presented the mildly socialist régime he was trying to overthrow as if it were the most extreme and dangerous Marxist communism, and just as communists represented social democrats as the social fascist traitors who were the worst foes of socialism, so in the face of all facts he represented the political parties of Germany as agents of the overlordship of international Judaism. His extreme flight and extreme success was his persuasion of multitudes that international finance-capitalism and the communism that was engaged in trying to overthrow capitalism were but two wings of the same army of destruction. Skillful emotional manipulation of symbols probably reached its climax for long ages in Hitler. If it is true, as is sometimes asserted, that he is himself pathological, it is certain that, in the phrase of the street, he is "crazy like a fox," since his own emotional disturbances, if they are there, are of a kind which enable him to arouse similar disturbances in others. As he says of his own teachings, "what the intellect of the intellectual could not see, was immediately grasped by the soul, the heart, the instinct, of simple primitive men." For good measure, he then added that the task of the education of the future is "to grasp the unity of feeling and intellect and return consciously to primitive instinct."

Blood, race, instinct, passion, in the vocabulary of Hitler, are names for life, for the vital; and they are a name for what move men to act *en masse*; leaders above meanwhile exercising with consummate skill the most approved methods of organization and control. The mass is not a new phenomenon. Neither is the authoritarian leader. What is new is a mass which is not a mere amorphous crowd but in which the most extraordinarily effective skill in every kind of organized effort is combined with the psychology of the crowd. There is nothing in the career of National Socialism which requires any change in the sentence of the next chapter, written over twenty-five years ago: "The chief mark of distinctively German civilization is its combination of self-conscious idealism with unsurpassed technical efficiency and organization." Only the locus of the "idealism" and the agents of its organization have altered.

That the content which fills and gives toughness to the idealism has moved from the intellectual (or quasi-intellectual) to the emotional and passionately impetuous, without losing its combination with technical efficiency and organization, is indeed new. It is the difference which has given victory in Germany to the ideology of Hitler. The transformation, it may be said with a large measure of truth, was anticipated by Heine in 1833. I quote again a passage cited in the second chapter of my original text. After saying that there will first be a time in which Germans will occupy themselves with systems of philosophy and that upon completion of this period a political revolution will follow, he goes on,

most to be feared are the philosophers of nature were they actively to mingle. . . . The Philosopher of Nature will be terrible in that he has allied himself with the primitive powers of nature, in that he can conjure up the demoniac forces of German pantheism and having done so, aroused that ancient Germanic eagerness which combats for the joy of the combat itself. . . . Smile not at my counsel as at the counsel of a dreamer. . . . The thought precedes the deed as the lightning the thunder. . . . The hour will come.

It had not come in 1914. At that time there did not seem to be any likelihood that it would ever come. As far as Heine had the philosophy of Schelling in mind, in that particular form, the hour has not come now; Hitler is doubtless innocent of any knowledge of Schelling. But the spirit of the remark is incarnate in the teachings and the actions of Hitler. The writings of Richard Wagner, in his return to primitive Teutonic mythology, probably have had more influence in giving shape to Hitler's hopes and ambitions than that of any other person. At all events, the saying of Hitler, reported by Rauschning, about the coming revival of the early nature worship of the German people reads like an almost literal reminiscence of the prophetic vision of Heine. For after Rauschning had said that the peasants of his district retained below the surface of Christianity beliefs inherited from olden times, Hitler replied, "That's what I'm counting upon. Our peasants have not forgotten their true religion. It is merely covered over. . . . They will be told what the Christian Church has deprived them of—the whole secret knowledge of nature, of the divine, the shapeless, the demonic."

We do not, however, need to depend upon this remark, nor yet upon Hitler's practical attempts to weaken the hold of the Lutheran and the Catholic churches, nor yet upon his coquettings with the ideas put forth by Rosenberg as to the necessity of a return to primitive Germanic gods and cults. The idea of a "religion rooted in nature and blood" (to use Hitler's words) is the only idea consonant with his whole appeal and with his efforts to give his National Socialism the emotional intensity, the symbols and the rites of a religion. There is more truth than appears on the surface in the comparison that has been suggested between Mohammed and Hitler in creation and propagation of a new and fanatical religion.

Hitler's whole philosophy of "blood and soil," the passion of his struggle for recovery of every one of German origin in the new community of Germans, his passionate struggle for new lands for Germans to settle and make their home, spring from his passionate faith in what he calls "nature." Such statements as these are typical of his appeal. He ascribed the rebirth of Germany to its response to the appeal he made in behalf of "the primacy of the eternal values of blood and soil *which have been raised to the level of the governing principles of our life*." And again he said, "Our worship is exclusively cultivation of that which is natural, *because what is natural is the God-willed*."

It is in this context that we have to understand Hitler's fervent belief that he is the Messiah commissioned to found a "new order" not only for Germany but for the whole earth. The values he calls "historic" are now old to the point of senility; they are artificial, lacking all support in "nature." They are to be replaced by biological values, by those of blood; that is, of life-force. His constant depreciation of "intellect," his assertion that the Germans were cultivated in excess, his reiterated appeal to raw primitive instincts, to the impetuous and unreflective, his supreme confidence in his own supreme leadership, are all of them aspects of his philosophy of nature and the natural—as he conceived them.

To win over captains of industry and socialist working-men (including abolition of their unions), peasants and Junkers, the old aristocracy and gangster upstarts, strong nationalists and the states-rights adherents of federated

states, required a world-outlook that cut below the "intel-
lectualism" of the traditional philosophy of Germany.
"Reason" had to be identified with "the most primitive manifestations of Nature." The earlier appeal was to an elite; as
long as an elite ruled a powerful and growing Germany it
sufficed. But with the defeat and humiliation of Germany,
power to rule was passing from the elite. It was the genius
of Hitler to grasp that fact. Commentators upon the German
scene, German born and bred, have noted that there are certain general industrial and political tendencies which are
breaking down class distinctions and creating a new force,
that of a more or less amorphous mass. The depression of
Germany, combined with traditional political ineptness of
the German populace in political matters, and with the ab-
staining remoteness of the scientifically educated part of the
population from political life, tremendously accentuated this
phenomenon in Germany. As events have demonstrated, it
became, under the skilled manipulations of Hitler, the decisive factor. An inverted democracy with authoritarian absolute leadership at the apex and the disciplined obedient mass
at the base, with a hierarchical order of intervening sub-
leaders, constitutes the political state of Nazi Germany. It is
an "inverted democracy" in which place and rank are made
dependent upon manifestation of fanatic zeal and resolute
energy in command and obedience rather than upon the
many feudal inheritances Germany had not thrown off.
Exhibition of zeal, devotion and fanaticism is what Hitler
understands by "the authority of personality," which in his
creed is an expression of the intensity attained in different
human beings by blood or natural life-force.

The change from the primacy of *Innerlichkeit* to
primacy of action is not what it seems to be upon the surface. What is more "inner" than "blood," and what is more
internal and intrinsic and at the same time more urgent for
utterance than the impulses and passions to which Hitler
successfully addressed his appeal? There is even more continuity between this appeal and the political philosophy and
the philosophy of history of Hegel than lies on the surface.
Hegel's constant use of the words Reason, Spirit, and the
alleged supremacy he accorded Logic (in his peculiar under-

standing of logic) have deceived the would-be elect. To get below the surface, we have to lay hold of the force of the distinction he drew between reason or *Vernunft* and *Verstand* or understanding. Reflection, inquiry, observation and experimentation to test ideas and theories, all that we of the lesser breeds call intelligence, belongs in the Hegelian scheme to mere "understanding," which reason scorns and leaves behind in its sublime flight.

Especial point is given to the sharp separation of reflective intelligence and what is called reason in the teachings of Hegel's *Philosophy of History*. "Understanding is the mode of mind which seeks precision and insists upon distinctions which are fixed." Accordingly it is at home in science (*mere* science as the Hegelian would say) and in all matters of calculation. Modern economic life is marked precisely by the manifestation of "understanding"; calculation and measurement are its determining factors. The bourgeois phase of society is accordingly identified by Hegel with operation of the understanding. According to him it has a necessary but strictly subordinate place in the structure of organized society. Beneath and above it is the creative work of reason which penetrates below distinctions to identities and rises above differences to unity.

History is the manifestation of this creative reason. In formation of historic peoples and in creation of their characteristic institutions, reason operates unconsciously. Human beings act according to their impulses, passions, desires and private egotisms. They suppose they are doing their own work and fulfilling their own destiny. Actually, they are organs, agents of the divine absolute spirit, and are realizing its purposes. Only after absolute rational will has done its work may reflection supervene, and see what has been accomplished, in its true, its philosophic, meaning. But intelligence cannot create; it can only register what absolute reason has created, in its poor use of passion, desire, and "finite" human purpose. Reflective intelligence is like the "owl of Minerva which takes its flight only when the shades of evening have fallen"—when, that is, creative reason has completed one historic phase of its unconscious creative work.

The fact that Reason, working according to the process to which Hegel gives the name "logic," operates blindly and unconsciously as far as the agents of its execution are concerned, provides a genuine bond between it, in spite of the high eulogistic phraseology of Hegel, and the reliance of Hitler upon instinct. The bond of continuity is reinforced when we learn that the supreme *historic* manifestation of Absolute Spirit is its creation of nations; and that, in the history of the world, "a particular nation is dominant in a given epoch, so that in comparison with its absolute right as the bearer of the current phase of development of absolute spirit, the spirits of other nations are void of authority and no longer count in history." No great difficulty stood in the way of translating Hegel's state, which he often calls "nation," into Hitler's Folk-community, and Hitler often expressly identifies nature, life, blood, with reason.

The chief bond of connection, however, is that after all Hegel's reason operates practically exclusively in the medium of the impulse, passion, desire, ambition, of personal or "subjective" wills, who unconsciously execute the will of absolute spirit, or Hegel's "God." It is perhaps worth noting that on one occasion Hegel, after mentioning the "cloudy undeveloped spirit of the Germans," went on to say, "If they are once forced to cast off their inaction, if they rouse themselves to action and realize the intensity of their inner life in contact with outward things, they will perhaps surpass their teachers"—the latter being, as the context shows, the French of the Revolutionary and the Napoleonic periods. Hitler might well claim to be the executor of the mission anticipated by Hegel. The one marked change is substitution of the "*volkische* society" for the political state—and even here Hegel's use of the word "nation" is loose enough to permit the transition.

In the course of the foregoing discussion, it was incidentally noted that Hitler holds the principle of democracy to be that of rule by a majority, and hence the subjection of "personality to mere numbers." He joins to this view of democracy on its political side, the view that, in its social phase, democracy is committed to an economic individualism which pulverizes all opportunity for social unity, and thereby weakens democratic countries so as to render them the easy prey of unified and "socialized" Germany. The democratic spirit of the United States has generally failed to make known abroad its working philosophy as a way of life. For while propaganda aims enter into what Hitler has said about democracy, what is just cited presents upon the whole his actual belief about democracy.

Hitler's failure to appreciate the philosophy of the democratic method of evolving social unity is the counterpart of his reliance upon authoritarian absolutistic force as the sole method of attaining social unity. Events have proved that there is something in German culture and education (Hitler calls it blood) which prevents Germans from appreciating and from trying the democratic method of attaining social unity, and which thereby evokes its response to appeal to achieve unity by the contrary method of force. An acute observer after years of association with Germans remarked to me that in no intellectual matter does the great mass of Germans have any use for discussion and conversation. They depend upon *ipse dixits*, upon finality of utterance, upon telling and being told. And this report of experience reminds me of what an engineer of European education told me: namely, that it required ten years of association with American engineers responsible for the conduct of a large productive industry to enable him to realize the force of the American method of back-and-forth give-and-take discussion until final decision represented a workable consensus of the ideas of all who took part. Until he reached that stage of development, he had felt it necessary, he said, to try to drive home *his* point.

I conclude, then, with expression of the belief that it is this method, the method of achieving community by processes of free and open communication, which is the heart and the strength of the American democratic way of living and that the weaknesses of our democracy all represent expressions of failure to live up to the demands imposed by this method. Prejudices of economic status, of race, of religion, imperil democracy because they set up barriers to communication, or deflect and distort its operation. This is not the place to go into the relation of socialization of industrial production and distribution to attainment of a genuinely democratic way of life. But we can at least be sure that so far as the methods of management of a shop, a factory, a railway, or a bank are autocratic and hence harmful to democracy, it is because these methods prevent or impede the processes of effective give-and-take communication, of conference, of consultation, of exchange and pooling of experiences—of free conversation if you will.

Compartmentalizing of "science" is a distinctive feature of German life. It is this compartmentalization which enables Hitler, along with the high technical scientific development of Germany, to reduce all forms of science, physical, psychological, and social, to sheer tools of Nazi policy. The lesson for democracy is that science places in our hands an immensely valuable resource for rendering the processes of communication genuinely intelligent, so as to take them out of the field of mere opinion as well as out of that of finality and *ipse dixit* "authority." While reduction of scientific method and scientific conclusions to a compartment that is external to social life is distinctively German, it is not confined to Germany. We have inherited that tendency; the heritage shows itself, with harm to democracy, whenever and wherever we fail to use science as a means of rendering communication more intelligent in all matters requiring social decision.

As yet we have no adequately developed American philosophy, because we have not as yet made articulate the methods and aims of the democratic way of life. Out and out use of force as the means of realizing the ideal of social unity should then, at the very least, remind us of the meaning of the alternative democratic method for the continuous developing of social unity. The philosophy which formulates that method will be one which acknowledges the primacy of communication in alliance with those processes of patient extensive observation and constant experimental test which are the human and social significance of science.

The concluding pages of the chapters written over

twenty-five years ago stated with emphasis that the situation which then existed "presents the spectacle of the breakdown of the whole philosophy of Nationalism, political, racial and cultural." They also suggested that our own country is not free from the guilt of swollen nationalism. Without reviving here the question of "isolationism" versus "interventionism" which events have decided, it is fitting to note that the isolationist plea for "America First," and the reasons it put forth in behalf of that plea, was animated by an uncurbed nationalist spirit of the sort which has brought the world to its present tragic state. The ever-increasing interdependence of peoples in every phase of modern life does not automatically bring understanding, amity and cooperation of the interdependent elements. As the state of the world proves, it may produce tensions and frictions, and these may lead each element to try at once to withdraw into itself and to establish peace and unity by forceful conquest of opposing elements.

The democratic principle of communication as the means of establishing unity applies to relations between nations as well as domestically. I do not think it is inappropriate to repeat the warning uttered many years ago about the danger of depending, when the war ends with victory over Fascist nations, exclusively upon judicial and political policies and agencies. They are necessary. But in the coming peace, as in the so-called peace of 1918, they will be effective only in connection with means and methods which make the inescapable facts of interdependence a positive and constructive reality in the lives of all of us, in "promoting the efficacy of human intercourse irrespective of class, racial, geographical and national limits." We shall play our own proper part in this work in the degree in which we make free communication a reality in all the phases and aspects of our own social life, domestic and trans-national.

I have tried in the foregoing pages to give an analysis of the theory and practice of Hitlerian Naziism in its own terms. Such an analysis has to be conducted in cool, dispassionate terms. But its outcome can and should produce an emotional response nonetheless intense because it is based upon understanding the nature of the enemy we have to meet. War with a totalitarian power is war against an aggressive way of life that can maintain itself in existence only by constant extension of its sphere of aggression. It is war against the invasion of organized force into every aspect and phase of life;—an invasion which regards its success within Germany as the sure promise of greater success throughout the whole world. And by use of the same methods of organizing every aspect of science and every form of technology to impose a servile straitjacket of conformity, to which the high title of social unity is given. We are committed by the challenge addressed to every element of a democratic way of life to use knowledge, technology, and every form of human relationship in order to promote social unity by means of free companionship and free communication. It is immensely clearer than it has ever been before that the democratic way of life commits us to unceasing effort to break down the walls of class, of unequal opportunity, of color, race, sect, and nationality, which estranges human beings from one another.

Appendixes

Appendix 1

THE PHILOSOPHY OF BIOLOGY: VITALISM *versus* MECHANISM[1]
by Ralph Stayner Lillie

In comparison with mathematicians and physicists, biologists have contributed little to philosophical literature, notwithstanding the close relations existing between their science and philosophy. The most notable instance of recent years has been Driesch, whose attempts at philosophical commentary and interpretation seem, however, to have given on the whole little satisfaction to either biologists or philosophers. Bergson—"the biological philosopher," as Driesch calls him—bases much of his doctrine on biological data, and the use of such data appears to be becoming more frequent among philosophers. Lately professed biologists have shown somewhat more tendency to enter the field of philosophical discussion; and it is remarkable that when they do so they often adopt a vitalistic point of view. Haldane's *Mechanism, Life and Personality* is one recent illustration of this tendency, and the present book of Johnstone's is another. As the author himself explains, the point of view and methods of treatment are largely those suggested by Driesch and Bergson. The book is not long; there are eight chapters entitled, respectively, the Conceptual World, the Organism as a Mechanism, the Activities of the Organism, the Vital Impetus, the Individual and the Species, Transformism, the Meaning of Evolution, the Organic and the Inorganic; there is also an appendix with a brief account of the chief principles of energetics. In the table of contents is given a concise yet complete and connected summary of each chapter. This makes it unnecessary for the reviewer to summarize the whole book, and this review will be confined chiefly to a criticism of the author's main contentions and especially

1. *The Philosophy of Biology*, by James Johnstone, D.Sc., Cambridge: University Press, 1914.

[First published in *Science*, n.s. 40 (1914): 840–46. For Dewey's discussion of this article, see this volume, pp. 3–13.]

of the arguments by which he seeks to support his vitalistic thesis.

The first chapter discusses the relation of conceptual reasoning to reality. The author agrees with Bergson in regarding intellect as essentially a biological function, which reacts in a characteristic manner on the flux of reality and dissociates this more or less arbitrarily into detached elements; the aim of this dissociation is practical—namely, to facilitate definite or effective action on the part of the organism. Scientific method follows an essentially similar plan; our scientific descriptions and formulations of natural processes are conceptual schemata; their correspondence with real nature is inevitably inexact; they necessarily simplify and diagrammatize. In reality, however, nature can not be regarded as a composite of separate processes, individually susceptible of exact description in intellectual terms, and interconnected in ways which are similarly definite and quantitatively determinable; it is rather a continuous or flux-like unitary activity, exhibiting a progressive and irreversible trend; hence actual duration is distinct from the conceptual time of physicists. Now the intellect, in making its characteristic conceptual transformation, neglects or ignores or even falsifies much of the essential character of reality. This is how it becomes possible to view the living organism as a mechanism: the physiologist substitutes for the real living organism the conception of a system of physico-chemical processes, conceived as interconnected in a definite way; by doing so he is enabled to view the organism as essentially a physico-chemical mechanism; but we must note that the conceptual elements out of which he builds up his scientific view of the organism inevitably determine the nature of this end-conception, which is physico-chemical or mechanistic only because his method does not permit him to regard the organism as anything but a summation or integration of the physico-chemical processes that form the elements of his synthesis. As a result, however, he really misses what is most distinctive of living beings, and reaches a point of view which is not only inadequate for scientific purposes— as shown by the failure of physico-chemical analysis in the case of many vital processes—but in its very nature far removed from the actuality itself.

This is the fundamental criticism which the author makes of the accepted scientific methods of investigating life-phenomena. In the remainder of his book he interprets the characteristics of the organism and of the evolutionary process from this general or Bergsonian point of view. He sees operative in life a distinctive agency, corresponding to the "élan vital" of Bergson or the entelechy of Driesch, which acts typically in a direction contrary to that characteristic of inorganic processes; these latter tend toward homogeneity and dissipation of energy; in living organisms, on the contrary, evolution tends toward the production of diversity, and the tendency of entropy to strive toward a maximum may be compensated or even reversed by vital activity.

Life, when we regard it from the point of view of energetics, appears as a tendency which is opposed to that which we see to be characteristic of inorganic processes. . . .The effect of the movement which we call inorganic is toward the abolition of diversities, while that which we call life is toward the maintenance of diversiti███████y are movements which are opposite in their direction (pag███).

It is here that the author's views become most seriously open to scientific attack; the evidence that the second law of thermodynamics does not always apply to life-processes is certainly inadequate; there is exact experimental evidence that the first law (that of conservation) holds for organisms; and the storing of solar energy by chlorophyll is in no sense evidence that the second law is evaded. There seems in fact to be a fundamental misconception in this part of the author's argument. He holds that life may play the part of the Maxwellian demon under appropriate circumstances (page 118), and defends this view on the ground that the laws of molecular physics are statistical in their nature and might be different if it were possible to control the movements of individual molecules; such control, it is implied, is possible to the vital entelechy. It seems to the reviewer, however, that the application of the second law to gases or solutions implies simply a tendency of the freely moving molecules to uniform distribution; the resulting homogeneity can be prevented only by adding energy to, or abstracting it from, part of the system; even Maxwell's demon has to work a partition which resists the impact of the faster molecules—

a consideration which shows that any coordination or sorting of molecules would in itself involve the performance of work. Johnstone's supposition, however, is that the vital entelechy can, without altering the total energy of the system, control or direct the otherwise uncoordinated motions of the individual molecules; and that the purposive or directed character of the individual organism's life, and also of the whole organic or evolutionary process, is conditional on the existence of such an agency, and is indeed the characteristic expression of its activity. He thus maintains, in effect, that physiological processes are unintelligible unless we can assume the existence of some such directive agency peculiar to life, which can vary the nature, intensity and direction of the physico-chemical processes and coordinate them in the interest of the organism. This "entelechy" is what imparts their distinctive quality to life-phenomena.

It has long seemed to the reviewer that failures or deficiencies in the physiological analysis of complex or delicately adjusted functions form no ses. The⬛⬛⬛⬛and for rejecting such methods of investigation ⬛e 314⬛⬛eir nature inadequate. Vitalists, however, are fond of this kind of attack; and both Haldane and Johnstone adduce instances which they believe make it incredible that physico-chemical processes, unguided by an entelechy, could ever form the basis of vitality. At present our knowledge of the physiology of embryonic development and of certain types of form-regulation is especially defective; and such phenomena are cited more frequently than any others as proving the inadequacy of physico-chemical analysis. Driesch's "logical proof of vitalism," quoted in the present book, is an instance of this tendency; even relatively simple processes like muscular contraction and nerve conduction remain largely mysterious, and we find also scepticism as to the possibility of any satisfactory account of these processes in physico-chemical terms (cf. page 100 of the present book).

A twofold reply to this type of vitalistic argument may be given. First, it is to be noted that the failure of physico-chemical analysis is often due to mere complexity of condition. But complexity, as such, does not introduce any essentially new problems; it simply makes more difficult, and may for a time make impossible, the task of analysis. Provided that the more elementary processes forming a complex process are characterized by *constancy* in their nature and in the conditions of their occurrence, any degree of complexity in the total process is possible. Ordinary experience with complex artificial systems, of a mechanical or other kind, verifies this contention; we find that there is no limit other than that set by practical expediency to the complexity of a system whose component parts operate and interact in a constant manner. In all such cases smaller and simpler parts are taken as units from which higher compound units are built up, and these secondary units are then similarly utilized for the construction of more complex systems; these may be still further combined, and so on. The one indispensable condition is that there should be an essential invariability in the operation and interaction of the parts of the system. Similarly with life and its manifestations: the complexity of organisms and of organic processes, so far from making us despair of the adequacy of physico-chemical analysis in dealing with vital phenomena, seems in fact to the reviewer the surest witness to their essential adequacy. For these vital processes, however complex and mysterious, are unfailingly *constant* in their normal manifestation; one has only to reflect on what is continually happening in the body of a healthy man in order to realize this; and the stability of conditions thus shown surely has the same basis as have the stability and constancy of the simpler non-vital processes which we everywhere find as components of the vital. The basis of this stability is simply the exactitude with which natural processes repeat themselves under identical conditions.[2] If this were not the case, how could a physico-chemical system of the vast complexity of (*e.g.*) the human organism ever exhibit stable existence or constant action? It is impossible to doubt that the constancy with which complex physiological processes operate is conditional on the constancy of the simpler component processes—those which form the subject-matter of physico-chemical science. Con-

2. Just why there is such repetition is rather a philosophical than a scientific question; but it seems probable that it is at bottom an expression of the homogeneity of the conditions of natural existence, space and time.

stancy in the character, mode of action, and interconnection of the component substances and processes is evidently indispensable to the constancy or stability of the product of their integration, the living organism. We find in fact that mysterious and unintelligible physiological processes, *e.g.*, the regeneration of the lens in the eye of a salamander, recur under appropriate conditions with the same constancy as the simplest and most intelligible, say the formation of a retinal image by that same lens. It is clear that if we admit the adequacy of physico-chemical methods in the one case we must be prepared to do so in the other.

Second, it is to be noted that the organic processes show evidence by their very limitations that the underlying mechanisms are strictly physico-chemical in character. Thus vitalists call especial attention to the instances of development and form-regulation which have so far baffled all attempts at physico-chemical analysis. "Does not this mean," Johnstone asks, "that in biology we observe the working of factors which are not physico-chemical ones?" The limits to the regulative power are less frequently cited by vitalists; yet surely evidence of this kind is equally relevant. Why, if an entelechy can restore the amputated arm of a salamander, can not it perform a similar miracle in the case of a man? The fact is that nothing is proved by citing such cases. But on the whole they seem clearly to imply that the properties of the organism are throughout the properties of physico-chemical systems, differing from inorganic systems simply in their complexity. The reviewer knows of no facts which, viewed without prepossession, necessitate or even un-equivocally favor the contrary view. Those vitalists who maintain that material systems are incapable, without the aid of an entelechy, of developing the characteristics of life —and who even hold that fundamental physical laws like the second principle of energetics are evaded by organisms— must adduce evidence of a less doubtful kind in support of their thesis. The peculiarities which organisms exhibit appear to the reviewer to lead to precisely the contrary conclusions, and to indicate that stable and constantly acting physico-chemical systems may exhibit a degree of complication, both of composition and of behavior, to which literally no limits can be assigned.

Another mode of reasoning popular among vitalists, and equally fallacious from the physico-chemical standpoint, is that an entelechy can, without the performance of work, guide or coordinate toward a definite end processes which themselves require the performance of work. This view implies that in the organism molecular movement may be directed, retarded, or accelerated at the will of the entelechy. But in Newton's first law of motion it is surely made clear that any deviation in the movement of a particle from a straight line, or any retardation or acceleration of its motion, involves work in precisely the same sense as does the initiation of the movement. Now it is evident that guidance or regulation of the sequence of events in any material system must involve one or other of these kinds of processes. In other words, it is physically impossible for any agency to modify the processes in any material system without modifying the energy-transfers in that system, and this can be done only by the introduction of compensating or reinforcing factors of some kind—*i.e.*, by altering the energy-content of the system—which is equivalent to the performance of work. One is forced to conclude that all such attempts at the solution of biological problems are based on fundamental misunderstandings. Dogmatism must be avoided in scientific criticism; nevertheless it seems to the reviewer that the following general considerations are incontrovertible, and that they are quite inconsistent with the type of vitalism represented by Driesch and Johnstone. First, the organism is a system whose development and continued existence are *dependent* on the rigid constancy of physico-chemical modes of operation; here, if anywhere in nature, stability of the internal or vital conditions is indispensable; otherwise it is inconceivable that the complex living system could persist, and maintain its characteristic activities and often delicate adjustment to the surroundings. Clearly the numerous and diverse processes whose integration constitutes life could not deviate far from a definite norm without fatal derangement of the whole mechanism. Second, the basis for this regularity is the regularity of physico-chemical processes in general. These, the more closely they are subjected to scientific scrutiny, appear the more definite and constant in their character: this conclusion is not—as many philosophical critics of scientific method maintain—an illusion resulting from the inherently classificatory nature of intellectual operations; it is simply a matter of observation and experimental verification. Repeat the conditions of a phenomenon and the phenomenon recurs. We find this to be equally the case in living organisms and in non-living systems; and it appears to be as true of psychical as of physical phenomena. The difficulty in dealing with organisms is to secure exact repetition of conditions, because organisms are in their nature complex, and complexity means a large number of factors which may vary. Regularity, in fact, may be said to be of the very essence of vital processes; special devices for securing regularity (e.g., constancy of body-temperature, of the osmotic pressure and reaction of the tissue-media, etc.) are highly characteristic of organisms. It would seem that an entelechy disturbing this regularity, however intelligently, would be not only superfluous but detrimental. Moreover, we must always remember that unequivocal evidence for the existence of such an agency is quite lacking.

Thus there seems to be no valid reason to believe that organisms differ essentially from non-living systems as regards the conditions under which the processes underlying vitality take place. The *conditions* of natural existence and happening appear everywhere and at all times to be homogeneous, whatever existence itself may be. This conclusion seems unavoidable to the impartial observer of natural processes; the repetition so characteristic of nature is apparently an expression of this central fact. The flux-like character of natural existence, so insisted upon by Bergson and the other Heracliteans, is to be admitted only in a highly qualified sense. Repetition and the existence of discontinuities and abrupt transitions are equally characteristic; and all of the evidence of physical science goes to show that a repetitious or atomistic construction lies at the very basis of things. So far from the intellect arbitrarily imposing a diagrammatic uniformity and repetition upon a nature which in reality is a progressive flux and never repeats itself—to the student of natural science it appears rather true that the conceptualizing characteristic of the reasoning process is itself one expression of this fundamental mode of natural occurrence—that it is, in fact, the derivative of a peculiarity which pervades nature throughout. Such a view, if well established, would refute the contention that scientific methods, being intellectual in their character, necessarily involve a falsification; and would dispose of attempts to discredit physiological analysis on the ground that life transcends intellect and hence is properly to be investigated by other than scientific methods.

The attempt to find in organisms evidence of special agencies not operative in the rest of nature seems to the reviewer to show less and less promise of success as physico-chemical and physiological science advances. Thus the author's attempt to limit the applicability of the second law of energetics to the non-living part of nature is quite un-justified by the evidence which he presents. The interception and accumulation of a portion of the radiant energy received by the green plant, in the form of chemical compounds of high potential, is in no sense an infringement of the second law; as well might one hold that the partial transformation of radiant energy into potential energy of position, as seen, e.g., in the accumulation of glaciers, is an instance of this kind. The partial transformation of energy at low potential into energy at high potential is in fact a frequent occurrence; thus the temperature of an electric arc far exceeds that of the furnace which generates the current; similarly the animal organism utilizes energy derived from oxidation of carbohydrates and proteins to build up compounds of much higher chemical potential, viz., the fats. If living organisms —systems which are specially characterized by utilizing chemical energy as the main source of their activity— exhibit such tendencies, there is in this fact nothing anom-alous from the point of view of physical science. To say on the basis of this kind of evidence that "life appears as a tendency which is opposed to that which we see to be charac-teristic of inorganic processes" (page 314) is surely un-warranted from any point of view.

This review is not necessarily an attack on vitalism, but only on certain current forms of vitalism. It can scarcely be denied that there is something distinctive about life; but at the present advanced stage of physical science it seems futile to argue that the vital process is the expression of an agency which is absent from non-living material systems. Viewed temporally or historically, the vital is seen to develop out of the non-vital; many of the steps in this process are still obscure; but with the progress of science it becomes more and more evident that the development is continuous in character. Hence, if we are to account for life, we must equally account for non-living nature. Now since nature exhibits itself as coherent throughout, we must conclude that in its inception[3] it held latent or potential within itself the possibility of life. This is not entirely an unbased speculation; even in the character of the chemical elements life is foreshadowed in a sense, as shown in Henderson's recent interesting book.[4] In a recent discussion,[5] in some respects related to the present, the reviewer has called attention to one implication of the scientific view of nature and the cosmic process. If we assume constancy of the elementary natural processes, and constancy in the modes of connection between them—as exact observation forces us to do—there seems no avoiding the conclusion that—given an undifferentiated universe at the outset—only one course of evolution can ever have been possible. Laplace long ago perceived this consequence of the mechanistic view of nature, and the inevitability of his conclusion has never been seriously disputed by scientific men. Nevertheless, this is a very strange result, and to many has seemed a *reductio ad absurdum* of the scientific view as applied to the whole of nature. The dilemma can be avoided only if we recognize that the question of ultimate origins is not, strictly speaking, a scientific question at all; and in saying this there is implied no disparagement of scientific method. As an object of scientific investigation nature has to be accepted as we find it; and why it exhibits certain apparently innate potentialities and modes of action which have caused it to evolve in a certain way is a question which really lies beyond the sphere of natural science. Such considerations, if they do not exactly

3. I do not use this term necessarily in a historical sense, but rather in the sense of ultimate origin of whatever kind,—which it may well be necessary to conceive as extra-temporal.
4. *The Fitness of the Environment,* Macmillan, 1913.
5. *Science,* n.s. 1913, page 337.

remove the vitalistic dilemma, yet separate sharply the scientific problems which organisms present from the metaphysical questions to which the phenomena of life— more than any others—give rise. If we consider the organism simply as a system forming a part of external nature, we find no evidence that it possesses properties that may not eventually be satisfactorily analyzed by the methods of physicochemical science; but we admit also that those peculiarities of ultimate constitution which have in the course of evolution led to the appearance of living beings in nature are such that we can not well deny the possibility or even legitimacy of applying a vitalistic or biocentric conception to the cosmic process considered as a whole.

Although disagreeing with the author's main contentions, the reviewer wishes to recognize the merits of the book as an interesting, enthusiastic and ingenious contribution to the literature of its subject. We have noted some errors in matters of biological detail, but these are not such as to affect the main argument. The brief account of certain physiological processes seems somewhat out of date; the account of the nerve impulse is unsatisfactory, and certainly few physiologists now hold that a muscle is a thermodynamic machine in the sense conceived by Engelmann; there is some evidence of unfamiliarity with biochemistry; the term "animo-acid" instead of amino-acid recurs a number of times, a mis-spelling perhaps appropriate to a book which is really a modern plea for animism.

Appendix 2

VOCATIONAL EDUCATION
by David Snedden

Some of us school men, who have profound respect for the insight of Dr. Dewey where the underlying principles of social organization and of education are under discussion, are somewhat bewildered on reading the contributions which he has recently made to the *New Republic*. Those of us who have been seeking to promote the development of sound vocational education in schools have become accustomed to the opposition of our academic brethren, who, perhaps unconsciously, still reflect the very ancient and very enduring lack of sympathy, and even the antipathy, of educated men towards common callings, "menial" pursuits and "dirty trades." We have even reconciled ourselves to the endless misrepresentations of numerous reactionaries and of the beneficiaries of vested educational interests and traditions. But to find Dr. Dewey apparently giving aid and comfort to the opponents of a broader, richer and more effective program of education, and apparently misapprehending the motives of many of those who advocate the extension of vocational education in schools designed for that purpose, is discouraging.

To many of us the questions of the so-called dual or unit control are not fundamental at all. The fundamental questions are, first, as to what constitutes sound pedagogic theories as to the aims and methods suited to vocational education in schools, and secondly, the most effective organization and administration of the means designed to realize them. There are fewer mysterious and uncertain features in vocational education, whether carried on by schools or by other agencies, when such education is rightly interpreted and defined, than in the fields of the so-called general or liberal education. Vocational education—not as

[First published in *New Republic* 3 (1915): 40–42. For Dewey's reply, see this volume, pp. 411–13.]

carried on in schools, of course—is the oldest as well as even yet the most widely distributed form of education of all, since all grown men and women have always had vocations for which, with some measure of purposiveness, they have been trained in the home, the field, the workshop, the commercial establishment or on shipboard. Vocational education is, irreducibly and without unnecessary mystification, education for the pursuit of an occupation. In all stages of social development men have always sought, with more or less conscious method, to train their youth efficiently to follow a vocation—to hunt, fight, fish, farm, work metals, weave, bake, trade, transport, teach, heal, lead in worship or to govern. Vocational education is not all of education— never was that fact more clearly recognized than to-day; but vocational education at the right time and of the right kind is supremely important—and of that fact we have recently been in danger of losing sight. Hence questions as to what constitutes right vocational education, when and by whom it shall be given, and how it shall be effectively correlated with other forms of education, are just now of the greatest importance.

It has long been recognized that vocational education for many of the leading callings could no longer be success- fully carried on by the historic methods of apprenticeship. Hence have appeared in succession vocational schools for the training of lawyers, theologians, military leaders, physi- cians, pharmacists, dentists, teachers, engineers, navigators, accountants, architects, telegraphers, stenographers and many others. Vocational schools for delinquents and for children without homes were organized many years ago by philanthropists. More recently the state itself has entered this field. In many of our cities far-sighted men have been active in establishing vocational trade schools as a means of extending educational opportunities.

Now, many of us have been forced, and often reluct- antly, to the conclusion that if we are to have vocational education for the rank and file of our youth as well as for the favored classes, we shall be obliged to provide special vocational schools for this purpose, because the historic agencies of apprenticeship training have in most cases become less rather than more effective as means of sound vocational education. A few industries are indeed still so organized as to be able to give good vocational education, and it may be that as a result of movements now taking place others will readjust themselves so that in them workers can be assured of progressive development of their capacities.

But in general, modern economic conditions are such as to impair rather than enhance the capacity of employers to give satisfactory vocational training. The mobility of labor has enormously increased in the western world, and more particularly in America. Competition among the various units of a given industry has, with rare exceptions, become keener, and the success of a given employer is often dependent upon his ability to attract immigrant labor or to lure skilled workmen away from his competitors. American manufacturers have long been accustomed to await a supply of foremen and competent workmen from European countries. Western railroads by paying higher wages attract firemen, engineers and mechanics away from Eastern roads. The city employer tempts country-trained hands.

There are some indications that a wise cooperation among employers, now beginning to be manifested in certain fields, will soon remedy this condition of affairs. Already the printers of America have joined forces to establish vocational schools for their apprentices. Railroads are stealing workmen from each other far less than formerly, and some of them now systematically train their own workmen. A few large manufacturers have established successful schools for machinists. But it is not yet clear just how far this movement can be carried, in view of the competitive conditions still persisting in such fields as the building trades, the manufacture of textiles, the food-packing industries and numerous smaller lines of manufacture. It is hardly to be expected that government can effectively force all employers to cooperate in the important function of training workers.

The function of the state in this as in other fields of education is clear. The state should consider the good of the individual and the needs of society, and where private agencies cannot accomplish a desired end the collective action of the state must be enlisted for this purpose. This is fundamentally the reason why the various commonwealths of the United States now, in greater or less degree, assist such special forms of vocational education as engineering, agriculture and even law and medicine. Massachusetts, usually conservative as regards state support of higher schools, nevertheless maintains a free agricultural college, makes large contributions towards engineering education, and supports three schools designed for the training of leaders in the textile industries.

In the light of recent experience it cannot be successfully contended that the state is unable to establish and maintain successful vocational schools for the various trades, for farming, for home-making, and for the different commercial pursuits. The pedagogic problems to be encountered are doubtless many and difficult, and are made doubly so by the academic prepossessions of the men who are likely to be put in charge of these vocational schools. It is not yet clear how economically state-supported vocational education can be administered, nor is it in every case demonstrated that it is expedient, as a matter of social policy, to have the state or the nation support such schools. But the time has passed when the feasibility of such training could be questioned.

When and under what conditions a youth should be permitted to enter a vocational school is yet debatable. In Massachusetts the law carefully provides that a youth shall be eligible to enter a vocational school only at the time when he is equally eligible to leave the regular public schools and to become a factory or farm hand. The administrative theory under which Massachusetts vocational schools are being conducted assumes that the youth ready to embark on wage-earning who instead turns aside for a period in a vocational school, should be able to concentrate his efforts largely in learning the occupation selected. It is not desirable to blend so-called liberal and vocational education at this period, it being always within the possibilities of the youth to continue in the regular or general elementary or high school if he so elects.

It is sometimes asserted that vocational education given by schools under state support is beneficial chiefly to employers. It is incredible that men acquainted with the economic conditions of our time, the competition of employers for labor and the mobility of labor itself, should take this view. In every occupation in the country there is constant competition for superior ability, as is manifested in the varying wage rates usually found. The only sound point of view is to regard vocational education as being primarily of significance to the boys and girls concerned, and ultimately, of course, to society as a whole. If vocational education does not result in greater productive capacity and if greater productive capacity does not result in a larger share to the laborer, then, indeed, are the times very much out of joint.

The question of so-called dual versus unit control is merely one of securing the greatest efficiency. In most states we already have the dual control, if we wish so to style it, of our various special vocational schools of agriculture, industrial training for delinquents, etc. In point of fact there can be no such thing as ultimate dual control of any stated type of school, since administrative bodies must owe their creation to some single state agency, such as the legislature, the governor as authorized by the legislature, or local administrative agencies as created by legislative enactment. Such so-called dual control as one finds in Wisconsin or as it existed in Massachusetts from 1906 to 1910, simply represents an attempt to put in immediate charge of a special form of education a group of persons who are primarily interested in its successful development, and who may be able to bring it to the point of view of practical men in that field. Business men generally are suspicious of the so-called academic mind in connection with vocational education. They feel assured neither of the friendliness nor of the competency of our schoolmasters in developing sound industrial education. For that reason they often favor some form of partially separate control, at least at the outset of any new experiment.

If vocational education is to be successfully established in those states where academic tradition strongly persists, it may prove absolutely essential that some form of separate control should, at least temporarily, be inaugurated with a view to obtaining best results. School men, however well-intentioned, are apt to be impractical and to fail to appreciate actual conditions.

Some successful beginnings of vocational education of the kind discussed in this paper have been made in Massachusetts. The present stage of development would not have been reached if it had not been for the activities of the Commission on Industrial Education during the years 1906 to 1910. The ultimate merger of this body with the Board of Education may have represented what should happen in every state after particular forms of development have arrived at some degree of maturity.

Appendix 3

EDITORIAL
by William C. Bagley

Under modern conditions the doctrines that dominate the public schools become the doctrines that dominate the nation. It is particularly important at the present time to inquire what type of educational theory is governing the development of our school system, and to determine the relation of this theory to the realization of the democratic ideal.

Contemporary educational theory in America is dominated by America's foremost philosopher—John Dewey. Not only is Dewey our foremost philosopher, but some of his contributions to educational theory are, we believe, the most significant that have been made since the generation of Pestalozzi, Froebel, and Herbart. His recently published book, *Schools of To-Morrow*, describes typical schools in which the theories for which he is largely responsible have been worked out—although he modestly refrains from stating this fact. His book also supplements these descriptions with chapters in which he discusses informally the educational doctrines involved.

It is not in derogation of Dewey's real and lasting contributions to educational theory that we would call into question the influence of his teachings. It is rather that his fundamental postulates may easily be made to sanction that type of individualism which most clearly imperils true democracy.

Dewey conceives the function of education exclusively in terms of growth or development, and his book (in so far as it is an exposition of educational theory) is a stimulating treatment of freedom, interest, and activity as means to this end. Freedom, interest, and activity are important factors

[First published in *School and Home Education* 35 (1915): 4–5. The last three paragraphs were written by George A. Brown. For Dewey's reply, see this volume, pp. 414–15.]

both in education and in democracy. But they are not the
only factors, and because Dewey stops with these, his treatment of democracy and education is partial and one-sided.
Just as democracy itself involves the peril of pernicious
individualism, so an educational theory which recognizes
freedom, interest, and activity as essential democratic factors, and then stops, makes inevitably in the same direction,
for both in democracy and in education, these are the
individualistic factors. An over-emphasis here means an
inevitable neglect of the balance-wheel which alone will
prevent democracy from self-annihilation.

This tendency in Dewey's teachings is most clearly
seen in his attitude toward the traditional educational
material—recorded knowledge. With this he will have no
commerce. The very notion that the child should be asked
or required to assimilate the experiences of others is repugnant to him. And this in spite of the fact that his own theory
is derived nine tenths from Rousseau and in spite of the fact
that his theory has been swallowed "lock, stock, and barrel,"
by many of the disciples whose efforts to put it into practice
he so well describes. This is in no wise derogatory to Dewey;
the one tenth that he has contributed gives him place as the
leading educational thinker of his generation; but the inconsistency is appalling.

The danger of this partial point of view lies in the fact
that it blinds one to an indisputable condition of democracy
—namely, the insuring of a community of knowledge among
all of the members of the democratic group. We have
referred in preceding discussions to the neglect of this factor
as revealed in contemporary reforms—which are largely
inspired by Dewey's teachings. Certainly an educational
theory which finds so small a place for recorded race-experi-
ence and which in addition insists that freedom and interest
shall govern the educative process will have a hard time
in adjusting its tenets to this fundamental need of common
elements in the people's culture.

A corollary from this derision of recorded knowledge is
an attack upon learning from books, and this in turn involves
a most significant implication. Dewey admits that "the text-
book method of education is well suited to that small group

of children who by environment are placed above the necessity for engaging in practical life and who are at the same time interested in abstract ideas." But he implies that those who do not happen to be interested in abstract ideas do not need them. This is tantamount to a denial of the possibility of mass or collective thinking on the conceptual level—an essential condition of effective democracy. It means, if it means anything, that the privilege of thinking in conceptual terms is to be limited to those who naturally "take to" this type of thinking; and this means, if it means anything, that constructive and far-reaching thought (which necessarily involves abstractions, and preparation for which necessarily involves training in abstract thinking) is not for the masses. It is at this point that any attempt to base the educational foundations of democracy exclusively upon the tenets of individual freedom and interest breaks down completely.

It is natural that Dewey should perpetuate the notion that discipline and obedience in childhood are fundamentally inconsistent with initiative and originality in adulthood. The inference is easy from his fundamental assumption. One who conceives education exclusively in terms of growth from within will find no sanction for coercion or direction from without. Initiative and originality imply freedom, but the kind of initiative that is worth while is the kind that builds on the gains that the past has made, and the kind of freedom that is worth while is the kind that has been achieved through discipline and sacrifice. Blind obedience and a blundering, thick-headed discipline will bring disaster,—just as unlimited freedom and unrestrained initiative will bring disaster. But one who asserts or implies that American children are so dangerously addicted to blind obedience as to imperil their originality is attempting to demolish a man of straw.

Much more significant from the point of view of its application in practice is Dewey's incessant insistence that instruction must always take its cue from the "felt needs" of the child. This is a most valuable pedagogical principle if applied within appropriate limits, and, together with the significance of activity to learning, it constitutes, we believe, Dewey's lasting contribution to educational theory. The danger lies in the plausible but fallacious inferences which it readily suggests. Carried beyond its proper sphere of application in educational method, it merges at once into the spirit of opportunism—that slavery to the immediate and the impending which, as we have pointed out, constitutes a serious handicap to effective democracy.

From the innumerable suggestions toward an improved technique of teaching which Dewey's book contains, American education will richly profit. It is in his fundamental postulates that the grave dangers are involved. If he were striking against a dominant educational doctrine which followed as a corollary from a harsh and Puritanical national philosophy, his basic principles would exert a most wholesome and salutary influence. But Dewey is not striking against the current of popular demands: on the contrary, he is himself the accepted prophet of the *Zeitgeist*, and quite contrary to his own wishes, no doubt, his teaching will be turned to the support of the dangerously individualistic tendencies of the hour. Inevitably many if not most of his readers will find in these teachings an authoritative justification of an extreme individualism and a radical reaction from effort and discipline and sacrifice that he perhaps would be the first to condemn.

GEO. A. BROWN

The Achilles heel of the God-protected logician is always in his premises. It is here that Dr. Bagley aims his shaft in the above discussion.

There is, however, in every discussion about public affairs an argument from facts that is of immediate interest to the people. The citizens are beginning to realize that Dr. Dewey and other critics of our schools would discredit the very aims of American education. These are aims that have seemed essential to the people for permanent welfare. The task they have given the teacher is to realize these aims. Is the task impossible? Are we not accomplishing it, in a way, and improving our methods and results with reasonable certainty? What are the probable results of the aim that Dr. Dewey and his followers would substitute? These are questions that ask for facts. Before we can get these facts we need to analyze many of the conditions of society and of teaching. But first we need to understand the position of these critics of American life.

Dr. Dewey has not stopped with criticisms of the methods and ends of teaching adopted in the school room. He even questions whether the American people have any fundamental aim for their civic and social life by which to determine the common elements of a liberal education for all. As he sees it, Americans are always "constructing the ends to be acted upon as well as experimenting in methods." If we must always be constructing a purpose for action, and can get no further with life under American conditions than that, of course we shall be forever experimenting without ever determining just what we wish to realize. In fact Dr. Dewey in his latest book, *German Philosophy and Politics*, contrasts this idea of "Americanism" with German "Nationalism" and proposes, if we understand him, that America become just the experiment station for the world's civic aims. Other nations may select the aims which seem most worthy and seek to realize them in full.

Appendix 4

PAROCHIAL SCHOOL EDUCATION
by Charles P. Megan

Sir: In your issue of April seventeenth there appears an article by John Dewey, of Columbia University, on vocational education, in which Professor Dewey attacks a bill on this subject, introduced into the last (1913) session of the Illinois legislature, under the auspices of the Commercial Club of Chicago, and now (1915) reintroduced. Of this bill Professor Dewey says:

It was publicly stated and not denied that at the previous session every member of the legislature of the Roman Catholic faith received a letter from a superior dignitary of that church urging support of the bill.

"And why not?" asks Professor Dewey. That is to say, here is a measure which every good citizen ought to oppose, but the Catholics are for it; and their reason is easily understood.

Professor Dewey has been grossly imposed upon in this matter. Inquiry among Roman Catholic members of the 1913 and 1915 legislatures of Illinois shows that no such letter was ever sent or received. As for the introductory statement "It was publicly stated and not denied" everybody ought to know that appeals to religious bigotry are not made publicly, where they can be denied, but secretly, in the dark; and this particular disreputable lie has not hitherto been denied, because no one who could have any occasion to make a denial has known that the lie was in circulation, until Professor Dewey let it out.

While it makes no especial difference, and one feels like apologizing for defending against such a charge, in the twentieth century, I may add that Mr. Cooley, the Com-

[First published in *New Republic* 3 (1915): 72. The Dewey article to which Megan refers, "Splitting Up the School System," appears in this volume on pp. 123–27. For Dewey's rejoinder to Megan's letter, see this volume, pp. 416–17.]

mercial Club's educational adviser, is a thirty-second degree
Mason, while the Chicago Teachers' Federation, the leading
opponent of the Commercial Club's bill, is probably seventy-
five per cent Catholic.

It may perhaps occur to Professor Dewey that his Illinois correspondents have misled him on other points also
in this vocational education controversy, and it may be
suggested to him respectfully that he inquire into the
accuracy of some more of the information he has received
from this state. I do not here call attention to any of these
points, but confine myself to the one sentence which I have
quoted. Roman Catholic citizens of this state feel a deep
sense of injustice at the suggestion that they have made an
effort, officially or unofficially, to use for their own purposes
the growing public interest in vocational education. The
great bulk of us are sincere well-wishers of the public
schools; and we can see no reason to doubt that a man may
be a good citizen and a good Roman Catholic at the same
time.

The conviction that a separate, but public, board should
be put in charge of these public vocational schools—as is
done with the State university, which in view of its special
problem has a separate, but public, board of management—
is independent of any religious question. It arises in part
from a study of the experience of countries which have tried
academic control, to their sorrow; in part from the experience
of Wisconsin, where a "dual" plan identical with that
proposed by the Commercial Club has been in successful
operation for three years; and in part from Professor Dewey's
own doctrine that the education of every individual should
not be a thing apart from life, but should grow out of the
experience of that individual, and be translated back again
into experience; so that after, not before, a boy has begun his
life-work in some occupation his further education should
grow out of that occupation and be applied again in it. This
is the principle on which the Commercial Club's vocational
education bill is drawn.

Appendix 5

POLITICAL PHILOSOPHY IN GERMANY
by William Ernest Hocking

In his book on *German Philosophy and Politics*, Professor Dewey has proposed an original view of what is wrong with the philosophy of the government responsible for the present war. It has been commonly felt that on Germany's part this war has a philosophy behind it, and a bad one. Many of us have been supposing that this philosophy stood in strong contrast with the idealism with which Germany began the nineteenth century. During the time when the present policies of the German government were shaping themselves, the prevalent state of mind was openly hostile to these idealistic teachings, and Germany was listening to leaders who learned far more directly from scientific experience and from the bitter examples of successful statecraft that were at hand, especially in English practise. We thought that Germany had learned these lessons only too well, and with native thoroughness had carried them to extremes at which we, who had in some measure been practising them, were forced to abhor them. As opposed to that early idealism, this philosophy was one which justified expediency as against principle; which had cured the German spirit of the weakness of sympathy and humanity; which had freed itself from the idea of absolute obligation toward treaties or elsewhere, and had become efficiently Darwinian and pragmatic.

In Professor Dewey's eyes we have been making a mistake, and a serious one. The trouble with Germany, he finds, is not in the rejection of its idealists, but in the vestige of their doctrines that it still retains. It is Kant in particular who has misled Germany, by giving a philosophic sanction to a certain native hypocrisy in the national blood which disposes it to revel in the inner flattery of idealistic sentiment

[First published in *New Republic* 4 (1915): 234–36. For Dewey's rejoinder, see this volume, pp. 418–20.]

while doing what it pleases in the outer world of hard facts. This was not quite foreseen or intended by Kant; but he had set up an absolute principle of duty, so formal and spectral that it could not be said to command anything in particular, and yet one which spurned instruction from experience. Such an absolute law, like the swept and empty house of Scripture, was open to occupancy by any usurping devil; and so Scharnhorst, Hegel, Bernhardi and others trooped in, setting up in the vacant sanctuary "the good of the State" as a concrete object of supreme devotion. Thus the nation has come to use the name and inner unction of the idealist's absolute duty to support the principles of Machiavelli, Frederick and Bismarck. This result is persuasive to the German mind chiefly because the German mind is disposed to have its absolute; abandon this "traffic in absolute," and the supreme good of the German state fails to impose on belief as an ultimate end; it becomes an end to be tested, like all others, in the crucible of experience. It must break down at last before the higher good, "furtherance of the depth and width of human intercourse." This, as I read it, is Professor Dewey's diagnosis of the German distemper.

He therefore recommends to American policy a more radical experimentalism; let us have done with absolute or fixed principles, such as "nationality" or "sacred rights"; let us regard everything as subject to test, discussion, measurement, compromise, adjustment, revision. Of course, while we are trying a theory out, we try it as if it were, for the time, worthy of complete confidence, and to become "established," for that is what giving a trial means. And we are forced to inquire whether the German government is not at the present moment faithfully following the experimental prescription: it is trying its own theories to see how they work. It believes firmly that its methods are the methods that succeed; and it believes so not because of anything that Kant taught, but because of the way in which it has recently been interpreting history, led by its series of economic historians from Marx (who precisely inverted Hegel's view of history) to Lamprecht and Schmoller. Perhaps official Germany still expects to find these principles confirmed by a successful issue of the war, and if such should be the case, would Professor Dewey have any argument from the armory of the experimental philosophy against them, as principles suitable for Germans? He might urge that what in such an event would work very well for the victors would work very badly for the victims; and unless a principle works all around, it cannot fairly be said to work. But this is exactly the test that Kant uses; it is, in fact, his "absolute law": any maxim, said he, that can be made universal is a good one, any other is a bad one. This law does not indeed prescribe any specific line of conduct; but, as the present instance shows, it would be highly inaccurate to infer that it is of no effect in guiding concrete action, or in distinguishing between a good course and a bad one. Germany's course might be defined as experimentalism without the Kantian corrective.

Upon close scrutiny of Professor Dewey's argument, however, the substance of his criticism seems to be, not that Germany has an absolute, but that it has the wrong absolute. Has he himself done more than to transfer the putative crown of the absolute moral end from "the good of the German state" to "the furtherance of human intercourse"? If it were true that Germany to-day believes in an absolute duty, the trouble would be, on Professor Dewey's showing, only that it gives this absolute too narrow a definition. But this is an error which can certainly find no sanction in the Kantian philosophy. For Kant did in fact try to fill his formally empty house with a maxim identical in effect with that which Dewey proposes: "Treat humanity as an end in itself, and never as a means only." Can anyone with the slightest historical justice credit the German government of to-day with following *this* Kantian principle? If this were taken by the government as an absolute of inflexible rule, would there have been any war? And would Professor Dewey have had anything to criticise?

The fact of the matter seems to be that the ruling party in Germany does not at heart believe in any absolute duty. It is radically experimental or pragmatic, which is what *Realpolitik* essentially means. It does indeed go about its work as desperate action always does, with relentless dogmatism and a liberal invocation of the name of God. It flourishes an absolute: but this absolute is not even verbally of Kantian origin—it has its roots in the ancient piety of Germany, transferred to the historically un-German doctrine of the divinity of the monarch and of the state. But assuming for the moment that this appeal to absolute right had a sidelong reference to Kant or Hegel, is anyone outside of Germany convinced by it that the German government believes in its own language, or is actuated by any idealistic faith? What most of us seem to feel here is rather a discrepancy between the profession and the actual belief exemplified in behavior, a mental dishonesty which can neither be traced to Kant's philosophy nor attributed to the normal character of the German people. And surely we cannot fairly judge the character of any philosophy by those who cloak themselves in its phrases without a shadow of faith in its substance.

The issue raised by Professor Dewey is not a slight one. It involves not only the good name of German idealism—which with all its strut and abstraction is worth defense, for we must allow Germany what spiritual asset she still has—it involves also our own American political thinking. The American people is becoming conscious of its need for a political philosophy which expresses its character. Largely through this war the conviction has become strong within us that we have a distinct character, and something to stand for. When Mr. H. G. Wells made the tour of America whose results were published in *The Future of America*, he failed to find any such conviction: he said we were "state-blind." This condition of things has come to an end. We have a political character, and are conscious of it. Is it expressed in the philosophy of experimentalism? Our national protests against submarine outrages have been based throughout on the ground of rights that are assumed stable. Experimentalism at this point would rob our national attitude of what punch it has. We need not, and do not, assume in these documents that we know in detail what is absolutely right and good; but we are bound to believe that there is such a thing as principle and right, and that there are certain rules which come so close to embodying it, in the existing cases, that we shall put an inflexible will behind them. They have been experimented with during all previous history, and they have been experimented with enough. We do not propose to experiment further with slavery, nor yet with our main positions upon the "rights of man," though we have much work to do in defining those rights. There can be no doubt that our own experiment in government has suffered from an overdose of absolute *a priori* theorems borrowed from England and France (surely not from Germany) in the framing of our constitution. It will take time, as Professor Dewey declares, to weed out this mass and determine what things they are to which we shall hold fast. Here an experimental temper will help us on. It is always easy to be absolute about too much, and the critic of the absolutist is always needful. But that is a far cry from the rejection of all absolutes— that is, of all fixed principle. I should prefer to accept the other side of Professor Dewey's faith, and adopt "the furtherance of human intercourse" as a good beginning toward defining an absolute end.

TEXTUAL APPARATUS
INDEX

TEXTUAL COMMENTARY

For John Dewey, the year 1915 was marked at the beginning and at the end by events connected with the American Association of University Professors: on 1 January 1915, he made an "Introductory Address" to the large group gathered to form that organization; on 31 December 1915, he delivered its first presidential address. These two addresses, along with two public letters Dewey wrote as president of the A.A.U.P., make up four of the fifteen articles that appear in the present volume. Only two years earlier, Dewey had actively participated in organizing the Teachers League of New York for elementary and secondary school teachers, but this national organization of college professors was a venture of even greater importance to him. Throughout much of the preceding year he had devoted many hours to discussing the possibilities with colleagues and to writing letters to key figures in the academic world.

Nevertheless, Dewey found time in late 1914 and in 1915 to write the fifteen articles and miscellaneous pieces that appear here. In addition, he published two new books—*German Philosophy and Politics* (New York: Henry Holt and Co.) and, with his daughter Evelyn, *Schools of To-Morrow* (New York: E. P. Dutton and Co.)—as well as the revised, expanded edition of his *School and Society* (Chicago: University of Chicago Press).[1]

Of the articles published in 1915, only four were

---

1. Although Dewey did, as the publisher advertised, revise the 1899 *School and Society* in 1915 by reworking and polishing the prose, the "expansion" included no new material. For the 1915 edition, the last chapter of the 1899 edition, "Three Years of the University Elementary School," was dropped and five new chapters, previously published as articles in the 1901 *Elementary School Record*, were added. The complete work, including the original last chapter, appears in *The Middle Works of John Dewey, 1899–1924,* ed. Jo Ann Boydston (Carbondale: Southern Illinois University Press, 1976), Volume 1.

printed more than one time. The single previous printing of
the remaining articles serves as copy-text for the present
edition.

Two of the articles that appeared more than once offer
no problems of copy-text. "Professorial Freedom," Dewey's
letter to the *New York Times*, 22 October 1915, was reprinted the following month by *School and Society*
2 (1915): 673, with the title "The Control of Universities."
The reprint derives directly from the *New York Times* with
no intervention by Dewey. Another letter by Dewey, as president of the American Association of University Professors,
also signed by Arthur Oncken Lovejoy, secretary, and
E. R. A. Seligman, chairman of the Committee of Inquiry,
appeared in *Nation*, 6 May 1915, with the title "The Situation at the University of Utah," and in *Science*, 7 May 1915,
with the title "Conditions at the University of Utah." The
two texts were undoubtedly printed from ribbon and carbon
copies of the same document and therefore have equal
authority. The *Nation* printing has provided the basic text
for the present edition simply because it is more complete:
Science omitted an extract from an earlier letter by Lovejoy,
stating that Lovejoy's letter had been published in full in
the previous week's issue of *Science*.

The two remaining articles in this volume that were
previously published more than once are "The Existence of
the World as a Logical Problem" and "The Logic of Judgments of Practice," both of which were revised extensively
for Dewey's 1916 collective volume *Essays in Experimental
Logic* (Chicago: University of Chicago Press, 1916). These
two articles and Dewey's two new books, *German Philosophy
and Politics* and *Schools of To-Morrow*, are discussed in the
sections that follow.[2]

"The Logic of Judgments of Practice"

"The Logic of Judgments of Practice" was first published in three parts in two issues of the *Journal of Philosophy, Psychology and Scientific Methods*: I, "Their Nature,"

2. The editorial principles and procedures used in preparing volumes of the *Middle Works* are discussed fully by Fredson Bowers
in *Middle Works* 1:347–60.

and II, "Judgments of Value," JP: *Journal of Philosophy* 12 (1915): 505–23; III, "Sense-Perception as Knowledge," *ibid.*, 533–43. That appearance serves here as copy-text.

To revise "The Logic of Judgments of Practice" for EE: *Essays in Experimental Logic*, Dewey changed a number of words and phrases to sharpen and clarify his meaning, and also made extensive additions. The largest class of accidental alterations accepted for the present edition are those within or caused by substantive revision or changes in close juxtaposition to such material. Also judged authorial are the frequent changes in emphasis, whether by adding italics, deleting italics, or adding quotation marks to call attention to a term. In addition, the following accidental revisions have been considered Dewey's own and have been adopted here: "doctrine" capitalized at 15.15; "One" lower-cased at 30.39; semicolon changed to comma, 15.17; commas deleted, 23.19, 39.10, 46.10, 52.8, 54.5; commas added, 15.34, 20.8, 38.3, 38.10, 46.8, 52n.2, 58.34, 64.6 (2); comma changed to colon, 31.26; hyphen added to "value standards", 46.27; "can not" joined, 20n.3, 20.26, 37.22, 50.31; "esthetic" changed to "aesthetic", 31.37, 52.6,8,n.3.

"The Existence of the World as a Logical Problem"

This essay originated as a paper Dewey read to the New York Philosophical Club. A carbon copy of the 20-page typescript for the address, not typed by Dewey himself, (TS), is in the papers of the Philosophical Club in Columbia University Special Collections; various notations and corrections appear in a hand other than Dewey's, including the name "John Dewey" at the conclusion of the paper.

The ribbon copy of this typescript can be hypothesized as the document that Dewey used to prepare printer's copy for first publication of the paper in PR: *Philosophical Review* 24 (1915): 357–70. He had, in fact, probably started correcting and marking his own copy even before he read the material to the Philosophical Club; important support is given this hypothesis by the fact that one of his listeners, the person who later deposited the carbon copy, wrote into the address at 87.18 the words "of the event with the momentariness," which did not originally appear in the carbon. The listener could have known this exact phrase only if Dewey read it thus at the Philosophical Club meeting.

In addition, Dewey subsequently reworked the paper, making extensive changes in both substantives and accidentals. Although many of the differences in accidentals between TS and PR are formal matters, such as changes in the relative position of punctuation, regularization of the size of the one-em dash, and substitution of footnote numbers for asterisks, there are enough clearly authorial accidental changes to warrant a conclusion that Dewey carefully and thoroughly revised the TS to prepare printer's copy for PR. The kinds of accidental changes that must be attributed to Dewey are different paragraphing, 87.29, 96.26; partial removal of italics in "*re*defining", 87.39; removal of italics at 85.35, 87.36, 88.10; and adding italics at 83.27, 86.13, 87.5, 91.3, 92.3, 93.34, 96.40. The first impression of the article in PR has therefore served here as copy-text. Except as noted, all variants between TS and PR in both substantives and accidentals appear in the Historical Collation for this article.

Dewey revised "The Existence of the World as a Logical Problem" for republication in EE in exactly the same way he revised "The Logic of Judgments of Practice"; the kinds of accidental changes accepted as emendations are therefore similar in both articles: accidental alterations within or caused by substantive revision and changes in close juxtaposition to rewritten passages. Other changes judged authorial are the frequent shifts in emphasis effected by adding italics, deleting italics, and adding quotation marks to a term or phrase. The following additional accidental revisions have also been considered Dewey's and have been adopted here as emendations: commas changed to parentheses, 95.8, 9; comma added, 86n.10; commas deleted, 85.4, 89.30; question mark changed to period, 84.32; lower-case letter changed to capital, 86.4; hyphens added, 90.8, 94.33; and "common sense" hyphenated at 85.3, 87.11, 93.23, 95.32, 96.38.[3]

3. At 84.29–30, "common-sense" is in a quotation from Russell; the hyphen was inadvertently deleted in TS and PR. The instance at 95.32 occurs in a sentence with other substantive revision. All

When the book of *Essays in Experimental Logic* (EE) was first suggested to Dewey, the University of Chicago editors considered it a routine republication of Dewey's essays in the *Studies in Logical Theory* (Chicago: University of Chicago Press, 1903), "with corrections and some minor additions."[4] The Press apparently thought of the "minor additions" in terms of a few paragraphs or even pages to be added to the previously published *Studies*; Dewey, however, responding to the repeated Press invitation to make such additions, doubled the size of the projected book by adding nine essays published earlier in various journals, among which were both "The Existence of the World as a Logical Problem," and "The Logic of Judgments of Practice."

Three printings of EE were made from a single set of plates, in 1916, 1918, and 1920; the book went out of print in December 1925. Machine collation of copies of the three impressions of the book[5] against the copyright deposit copy (A433372) revealed that for the 1920 printing two changes were made in "The Existence of the World as a Logical Problem," to eliminate line-end hyphenation. In "The Logic of Judgments of Practice," four typographical errors were corrected: 15.1, "assuerdly"; 42.39, "suppresssing"; 80.19, "mathmatical"; 81.12, "thinikng".

German Philosophy and Politics

German Philosophy and Politics (New York: Henry Holt and Co., 1915) is based on Dewey's series of three

---

cases of accepting hyphens in "common-sense" are listed here, however, to call attention to a general class of emendations made on the authority of Dewey's usual practice of distinguishing between "common-sense" used as an adjective and "common sense" as a noun. The 1914 Chicago *Manual of Style* in use when EE was edited preferred the consistent use of the hyphen, which was supplied wholesale throughout this book. The present edition has accepted those listed in the Textual Commentary and has allowed the copy-text noun "common sense" to stand at 96.23, 96.39, 97.8.

4. The genesis and history of *Essays in Experimental Logic* are discussed in the Textual Commentary to Volume 2 of the *Middle Works*. The account in the present volume is a summary of that discussion.

5. First impression, Dewey Center; second impression, University of Minnesota, 1329092; third impression, University of Chicago Press Collection of Record Copies.

lectures on the John Calvin McNair Foundation at the University of North Carolina in February 1915. Although in later years this book has been generally conceded to be among Dewey's least valuable, reviewers praised it at the time of its publication.[6] The *American Review of Reviews*, for instance, said, "It is a most lucid and well-reasoned survey of the philosophical principles that have by saturation motivated the development of the German nation" (p. 248). The *Nation's* reviewer added, "The treatment is impersonal, but the collocation of facts forms a telling piece of sarcasm" (p. 152). Dewey's contemporaries in the field of philosophy also reviewed the book: James H. Tufts wrote in the *International Journal of Ethics*, "The book is arresting and suggestive—important out of proportion to its size" (p. 133); George Santayana said in the *Journal of Philosophy, Psychology and Scientific Methods*, "It is a fair, candid, and generous presentation of the political philosophy of Kant, Fichte, and Hegel, yet independent in its attitude and not, on the whole, favorable in its judgment" (p. 645); and F. C. S. Schiller said in *Mind* that together these "eminently sane and stimulating lectures" (p. 253) result in an argument that is "closely knit and highly instructive" (p. 251).

German Philosophy and Politics was registered for copyright (A401196) following publication 28 May 1915. The copyright deposit copy has served as copy-text for the present edition.

Examination of the volumes themselves makes it possible to distinguish at least two impressions of this book, although Holt Publishing Company records (Princeton Uni-

6. Reviews of *German Philosophy and Politics* were: *A.L.A. Booklist* 12 (1915): 6; *American Review of Reviews* 52 (1915): 248; *Independent* 83 (1915): 24–25; *New York Times Book Review*, 18 July 1915, p. 257; *Springfield Daily Republican*, 10 June 1915; Francis Hackett, *New Republic*, 17 July 1915, pp. 282–84, with a Footnote by Walter Lippmann, pp. 284–85; William Ernest Hocking, "Political Philosophy in Germany," *New Republic*, 2 October 1915, pp. 234–36; Reply by Dewey, ibid., p. 236 (both in this volume); Frank Thilly, *Philosophical Review* 24 (1915): 540–45; James H. Tufts, *International Journal of Ethics* 26 (1915): 131–33; George Santayana, *Journal of Philosophy, Psychology and Scientific Methods* 12 (1915): 645–49; F. C. S. Schiller, *Mind*, n.s. 25 (1916): 250–55; *Nation*, 29 July 1915, p. 152.

versity) include only sales figures and no information about the number or size of the printings. Four copies with 1915 on the title page and two copies with no date except on the copyright page (1915) were compared on the Hinman collating machine and found to be invariant. However, the exemplars without title-page date show much more broken and worn type. The sales figures indicate that the printings were probably small; some 200 copies of the book were sold in 1916, 1920, 1921, with sales dwindling to around 100 for 1922 and 1923. The sales records appear to be continuous for the years mentioned, which leaves unexplained the fact that no sales for 1917, 1918 and 1919 are listed. In 1936, Holt Publishing Company asked Dewey's permission to remainder the book because it was selling poorly. Dewey gave his permission and the last 375 copies were remaindered.

In May 1942, Earle Balch of G. P. Putnam's Sons inquired of Holt whether plates for *German Philosophy and Politics* could be stored at Putnam's for Dewey. Holt replied that the book plates had been melted down some time before and that only the rights could be conveyed to Dewey. Dewey in turn conveyed the rights to Putnam's, who then completely reset the type, and the book was "reprinted without change, save for a few slight verbal corrections" and the addition of a new 10,000 word Introduction, "The One-World of Hitler's Socialism." The new Introduction to *German Philosophy and Politics* (this volume, pp. 421–46) will appear in its proper chronological setting in the *Later Works of John Dewey*; however, the full text will not be reprinted. Therefore, Dewey's 1942 changes in both substantives and accidentals appear here in the "List of 1942 Variants."

Schools of To-Morrow

The genesis of *Schools of To-Morrow* (New York: E. P. Dutton, 1915), one of the two Dewey titles published by E. P. Dutton, has been described in detail by Burges Johnson, who was then manager of the educational department.[7]

7. Burges Johnson, *As Much as I Dare: A Personal Recollection* (New York: Ives Washburn, 1944), pp. 186–87.

Johnson says that after the manuscript was developed and
sent to him, he found the first chapter "rather forbidding,"
but the second chapter seemed "simply expressed" and clear.
When Johnson asked Dewey about switching the order of
these two chapters, "He listened to me quietly and said in his
gentle voice, 'What you say interests me greatly. I wrote the
first chapter and my daughter Evelyn wrote the second.'"
Despite Johnson's suggestion, the order of the chapters remained undisturbed.

Fourteen reviews of *Schools of To-Morrow* appeared
in 1915 and 1916.[8] Although Dewey specifically states in his
Preface that Evelyn Dewey "is responsible for the descriptive
chapters of the book," reviewers without exception attributed
the entire work to Dewey. In their unanimous, sometimes
even fulsome, approbation, Evelyn Dewey's name is not
mentioned at all. For example, the *Modern School* reviewer
wrote, "Professor John Dewey has at last achieved a popular
book" (p. 90); *New Republic* said, "Professor Dewey gives
the whole historical setting of the American school in his
masterly fashion" (p. 211); and T. P. Beyer wrote in *Dial*
that

there are philosophers who know little of the art of teaching. A
great shout of welcome should therefore go up when a profound
thinker sets himself the task of a practical exposition of the most
practical, as it is the most important, art in life,—the art of
education. . . . The ripe scholarship, the scrupulous soundness
of the logic, and the art shown in presenting and massing the
concrete in a bath of luminous and consistent theory make of
"Schools of To-morrow" a contribution of great importance (p.
109).

With Beyer, a number of reviewers commented on the simplicity and readableness of the style, attributing it, however,

---

8. Nine unsigned reviews were: *A.L.A. Booklist* 12 (1915): 9;
American Review of Reviews 52 (1915): 248–49; *Independent* 83
(1915): 198; *Literary Digest* 51 (1915): 537; *Nation*, 9 Septem-
ber 1915, pp. 326–27; *New Republic*, 26 June 1915, pp. 210–11;
New York Times Book Review, 15 August 1915, p. 291; *Outlook*
110 (1915): 875; *Wisconsin Library Bulletin* 11 (1915): 367.
Five signed reviews were written by: Florence Finch Kelley,
Bookman 42 (1915): 88–89; Thomas Percival Beyer, *Dial* 59
(1915): 109–11; Adoniram J. Ladd, *Quarterly Journal of the
University of North Dakota* 6 (1916): 272–75; Ernest Carroll
Moore, *Survey* 35 (1916): 438; Carl Zigrosser, *Modern School*
2 (1915): 90–91.

exclusively again to Dewey, as did the *New Republic*: "Popular and unpretentious as is its style, this book is perhaps the most useful he has written. From no other does one get so much that feeling of clean insight, widely searching command of the situation, absolutely steady and relevant interpretation, that are his genius" (p. 211).

A number of reviewers of *Schools of To-Morrow* described it with superlatives: "—probably the most important social book of the year" (*Independent*, p. 198); "of preeminent importance" (*Outlook*, p. 875); Ernest C. Moore in *Survey*, "I regard the appearance of this book as the most significant educational event of the year" (p. 438); Moore's statement was repeated by the *Wisconsin Library Bulletin*, which said, "undoubtedly the most significant educational record of the day, it will probably have a marked influence on school curricula everywhere" (p. 367).

It would be difficult to measure the book's predicted direct impact on "school curricula everywhere." What can be said unequivocally, however, is that *Schools of To-Morrow* was a popular book with outstanding sales. A handwritten notation on a 1930 company letter indicates that the first printing was 1500 copies and that from 1915 through 1928, 24,000 copies were sold.[9] John Macrae, president of E. P. Dutton, wrote to Dewey on 20 April 1917,

As you will observe [from the size of the royalty check], and, I think, frankly admit, the sale of this book is most gratifying; and I congratulate you and felicitate ourselves on the continuing sale of this remarkably good book on the subject of education.

Three days later, Dewey responded,

I certainly am much pleased with the continued large sale of the book, and wish to thank you for the pains which you have taken with pushing the book. It is most gratifying that the sale continues at any such pitch.

9. Macrae to Dewey, 14 April 1930, Dutton Publishing Company Archives, Syracuse University, Syracuse, New York. Mr. Elliott Graham, president of the company, generously arranged to make available all correspondence and other documents associated with the publication of works by Dewey, Evelyn Dewey, and Marie Harvey Turner. The letters cited here are among those papers.

Dutton records indicate that as late as 1923, J. M. Dent, British distributor of *Schools of To-Morrow*, ordered 300 copies.

But by 19 March 1927, Dewey thought sales of the book had slackened too much. He wrote to Macrae,

I am somewhat disappointed that the sale of Schools of Tomorrow doesn't keep up better; is it not possible to press the sale in Normal and Training Schools? My School and Society, altho published almost thirty years ago still keeps up a sale of nearly a thousand a year, just because it is used as a text or collateral reading in schools. My experience is that use as a text is what keeps up an even sale year after year.

Macrae answered on 21 March 1927 that

We have been making some additional effort to increase the sale of SCHOOLS OF TOMORROW. . . . There has been an effort [by some] to show that SCHOOLS OF TOMORROW was written a long time ago; and that the inspiration and machinery of education has changed considerably since the book was written. . . . Would an additional chapter, to be used as an introduction, bringing the book up to date, give the book that added impetus which it needs at this time?

Whether SCHOOLS OF TOMORROW is hampered because it is somewhat out of date or not, is not the real problem. The problem is that people are saying that it is old and behind the times.

If you will give me your reaction to this complaint, or better still, if you would give me an introductory chapter as long or as short as your good judgment would dictate, I feel that we can do precisely what you suggest in your letter of March 19th, and reinstate it as a text-book where it was formerly used.

Dewey apparently did not reply to Macrae's invitation to write a new Introduction. On 14 April 1930, Macrae's suggestions were more extensive:

SCHOOLS OF TOMORROW . . . made a deep impression on educators at the time it came out; and it has had a very important and far-reaching influence on education in the English-speaking world during all the years of its life. It has seemed to me that this book might be entirely revised. Possibly you may think that the book should not be revised, but that a new book should be written from today of the schools of tomorrow.

Although Dewey answered at once, "I shall talk over with Evelyn the possibility of a revision of Schools of To-

Morrow with new material," no such revision was ever undertaken.

Starting with what Dutton labeled the sixth printing, in July 1916, a list of previous impressions and their dates appeared on the copyright page of *Schools of To-Morrow*. This listing shows that a second printing was made in August 1915, four printings in 1916—two in March and two in July—and two more in January 1917. Whether two separate printings were in fact made within a single month three different times is not known; this somewhat unusual procedure may be explained by the fact that the publisher labeled two different bindings (and therefore different states) as separate printings each time. The last printing examined in preparing the present edition was dated February 1929 and labeled by Dutton as the sixteenth.

The copyright deposit copy of *Schools of To-Morrow* (A406047) was machine-compared with the last impression; no variants appear between the two. The copyright deposit copy serves as copy-text for the present edition. Three errors in the book, called to Dewey's attention on 4 June 1915 by Scudder Klyce,[10] have been checked in twenty-four copies of undated printings (1–6?) and found not to have been corrected, either in these early printings or in the later dated printings. These errors were: plane for plan, 261.11; meters for decimeters, 306.10; and turn for turn out, 404.23.

10. Klyce to Dewey, 14 July 1915, Scudder Klyce Papers, Manuscripts Division, Library of Congress.

LIST OF SYMBOLS

Page-line number at left is from present edition; all lines of print except running heads are counted.

Reading before bracket is from present edition.

Square bracket signals end of reading from present edition, followed by the symbol identifying the first appearance of reading.

W means Works—the present edition—and is used for emendations made here for the first time.

The abbreviation [*om.*] means the reading before the bracket was omitted in the editions and impressions identified after the abbreviation; [*not present*] means the reading before the bracket was added to earlier material.

The abbreviation [*rom.*] means roman type and is used to signal the omission of italics.

Stet indicates a substantive reading retained from an authoritative edition or impression subsequently revised; the rejected variant follows the semicolon.

The asterisk before an emendation page-line number indicates the reading is discussed in the Textual Notes.

For emendations restricted to punctuation, the curved dash ~ means the same word(s) as before the bracket, and the inferior caret ʌ indicates the absence of a punctuation mark.

EMENDATIONS LIST

All emendations in both substantives and accidentals introduced into the copy-texts are recorded in the list that follows, with the exception of certain regularizations described and listed in this introductory explanation. The reading to the left of the square bracket is from the present edition. The bracket is followed by the abbreviation for the source of the emendation's first appearance and by abbreviations for subsequent editions and printings collated that had the same reading. After the source abbreviations comes a semicolon, followed by the copy-text reading. Substantive variants in all texts collated are also recorded here; the list thus serves as a historical collation as well as a record of emendations.

The copy-text for each item is identified at the beginning of the list of emendations in that item; for items that had a single previous printing, no abbreviation for the copy-text appears in the list itself.

The following formal changes have been made throughout:

1. Book and journal titles are in italic type; articles and sections of books are in quotation marks. Book titles have been supplied and expanded where necessary.

2. Superior numbers have been assigned consecutively throughout an item to Dewey's footnotes; the asterisk is used only for editorial footnotes.

3. Single quotation marks have been changed to double when not inside quoted material; opening or closing quotation marks have been supplied where necessary, and recorded.

The following spellings have been editorially regularized to the known Dewey usage appearing before the brackets:

aerial] aërial 176.40
bookkeeping] book-keeping 371.16–17

cannot] can not 298.8, 300.14, 303.4, 311.17, 314.14, 317.6,
    317.31, 319.12, 323.17, 330.3, 340.19, 366.30–31,
    368.38, 375.19, 380.27, 383.20, 384.12, 396.13, 397.33
centre (all forms)] center 81.31, 107.29, 119.24, 120.14, 120.36,
    125.33, 131.39(2), 184.19, 248.6, 249.21, 280.25,
    303.11, 305.5, 344.32, 349.10(2), 350.11, 350.23,
    351.40, 352.14, 358.32, 359.22, 360.12
clue] clew 147.21, 254.35, 303.20, 398.12
coadaptation] co-adaptation 423.34
cooperate (all forms)] coöperate 105.9, 106.2–3, 203.38, 204.11,
    271.9, 289.36, 312.10, 312.18, 326.7–8, 326.33, 326.37,
    327.17, 328.4, 333.20, 349.20, 374.15, 383.27, 383.35,
    384.23, 385.8
cooperation] co-operation 111.13, 116.21, 116.27
coordinate (all forms)] coördinate 232.14, 234.24, 306.3, 366.3–4,
    369.30
coordinating] co-ordinating 61.5
detour] détour 196.5
every-day (adj.)] every day 278.32, 363.31
fantasy] phantasy 71.27
far-reaching] far reaching 207.18
fibre] fiber 396.20, 396.22
first-rate] first rate 426.39
foodstuffs] food stuffs 394.1
guarantee] guaranty 82.39
handwork] hand work 227.33, 230.2, 342.10–11, 377.19–20
handwork] hand-work 368.5–6, 368.14, 370.22
high-school (adj.)] high school 235.17, 235.18, 247.17, 366.9,
    366.32, 373.26, 380.30
meagre] meager 219.37, 340.18
molding] moulding 210.5
object-lesson (adj.)] object lesson 282.34
part-time] part time 118.11, 118.38
playground] play ground 282.40
preestablished] pre-established 422.1
present-day (adj.)] present day 395.31, 404.22, 435.26
prima-facie] prima facie 16.6, 69.29, 73.13
public-school (adj.)] public school 123.11, 123.26, 225.18, 247.5,
    263.8, 320.16–17, 369.22, 403.38, 404.28–29, 414.21
reenforce (all forms)] reënforce 215.32, 287.36, 305.10, 394.5,
    398.36
régime] regime 130.26, 412.31, 412.32, 436.38
role] rôle 25.40, 145.19, 208.15, 232.35, 284.17, 298.36, 306.34,
    307.21, 318.36, 320.2, 320.3
Schoolhouses] School-Houses 209.13
school-teacher] schoolteacher 388.14–15, 391.27
self-enclosed] self-inclosed 28.8
shop work] shop-work 368.27

short-cut] short cut 219.13, 373.14, 381.5, 412.39
storekeeping] store keeping 371.10
subject-matter] subject matter 233.10, 254.11, 412.5
taxpayers] tax-payers 323.10
text-book] text book 207.4–5, 209.2, 263.31
well-developed] well developed 267.15
well-known] well known 424.4
well-planned] well planned 131.9
zoology] zoölogy 374.8

"The Subject-Matter of Metaphysical Inquiry"

Copy-text is the only previous publication of this article, in *Journal of Philosophy, Psychology and Scientific Methods* 12 (1915): 337–45.

3n.3	Biology:] W; ~—
8.4	his] W; this
11.37	found‿] W; ~,
12.10	peculiar] W; pecular

"The Logic of Judgments of Practice"

Copy-text for "The Logic of Judgments of Practice" is the first publication, in JP: *Journal of Philosophy, Psychology and Scientific Methods* 12 (1915): 505–23, 533–43. The copyright deposit copy of EE: *Essays in Experimental Logic* (Chicago: University of Chicago Press, 1916) serves as copy-text for 64.30 to 82.40. Emendations have been adopted from the revised, expanded version in EE. Superscript numbers distinguish among the three printings of EE (EE[16], EE[18], EE[20]) where variants occur.

14.1	PRACTICE] EE; PRACTISE
14.2	*I. Their Nature*] W; THEIR NATURE EE; I. THEIR NATURE
14.6	"practical judgment"] EE; ‿~‿
14.12	a type] EE; an alleged type
14.15	Propositions exist] EE; There are propositions
14.16	situation] EE; situation as
14.24	SP] EE; S is P
14.25–26	meanwhile the] EE; meanwhile there is a

14.26   is] EE;   which is
14.28   is] EE;   is involved
15.1   form *SP* or *mRn*] EE;   form of *S P* and mathematical
           propositions
15.1   as gratuitous] EE;   quite as gratuitous
15.2–4   It . . . time.] EE;   [*not present*]
15.4   exhibits, if not a] EE;   exhibits not, indeed, a
15.5   at least] EE;   but
15.5–6   this type] EE;   the type mentioned above
15.8   propositions.¹ It] EE;   propositions,¹ and it
15.9   this kind] EE;   any of the above sort
15.10   this omission] EE;   omission of this type
15.10   discussion] EE;   success and efficacy
15.11   other kinds] EE;   the exposition of other types
15.15   Doctrine] EE;   doctrine
15.17   wrong,] EE;   ~;
15.17   etc.] EE;   etc., etc.
15.17   is] EE;   seems
15.18   importance] EE;   importance in our lives
15.20   arouses] EE;   arouses curiosity and even
15.20   the grounds of] EE;   [*not present*]
15.20   neglect] EE;   relative neglect
15.20–21   discussion] EE;   the discussion
15.21   of] EE;   of the theory of
15.21   in general] EE;   [*not present*]
15.30–31   by opponents] EE;   opponents
15.34   unfinished,] EE;   ~∧
15.35–16.26 Moreover . . . discussion.] EE;   [*not present*]
15n.1   p.] EE;   page
16.28   carrying] EE;   in carrying
16.31   subject-matter] EE;   content
16.33   the way] EE;   the way of treating
16.36   *in*] EE;   [*rom.*]
16.37   in] EE;   as
16.38   force] EE;   import or force
16.38   *prima-facie*∧] W;   prima∧facie∧ EE;   *prima∧facie,*
16.40   *SP*] EE;   *S-P*
17.5   which has] EE;   having
17.5   He] EE;   he
17.5   house";] EE;   ~;"
17.6   The] EE;   the
17.6   burning";] EE;   ~;"
17.6   It] EE;   it
17.7   implied] EE;   stated
17.8   proposition] EE;   statement
17.15   *descriptive*] EE;   [*rom.*]
17.15   a] EE;   or any
17.17   it] EE;   hence it

17.17   help] EE;   either help
17.17–18   its development . . . development] EE;   [*not present*]
17.24   it‸] EE;   is,
17.25   It] EE;   This is to say that it
17.27   means] EE;   means—of the given situation and the
             proposed act as conditions of the outcome
17.27   disconnect] EE;   take
17.27   discussion] EE;   matter
17.28   from] EE;   out of connection from
17.29   thereby] EE;   also
17n.1   analytic realists] EE;   neo-realists
17n.6   but] EE;   simply
17n.6   logical reference,] EE;   acts of thought having a
             reference?
17n.6–9   leaving . . . future?] EE;   [*not present*]
18.3   concerns] EE;   is of
18.5   elements] EE;   the elements
18.11   pursuits] EE;   pursuit
18.19   given] EE;   statement of the given
18.19   exhaustively] EE;   and exhausts
18.20   practical] EE;   the practical
18.21   it."] EE;   it" so far as intelligence is concerned.
18.23   *of*] EE;   [*rom.*]
18.33   and] EE;   and of
18.34   course] EE;   mode of action
18.37   death] EE;   its continuance or death
18.38–39   render . . . cases] EE;   render similar cases in the
             future
19.1   is] EE;   is of course
19.2, 5; 20n.3; 20.26; 22.5; cannot] EE;   can not
36.26; 37.22; 47.12; 50.31
19.4   propositions about] EE;   the judgment of
19.7   it,] EE;   ∼.
19.8   much . . . propositions.] EE;   [*not present*]
19.9   method] EE;   assertion is
19.9   begs] EE;   to beg
19.9   question] EE;   question at issue
19.10–11   preconception,] W;   ∼‸
19.13   doctrine of a] EE;   [*not present*]
19.17   the] EE;   which is the
19.19   slight] EE;   extremely slight
19.24   the] EE;   what is
19.24   *as*] EE;   [*rom.*]
19.26   development of] EE;   [*not present*]
19.26–27   situation] EE;   movement
19.30   recognition] EE;   the recognition
19.31   redirection] EE;   intelligent control
19.31   events] EE;   events which are

19.34   utilizing] EE;   the utilization of
19.35   means] EE;   as a method of knowledge is
19.36   It] EE;   That is, it
19.36   import,] W;   ~∧
20.4   is] EE;   would be
20.8   done),] EE;   ~)∧
20.14   taken] EE;   taken both
20.15   of] EE;   as furnishing
20.15   Such a] EE;   This
20.17   For] EE;   But it is important to note that
20.20   respects] EE;   respects decision as to
20n.1   ³Supposing] EE;   ³I may refer in passing to the bearing
           of this upon a point in my recent paper (this JOURNAL,
           Vol. XII., page 337). Supposing
20n.8   mechanical condition] EE;   mechanism
20n.11   is] EE;   is quite as much
20n.12   statement] EE;   complete statement
20n.12   history] EE;   history as is its molten, non-living state
           at a given date
20n.15–18 That . . . future.] EE;   [not present]
21.1   qualifications] EE;   terms
21.3   terms of the proposition] EE;   statement
21.7   yet] EE;   yet they
21.7   of] EE;   [rom.]
21.10   or in] EE;   or with
21.12   making] EE;   in being
21.18   his propositions] EE;   propositions
21.18–19   breeding . . . domestication.] EE;   breeding.
21.22   Logically] EE;   Logically speaking
21.22   any] EE;   the
21.23   when . . . inference] EE;   in that connection
21.27   (constituting] EE;   ∧which constitutes
21.28   terms and relations] EE;   content
21.28   proposition)] EE;   ~∧
21.35   the] EE;   my
21.36   other matters] EE;   value-judgments
21.39   all propositions of] EE;   given
22.4   is] EE;   is altogether
22.4   in] EE;   as
22.4–5   incidental way] EE;   appendage
22.6   worth] EE;   worthy of
22.7   frame at least] EE;   at least frame
22.9   and to] EE;   and
22.9   realization] EE;   attempted realization
22.12   would] EE;   would then
22.19   would] EE;   might
22.21   its result] EE;   the results
22.24   truths] EE;   truth

22.26	this] EE; this statement
22.26	origin] EE; context of the origin
22.29	such] EE; these
22.33	as are used] EE; used
22n.1	pp.] EE; pages
22n.1	104,] EE; 104 and
23.1	*If*] EE; *If* then
23.2	are then] EE; are
23.3	done,] EE; done (if only as to some inference to be made)
23.3	are themselves] EE; themselves are
23.6	would be] EE; is
23.7	but] EE; but one
23.7	expounded] EE; conceived
23.8–9	For . . . verifiability.] EE; [*not present*]
23.10	*II. Judgments of Value*] W; JUDGMENTS OF VALUE EE; II JUDGMENTS OF VALUE
23.14	First,] EE; First, however,
23.15	misunderstanding.] EE; misunderstanding. I am not concerned with the *nature* of value as that has recently been the object of controversy. For my purposes it makes no difference whether value is comprised within consciousness, independent of consciousness, or a relation between an object and some form of consciousness. I am going to deal with valuation, not with value.
23.17	value] EE; value so
23.19	amount$_\wedge$] EE; ~,
23.21	mediaeval] EE; medieval
23.31	were then] W; were them EE; could then be
23.34	it was] EE; he makes it
24.1	conclusion] EE; inference
24.4	are] EE; are quite
24.20	$_\wedge$When] EE; "~
24n.1	p.] EE; page
24n.4	that] EE; that the
24n.5	used] EE; [*ital.*]
24n.5	*evidences*] EE; [*rom.*]
24n.9–10	pretension] EE; pretensions
24n.10	acquire] EE; have
24n.10	status] EE; only
24n.14–17	qualities . . . qualities.] EE; qualities as such.
25.1	further] EE; farther
25.2	currency] EE; uncriticized currency
25.5	in having] EE; [*not present*]
25.26	"acquaintance"] EE; $_\wedge$~$_\wedge$
25.26	"familiarity"] EE; $_\wedge$~$_\wedge$
25.26–27	"recognition"] EE; $_\wedge$~$_\wedge$

25.27–28   ambiguity.] EE;   ambiguity. [◖] By a value judgment,
then, I mean simply a judgment having goods and bads
for its subject-matter. Such being the case, it may
well be asked: Why give it any special consideration?
Why should logic, in addition to a theory of judgment,
bother with value-judgments as a special class any
more than with dog-judgments or granite-judgments?
And my answer is there is no reason, save that value-
judgments are a species of practical judgments (which
present specific problems for consideration); and that
the failure to observe this fact has resulted—so it seems
to me—in much confusion, especially in moral theories
about the judgment of good, right, and standards. And,
I have no doubt, the same confusion has affected for
evil the economic theory of valuation of commodities
and services.

25.29–30.34   In . . . examination.] EE;   [*not present*]
26.10   thinking$_\wedge$] W;   ~,
27.37   physician] EE[20];   physican EE[16,18]
30.39   one] EE;   One
31.3   previously] EE;   as yet
31.4   to$_\wedge$be$_\wedge$given] EE;   ~-~-~
31.5–18   This . . . on. [◖] Practical] EE;   Practical
31.19   not therefore] EE;   not
31.20   value] EE;   question of the value
31.20   *objects*;] EE;   ~.
31.20   but with] EE;   They deal primarily with fixing upon
31.26   clothes:] EE;   ~,
31.32   in] EE;   as
31.37; 52.6,8,n.3   aesthetic] EE;   esthetic
32.3   for knowledge] EE;   in judgment
32.5–6   provided] EE;   provides
32.20   *not*] EE;   [*rom.*]
32.21   valuation;] EE;   ~,
32.21   they are] EE;   but
32.21   a valuation] EE;   valuation
32.23–24   a subsequent] EE;   a
32.25   they would not] EE;   the traits would not
32.30   action,] EE;   ~$_\wedge$
32.33   *the . . . judgment*] EE;   [*rom.*]
32.36   an existence merely] EE;   merely an existence
32.37   claim] EE;   certain claim
32.37   judgment] EE;   the judgment to be formed
33.3–35.29   fanciful. I . . . efficiencies.] EE;   fanciful. It is
existential, but it exists *as* something whose good or
value resides (first) in something to be attained in action and (secondly) whose value both as an idea and
as existence depends upon judgment of what to do.

Value is "objective," but it is such in an active or practical situation, not apart from it. To deny the possibility
of such a view, is to reduce the objectivity of every tool
and machine to the physical ingredients that compose
it, and to treat a distinctive "plow" character as merely
subjective. *Value-in-judgment* always has to do with
something *as* tool or means, and instrumentality is an
added (and selective) specification.

35.30	whatever risk of] EE; the risk of whatever
36.16	There] EE; These
36.16	are] EE; are undoubted
36.21	practical judgment] EE; practical judgment of what is to be done
36.23	judgment.] EE; judgment. It is precisely this character which constitutes the necessity of the reference of the subject-matter of judgment beyond judgment: which makes it impossible for a practical judgment as judgment to have a self-contained meaning and truth.
36.26	now go] EE; go
36.27	III] EE; II
36.29–30	decisive . . . what] EE; determination of what
36.36	a prior] EE; a
36.37	comparing] EE; equating
36.37	the supreme] EE; a supreme
36.38	value] EE; unquestioned value
37.1	the] EE: the practical
37.1	judgment . . . do] EE; judgment
37.2	ready-made] EE; ready-made outside the valuation
37.12	recognition] EE; judgment
37.16	"end."] EE; ∧~·∧
37.19	a] EE; the
37.20	things] EE; of things
37.23	"end"] EE; ∧~∧
37.29	sense,] EE; ~∧
37.30	a] EE; the
37.30	kind] EE; kind of judgment
37.31	discussing or that] EE; discussing, so that as value
37.32	given by which] EE; employed
38.1	possessive, sense∧] EE; ~∧~,
38.2	an end not] EE; not an end
38.3	begins,] EE; ~∧
38.10	that,] EE; ~∧
38.19	*aims*] EE; [*rom.*]
38.26	suit] EE; given suit
38.28	by] EE; by means of
38.28	various] EE; the various
38.29	comparing . . . respect] EE; weighing the claims
38.29–30	cheapness] EE; the cheapness

38.30   adaptability] EE;   adaptability of various suits
38.30   *with*] EE;   against
38.30   *one another*] EE;   [*rom.*]
38.37   but] EE;   but simply
38.37–38 act . . . action.] EE;   act.
39.10   it₍ₐ₎] EE;   ~,
39.12–44.31 IV . . . skepticism.] EE;   [*not present*]
41n.15   supplies] W;   supply
42.8   pangs₍ₐ₎] W;   ~,
42.16   which,] W;   ~₍ₐ₎
42.39   suppressing] EE²⁰;   suppresssing EE¹⁶,¹⁸;   [*not present*]
43.31   notion] W;   motion
44.19–20 they analyzed] W;   analyzed
44.30   them₍ₐ₎] W;   ~,
44.32   may be contended, however,] EE;   may, however, be
          contended
44.32   all this] EE;   this
44.33   earlier statement] EE;   statement made to the effect
45.14   about] EE;   about the worth of
45.17   the specific] EE;   the
45.18   it] EE;   it still
45.20   life] EE;   life as such
45.20   by definition it] EE;   it by definition
45.22   by suggesting or] EE;   by
45.23   make] EE;   made
45.23   living;] EE;   ~,
45.24   *direct*] EE;   [*rom.*]
45.27   and] EE;   or
45.29   Every] EE;   But nevertheless every
45.30   the] EE;   on the contrary, the
45.30   is] EE;   is always
45.31   the situation] EE;   this situation
45.40–46.1 whatever in . . . be] EE;   whatever is not and can
          not be in the situation at hand
46.2   and which] EE;   and
46.3–5   judgment. . . . limit.] EE;   judgment. Unfortunately
          for discussions, "to value" means two radically different
          things: to prize and appraise; to esteem and to estimate.
          I call them radically different because to prize names
          a practical, non-intellectual attitude, and to appraise
          names a judgment. That men love and hold things dear,
          that they cherish and care for some things, and neglect
          and contemn other things, is an undoubted fact. To
          call these things values is just to repeat that they are
          loved and cherished; it is not to give a reason for their
          being loved and cherished. To call them values and
          then import into them the traits of objects of valuation,
          or to import into values, meaning valuated objects, the

traits which things possess as held dear is to confuse
the theory of judgments of value past all remedy.

46.6   V] EE;   III
46.8   is,] EE;   ~∧
46.10   action)∧] EE;   ~),
46.15   previously chosen] EE;   chosen previously
46.16   valuation] EE;   value
46.17–18   Situations] EE;   In *that* situation one thing *is* better
            than another. Moreover, situations
46.23   or valuables thus] EE;   thus
46.24–25   Moreover, . . . operation, the] EE;   Moreover, the
46.26   standardized values.] EE;   standard values, by the
            same kind of operation.
46.27   value-standards] EE;   ~∧~
46.29   a] EE;   the
46.30   rapidly] EE;   a rapidly
46.31   of identical] EE;   of
46.32   one's self] EE;   oneself
46.33   valuables] EE;   values
46.38   *they*] EE;   [*rom.*]
46.38   critically made;] EE;   made critically, and
47.3–4   the . . . verification] EE;   the verification the prior
            estimate of it has received
47.5   place] EE;   place at all
47.6   reminiscence] EE;   thought
47.7   to present] EE;   to
47.10   he had] EE;   he
47.14   arouses] EE;   will arouse
47.15   appears] EE;   will appear
47.16   epistemology. . . . three] EE;   epistemology. But I am
            talking about practical judgments—judgments where
            the object of judgment is something to be done. I see
            but three
47.17   practical] EE;   such
47.19   past∧ or] EE;   past,
47.20   realm (] EE;   ~,
47.21   logically),] EE;   ~∧;
47.23   the change] EE;   which change
47.23   depending] EE;   depends
47.23–24   judgment] EE;   judgment itself
47.24   constituting its] EE;   constitutes the
47.24   subject-matter] EE;   subject-matter of judgment
47.26–27   not merely that] EE;   that not merely do
47.27–28   make . . . after-effect] EE;   as after effect make a
            difference in things
47.28   admit] EE;   accept about many propositions
47.29   validity] EE;   the validity
47.29   judgments] EE;   the judgments

48.2   claim] EE;   hold
48.5   things,] EE;   ~∧
48.6   in . . . made] EE; actually made in consequences
              which issue
48.6–21   And . . . appear.] EE;   [*not present*]
48.23   difference in things. In] EE;   difference. The point is
              purely logical, and is twofold. In
48.25   and,] EE;   ~∧
48.25   place,] EE;   ~∧
49.17   *III. Sense∧Perception as Knowledge*] W;   SENSE∧PER-
              CEPTION AS KNOWLEDGE EE;   III. SENSE-PERCEP-
              TION AS KNOWLEDGE
49.18   I] EE;   I have
49.18   incidentally∧] EE;   ~,
49.18   the first section] EE;   my former article,
49.19   failure] EE;   the failure
49.19   to] EE;   to the logical form of
49.21   types.∧] EE;   forms.[1] . . . [1]See this JOURNAL, Vol. XII.,
              page 506.
49.22, 28; 50.22; 54.1–2; 58.15   sense∧perception] EE;   ~-~
49.25   I] EE;   I shall
49.32   image] EE;   optical image
49n.1–4   See . . . pp. 103–22].] W; See IX and X, *ante.* EE;
              See this JOURNAL, Vol. VIII., page 393 in an article en-
              titled "Brief Study in Realism."
49n.5   "image"] EE;   ∧~∧
50.1   conditions] EE;   the conditions
50.1   of logic, of truth] EE;   of truth
50.7   or else] EE;   or
50.13   ∧appearance∧] EE;   "~"
50.14   or] EE;   [*ital.*]
50.14   water-bubble] EE;   water-bubbles
50.16   This] EE;   The
50.16   thus] EE;   which I have
50.16   needs to be] EE;   was not, however,
50.20   a sense] EE;   sense
50.22   is not] EE;   was also taken to imply what I did not
              mean—
50.22–23   thereby exhausted] EE;   exhausted in this mode of
              treatment
50.25   mean] EE;   meant
50.25   holding] EE;   showing
50.26   is] EE;   was
50.36   more than five] EE;   five
50.37   This] EE;   That this
50.39   falsity.] EE;   falsity, was assumed by me, but un-
              doubtedly the assumption was not made sufficiently
              clear.

51.4	judgment] EE; judgments
51.5	as] EE; as these have been defined—
51.5	of] EE; as to
51.6	a street] EE; the street
51.17	an] EE; any
51.19–20	conception . . . do] EE; class
51.21	to . . . it] EE; to do so
51.32	for] EE; for the
52.8	non-cognitive∧] EE; ~,
52.9	place,] EE; place, some
52.9	operation] EE; existence
52.10	signifying] EE; sign
52.10–11	surplusage] EE; it
52.13	*alternatives*] EE; [*rom.*]
52.19	grounds] EE; ground
52.19	them.∧] EE; them.⁵ . . . ⁵See my article on "Perception and Organic Action," this JOURNAL, Vol. IX., page 645.
52.20	hard-and-fast] EE; ~∧~∧~
52.21	postulated] EE; supposed
52.23	in order to] EE; to
52.25	does not] EE; it does not
52.26	Sense] EE; We may fairly conclude that sense
52n.2	function,] EE; ~∧
52n.6	be] EE; have been
52n.6–7	perception . . . should] EE; perception should
52n.10	*Alternative*] EE; They are *alternative*
52n.11	change] EE; which change
52n.12–14	possibilities . . . datum.] EE; possibilities.
53.6	for an inference] EE; of how to act
53.8	were it] EE; if it were
53.9	inferences] EE; inferences made on the basis of data which were not as perceived *definite* shapes
53.12	function] EE; outcome
53.13–14	the . . . organic] EE, the organic result of a
53.14	which has occurred] EE; occurring
53.19	having . . . of] EE; having the character, as perceived, of
53.32	*brain*] EE; [*rom.*]
53.35	organic conditions] EE; conditions
53.35–36	the occurrence] EE; occurrence
53.36	an act of perception] EE; something
53.37	results] EE; results thus far reached
53.40	which produces] EE; in giving
54.3–4	Such . . . them.] EE; [*not present*]
54.5	unrefracted∧] EE; ~,
54.10	to perform] EE; of the performance of
54.11	stimuli] EE; the stimuli

54.11   occur] EE; have occurred
54.13   indexes] EE; indices
54.13   set up has] EE; have
54.15   inference] EE; inferred action
54.31–33   There . . . it.] EE; [*not present*]
54.37   practical] EE; usual
54n.1–2   *Journal of Philosophy, Psychology and Scientific Meth-
           ods*] W; *Journal of Philosophy and Psychology* EE;
           this JOURNAL
55.1   causes] EE; chief causes
55.6   because] EE; just because
55.8   themselves become] EE; become themselves
55.10   Inference] EE; The inference
55.10   will usually] EE; will
55.16   inference] EE; the inference
55.16   data, the] EE; data—but the
55.16   being] EE; are
55.17   determined, however,] EE; determined
55.24   sense] EE; given sense
55.25   must] EE; [*ital.*]
55.26   for . . . appear] EE; appear for the most part
55.29–30   indicates] EE; leads to
55.31   are] EE; [*ital.*]
55.33   where . . . appear] EE; [*not present*]
55.35–36   practical judgments,] EE; these
55.36   as open] EE; open
55.36–37   above board . . . it] W; aboveboard as it is the
           sensory quality: it EE; above board—it
55.40   she . . . in] EE; there is
55.40   error,] EE; ~∧
56.1   sound] EE; the sound
56.2   and] EE; while
56.2   fact] EE; fact it
56.6   this practical] EE; this
56.7   them] EE; inferences of the practical type
56.10   knowledge-object] EE; "object"
56.15   had] EE; had so
56.16   would] EE; might only
56.19   lie] EE; [*ital.*]
56.22   inference] EE; it
56.29   conditions] EE; its conditions
56.35   will] EE; are of a character to
56.35   which] EE; to
56.39   necessary, for I] W; necesary, for I EE; necessary. I
57.1   or] *stet* JP; nor EE
57.5   depends] EE; depends, however,
57.9   was] EE; was for
57.10   derived] EE; of construction

57.15   treated] EE;   presented
57.16   inference] EE;   the control of inference
57.16   were a] EE;   were
57.17–18   beliefs. [⟦] The] EE;   beliefs. The
57.19   unrecognized] EE;   unperceived
57.19   of] EE;   of the
57.19   Perception] EE;   That is, perception
57.20   experimentally] EE;   itself critically
57.20   present] EE;   present a
57.20   wide] EE;   wide scope of
57.25–26   production . . . present] EE;   production
57.28   to] EE;   to its
57.35   so] EE;   as
57.38   unjustifiable] EE;   undue
57.38–39   over-simplification] EE;   simplification
58.2   all] EE;   the
58.3   The remedy] EE;   with reference to ambiguity of
           verbal symbols. The remedy
58.5   "elements."] EE;   "elements," that is, into more ulti-
           mate simples.
58.10   spectrum] EE;   spectrum as that is
58.14   Locke . . . Russell] EE;   Locke
58.14   They] EE;   They are not prior to sense-perception, but
58.15–16   discriminated . . . inferences] EE;   elaborately dis-
           criminated
58.17   original,] EE;   ~∧
58.19   irreducible] EE;   irreducibles
58.23   customary] EE;   historical-psychological
58.25   through] EE;   by
58.26   wide] EE;   a wide region of
58.28   i.e.] EE;   i. e.
58.34   initial,] EE;   ~∧
58.35   perceived to be given] EE;   perceived
58.38   established,] EE;   ~∧
58.38–39   detection . . . exacts] EE;   whose determination in-
           volves
58.40   propositions] EE;   propositions deductively brought to
           bear
59.2   current] EE;   the current empirical
59.3   mistaking] EE;   taking
59.4   for] EE;   as if they were
59.13   logical] EE;   wholly logical
59.14   in] EE;   to
59.20   knowledge was] EE;   knowledge is
59.23   "work of nature"] EE;   "work" of nature
59.29   such deistic] EE;   such
59.34   and to] EE;   and
59.37   of] EE;   of the

59.38   their compoundings] EE;   connections by which they
             are reached
60.1–2   inference . . . knowing] EE;   inference
60.3   make him] *stet* JP;   make EE
60.10–12   observation . . . primitives] EE;   observation
60.13   or simple] EE;   which is directly given in simple
60.14–15   inference.] EE;   inference. The forcing of problems of
             epistemology into logic is an inevitable consequence. If
             what is given in sense is taken as a kind of knowledge,
             one has to raise the problem of the place and office of
             the organism in its being given or presented: the mind-
             body problem henceforth haunts the foundations of
             logic.[8] . . . [8]See, for example, Kemp Smith, this JOUR-
             NAL, Vol. IX., page 113. Moreover, since the propositions
             of physics can not be found among these simple data
             and these scientific propositions give us the constitution
             of nature, we have on our hands the problem of the
             reconciliation of the "world" of sense-perception and
             the "world" of science. Shall we take the former as an
             appearance of the latter? If so, how can we argue from
             appearance—that is, sense perceptions—to reality? How
             can we transcend the given which is appearance and
             infer a reality behind, much less make any verifiable
             judgments about what it is? Relativism or a psychic
             idealism are fruits. Or at all events the question of the
             possible validity of scientific propositions becomes a
             problem.[9] . . . [9]Compare Mr. Russell's discussion of
             "Our Knowledge of the External World." Moreover, the
             given in sense varies with the position and structure of
             the "percipient." Consequently we have the epistemo-
             logic problem of the relation of a number of private
             worlds of knowledge to the one public and impersonal
             world of science. And so it goes.
60.15–63.23 Note . . . believed in.] EE;   [*not present*]
60.17   were,] W; $\sim_\wedge$
60.18   it,] W;   its$_\wedge$
62.10   data$_\wedge$] W; $\sim,$
63.26   show that] EE;   show
63.27   datum] EE;   datum which is
63.28   to] EE;   to inference and for the
63.28   inference$_\wedge$] EE; $\sim,$
63.28   with] EE;   as
63.28–29   self-sufficient knowledge-object] EE;   knowledge-mode
63.32   existent, perceived] EE;   existent it contains already
             in its giveness functions of inference. Psychologically
             or historically these are primarily inferences as to what
             to do in given situations, where the perceived objects
             supply the signs (indications or evidence), instead of

operating, as do unperceived objects, simply as direct
stimuli to reactions. The perceived

63.33   whole scope of the] EE;   whole
63.34   extent] EE;   empirical extent
63.34–35   necessary] EE;   necessary, however,
63.35   this complex] EE;   the
63.36   is irrelevant] EE;   isn't
63.37   resolution] EE;   resolution of what seem to be wholes
63.38–39   microscopic, telescopic,] EE;   microscopic and tele-
             scopic$_\wedge$
64.3   a] EE;   institute discriminations of
64.6   regarding, say,] EE; $\sim_\wedge$ $\sim_\wedge$
64.8   a false] EE;   false
64.8   it,] EE; $\sim_\wedge$
64.9   as merely] EE;   as
64.10   Instead] EE;   That is, instead
64.11   this] EE;   all this
64.11   as a] EE;   a
64.13   order] EE;   order in the end
64.28–29   discovery and fixation] EE;   determination
64.29–64n.2 data![20] . . . [20]See . . . pp. 83–97.] W;   data![1] . . .
             [1]See the essay on *The Existence of the World as a
             Logical Problem.* EE;   data!$_\wedge$ / John Dewey. / Colum-
             bia University.
64.30   IV.] W;   [*not present*]
64.30–82.40 *Science* . . . theorist.] EE;   [*not present*]
64.31   angle,] W; $\sim_\wedge$
69.16   To say that] W;   That
69.25   referred] W;   re-/referred
71.2   liabilities,] W;   liabilites$_\wedge$
71.6   "falsity,"] W;   "$\sim$",
71.15   "true."] W;   "$\sim$".
71.26   fantasy,] W;   phantasy;
78.30   V. *Theory*] W;   THEORY
80.19   mathematical] EE[20];   mathmatical EE[16,18]
81.12   thinking] EE[20];   thinikng EE[16,18]
81.12   point out] W;   point

"The Existence of the World as a Logical Problem"

Copy-text is the first printing as "The Existence of the
World as a Problem" in *Philosophical Review* 24 (1915):
357–70. Emendations have been adopted from the revised
edition in EE: *Essays in Experimental Logic* (Chicago: University of Chicago Press, 1916); the typescript, TS, is also
noted as the first appearance of one change that would have

been made editorially and of nine changes that have been accepted from EE.

83.1–2   THE EXISTENCE . . . PROBLEM] W;   XI / THE EX-
           ISTENCE OF THE WORLD AS A LOGICAL PROBLEM
           EE;   THE EXISTENCE OF THE WORLD AS A PROB-
           LEM. PR;   THE EXISTENCE OF THE WORLD AS A
           PROBLEM OF KNOWLEDGE.
83.3   is a] EE;   is the significant one. As a
83.4   analysis. It] EE;   analysis, it
83.6   point] EE;   sole point
83.7–8   stated so] TS, EE;   so stated
83.16   first] EE;   first contention
84.11   p. 75).] W;   *op. cit.*, p. 75). EE, PR
84.15   I shall] EE;   As already indicated, I shall
84.15, 85.25   that] EE;   that the
84.16   as . . . generate] EE;   for the purposes of generating
84.17   involves] EE;   already involves
84.18   question] EE;   [*ital.*]
84.31   83] W;   85
84.32   sense."] EE;   ~"?
84.36   objection] EE;   objections
85.1   ask, Whence] EE;   ask$_\wedge$ whence
85.3; 87.11; 93.23; 95.32; 96.38   common-sense] EE;   ~$_\wedge$~
85.4   left] EE;   supposedly left
85.4   visual$_\wedge$] TS, EE;   ~,
85.6–7   Visible . . . term.] EE;   [*not present*]
85.9   fact] EE;   the bare statement
85.10   presupposes] EE;   presupposes as a condition of the
           question
85.12   another] EE;   a like
85.18   supposititious] EE;   suppositious
85.18   matter] EE;   whole matter
85.21   definite] EE;   certain
85.22   assigned to] EE;   of
85.23   taking] EE;   directly taking
85.29, 31, 32   color] EE;   the color
85.39   Without] EE;   It may be questioned whether without
85.39   "immediate"] EE; $_\wedge$~$_\wedge$
85.39–40   could not] EE;   could
85.40   *object*] EE;   [*rom.*]
86.1–2   If . . . itself.] EE;   [*not present*]
86.4   It] EE;   it
86.12   belief$_\wedge$] EE;   ~,
86.12   means here:] EE;   mean here;
86.15   what] EE;   what is
86.16   is a] EE;   a
86.17   in getting] EE;   in order to get
86.24   neglected] EE;   logically neglected

86.25   question$_\wedge$—] EE; $\sim$;—
86.26   give it] EE;   give
86n.1   Contrast] EE;   Compare
86n.7   offers] EE;   offers to belief
86n.8–9   between the] EE;   between
86n.9   the believed in] EE;   believed
86n.10   is,] EE; $\sim_\wedge$
86n.13   Meanings] EE;   Meaning
86n.14   dubious] EE;   very dubious
87.6 $(a)_\wedge$] TS, EE; $(\sim)$,
87.6   time$_\wedge$] TS, EE; $\sim$,
87.6 $(b)_\wedge$] TS, EE; $(\sim)$,
87.7   time$_\wedge$] TS, EE; $\sim$,
87.7   fact] EE;   bare fact
87.7–8   of existence of color] EE;   of color
87.19   grounds] EE;   other ground
87.20   and] EE;   or
87.21–23   seeing. . . . [¶] How] EE;   seeing.   How
87.25   discovering] EE;   assuming
87.27   are] EE;   appear to be
87.29   be only] EE;   not be
87.35–36   object . . . and] EE;   object perceived and
88.4   qualities] EE;   quality
88.6 $_\wedge a$)] EE; $(\sim)$
88.13   the discovery of which] EE;   whose discovery
88.17   them] TS, EE;   these
88.20   its perception] EE;   the perception
88.22 $_\wedge b$)] EE; $(\sim)$
88.28   ceases] EE;   ceases to exist
88.29   way then] EE;   way
88.30–31   innocently. It is taken] EE;   innocently, but
88.33   *mental*] EE;   [*rom.*]
88.38   of one] TS, EE;   one of
89.2   *inference*] EE;   [*rom.*]
89.3   have already] EE;   have
89.3   describe,] EE;   describe or
89.3   define, and delimit] EE;   define
89.10   *thing*] EE;   [*rom.*]
89.12–14   Or . . . cessation.] EE;   [*not present*]
89.21–89n.1–3   known[4] . . . [4]"Really . . . beyond.]   EE;
           known
89.25   visual,] EE; $\sim_\wedge$
89.27   which also] EE;   which
89.30   involve$_\wedge$—] EE; $\sim$,—
89.32   statement,] EE; $\sim_\wedge$
90.8   point-to-point] EE; $\sim_\wedge\sim_\wedge\sim$
90.12–13   on account of] EE;   to account for
90.15–16   upon the basis of necessity for] EE;   upon the neces-
           sity of

90.16   correlations] EE;   assumptions of correlation
90.17   sensationalist] EE;   sensationalistic
90.18   qualities] EE;   relations
91.4   continuum] EE;   temporal continuum
91.9   the determination] EE;   it
91.12   already belongs to] EE;   *is* part of
91.17   definition of an object] EE;   definition
91n.1   all-at-once$_\wedge$] EE; $\sim_\wedge\sim_\wedge\sim$,
91n.2   writers$_\wedge$] EE; $\sim$,
91n.7   limitations is] EE;   limitations are
91n.10   "self-evident"] EE; $_\wedge\sim_\wedge$
91n.12   inference in process of] EE;   inference
91n.19   existence of] EE;   existence, and conditions of
91n.20   "muscular sensations"] EE;   quales of bodily move-
             ment
91n.21–23   Anatomical . . . question.] EE;   [*not present*]
91n.23–24   such questions] EE;   question
92.22   worlds] EE;   world
92.36   from] EE;   between
92.36   *within*] EE;   [*rom.*]
92.36   a] EE;   some one
92.36   *between*] EE;   [*rom.*]
93.2   and which] EE;   which
93.4–8   Having . . . them.] EE;   [*not present*]
93.13   usual crude] EE;   crude usual
93.17   objects] EE;   data
93.25   but is] EE;   but
94.2   reason$_\wedge$] EE; $\sim$,
94.3   facts$_\wedge$] EE;   real facts,
94.8   that] EE;   those
94.19–20   controlled] EE;   accurate
94.20   observation$_\wedge$] TS, EE; $\sim$,
94.33   matter-of-fact] EE; $\sim_\wedge\sim_\wedge\sim$
95.4   but] EE;   and
95.5   the mind] EE;   it
95.8   improbability (] EE; $\sim$,
95.9   system)] EE; $\sim$,
95.12   sense-organ] TS; $\sim_\wedge\sim$ EE
95.13   conscious experience] EE;   experience
95.14   itself] EE;   it
95.14   will be] EE;   is
95.19   event] EE;   datum
95.21   exists$_\wedge$] EE; $\sim$,
95.21   kind$_\wedge$] EE; $\sim$,
95.22   a trivial] EE;   an insignificant
95.22–23   that psychological] EE;   that the type of psycholog-
             ical

95.23   perception] EE;   perception with which we have been
           dealing
95.24   that] EE;   the introduction of the
95.26   discovery of any] EE;   any discovery of a
95.27–28   different] EE;   a different
95.28   data] EE;   sort of data
95.29   objects] EE;   data
95.32   objects] EE;   objects as data for inference
95.33   minute,] EE;   ∼∧
95.37   diversity;] EE;   diversity, and
95.37   that] EE;   the fact that
95.38   influence] EE;   their influence
95.38   habits),] EE;   ∼)∧
95.40   objects] EE;   knowledge
95.40   It was] EE;   It
96.1   chance, habit, and] EE;   chance and
96.2–3   influences . . . world] EE;   influences in determining
           what men currently believed about the world than was
           intellectual inquiry
96.3   What] EE;   What the
96.6   which] EE;   as that
96.10   movement] EE;   same movement
96.13   dialectical] EE;   dialectic
96.14   the fact that] EE;   that
96.16   is now] EE;   I have now
96.17   marks] EE;   effects
96.18   the resources of] EE;   our resources in
96.18–19   improving] EE;   improvement of
96.21   they leave] EE;   leave
96.27   connected with] EE;   related to
96.27   things] EE;   elements
96.28   gets] EE;   enables us to get
96.29   relations.] EE;   relations than present themselves in
           their crude form.
96.31   objects discriminated] EE;   discriminated objects
96.32   improving, reorganizing,] EE;   improvement, reorgani-
           zation∧
96.32   testing] EE;   testing of
96.34   which] EE;   of which
96.35   noted∧] EE;   treated,
96.37   customary yet] EE;   customary
96.39   as] EE;   [ital.]
96.40   never] EE;   we never
97.1   inquiry do we] EE;   inquiry
97.3   We doubt] EE;   What we do is to doubt
97.6   determining unambiguous] EE;   detection of elemen-
           tary
97.6   and eliminating] EE;   and of

97.7	influences . . . habit] EE; influences
97.7	control] EE; determine
97.8	aid in] EE; aid to

"Faculty Share in University Control"

Copy-text is the only previous publication of this article, in *Journal of Proceedings and Addresses of the Seventeenth Annual Conference* [of the Association of American Universities], 1915, pp. 27–32.

113.32	trustees] W; trustee
113.38	do] W; does
115.27	colleagues] W; colleague

"Industrial Education—A Wrong Kind"

Copy-text is the only previous publication of this article, in *New Republic* 2 (1915): 71–73.

118.14	complementary] W; complimentary

German Philosophy and Politics

Copy-text for this work is the copyright deposit copy (New York: Henry Holt and Co., 1915). The second edition, G42: *German Philosophy and Politics* (New York: G. P. Putnam's Sons, 1942) is cited as the first appearance of a number of corrections that would have been made editorially for the present edition.

144.22	world—] W; ~,
160.11	set] W; [*not present*]
162.28	fall] W; falls
162.29	instinct or] W; instinct
163.32	each] G42; which
164.9	get] G42; gets
165.17	adapts itself] W; adopts herself
166.14	or] G42; and
166.19	Trafficking in] W; Trafficking
167.21	that is∧] W; ~,

167.39   gives] W;   give
167.40   show] W;   show in
168.32   other hand] W;   other
169.20   Weltanschauung] G42;   Welt-Anschauung
175.9   labor,] G42;   ~∧
176.1   Lassalle] W;   Lasalle
176.3   *The Working Man's Programme,*] W;   "Programme of
           Workingmen,"
178.21   science] G42;   philosophy
184.11   bequeaths] W;   bequeathes
188n.17   have] W;   has
191.6   their] G42;   his
191.27–28 *The German Enigma*] W;   the "German Enigma"
191.35   "That which *is,*"] W;   ∧~,∧
191.35   "is reason realised."] W;   ∧~·∧
192.21   *Philosophy of Right*] W;   "Philosophy of Law"
192.35   "the] W;   ∧~
193.21–22 *Philosophy of History*] W;   History
194.11–12 *Outlines of a Philosophy of the History of Man*] W;
           "Ideas for a Philosophy of the History of Humanity"

Schools of To-Morrow

Copy-text for this work, which was co-authored by
John and Evelyn Dewey, is the copyright deposit copy
(New York: E. P. Dutton and Co., 1915).

217.9–10   are intended] W;   intended
250.19   illustrated∧ again,] W;   ~, ~∧
261.11   plan] W;   plane
262.8   provide] W;   provides
290.39   God Is Also"] W;   Is God"
300.28   life;] W;   ~,
306.10   decimeters] W;   meters
307.11   other] W;   others
327.20   per cent∧] W;   percent.
332.15, 28; per cent∧] W;   ~.
341.25; 372.27
334.32   distribute] W;   distributing
346.25   for.] W;   ~∧
350.6   Girls] W;   girls
381.18   pupil] W;   pupils
389.3–4   representative] W;   representive
404.23   turn out] W;   turn

"Letter to William Bagley and the Editorial Staff
of School and Home Education"

Copy-text is the first appearance of the article in *School*
and Home Education 35 (1915): 35–36.

414.12–13   ∧*Schools of To-Morrow,*∧] W;   "Schools of Tomor-
            row,"
414.22   Meriam's] W;   Merriam's
414.27   Leete, etc.] W;   Leete∧ &c.

"Reply to 'Parochial School Education'
by Charles P. Megan"

Copy-text is the only previous appearance of this letter,
in *New Republic* 3 (1915): 72.

416.28   schools'] W;   ∼∧

"The One-World of Hitler's National Socialism"

Copy-text is the only previous appearance of this Introduction, in the second edition of *German Philosophy and*
Politics (New York: G. P. Putnam's Sons, 1942), pp. 13–49.

425.36   Party] W;   party
438.24   now;] W;   ∼,
440.22   constitutes] W;   constitute
440.34   at the] W;   the
441.11   *Philosophy of History*] W;   philosophy of history

LIST OF 1942 VARIANTS IN *GERMAN PHILOSOPHY AND POLITICS*

In 1942, *German Philosophy and Politics* (New York: Henry Holt and Co., 1915) was reset and "reprinted without change, save for a few slight verbal corrections," and with a new Introduction, "The One-World of Hitler's National Socialism" [this volume, pp. 421–46], by G. P. Putnam's Sons. The variants between the 1915 and 1942 texts appear below; the copy-text reading appears before the bracket and does not coincide with the reading of the present edition if an emendation has been made. The later reading is to the right of the bracket. In the eight instances of corrections that would have been made editorially for the present edition (163.32, 164.9, 166.14, 169.20, 175.9, 178.21, 179.36, 191.6), the 1942 reading coincides with the emended text.

140.32   we are dealing with] with which we are dealing
141.16, 17, 36   esthetic] æsthetic
142.38   reality, or] reality‚ and
143.28   which] whiich
145.19   rôle] role
147.26   reason by which are marked] reason which marks
147.27   that of science and] one of science, the others
149.3   philosophy not only frees] philosophy seemed to his followers not only to free
149.5   gives] to give
152.35   technically] rigidly and narrowly
154.13   esthetic] æsthetic
157.11–12   the enlightenment] enlightenment
158.26   moral] normal
158.28   deduced] deducted
158.32   a resource] resource
163.32   which] each
163.34   to] of
164.9   gets] get
166.14   and] or
167.17   conquest] the conquest
169.20   Welt-/Anschauung] Weltanschauung
170.14   ‚Society‚] "~"

172.4   quality] quantity
173.2   may] must
175.9   labor_∧] ~,
178.2–3   the mighty Napoleon] Napoleon
178.21   philosophy] science
178.36   State] state
179.36   ourselves] themselves
180.8   demoniac] domestic
180.11   my] any
180.13   come.] ~,
184.28–29   protested because] protested against the abstract
             character of the French doctrine of rights founded in
             natural reason because
184.29   interference] its interference
184.29   established] or historically established
184.30   the Germans,] while the Germans_∧ protested
185.7   freedom] abstract formal freedom
191.6   his] their
195.35   object] subject
196.5   back] by Hegel
198.37   this] his
202.26   philosophy] [ital.]

HISTORICAL COLLATION

"The Existence of the World as a Logical Problem"

In the following list appear all variants in substantives and accidentals between the copy-text first publication of this article with the title "The Existence of the World as a Problem" in PR: *Philosophical Review* 24 (1915): 357-70, and TS, a carbon copy of the typescript for Dewey's paper "The Existence of the World as a Problem of Knowledge" in Butler Library, Columbia University, in the papers of the New York Philosophical Club. Omitted from the tabulation are the instances of faulty spacing, chiefly words run together, the substitution of numbers for asterisks to key the footnotes, and the TS use of a spaced hyphen for a dash. The reading to the left of the bracket is from PR and will not coincide with the text of the present edition if an emendation has been made; the reading following the bracket is, in all cases, that of TS.

83.1-2	THE EXISTENCE OF THE WORLD AS A PROBLEM.] THE EXISTENCE OF THE WORLD AS A PROBLEM OF KNOWLEDGE.
83.7	self-contradiction:] ~;
83.7-8	so stated] stated so
83.12-13	concerned,] ~∧
83.16	contention] contentions
83.20	examinations] examination
83.21	∧Our] "Our
83.21-22	*Knowledge . . . in*] [*rom.*]
83.22	*Philosophy*∧.] Philosophy".
83.24	importance,] ~∧
83.27	*a fortiori*] [*rom.*]
84.1	somewhere.] ~,
84.5	reader∧] ~,
84.10	formulation] statement of it
84.10	sense∧ . . .] ~. . . .
84.11	p. 75).] ~)∧

84.13	own¹] ~ₐ
84.14	(pp. 73 and 83).] (p. 73 and p. 83.)
84.15	I shall] I. As already indicated, I shall
84.25	eyes"ₐ] ~".
84.30	doubtₐ] ~.
84.35	would be] are
84.36	But if] If
84n.4	established] estahlished
85.2	visual,] ~ₐ
85.11	a 'sensory'] 'sensory'
85.13	involving,] ~ₐ
85.13	existence] of existence
85.25	'being seen'] ₐ~ₐ
85.31	fulfills] fulfils
85.35	color] object
85.35	noting] [ital.]
86.4	'known.'] "~".
86.4	example:] ~,
86.6	[believed] (~
86.7	evidence]] ~)
86.9	self-evident"ₐ] ~".
86.11	logicₐ] ~.
86.13	fact] [rom.]
86.14	application] applications
86.16	Again,] ~ₐ
86.18	into] in
86.18–19	not made] not
86.20	relation,] ~ₐ
86.21	three-term] ~ₐ~
86.22	inexplicableₐ] ~.
86.23	We] But we
86.24	'visual,' 'sensory,'] ₐ~,ₐ ₐ~,ₐ
86n.1	a fact] fact
86n.2	world.] ~,
86n.4	relationₐ"] ~."
86n.6	that] of
86n.7	offers] offering
86n.13	Meaning] [ital.]
86n.14	distinct] distinct ideas
86n.14	dubious.] dubious. The terms of a lie may be self-evident.
87.2	timeₐ"] ~?"
87.2	75)?] ~).
87.5	problem] [rom.]
87.6	(a),] (a)ₐ
87.6, 7	time,] ~ₐ
87.6	(b),](b)ₐ
87.9	"a] ₐ~

87.9   seen"ʌ] ~".
87.12   that] the
87.17   context,] ~ʌ
87.24   'momentary'?] '~?'
87.24   no] no other
87.25   by assuming] to assume
87.29   matter that] matter. [▌] (a). If anything is an eternal
         essence it is surely such a thing as matter that
87.34   as matter of fact] [not present]
87.34-35 'the patch of color'] ʌ~ʌ
87.36   vice-versa] viceʌversa
87.37   engaged,] ~ʌ
87.39   redefining] redefining
87.39   object,] ~ʌ
88.1   this] the
88.6   (a)] (a)
88.8   Russell.] ~ʌ
88.10   might] [ital.]
88.15   4] four
88.17   these] them
88.18   datum] data
88.21   a] any
88.22   (b)ʌ] (b).
88.22   Suppose] Supposed
88.28   an atom] atom
88.30   'sense'] 'sensory'
88.30   innocently,] ~ʌ
88.36   which is] [not present]
88.38   one of] of one
89.2   no] now
89.2   times."] ~".
89.4   (brief)] ʌ~ʌ
89.15   Mr. Russell] 3. Mr. Russell
89.17   common-sense] ~ʌ~
89.20-21 to be something to be stated] [not present]
89.23   sensations"ʌ] ~".
89.23   77).] ~)ʌ
89.24   objects,] ~ʌ
89.28   that was] [not present]
89.29   belief,] ~ʌ
89.30   involve,—] ~,ʌ
89.31   contrary,] ~ʌ
89.31-32 complex,] ~ʌ
90.1   Note,] ~ʌ
90.2   three-fold,] ~ʌ
90.12   sense,] ~;
90.15   upon] upon the basis of
90.16   the rationalists] rationalists

90.17   sensationalistic] introspective
90.21   rather∧ (i)∧] ∼, ∼,
90.25   historical] historic
90.25   but is] but
90.37   ordered∧] ∼,
90.38   conception] assumption
90.38   perception,] ∼∧
90.38   so that] and
90.39   inferring from it] making an inference
91.1   beyond] beyond it
91.3   perceptual] perceptive
91.3   can] can itself
91.3   *determined*] [*rom.*]
91.3–4   as . . . structure] [*not present*]
91.4   objects. That is,] perceptions. Or, from the side of the
           object,
91.5   determined] identified
91.6   just . . . series] [*not present*]
91.6   of specific∧] a specific,
91.6–7   elements, . . . end, only] single series only
91.7–8   a temporal . . . things] other objects
91.8   succeeding] following
91.9   Moreover, it] By description the continuous and ordered
           series constitutes something delimited as a single ob-
           ject. This delimited determination involves location
           within a larger series.
91.9–11   involves . . . word,] [*not present*]
91.12   extends] extends, in logical reference,
91.12   itself;] ∼.
91.12–13   it *is* part of a larger world] The same considerations
           apply, on the side of a spatial continuum, to the de-
           limited shapes of the visible series.
91.14   (ii)∧] ∼.
91.14   A sensible] Such an
91.14   which can be] as is
91.14   described as] described in the quoted passage
91.14–15   ∧a correlation] (∼
91.16   objects∧ presents] objects) represents
91.17   What] It
91.18   stated is the] a
91.18   an object,] ∼—
91.18–19   of . . . Barring] and, as it seems to me (barring
91.19   ambiguities[1]] ∼∧
91.19   terms] term
91.19   'muscular'∧] '∼')
91.19–20   and . . . be] [*not present*]
91.20–21   But . . . poor,] [*not present*]
91.21   it states] It is

91.21   datum] perceived object
91.21–22   ∧as . . . definite] —definite
91n.1   exhaustive] complete
91n.2   idealistic writers] writers
91n.3–4   for the sake of] in order to
91n.4   identifying] identify
91n.4   thinkers] writers
91n.5   that the] that while it is true that the
91n.5   empirical data] data
91n.6   inference.] inference, the recognition of specified limita-
            tions assumes that the data in question are already
            described as portions of a
91n.6–9   But . . . to the] [*not present*]
91n.9–12   Hence . . . making] [*not present*]
91n.13–24   ¹The . . . have arisen.] [*not present*]
92.3   If] [*rom.*]
92.13   correct,] ~∧
92.15   tacitly been] been tacitly
92.19   His] The
92.19   "peculiar,"] "peculiar∧" or
92.21   projectional] profectional
92.38   their] their degree of
92.38   thing] thing is what
93.9–10   'empirical datum'?] '~?'
93.16   analysis∧] ~,
93.18   changes∧] ~,
93.19   great . . . over] great—so it seems to me—advance over
93.31   character.] ~,
93.34   fact] [*rom.*]
93.37   criticisms] criticisms made
94.2   treatment.] ~,
94.3   to] to what are
94.4   by] in
94.10   sounds] particular sounds
94.10   kinesthetic] esthetic
94.11   etc.,] &c.∧
94.18   careful,] ~∧
94.19   anatomy,] ~∧
94.20   observation,] ~∧
94.23   data of experience,] data
94.23   infancy,] ~∧
94.26   innocent] onnocent
94.38   represent] present
94.39   discriminations] subsequent discriminations brought to
            bear by other experienced objects
94.39, 40   data,] ~∧
95.6   inferring] inferring such
95.7   psychology] psychogygy

95.12	sense‸organ] ~-~
95.28	sort] kind
95.29	—or customary—] ‸~‸
96.6	world,] ~‸
96.7	believed in,] believed
96.8	Analysis] The analysis
96.24	are,] ~‸
96.26	They] [◖] They
96.26–27	always—] ~,
96.27	given—] ~,
96.31–32	purposes] purpose
96.34	this] the
96.38	doubtful,] ~‸
96.38	or which is] or
96.40	specific] the specific
96.40	in] [rom.]
97.2	doubt,] question—
97.3	received piece of] piece of received
97.4	of] in
97.4	then set] set
97.8	aid] contribution

LINE-END HYPHENATION

I. Copy-text list.

The following are the editorially established forms of possible compounds which were hyphenated at the ends of lines in the copy-text:

12.10	physico-chemical	261.28	playground
17.3	subject-matter	262.14	text-book
24n.14	non-cognitive	265.20	schoolrooms
26.36–37	subject-matter	268.4	backyards
40.20	common-sense	271.19	classroom
42.5–6	extra-organic	271.27	playgrounds
43.10	subject-matter	284.40	mid-morning
57.37	standpoint	293.22	Gradgrind
60.18	subject-matter	300.36	classroom
67.20	boatmaker	303.34	subnormal
73.11	subject-matter	305.11	Sandpaper
80.20–21	subject-matter	317.20	subject-matter
103.36	underestimates	317.38	steamboats
120.38	pre-vocational	318.25	text-books
133.7	middleman	323.39	classroom
142.21	non-reflective	324.28	classroom
159.32	pigeon-hole	324.32	playground
164.2	thoroughgoing	335.4	bookkeeping
175.14	workingmen	335.30	text-book
190.22	warlike	342.28	bookcases
203.8	breakdown	345.5–6	woodwork
219.11	Text-books	345.23	cooperation
226.11	classroom	350.11	housework
228.1	classroom	351.14	cooperation
231.35–36	text-books	356.6	housekeeping
231.39	watersheds	358.14	text-book
243.35	text-book	359.29	workingmen
255.16	text-book	369.5	dressmakers
255.24	text-book	371.11	storerooms
255.36	handwork	374.3	dressmaking
259.2	text-book	375.12	newcomer
259.9	classroom	379.39	housekeeping

402.22–23	short-sighted	437.38–438.1	quasi-
428.12	preoccupations		intellectual
430.26	thoroughgoing	439.38–39	workingmen
434.22	quasi-mystical	444.7	railway

II. Critical-text list.

In transcriptions from the present edition, no line-end hyphens in ambiguously broken possible compounds are to be retained except the following:

6.21	pseudo-science	219.16	sure-footedness
6.30	subject-matter	222.28	to-day
26.36	subject-matter	231.35	text-books
30.29	so-called	285.40	mid-morning
41.12	ultra-empirical	290.30	subject-matter
42.5	extra-organic	323.13	up-keep
43.28	ready-made	358.4	ready-made
57.38	over-simplification	364.19	bread-winning
80.20	subject-matter	388.14	school-teacher
102.27	right-minded	402.22	short-sighted
128.26	purse-strings	432.7	sub-leaders
140.6	hard-headed	440.21	sub-leaders
207.4	text-book		

CORRECTION OF QUOTATIONS

Dewey represented source material in varying ways, from memorial paraphrase to verbatim copy, sometimes citing his source fully, in others mentioning only authors' names, and in still others, omitting documentation altogether.

To prepare the critical text, all material inside quotation marks, except that obviously being emphasized or restated, has been searched out and the documentation has been verified and emended when necessary. Steps regularly used to emend documentation are described in "Textual Principles and Procedures" (*Middle Works* 1:358), but Dewey's substantive variations from the original in his quotations have been considered important enough to warrant a special list.

All quotations have been retained within the texts as they were first published, except for corrections required by special circumstances and noted in the Emendations List. Substantive changes that restore original readings in cases of possible compositorial or typographical errors are similarly noted as "W" emendations. The variable form of quotation suggests that Dewey, like many scholars of the period, was unconcerned about precision in matters of form, but many of the changes in cited materials may have arisen in the printing process. For example, comparing Dewey's quotations with the originals reveals that some journals housestyled the quoted materials as well as Dewey's own. In the present edition, therefore, the spelling and capitalization of the source have been reproduced, except in concept words where Dewey changed the form of the source.

The sources of John Dewey's and Evelyn Dewey's quotations from Fichte, Froebel, Heine, Kant, Lassalle, Pestalozzi, and Spengler appear in the Checklist of References, but no correction of the quotations is included here because both authors translated from the original works in French and German. In the cases of Hegel and Rousseau, John and Evelyn Dewey both quoted directly and also translated from the same works. Both German and English versions are listed in the Checklist of References and corrections entries for quotations that do not seem to be translations appear in the following list. For a fuller discussion of Dewey's translation methods, see *The Early Works of John Dewey* 1: lxi–lxiv, xc–xcii.

Dewey's most frequent alteration in quoted material was changing or omitting punctuation. No citation of the Dewey material or of the original appears here if the changes were only of this kind. He also often failed to use ellipses or to separate quotations to show that material had been left out. In the case of Dewey's failure to use ellipses, omitted short phrases appear in this list; if a line or more has been left out, an ellipsis in brackets calls attention to the omission. When a substantive difference between Dewey's material and its source has been caused by the context in which the quotation appears, that difference is not recorded.

Italics in source material have been treated as accidentals. When Dewey omitted those italics, the omission is not noted; his added italics, however, are listed. If changed or omitted accidentals have substantive implications, as in the capitalization or failure to capitalize concept words, the quotation is noted.

The form used in this section is designed to assist the reader in determining whether Dewey had the book open before him or was relying on his memory. Notations in this section follow the formula: page-line numbers from the present text, followed by the text condensed to first and last words or such as make for sufficient clarity, followed by a bracket. Next comes the necessary correction, whether of one word or a longer passage, as required. Finally, in parentheses, the author's surname and shortened source-title from the Checklist of Dewey's References are followed by a comma and the page-line reference to the source.

"The Subject-Matter of Metaphysical Inquiry"

3.14   even biocentric] biocentric (Lillie, "The Philosophy of Biology," 846.22)

3.15   as] considered as (Lillie, "Philosophy of Biology," 846.23)

3.29   ultimate peculiarities] peculiarities of ultimate constitution (Lillie, "Philosophy of Biology," 846.17)

8.1   start] outset (Lillie, "Philosophy of Biology," 845.28)

8.11   start] outset (Lillie, "Philosophy of Biology," 845.28)

"The Logic of Judgments of Practice"

23.33   for] merely for (Descartes, *Philosophical Works,* 194.12)

23.33   *signifying*] [*rom.*] (Descartes, *Works,* 194.12)

23.33   what] to my mind what (Descartes, *Works,* 194.12–13)

23.34   harmful.] hurtful$_\wedge$ (Descartes, *Works,* 194.13)

24.22   feet] foot (Hume, *Human Nature,* 1:248.29)

"The Existence of the World as a Logical Problem"

87.14   of] consisting in (Russell, *Knowledge of the External World,* 76.2)

92.28   others] previous worlds (Russell, *Knowledge,* 88.3)

German Philosophy and Politics

155.1–3   *all . . . rest:*] [*rom.*] (Bernhardi, *Germany and the Next War,* 73.5–6)

155.3   *mankind*] man (Bernhardi, *Germany,* 73.6)

155.8   capacities] capacity (Bernhardi, *Germany,* 73.11–12)

155.9   the way in which] in what way (Bernhardi, *Germany,* 73.12–13)

155.13   thus to] to (Bernhardi, *Germany,* 73.17)

155.18   leader] leaders (Bernhardi, *Germany,* 73.31)

155.22   leadership] the leadership (Bernhardi, *Germany,* 74.14)

155.23   domain$_\wedge$] world, (Bernhardi, *Germany,* 74.15)

155.23–24   *imposes . . . position*] [*rom.*] (Bernhardi, *Germany,* 74.15–16)

163.29–30 the critical] critical (Bernhardi, *Germany*, 64.1)
163.35   claims] claim (Bernhardi, *Germany*, 64.7)
165.8   of] for (Eucken, *Meaning and Value of Life*, 104.11)
176.34   development started] development, more regular than
           that of ancient Hellas, started (Lange, *History of
           Materialism*, 2:236.10–11)
177.13   wiped] lost and wiped (Von Sybel, *Founding of the
           German Empire*, 1:36.4)
177.15   everybody] every one (Von Sybel, *Founding*, 1:36.6)
177.30   was] were (Von Sybel, *Founding*, 1:36.24)
184.24   principle] political principle (Burke, *Works*, 3:25.25)
185.15   end] aim (Hegel, *Lectures*, 368.8)
185.19   struggle, its harmony] struggle∧ and its harmonization
           (Hegel, *Lectures*, 369.1–2)
191.38   is] was (Bourdon, *German Enigma*, 289.7)
191.38   could] should (Bourdon, *German Enigma*, 289.9)

Schools of To-Morrow

211.3   notions of it] notions (Rousseau, *Émile*, 1.33)
211.3   go in education] advance (Rousseau, *Émile*, 1.34)
211.3   more] further (Rousseau, *Émile*, 1.34)
212.15   indeed know] know (Rousseau, *Émile*, 141.29)
212.16   child. Must] child, but need (Rousseau, *Émile*,
           141.29–30)
212.16   can] or can (Rousseau, *Émile*, 141.30)
212.16   he learn] he indeed learn (Rousseau, *Émile*, 141.30)
212.17   teach a] teach the (Rousseau, *Émile*, 141.31)
212.17   to him as] to (Rousseau, *Émile*, 141.31)
212.22   know;] do know, (Rousseau, *Émile*, 141.36)
212.24   adult] [*not present*] (Rousseau, *Émile*, 141.38)
212.24   *him*] a man (Rousseau, *Émile*, 141.38)
212.24   his] its (Rousseau, *Émile*, 141.38)
213.20–21 education∧ is] education? It is (Rousseau, *Émile*,
           57.26)
213.21   it. If] it. [. . .] If (Rousseau, *Émile*, 57.27–
           34)
213.23   present education] present type of education (Rous-
           seau, *Émile*, 57.35)
214.4   ill. Give] ill. Leave exceptional cases to show them-
           selves, let their qualities be tested and confirmed, be-
           fore special methods are adopted. Give (Rousseau,
           Émile, 71.14–16)
214.4–5   upon yourself] over (Rousseau, *Émile*, 71.16)
214.9   excellence] virtue (Rousseau, *Émile*, 71.20)
214.11   jump and run] run and jump (Rousseau, *Émile*,
           71.23)

214.19   children be children] them children (Rousseau, *Émile*, 54.27)

214.21   that rots] which will be rotten (Rousseau, *Émile*, 54.29)

217.3   man's] a man's (Rousseau, *Émile*, 89.49)

217.3   upon] with (Rousseau, *Émile*, 89.49)

217.4   find] discover (Rousseau, *Émile*, 90.1)

217.4   the] those sensible (Rousseau, *Émile*, 90.1)

217.7   own] proper (Rousseau, *Émile*, 90.5)

217.8–9   limbs and keen senses] limbs (Rousseau, *Émile*, 90.5)

217.10   act$_\wedge$ is] act, while his senses are keen and as yet free from illusions, then is (Rousseau, *Émile*, 90.7–8)

217.10   senses] both limbs (Rousseau, *Émile*, 90.8)

217.10   limbs] senses (Rousseau, *Émile*, 90.8)

217.11   business—the] business. It is the (Rousseau, *Émile*, 90.8–9)

217.11   learn the relation] learn to perceive the physical relations (Rousseau, *Émile*, 90.9)

217.11   themselves] ourselves (Rousseau, *Émile*, 90.10)

217.12   things. Our] things. [. . .] our (Rousseau, *Émile*, 90.10–13)

217.16   can get] can practise (Rousseau, *Émile*, 90.18)

217.17   your] those (Rousseau, *Émile*, 90.19)

217.18–19 accordingly] therefore (Rousseau, *Émile*, 90.20–21)

217.20   for these] which (Rousseau, *Émile*, 90.21)

217.20   intellect. To] the intellect; and to (Rousseau, *Émile*, 90.22)

217.21   these tools] them (Rousseau, *Émile*, 90.23)

217.21–22 kept strong] strong (Rousseau, *Émile*, 90.23)

217.22   a] quite a (Rousseau, *Émile*, 90.24)

218.35   We] You (Rousseau, *Émile*, 71.37)

218.36   ease] facility (Rousseau, *Émile*, 71.38)

218.37   merely reflects] reflects (Rousseau, *Émile*, 71.39)

218.37   we] you (Rousseau, *Émile*, 71.39)

221.8   between] already between (Rousseau, *Émile*, 134.24)

221.9   pupils] scholars (Rousseau, *Émile*, 134.24)

228.12   way. Too] way. [. . .] Too (Rousseau, *Émile*, 127.14–20)

228.15   they answer] reply (Rousseau, *Émile*, 127.22)

295.41   the force of conditions] force (Rousseau, *Émile*, 55.28)

303.29   objects representing] *objects* (which I do not here wish to speak of in the technical language of psychology as stimuli) representing (Montessori, *Method*, 169.2–4)

307.6   the teacher] *she* (Montessori, *Method*, 226.10)

307.13   associations] association (Montessori, *Method,* 226.17)
307.17   others,]   others (such as smooth or rough),   (Montes-
           sori, *Method,* 226.23)

"The Situation at the University of Utah"

The original Lovejoy letter, which both the *Salt Lake City Herald-Republican* and *Science* magazine published in full, has not been located. Collation of the two published versions shows that a number of modifications were made in the letter for publication in "The Situation at the University of Utah." The deletions and other substantive variants are listed below; the basic reference is the *Herald-Republican,* with the one S (*Science*) variant from that version shown in brackets.

409.24   periodicals. It]   periodicals. In particular, the state-
           ments [made] upon the two sides of the controversy
           appear to have failed specifically to join issue upon
           certain points of interest. It (*Salt Lake City Herald-
           Republican,* "Lovejoy Writes Letter," 9 April 1915,
           3.1.29–34; Dewey and Lovejoy, "Conditions at the
           University of Utah," *Science,* n.s. 41, 637.1.25–28)
409.26   Professors to] Professors, Dr. John Dewey, to
           (*Herald-Republican,* "Lovejoy," 3.1.36–37; Dewey and
           Lovejoy, "Conditions," 637.1.30–31)
409.27   to secure]   to interview yourself and others concerned,
           with reference to the matters in controversy, and to
           endeavor to secure (*Herald-Republican,* "Lovejoy,"
           3.1.38–41; Dewey and Lovejoy, "Conditions," 637.1.32–
           34)
410.8   charges]   changes (*Herald-Republican,*   "Lovejoy,"
           3.2.35)
410.10   conduct or policy]   policy or conduct (*Herald-Repub-
           lican,* "Lovejoy," 3.2.36–37; Dewey and Lovejoy, "Con-
           ditions," 637.2.3)
410.11   ascertained]   determined (*Herald-Republican,* "Love-
           joy," 3.2.40; Dewey and Lovejoy, "Conditions," 637.2.4)
410.12–13 controversies]   controversy (*Herald-Republican,*
           "Lovejoy," 3.2.42; Dewey and Lovejoy, "Conditions,"
           637.2.6)
410.15   the present]   this (*Herald-Republican,* "Lovejoy,"
           3.2.46; Dewey and Lovejoy, "Conditions," 637.2.9)

CHECKLIST OF DEWEY'S REFERENCES

Titles and authors' names in Dewey references have been corrected and expanded to conform accurately and consistently to the original works; all corrections appear in the Emendations List.

This section gives full publication information for each work cited by Dewey. When Dewey gave page numbers for a reference, the edition he used was identified exactly by locating the citation. Similarly, the books in Dewey's personal library have been used to verify his use of a particular edition. For other references, the edition listed here is the one from among the various editions possibly available to him that was his most likely source by reason of place or date of publication, or on the evidence from correspondence and other materials, and its general accessibility during the period.

Aristotle. *The Nicomachean Ethics of Aristotle*. Translated by F. H. Peters. 2d ed. London: Kegan Paul, Trench and Co., 1884.

Bernhardi, Friedrich von. *Germany and the Next War*. Translated by Allen H. Powles. New York: Longmans, Green, and Co., 1914.

Bourdon, Georges. *The German Enigma: Being an Inquiry among Germans as to What They Think, What They Want, What They Can Do*. Translated by Beatrice Marshall. London: J. M. Dent and Co., 1914.

Brandes, George. *Main Currents in Nineteenth Century Literature*. Vol. 2. London: William Heinemann, 1902.

Burke, Edmund. *The Works of Edmund Burke*. Vol. 3. Boston: Little, Brown and Co., 1817.

Chamberlain, Houston Stewart. *The Foundations of the Nineteenth Century*. Translated by John Lees. New York: J. Lane Co., 1911.

Descartes, René. *The Philosophical Works of Descartes*. Vol. 1. Translated by Elizabeth S. Haldane and G. R. T. Ross. Cambridge: University Press, 1911.

Dewey, John. *German Philosophy and Politics*. New York: Henry

Holt and Co., 1915. [*The Middle Works of John Dewey,*
1899–1924, edited by Jo Ann Boydston, 8:135–204. Carbon-
dale: Southern Illinois University Press, 1979.]
————. "The Existence of the World as a Problem." *Philosophical
Review* 24 (1915): 357–70. [*Middle Works* 8:83–97.]
————, and Dewey, Evelyn. *Schools of To-Morrow.* New York:
E. P. Dutton and Co., 1915. [*Middle Works* 8:205–404.]
Eucken, Rudolf. *The Meaning and Value of Life.* Translated by
Lucy Judge Gibson and W. R. Boyce Gibson. London: A. and
C. Black, 1910.
Fichte, Johann Gottlieb. *Sämmtliche Werke.* 8 vols. Berlin: Veit
and Co., 1845.
Froebel, Friedrich. *Froebels kleiner Schriften zur Pädagogik.*
Leipzig: K. F. Koehler, 1914.
Hegel, Georg Wilhelm Friedrich. *Grundlinien der Philosophie
des Rechts. Werke.* Vol. 8. Edited by Eduard Gans. Berlin:
Duncker and Humblot, 1833.
————. *Hegel's Philosophy of Right.* Translated by S. W. Dyde.
London: George Bell and Sons, 1896.
————. *Lectures on the Philosophy of History.* Translated by
J. Sibree. London: George Bell and Sons, 1902.
Heine, Heinrich. *Sämmtliche Werke.* 22 vols. Edited by Adolph
Strodtmann. Hamburg: Hoffman and Campe, 1861–65.
Hume, David. *A Treatise of Human Nature: Being an Attempt
to Introduce the Experimental Method of Reasoning into
Moral Subjects.* Vol. 1. London: John Noon, 1739.
Irving, Washington. *The Sketch Book of Geoffrey Crayon, Gent.*
New York: C. S. Van Winkle, 1819–20.
Kant, Immanuel. *Idee zu einer allgemeinen Geschichte in welt-
burgerlicher Absicht.* Wiesbaden: H. Staadt, 1914.
————. *Kritik der praktischen Vernunft. Immanuel Kants sämm-
tliche Werke.* Vol. 5. Edited by Gustav Hartenstein. Berlin:
L. Voss, 1867.
————. *Kritik der reinen Vernunft.* Riga: Johann Friedrich Hart-
knoch, 1781.
Kipling, Rudyard. *Just So Stories.* Garden City, N.Y.: Doubleday
and Page Co., 1912.
Lange, Frederick Albert. *History of Materialism and Criticism of
Its Present Importance.* Vol. 2. Translated by Ernest Chester
Thomas. London: Trübner and Co., 1880.
Lassalle, Ferdinand. *Arbeiterprogramm.* Zurich: Meyer and Zeller,
1863.
Lillie, Ralph S. "The Philosophy of Biology: Vitalism *versus*
Mechanism." *Science,* n.s. 40 (1914): 840–46.
Montessori, Maria. *The Montessori Method.* Translated by Anne E.
George. 4th ed. New York: Frederick A. Stokes Co., 1912.
Moore, Ernest Carroll. *How New York City Administers Its
Schools.* School Efficiency Series, edited by Paul H. Hanus.
New York: World Book Co., 1913.

New York Times. "The Philadelphia Martyr." 10 October 1915, p. 16.

Nietzsche, Friedrich. *The Will to Power.* Vol. 14. Translated by Anthony M. Ludovici. Edinburgh: T. N. Foulis, 1910.

Pestalozzi, Johann Heinrich. *Pestalozzis sämmtliche Werke.* 12 vols. Edited by L. W. Seyffarth. Liegnitz: C. Seyffarth, 1899–1902.

Plato. *The Dialogues of Plato.* Translated by B. Jowett. 4 vols. Boston: Jefferson Press, 1871. [*The Republic* 2:1–452.]

Rousseau, Jean Jacques. *Émile.* Translated by Barbara Foxley. New York: E. P. Dutton and Co., 1911.

——. *Émile; ou de l'éducation.* Paris: Hector Bossange, 1829.

Russell, Bertrand. *Our Knowledge of the External World as a Field for Scientific Method in Philosophy.* Chicago: Open Court Publishing Co., 1914.

——. *Philosophical Essays.* New York: Longmans, Green, and Co., 1910.

Salt Lake City Herald-Republican. "Lovejoy Writes Letter." 9 April 1915, p. 3.

Spencer, Herbert. *First Principles of a New System of Philosophy.* New York: D. Appleton and Co., 1864.

Spengler, Oswald. *Der Untergang des Abendlandes.* Munich: Beck, 1919–22.

Sybel, Heinrich von. *The Founding of the German Empire by William I.* Vol. 1. Translated by Marshall Livingston Perrin. New York: Thomas Y. Crowell Co., 1890.

Tacitus, Publius. *Dialogus, Agricola, Germania.* Translated by William Peterson. Cambridge: Harvard University Press, 1914.

Tolstoy, Leo. *Master and Man and Other Parables and Tales.* New York: E. P. Dutton and Co., 1910.

Woodbridge, Frederick J. E. "The Deception of the Senses." *Journal of Philosophy, Psychology and Scientific Methods* 10 (1913): 5–15.

——. "Evolution." *Philosophical Review* 21 (1912): 137–51.

INDEX